THE GREAT TANG DYNASTY RECORD OF THE WESTERN REGIONS

BDK English Tripiṭaka 79

THE GREAT TANG DYNASTY RECORD OF THE WESTERN REGIONS

Translated by the Tripiṭaka-Master Xuanzang
under Imperial Order
Composed by Śramaṇa Bianji
of the Great Zongchi Monastery

(Taishō, Volume 51, Number 2087)

Translated into English
by
Li Rongxi

Numata Center
for Buddhist Translation and Research
1996

First Printing, 1996
ISBN: 1-886439-02-8
Library of Congress Catalog Card Number: 96-069942

Published by
Numata Center for Buddhist Translation and Research
2620 Warring Street
Berkeley, California 94704

Printed in the United States of America

A Message on the Publication of the English Tripiṭaka

The Buddhist canon is said to contain eighty-four thousand different teachings. I believe that this is because the Buddha's basic approach was to prescribe a different treatment for every spiritual ailment, much as a doctor prescribes a different medicine for every medical ailment. Thus his teachings were always appropriate for the particular suffering individual and for the time at which the teaching was given, and over the ages not one of his prescriptions has failed to relieve the suffering to which it was addressed.

Ever since the Buddha's Great Demise over twenty-five hundred years ago, his message of wisdom and compassion has spread throughout the world. Yet no one has ever attempted to translate the entire Buddhist canon into English throughout the history of Japan. It is my greatest wish to see this done and to make the translations available to the many English-speaking people who have never had the opportunity to learn about the Buddha's teachings.

Of course, it would be impossible to translate all of the Buddha's eighty-four thousand teachings in a few years. I have, therefore, had one hundred thirty-nine of the scriptural texts in the prodigious Taishō edition of the Chinese Buddhist canon selected for inclusion in the First Series of this translation project.

It is in the nature of this undertaking that the results are bound to be criticized. Nonetheless, I am convinced that unless someone takes it upon himself or herself to initiate this project, it will never be done. At the same time, I hope that an improved, revised edition will appear in the future.

It is most gratifying that, thanks to the efforts of more than a hundred Buddhist scholars from the East and the West, this monumental project has finally gotten off the ground. May the rays of the Wisdom of the Compassionate One reach each and every person in the world.

NUMATA Yehan
Founder of the English
Tripiṭaka Project

August 7, 1991

Editorial Foreword

In January, 1982, Dr. NUMATA Yehan, the founder of the Bukkyō Dendō Kyōkai (Society for the Promotion of Buddhism), decided to begin the monumental task of translating the complete Taishō edition of the Chinese Tripiṭaka (Buddhist Canon) into the English language. Under his leadership, a special preparatory committee was organized in April, 1982. By July of the same year, the Translation Committee of the English Tripiṭaka was officially convened.

The initial Committee consisted of the following members: (late) HANAYAMA Shōyū (Chairperson); BANDŌ Shōjun; ISHIGAMI Zennō; KAMATA Shigeo; KANAOKA Shūyū; MAYEDA Sengaku; NARA Yasuaki; SAYEKI Shinkō; (late) SHIOIRI Ryōtatsu; TAMARU Noriyoshi; (late) TAMURA Kwansei; URYŪZU Ryūshin; and YUYAMA Akira. Assistant members of the Committee were as follows: KANAZAWA Atsushi; WATANABE Shōgo; Rolf Giebel of New Zealand; and Rudy Smet of Belgium.

After holding planning meetings on a monthly basis, the Committee selected 139 texts for the First Series of translations, an estimated one hundred printed volumes in all. The texts selected are not necessarily limited to those originally written in India, but also include works written or composed in China or Japan. While the publication of the First Series proceeds, the texts for the Second Series will be selected from among the remaining works; this process will continue until all the texts, in Japanese as well as in Chinese, have been published.

Frankly speaking, it will take perhaps one hundred years or more to accomplish the English translation of the complete Chinese and Japanese texts, for they consist of thousands of works. Nevertheless, as Dr. NUMATA wished, it is the sincere hope of the Committee that this project will continue unto completion, even after all its present members have passed away.

It must be mentioned here that the final object of this project is not academic fulfillment, but the transmission of the teaching of the

Buddha to the whole world in order to create harmony and peace among mankind. Therefore, any notes, such as footnotes and endnotes, which might be indispensable for academic purposes, are not given in the English translations, since they might make the general reader lose interest in the Buddhist scriptures. Instead, a glossary is added at the end of each work, in accordance with the translators' wish.

To my great regret, Dr. NUMATA passed away on May 5, 1994 at the age of 97, entrusting his son, Mr. NUMATA Toshihide, with the continuation and completion of the Translation Project. The Committee also lost its able and devoted Chairperson, Professor HANAYAMA Shōyū, on June 16, 1995, at the age of 63. After these severe blows, the Committee elected me, Vice-President of the Musashino Women's College, to be the Chair in October, 1995. The Committee has renewed its determination to carry out the noble intention of Dr. NUMATA, under the leadership of Mr. NUMATA Toshihide.

The present members of the Committee are MAYEDA Sengaku (Chairperson), BANDŌ Shōjun, ISHIGAMI Zennō, ICHISHIMA Shōshin, KAMATA Shigeo, KANAOKA Shūyū, NARA Yasuaki, SAYEKI Shinkō, TAMARU Noriyoshi, URYŪZU Ryūshin, and YUYAMA Akira. Assistant members are WATANABE Shōgo and MINOWA Kenryō.

The Numata Center for Buddhist Translation and Research was established in November 1984 in Berkeley, California, U.S.A. to assist in the publication of the BDK English Tripiṭaka First Series. In December 1991 the Publication Committee was organized at the Numata Center, with Professor Philip Yampolsky as the Chairperson. The Numata Center has thus far published seven volumes and has been distributing them. All of the remaining texts will be published under the supervision of this Committee, in close cooperation with the Translation Committee in Tokyo.

MAYEDA Sengaku
Chairperson
Translation Committee of
the BDK English Tripiṭaka

November 1, 1995

Publisher's Foreword

In December, 1991, at the Numata Center for Buddhist Translation and Research in Berkeley, California, a publication committee was established for the purpose of seeing into print the translations of the Buddhist works in the BDK English Tripiṭaka Series. This committee processes the translations forwarded by the Translation Committee in Tokyo. It performs the duties of copyediting, formatting, proofreading, indexing, consulting with the translators on questionable passages, and so on—the routine duties of any publishing house. No attempt is made to standardize the English translations of Buddhist technical terms; these are left to the discretion of the individual translator. Represented on the committee are specialists in Sanskrit, Chinese, and Japanese, who attempt to ensure that fidelity to the texts is maintained.

This Publication Committee is dedicated to the production of lucid and readable works that do justice to the vision of the late Dr. NUMATA Yehan, who wished to make available to Western readers the major works of the Chinese and Japanese Buddhist canon.

"Taishō" refers to the *Taishō Shinshū Daizōkyō* (Newly Revised Tripiṭaka Inaugurated in the Taishō Era), which was published during the period from 1924 to 1934. This consists of one hundred volumes, in which as many as 3,360 scriptures in both Chinese and Japanese are included. This edition is acknowledged to be the most complete Tripiṭaka of the Northern tradition of Buddhism ever published in the Chinese and Japanese languages. As with all books in the BDK Series, the series number on the spine and title page of each work corresponds to the number assigned to it by the Translation Committee of the BDK English Tripiṭaka in Tokyo. A list of the volume numbers is appended at the end of each volume. For the convenience of scholars who may wish to turn to the original texts, Taishō page and column numbers are provided in the margins of each volume.

Those participating in the work of this committee are Diane Ames, Brian Galloway, Nobuo Haneda, Charles Niimi, and Rev. Kiyoshi S. Yamashita.

Philip Yampolsky
Chairperson
Publication Committee

July 1, 1996

Contents

Thirty-four Countries, from Agni to Kāpiśī
    Agni; Kuci; Bālukā; Nujkend; Shash; Feihan; Sutrūshana;
    Samarkand; Mimohe; Kapūtānā; Kuṣāṇika; Khagan; Bukhārā;
    Betik; Horiṣmīka; Kasanna; Tirmidh; Sahāniyan; Kharūn;
    Shūmān; Kuvāyāna; Wakhsh; Khuttalān; Komidai; Baghlan;
    Hrum-Simingān; Khulm; Baktra; Zumathān; Gūzgānān;
    Talaqān; Kacik; Bāmīyāna; Kāpiśī

Three Countries, from Lampā to Gandhāra
    Lampā; Nagarahāra; Gandhāra

Eight Countries, from Udyāna to Rājapura
    Udyāna; Balūra; Takṣaśilā; Siṃhapura; Uraśā; Kaśmīra;
    Parṇotsa; Rājapura

Translator's Introduction

The Great Tang Dynasty Record of the Western Regions is the itinerary of the journey undertaken by the Tripiṭaka Master Xuanzang, in India and some parts of Central Asia in 629–45 C.E. An epoch-making figure in the history of Chinese Buddhism, the Master was born at Chenliu (in the suburbs of the present Kaifeng Municipality in Henan province) in 600 C.E. with the family name of Chen. His ancestral line, according to Bianji's "Eulogy" appended at the end of this *Record*, is said to be traceable as far back as the legendary Emperor Shennong, who is supposed to have reigned around 3000 B.C. But according to ascertainable historical data, the Master was the progeny of Chen Shi, alias Zhonggong, who once served as magistrate of the ancient Taiqiu county during the reign of Yongping (58–75 C.E.) of Emperor Ming of the Later Han dynasty. His great-grandfather, Chen Xin, was the governor of Shangdang prefecture during the Northern Wei dynasty (386–534 C.E.), while his grandfather, Chen Kang, served as an official at the court of the Northern Qi dynasty (561–77 C.E.). His father, Chen Hui, was a learned scholar who devoted himself to the study of Confucian classics and refused to accept government appointments at a time when the country was in turmoil.

The Master was the youngest of the four children of the family. After becoming a novice while he was a youth, he lived with his second brother, Chen Su, who had become a monk previously with the religious name of Changjie at the Jingtu Monastery in Luoyang, where the Master started his career as a student of Buddhist doctrines under the instruction of various teachers. At the age of twenty he was fully ordained as a *bhikṣu* at Chengdu in the fifth year of the Wude period (622 C.E.). In the course of his study he was bewildered by the various theories in the Buddhist texts available in Chinese translations. He had a strong impulse to solve these theoretical uncertainties by searching for the missing, untranslated original Sanskrit texts, particularly the *Yogācāra-bhūmi-śāstra*; thus he braved all hardships lying ahead on the journey to India. Violating a government ban on emigration, he slipped out of the empire without official permission. During his sojourn of sixteen years in India, he studied the said *śāstra* and other texts under the tutelage of the Venerable Śīlabhadra, a well-known Buddhist scholar of Nālandā Monastery near Rājagṛha. He visited all the important Buddhist sites and ruins, enjoyed great popularity in India through his learning as an outstanding Buddhist scholar, and he won the support of the reigning monarchs such as Śīlāditya and others of India.

When he reached Khotan on his way back to China, he brought with him as many as six hundred fifty-seven books bound in five hundred twenty bundles that he had acquired in India, carried by twenty packhorses. He sent a message by a merchant to inform Emperor Taizong (r. 627–49) of his forthcoming arrival in the capital. The Emperor immediately dispatched a reply, urging the Master to quicken his speed in his home-bound journey. Upon his arrival in the capital on the seventh day of the first month in the nineteenth year of Zhenguan (645 C.E.), the Master was given a warm and lively welcome by the Emperor. In the course of the conversation the Emperor inquired about the conditions in the various regions and countries the Master had visited. In reply the Master informed the Emperor of what he had seen or heard concerning the religion, geography, local products, habits and customs, climates, and legends and fables of the different localities of India and Central Asia. Fascinated by his account, the Emperor right away requested the Master to write a book about the journey for his reference. This was the cause of the compilation of this *Record*, which the Master completed in 646 C.E., the year after his return to the capital, with the assistance of Bianji, a monk-scholar of Zongchi Monastery, who was invited by imperial order to help the Master in his translation tasks. Bianji was not merely a stenographer who took down the Master's dictation, as he modestly says in his "Eulogy," but also an editor who put the Master's oral recital into the classical style of the Chinese written language. This is why Bianji's name appears on the title page as the compiler of the *Record*.

The name of the Master appears as the translator, perhaps because certain passages of the *Record*, such as the Jātaka stories, were not his but the work of earlier writers. (For further details of Xuanzang's life, see *The Biography of the Tripiṭaka Master of the Great Ci'en Monastery of the Great Tang Dynasty,* BDK English Tripiṭaka.)

Here I should like to mention that the passage at the end of Fascicle XI is an addition appended some seven hundred years after the time of Xuanzang. This passage deals with Zheng He's visit to Sri Lanka during the reign of Emperor Chengzu (r. 1403–24) of the Ming dynasty. Zheng He (1371–1435) was an influential eunuch at the court, and in 1405 he was ordered to lead an official mission to visit various countries in South Asia and around the Indian Ocean. In the course of his voyage, he visited King Bhuvanaikabāhu V (r. 1372–1408) of Sri Lanka. Thus it seems that Zheng He was probably the person who wrote this passage.

From the second half of the nineteenth century onwards, when French and English translations of the *Record* appeared, Indian and Western historians and archaeologists found this work of great value in filling certain gaps in the history of India and locating the sites of former glories of ancient India. With its exact descriptions of distances and locations of different places, the *Record* served as a guidebook for the excavation and rediscovery of such important ancient sites as the old city of Rājagṛha, the Temple of the Deer Park at Sarnath, the grottoes of Ajantā, the ruins of the well-known Nālandā Monastery in Bihar, etc. Thus it is not merely a book to be studied by students of Buddhism but also a substantial and interesting book of reference providing rich information about medieval India for the general reader.

Li Rongxi

March 10, 1995
Beijing

Preface

by Jing Bo

I venture to consider that the vast space between heaven and earth is so extensive, and that the dissimilarities of human beings endowed with consciousness and intelligence are so variant, that the *Talk on Heaven* could not trace their limits, nor could the *Comprehensive Map of the Earth* distinguish their original sources. From this we may know that it is impossible to relate all the places that are not mentioned in the regional records and lie beyond the reach of the influence and education of the imperial court. 867b

As regards India, it has a long history since its establishment as a country. There saints and sages spring up generation after generation, and the morality of kindness and justice is their common custom. But in the past we never had contacts with that country, and its territory is not conjoined with the Middle Kingdom. It is neither recorded in the *Shan-hai-jing* (Book on mountains and seas) nor mentioned in the *Wang-hui-pian* (Chapter on the royal meeting). Although Zhang Qian, the Marquis of Bowang, opened the road to the Western Regions, he was inspired in vain by the sight at Bactria of bamboo sticks produced at Qionglai Mountain in China. The Kunming route was obstructed by the mountainous region of Yuexi in the southwest, and so Emperor Wu of the Han dynasty could only excavate the Divine Lake at Chang'an to train his navy, but to no effect. Therefore even though astrological signs had shown the good omen of the birth of the Buddha, his abstruse teachings were impeded from being introduced to China for a thousand years. Emperor Ming of the Han dynasty dreamed of a golden figure with a sunlike halo behind its head, but the divine light of Buddhism was still enshrouded in secret ten thousand *li* away. When Cai Yin was dispatched to the Western Regions in search of the Buddhist religion, he invited Kāśyapa-Mātaṅga to Luoyang with Buddhist scriptures, which were preserved at the Rock Chamber but were not as profound as the texts kept in the Nāga Palace in India. The Buddha's portrait was drawn at the Terrace of Coolness, but it was not as fine as the statue erected at Vulture Peak.

After that the governance of the state became faulty, and eunuchs and men of ignoble character swayed the realm. They brought disaster upon the Eastern Capital and disrupted the country. The Empress and Empress Dowager started disturbances and split the nation as one tears a piece of silk into pieces. Political institutions and decrees died out at Hangu Pass and Luoyang, and beacon fires were set to give the alarm at the strategic watchtowers. Thus the cities became blockaded by fortresses at the four suburbs.

India was separated from here by a very great distance. There were, however, occasional inquisitive travelers who visited that country to hunt for novelty. Although they have left us some records, they did not make a full account of the products and topography of the places they visited. They merely quoted passages from books of strange stories and did not make a thorough study of the truth of *Bhūtatathatā* (Absolute truth).

Even at the time of the Sui dynasty, when the empire was
867c unified and the domain considerably expanded, people could only gaze at the sea in the West and regret that they were unable to proceed further. They had to ponder over the situation while looking at the country of Dongli (Tāmraliptī?). It is true that many a man has hoisted banners and flags outside the Yumen Pass, but no record can be found about anyone who successfully crossed the Pamir Range. How could anyone ride through the Snow Mountains and halt for a while beside the Dragon's Lake? This was really because the virtue of the Sui rulers was not pervasive and their prestige not far-reaching.

The House of Great Tang, holding sway over the empire, has opened up the world for the initiation of imperial prospects. The comets [of rebels] have been swept away, and the fortune of the nation has been brightened. Its achievements are as great as the creation of the universe, and its brilliance is equal to the light of the sun and the moon. All people are grateful for having gained a new life, as if they had been saved from the mouths of jackals and wolves. Every family is glad about having a new lease on life, as if their souls had returned from the sphere of ghosts and monsters. Alien residents of different nationalities reside on Gao Street in the capital, and all distant and desolate places are included in the imperial territory. It may be said that the Ten Fairy Islands are parts of the Imperial Garden, and that the four seas are regarded as its ponds and pools. The Five Emperors of old are slighted and the monarchs of ancient ages are held in scorn.

Having entered the Gate of the Dharma in his childhood, the Dharma-master [Xuanzang] regretted that he had not been to the Jetavana Garden; and when he grew up, he thought about the traces left by the Buddha and eagerly looked forward to visiting the Deer Park. Thus he lifted up his robe to start the journey to the Land of Purity; this was his long-cherished desire.

At a time when the general mood of honesty was prevailing westwards, and in the season when the climate was suitable for officials to take home-bound trips to the east, he started his journey with his pewter staff in hand in the third year of Zhenguan. Under the spiritual protection of his ancestors, he was able to reach lands with various customs, and he met with many dangers that he eventually weathered safely. With the aid of deities, he traversed risky paths, from which he barely escaped with his life. He suffered the abrupt changes of scorching heat and bitter cold, passing through many places before he reached his destination. If we speak of inquiring into the truth, it depends on whether one sees or does not see the difference between the theories of voidness and existence; and research into the sublime teachings lies in whether one has or has not heard about the doctrine of birth and death. Doubts about the sea of truth must be solved to enable all living beings to awaken from the stream of delusion. Thus he collected various scriptures, of which not a single word did he not understand, and he visited all the holy sites, none of which did he not see in person. After having travelled for many years, he returned home and reached Chang'an in the first month of the nineteenth year [of Zhenguan], bringing back six hundred fifty-seven books, which he translated into Chinese by imperial decree.

He personally visited one hundred ten countries and heard information about twenty-eight countries. Some of them are mentioned in the historical records of previous dynasties, while others are known to us for the first time in the present age. All of them are influenced by the spirit of harmony and enjoy the benevolence of Great Tang. They have paid homage and submitted to the authority of the Emperor, beseeching him to dispatch officials to reform their language. They climbed mountainous paths to come to offer tribute, and they were so merrily entertained at the imperial court that they clapped their hands; dressed in the costume of the Tang, they formed into groups. Regarding their different products and local conditions, as well as their social customs and mountains and rivers, we have to refer to their books, for ancient times; for recent times, we can inquire of elderly people. Distant are those alien countries, but they appear clearly before our eyes. We need not take the trouble to write letters to find out details that are already written on white silk and entitled *The Great Tang Dynasty Record of the Western Regions* in twelve fascicles kept in one cloth slipcase. I humbly consider that the information provided in this book is quite detailed, while certain trivial matters and minor events will, I hope, make up what is missing in former historical works.

This is the preface composed by Jing Bo, Assistant Writer of the Imperial Secretarial Department.

Preface

by Yu Zhining, Duke of Yanguo and Left Premier of the Board of Ministers

As the ray emitted from the white curl between the Buddha's eyebrows illuminates the whole earth, so the sweet dew of his teachings spreads over the Great Chiliocosm. Like a golden mirror that shines brightly, the great order of the Tang Empire prevails over the whole domain. Having manifested the three spheres of the world, the Buddha-dharma may be considered the most venerable of all religions. With the light of virtue shining upon the four quarters, the Tang Empire possesses the largest territory in the world. After the shadow of the Buddha, the Sun of Wisdom, disappeared, his teachings were introduced to China in the East, and the Way of the Emperor was so glorious that his moral influence reached far to the West. 868a

The Tripiṭaka-master of the Ci'en Monastery is named Xuanzang and has the family name of Chen; his ancestors were natives of Yingchuan. When the Yellow Emperor ascended the throne at Youxiong, he controlled Huazhu and established the Chen family. Emperor Shun threw open the doors at the four sides of his audience hall to receive the princes and dukes under his sovereignty, and he laid the foundation of his lofty structure even when he was farming at Lishan. King Wu of the Zhou dynasty conferred the fief of Chen on a descendant of Emperor Shun and made his offspring one of the three respectable families. Chen Ping's six ingenious stratagems played a glorious part in the establishment of the Han dynasty, and the petitions submitted by Chen Chong and his son Chen Zhong to the emperors of the Later Han dynasty were like brilliant moonlight shining upon the world after sunset. When Chen

Shi and his sons and nephews visited Xun Shu and his sons, Jupiter, the Star of Virtue, appeared in the sky to mark the meeting of virtuous people of great talent. Prominent figures emerged in the Chen clan in successive generations, like huge fishes swimming freely side by side in the sea, or enormous rocs flying high with wings fully extended. By their traditional virtue, not only did the stock of the Chen family prosper but also its branches flourished as those of a distinguished clan.

The Master was born under the favorable auspices of the light of harmony and the appearance of the Star of Virtue. He has deep roots with exuberant foliage, and the source of his Way is profound and long-lasting. In his infancy he had a lofty bearing like the glow of the rising sun and moon, and in childhood he proved to be a good son as admirable and fragrant as orchids and osmanthus. When he had grown up, he studied well the ancient books, and his fame spread all over the country, so much so that the local governments of various places vied with each other in inviting him to serve in their offices. But he could discern truth from falsehood at an early age and always had compassion and wisdom. He longed to gain a clear understanding of truth and sighed at the limitations of human life. He regarded the red silk ribbon attached to the official seal and the purple belts worn by government officials as snares of the material world, and he thought that those Precious Vehicles the *Ekayāna* (One Vehicle) and the esoteric texts were truly the ways leading one out of the world. Therefore he despised all worldly things as dust and rubbish, and talked only about serene and broadminded principles.

His elder brother, the Venerable Changjie, a pillar of the Gate of Buddhism, was as energetic as a Nāga (dragon or elephant) in practicing the Way, and his wisdom might be compared with that of Śāriputra of yore. Both those who held office at court and those who were not in office respected him for his good demeanor and learning, and his repute and literary talent were admired by people both at home and abroad. The two brothers had a deep feeling of fraternity in concordance with the ethical relationships between members of a family. The Master was diligent in serving his elder brother and in receiving instruction from him without wasting a single moment. His accomplishments in learning qualified him to be a Chief Monk and thus occupy an outstanding position in a monastery. His virtue coincided with the principle of the Middle Way, and he was well-known among his fellow monks. He galloped along the Path of Equality and comprehended the nine classes of the Buddhist texts, his scope of learning being as extensive as the marshland of Yunmeng. He rowed his way in the sea of abstruse teachings, looking down upon the Four Vedas, which appeared to him insignificant. After that he travelled for several years to various places to attend lectures on Buddhist theories, until he succeeded in his studies and gained achievement in learning.

In the remote past, at the beginning of time, the sun and moon shone upon the Terrace of Spirituality, and Yang Xiong deliberated about the Way of Heaven, which called for deep thought in one's mind. Then the teachings of the Buddha were gradually revealed, waiting to be spread far and wide. Holding the jade handle of his 868b
chowrie, the Master waved off the mist on the sea to unveil the billows, just like an experienced wheelwright who knows the essence of his craft or a zither maker who understands the knack of producing musical instruments. He was so well informed that he instructed people with the fluency of water pouring out of a bottle, and he travelled alone far away from his native place in a small boat. While he was still at home, he defeated a boastful man who bragged that he had to wear a copper belt around his waist lest his abdomen should burst under the pressure of the knowledge he had in his possession; and when he came to the region of Shu, he informed his elder brother that he had the desire to travel abroad. People far and near said to him, "We have heard that the Xun family of old had eight prominent sons, and now we see that the Chen clan has two outstanding brothers. It is true that many distinguished persons have emerged in the region between Ruzhou and the Ying River!"

From his youth until he arrived at manhood, the Master engaged himself in studying abstruse Buddhist books. Well-known scholars and predecessors grasped the theories of different sects of Buddhism, performing detailed research into side issues and forgetting about the root, plucking flowers while neglecting the fruits. Thus they gave rise to the southern and northern schools with various tenets and contradictory arguments. In the long-standing theoretical contentions, he was at a loss what to do, and feared that the translators might have made mistakes and caused confusion, so that he might not be able to get a thorough understanding of the ultimate truth. With this view in mind, he wished to read all Buddhist texts at the Nāga Palace in India.

At a time when the country was most prosperous, and equipped with unparalleled virtue, he started his journey to the remote lands carrying his pewter staff and whisked the dust off his robe. In this manner he left Chang'an behind to proceed with big strides toward the Pamir Range. In his long journey over land and water, he experienced all sorts of hardships and risks. He considered the journey undertaken by the Marquis of Bowang not a long one and regarded Faxian as having travelled only in a limited area. Wherever he went he studied the local dialect and conducted research into the profound theories there; and he probed into the essence of the Buddhist teachings in a marvelous way. Thus he was eloquent in debate and became famous in India, and he brought back to China the Buddhist scriptures written on palm leaves.

Emperor Taizong, who ascended the precious throne as a Gold Wheel King, was a person of elegant character. He granted an interview to the Master in the inner chamber of the imperial palace, showing the consideration due to a learned scholar, and listened attentively to what he said. He personally wrote decrees to express his friendly feeling to the Master and sent palace messengers incessantly to inquire after his health. At the request of the Master, the Emperor composed the *Preface to the Holy Teachings of the Tripiṭaka* in seven hundred eighty characters. When the reigning Emperor [Gaozong] was crown prince and living at the Spring Palace, he wrote *A Record Relating the Preface to the Holy Teachings of the Tripiṭaka* in five hundred seventy-nine characters.

If the Master had not cast the light of his prestige upon the Kukkuṭārāma Monastery and had not spread his fame over Vulture Peak in India, how could the Emperors have condescended to write such ornamental compositions for the commendation of a contemporary scholar?

Under imperial edict, the Master translated six hundred fifty-seven Sanskrit texts into Chinese. Having witnessed the strange customs of distant lands, the typical scenes of remote countries, the special products of different places, the peculiar orders of human relations, the regions where the Chinese almanac has been adopted, and the localities where Chinese culture and influence have reached, he wrote *The Great Tang Dynasty Record of the Western Regions* in twelve fascicles, in which he cited passages from profound and obscure texts and included comprehensive investigations and detailed textual researches done in such a way as to render it a work of lasting value.

Fascicle I

Thirty-four Countries, From Agni to Kāpiśī

1. The Country of Agni
2. The Country of Kuci
3. The Country of Bālukā
4. The Country of Nujkend
5. The Country of Shash
6. The Country of Feihan
7. The Country of Sutrūshana
8. The Country of Samarkand
9. The Country of Mimohe
10. The Country of Kapūtānā
11. The Country of Kuṣāṇika
12. The Country of Khagan
13. The Country of Bukhārā
14. The Country of Betik
15. The Country of Horiṣmīka
16. The Country of Kasanna
17. The Country of Tirmidh
18. The Country of Sahāniyan
19. The Country of Kharūn
20. The Country of Shūmān
21. The Country of Kuvāyāna
22. The Country of Wakhsh
23. The Country of Khuttalān
24. The Country of Komidai
25. The Country of Baghlan
26. The Country of Hrum-Simingān
27. The Country of Khulm
28. The Country of Baktra
29. The Country of Zumathān
30. The Country of Gūzgānān
31. The Country of Talaqān
32. The Country of Kacik
33. The Country of Bāmīyāna
34. The Country of Kāpiśī

By counting the grand strategies of successive Emperors and read- 868c
ing the records of remote events of the past monarchs, we know
that when Emperor Fuxi first ascended the throne, and when the
Yellow Emperor began to rule over the country, they managed the 869a
affairs of the people and divided the country into administrative
regions. When Emperor Yao of Tang received the Mandate of Heaven
to be the sovereign, his glory reached the four quarters, and when

Emperor Shun of Yu accepted the map of the empire, his virtue spread over all the nine districts. Since then only the memoranda recording past events have been transmitted, and if one wishes to hear from the former sages, one can only listen to the historians who recorded their words. How can these be compared with our time, when good government prevails in the empire under a monarch who reigns without ruling?

As to our great Tang dynasty, it has held sway over the empire in accordance with the Mandate of Heaven; taking advantage of the times, it has controlled the power of governance. The Emperor has united the six quarters into one domain and filled it with his glory, and he has succeeded to the virtuous deeds of the three ancient Emperors as the fourth one in order, illuminating the world with his light. His subtle influence has permeated widely, and his auspicious edification has extended far. He possesses the power of covering and carrying all things like heaven and earth, and he acts with the functions of both the stimulating wind and the moistening rain. With the Yi tribe at the eastern border coming to present tribute, and the Rong people of the western frontier arriving to pledge allegiance, he has founded an imperial heritage for his posterity; and in quelling rebellion to restore order, he certainly has surpassed former kings. His great deeds have included all those achieved by previous dynasties. Now the whole empire is in such a uniformity that we use the same characters in writing and our carriages have standard wheels to go in the same ruts. This is the marvellous achievement of his consummate government. If I did not mention all these points in my *Record*, I should have nowhere to praise his great exploits, and if I did not publish them abroad, how could I shed light on his profuse merits? Wherever I went in my journey, I inquired about the local conditions and customs; and although I did not do research into their locations, nor did I differentiate their social institutions, I believe that the great merits of the Emperor [Taizong] have surpassed those of the three ancient Emperors and the five monarchs of old. All living creatures are benefitted by his genial influence, and every human being who can speak extols his merits. From the Tang Empire up to the land of India, all the people either of secluded regions with different customs, or of isolated places and alien countries, accept the Chinese calendar and enjoy the fame and teachings of the Emperor. The praise of his military feats has become a topic of conversation, and the commendation of his civic virtue is the most popular theme. I examined various books but found no records of these things, and I presume that there is no similar instance mentioned in the genealogical tables. Had I not made this narration, how could I record the beneficial influence of the Emperor? The narratives I have now composed are based on what I saw and heard.

Now the Sahā world, consisting of one Great Chiliocosm, is the sphere of the spiritual influence of one Buddha. The four continents under the illumination of one sun and moon within the Great Chiliocosm are the places where the Buddhas, the World-honored Ones, emerge in their incarnation bodies and manifest birth and death to enlighten saints and ordinary beings. Mount Sumeru, meaning the Wonderful High Mountain, is composed of the four precious substances. It is located in the sea, standing on the golden wheel, under the illumination of the sun and moon in rotation, being the residence of heavenly beings, surrounded by a ring of seven mountains and seven seas. The water in the seas between the mountains possesses the eight virtues. Beyond the seven golden mountains is the Salt Sea. Roughly speaking, there are four habitable continents in the seas, namely, the Videha continent in the east, the Jambu continent in the south, the Godānīya continent in the west, and the Kuru continent in the north. A Gold 869b
Wheel King rules over all these four continents, a Silver Wheel King administers all except the Kuru continent in the north, a Copper Wheel King's domination does not include the Kuru continent in the north or the Godānīya continent in the west, while an Iron Wheel King controls only the Jambu continent in the south. When a Wheel King is about to ascend the throne, a great precious wheel of gold, silver, copper, or iron will appear in the air according to his merits, to empower him to rule over four, three, two, or

one continent as the case may be. As the wheel is an auspicious symbol, it is adopted as the title of the kings.

In the center of the Jambu continent is the Anavatapta Lake, meaning "No Trouble of Heat," which is south of the Fragrant Mountain and north of the Great Snow Mountains, with a circuit of eight hundred *li*. Its banks are adorned with gold, silver, lapis lazuli, and crystal. It is full of golden sand, and its water is as pure and clean as a mirror. A Bodhisattva of the eighth stage, having transformed himself into a Nāga king by the power of his resolute will, makes his abode at the bottom of the lake and supplies water for the Jambu continent. Thus from the mouth of the Silver Ox at the east side of the lake flows out the Ganges, which after going round the lake once enters the Southeast Sea; from the mouth of the Golden Elephant at the south side of the lake flows out the Indus, which after winding round the lake once enters the Southwest Sea; from the mouth of the Lapis Lazuli Horse at the west side of the lake flows out the Oxus, which after meandering round the lake once enters the Northwest Sea; and from the mouth of the Crystal Lion at the north side of the lake flows out the Sītā, which after encircling the lake once enters the Northeast Sea, or it is said that it flows by a subterranean course to the Jishi Mountain, where the water reappears as a tributary of the Sītā and becomes the source of the Yellow River in China.

As there is no ruler now destined to be a Wheel King, the Jambu continent is reigned by four lords. The dominion under the sovereignty of the Lord of Elephants in the south is hot and humid in climate, and it is fit for breeding elephants. In the west the Lord of Treasure rules over the land beside the sea, where there are plenty of precious substances. The place of the Lord of Horses in the north is cold and bracing, and it is good for rearing horses. The country of the Lord of Men in the east is well-populated with amiable inhabitants. The people of the Lord of Elephants are impetuous by nature, but they are devoted to studies and are especially skillful in miraculous arts. They wear a piece of cloth across the body, leaving the right shoulder bare. Their hair is made into a topknot with tufts falling down on the sides. They live in groups of clans in towns, and their houses are multi-storied. In the country of the Lord of Treasure, the people know nothing of propriety and righteousness and overestimate wealth and property. They wear short jackets fastened on the left side and cut their hair short but keep long moustaches. They live in towns and gain profit by engaging in trade. The people under the rule of the Lord of Horses are of a furious disposition and are cruel man-slayers. They live in felt yurts and are migratory herdsmen. In the land of the Lord of Men, the people are clever and skillful with obvious sentiments of kindness and righteousness. They wear hats and belts, and their garments are buttoned on the right side. Their carriages and clothes are classified according to the ranks and orders of the people, and they are attached to their native land and unwilling to leave it. They have a class of people specially devoted to commerce.

Excluding the Lord of Men, the other three lords hold the east
as the superior direction. Their people build houses with doors 869c
opening to the east, and early in the morning they pay reverence toward that direction. In the land of the Lord of Men, the people respect the southern direction. Such is the general condition of the different customs and modes of living in the diverse countries. As regards the etiquette observed between a monarch and his subjects and that between the superior and the inferior, and the cultural institutions and political systems, the land of the Lord of Men excels all the other countries; while as to instructions concerning the purification of the mind, and liberation from worldly burdens, as well as teachings to relieve one from birth and death, the theories are the best in the country of the Lord of Elephants. All these matters are recorded in classical works and imperial mandates and are also heard from the local people. I have made a careful check about what I saw and heard.

Though the Buddha was born in the West, his Dharma has spread to the East. In the course of translation, mistakes may have crept into the texts, and idioms may have been misapplied. When the words are wrong, the meaning is lost, and when a phrase is mistaken, the doctrine becomes distorted. Hence the saying, "It is necessary to use correct names." What is valuable is the absence of faults!

Human beings are of different dispositions, stubborn or pliable, and speak different languages. This is caused by climatic conditions and by customary usage. As to the varieties of physical features and natural products of the land of the Lord of Men, and the different customs and temperaments of its people, they are recorded in detail in our national histories. As to the customs of the land of the Lord of Horses and the country of the Lord of Treasure, they are fully described in historical records, and we can give a brief account of them. But as to the country of the Lord of Elephants, it has never been described accurately in our ancient literature. Some said that it was mostly a hot and humid country, and others depicted its people as customarily fond of kindness and compassion. These are mentioned in topographies, but no detailed information can be found. As the Way is sometimes prevalent and sometimes in hiding, do not human affairs also have changes of fortune? Thus we may know that it is difficult to describe all those who predict the right season to pledge allegiance and who come to submit to the benevolence of the Emperor, or who passing one danger after another seek admittance at Yumen Pass and bearing tribute of native rarities, bow before the gate of the imperial palace. That is why, in the intervals of my studies during my long journey inquiring for truth, I took notes on the conditions and customs along the way.

Up to the Black Range, the customs of the Hu people are prevalent. Although they live together with the Rong people in the same localities, they are distinct in tribes, and their territories are demarcated. They are mostly aborigines, living in walled cities, engaging in agriculture and rearing cattle. They value wealth and property, and to despise kindness and righteousness is their custom. They have no ceremony for marriage and no distinction between the superior people and the inferior. The wife's word is authoritative, and the husband occupies a low position. They cremate the bodies of the dead and have no fixed period of mourning,

but they scrape their faces, mutilate their ears, cut off their hair, and rend their garments. They slaughter domestic animals as sacrifices offered to the manes of the dead. On happy occasions they put on white clothes, while at sorrowful events they are dressed in black. This is a brief account of the common or similar 870a
customs of the tribes; the different politics and various institutions of diverse countries will be described separately as the occasion arises, and the manners and customs of India will be narrated in the following *Record*.

Going out of what was formerly the land of Gaochang, I started my journey with the nearest country, called Agni (formerly known as Yanqi).

The country of Agni, which is more than six hundred *li* from east to west and over four hundred *li* from south to north, its capital city being six or seven *li* in circuit, is surrounded by hills on four sides with perilous tracks that are easily defended. Spring water flows in a network of channels, leading the water to irrigate cultivated fields. The soil is suitable for growing millet, broomcorn, winter wheat, fragrant jujubes, grapes, pears, crabapples, and other fruits. The climate is moderate and pleasant, and the people are honest and straightforward by social custom. Their alphabet is taken from that of India with slight modifications. The garments of the people are made of felt and hempen cloth. The men cut their hair short without wearing any headdress. As to their currency, they use gold, silver, and small copper coins. The king, a native of the country, is a man of bravery but short of resourcefulness; he indulges in bragging about his own merits. The country has no guiding principle or discipline, and government orders are imperfect and not seriously implemented. There are more than ten monasteries with over two thousand monks, who are followers of the Sarvāstivāda school of the Hinayana teachings. Since they practice the scriptural theories and observe the Vinaya discipline of India, the students carefully study these subjects in Indian texts. They are pure and strict in observing the

Vinaya rules, but they take the three kinds of pure meat together with other foodstuffs, which shows that they are stagnating in the stage of the gradual teaching.

Going from here toward the southwest for more than two hundred *li*, I climbed over a hill and crossed two large rivers, and then I reached a plain in the west. After proceeding for more than seven hundred *li*, I arrived in the country of Kuci (formerly known as Qiuci).

The country of Kuci is over one thousand *li* from east to west and over six hundred *li* from south to north, and its capital city is about seventeen or eighteen *li* in circuit. The soil is fit for growing millet and wheat. It yields round-grained rice, grapes, and pomegranates, and plenty of pears, crabapples, peaches, and apricots. It produces gold, copper, iron, lead, and tin. Its climate is mild and the people are honest and upright by nature. Their writing is taken from that of India but with minor alterations. Their skill in playing wind and stringed instruments is well known in various countries. They dress in brocade and hempen clothes, cut their hair short, and wear turbans. For currency they use gold, silver, and small copper coins. Being a man of the Kuci race, the king has little resourcefulness and is under the control of powerful ministers. It is their custom to press the heads of their babies into a flat shape with wooden planks. There are over one hundred monasteries with some five thousand monks, who study the Sarvāstivāda school of the Hinayana teachings. Their scriptural teachings and Vinaya discipline follow the example of India, and so they study the books on these subjects in the original Indian language. As they eat the three kinds of pure meat together with other foodstuffs, they are still stagnating in the stage of the gradual teaching. But they are pure in conduct and deeply engrossed in studies, and they compete with one another in their achievement of spiritual cultivation.

In front of a deva-temple to the north of a city in the eastern part of the country there is a big dragon pond. The dragons of the pond often changed their form to mate with mares and gave birth to dragon-colts, which were fierce and unruly. But the offspring of the dragon-colts were tamable. That is why plenty of fine horses

are bred in this country. I heard some old people saying that there 870b
was recently a king named Golden Flower, who by his sagacious administration and sharp insight into political affairs moved one of the dragons to pull his carriage for him. When the king was approaching his death, he touched the dragon's ear with his whip, and then it submerged into the pond and hid itself to the present time. As there was no well in the city, the people drew water from this pond. The dragons transformed themselves into the forms of men and mated with the women. Their descendants were strong and courageous and could run as fast as a galloping horse. In this manner the blood of the dragons was diffused, and everybody became a man of the dragon race. Relying upon their physical strength, they rode roughshod over others and paid no heed to the king's orders. Thus the king colluded with the Turks to slaughter all the inhabitants old and young in the city. After the massacre, not a single man was left living in the city, which is now a deserted place without a trace of human habitation.

More than forty *li* to the north of the deserted city, there are two monasteries separated by a river close to the corner of a mountain. Both monasteries, one on the east side and the other on the west side of the river, are named Cakuri. The images of the Buddha and the ornaments are so beautifully made that they almost excel human craftsmanship. The monks are pure and austere in conduct and are sincere and diligent in studies.

In the Buddha hall of the Eastern Cakuri Monastery, there is a jade stone about two feet in width, yellowish white in color, in the shape of a sea clam. On the stone there is a footprint of the Buddha, one foot eight inches in length and more than six inches in breadth. On the fast days it sometimes issues a brilliant light.

There are two standing statues of the Buddha, more than ninety feet in height, one at each side of the road outside the west gate of the capital city. It is at this place in front of the statues that the great quinquennial congregations are held. For several tens of days around the autumnal equinox every year, all the monks in the whole country come here to attend a meeting. From the monarch and princes on top down to the commoners, all suspend their secular affairs and observe the precepts; and they study the scriptures and listen to the discourses on the Dharma for a whole day at a time without feeling fatigue. All the monasteries decorate their images of the Buddha with jewels and gems and dress them in brocade and damask, and carry them in handcarts, counted by the thousand, to conduct what is known as the procession of images, flocking to the place of the meeting. The king always discusses state affairs with his ministers on the fifteenth and the last day of the lunar month, and after consulting with the eminent monks about their discussion, they make a proclamation.

At the northwest of the meeting place I crossed a river and reached the Āścarya (Marvellous) Monastery. The buildings and courtyards of the monastery are splendid and spacious, and the Buddha images are well adorned. The monks, quiet and austere in appearance, are diligent in studies and without negligence. Old people of virtue with much learning and great talents are venerated. In admiration of their good conduct, brilliant scholars come here from distant lands to stay with them. The king and his ministers as well as the common people and magnates provide the monks with the four monastic requisites with increasing respect as time goes on.

I heard some old people saying that once a previous king of this country, who revered the Triple Gem, wished to go on tour to worship various holy sites at different places and had his younger brother act as regent during his absence. Upon receiving the order of the king, the younger brother secretly cut off his own genital organ and put it in a golden casket as a precaution against possible calumniation. He sent the casket to the king, who asked, "What is it?" His younger brother said in reply, "Upon your re-
870c turn, Your Majesty may open it and see." The casket was then handed to a guard of the king's retinue for safekeeping during the journey. When the king returned from his trip, a slanderer actually accused the regent, saying, "The regent appointed by the king committed adultery in the inner palace." On hearing this accusation,

the king was enraged and intended to impose a heavy punishment on the culprit. His younger brother said, "I would not dare evade the responsibility, but I hope the golden casket can be opened." When the king opened the casket and found a severed male organ contained in it, he asked, "What is this strange thing? What do you want to say about it?" His younger brother said, "When Your Majesty went out on tour and appointed me as regent, I feared that the disaster of possible calumniation might befall me, and so I cut off my organ to prove my innocence. Now this misfortune has actually happened to me. I hope Your Majesty will make a clear investigation into the case." The king was deeply surprised to hear this, and since then his fraternity toward his younger brother became more profound, so that he was allowed free admission to the inner palace without hindrance.

Later, when the king's younger brother was walking on the road, he met with a herdsman driving a herd of five hundred bulls to be castrated. On seeing these animals that were to suffer the same impairment as he had, the king's younger brother reflected on his own fate and thought, "Is it not due to my past evil deeds that I am now in this life a deformed man?" Thus he redeemed the herd of bulls from mutilation with money and valuables, and by the power of his compassion his genital organ was gradually restored. As he regained masculinity, he refused to enter the inner palace any more. When the amazed king asked him why, he told the king all the details. Regarding it as a marvellous affair, the king constructed this monastery in a beautiful style to transmit [his brother's] good reputation to posterity.

From here going westwards for more than six hundred *li*, I crossed a small desert and arrived in the country of Bālukā (formerly known as Gumo or Jimo).

The country of Bālukā is over six hundred *li* from east to west and more than three hundred *li* from south to north, its capital city being five or six *li* in circuit. The native products, climate, temperament of the people, customs, written language, and law are the same as in the country of Kuci, but the spoken language is somewhat different. Its fine cotton and hempen cloth is much valued in the neighboring countries. There are several tens of monasteries with more than a thousand monks, who study the Sarvāstivāda school of the Hinayana teachings.

From this country proceeding northwest for more than three hundred *li*, I crossed a stony desert and reached the Ice Mountains, which are located at the northern side of the Pamir Range, where most of the streams flow eastwards. Snow is accumulated in the valleys, which are freezing even in the spring and summer seasons, and although they sometimes melt a little, they become frozen very soon. The path is dangerous and the cold wind blows with a piercing vehemence. There are frequent disasters caused by ferocious dragons that give trouble to travellers. Passengers going by this path should not wear garments of reddish brown color, nor should they carry calabashes, nor shout loudly. The slightest in-
871a fringement of the taboos will cause immediate disaster. A fierce wind will arise all of a sudden with sand flying in the air and pebbles raining down from the sky. Those who encounter such a catastrophe are sure to die, [or at least] it is difficult for them to escape alive.

Going among the mountains for over four hundred *li*, I reached the Great Pure Lake (also known as the Hot Sea or the Salt Sea), which is more than one thousand *li* in circuit. It is long from east to west and narrow from south to north. There are hills around the lake with many streams flowing into it. The water is bluish dark in color and brackish and bitter in taste. It is a vast expanse of water with huge and boisterous billows. Fish and dragons live together in the lake, and supernatural monsters sometimes appear in it. Therefore passing travellers pray to them for good fortune, and there are plenty of aquatic animals, but nobody would venture to catch them.

From the Pure Lake going northwest for more than five hundred *li*, I reached the City of the Sushe River, which is about six or seven *li* in circuit, a place where traders of the Hu tribes from different countries mingle their abodes. The soil is good for growing millet, wheat, and grapes, but fruit trees are scarce. The climate is windy and cold, and the people wear clothes made of felt and hemp. To the west of the Sushe River are some tens of isolated cities, each having its own ruler, but they do not obey one another, and all of them are under the domination of the Turks.

The region stretching from the City of the Sushe River up to the country of Kasanna is called Suli, and the people are known by the same name. Their language is also known as Suli. The alphabet of their language is brief and simple, having only twenty-odd rudimentary letters, with which a vast vocabulary is formed by a methodical spelling system. The people have rough written records, which are read vertically and are transmitted from teacher to pupil without interruption. They dress in felt and hempen clothes and put on fur and cotton garments. Both their undergarments and their upper clothes fit tightly. They cut their hair trimly and expose their tops, or shave their heads, tying a colored silk band on their forehead. They are tall and sturdy in stature but timid in disposition. Their general mood is perfidious and deceptive. They are mostly avaricious and take account of money matters even between father and son. Rich men are honored and esteemed, and there is no distinction between the well-born and the low-born. A millionaire, however, may lead a simple and coarse life. Half of the population are farmers and the other half traders.

Going westward from Sushe City for more than four hundred *li*, I arrived at the Thousand Springs. The district known by this name is over two hundred *li* square, facing the Snow Mountains in the north, with plains on the three other sides. The soil is fertile and damp and there are luxuriant trees. In late spring various flowers bloom as beautifully as embroidered silk. As there are a thousand springs, the district is named as such. The Turkish Khan often comes here in the summer season to avoid the heat. There are flocks of deer, most of them wearing bells and rings. They are docile and friendly with men and do not easily become so afraid as to flee. These animals are pets of the Khan, who has forbidden his subjects to slaughter them on penalty of death; and so they can live out their natural lifetimes.

Going westward from Thousand Springs for one hundred forty or fifty *li*, I reached the city of Taras, which is eight or nine *li* in circuit, being a place where traders of the Hu tribes from different countries make their abodes together. The natural products and climate are roughly the same as in Sushe. Going southward for about ten *li* is the Small Isolated Town, in which live more than three hundred families of Chinese who were formerly taken prisoner by the Turks. Afterward they gathered together all their compatriots and safeguarded this town, in which they settled. They
871b adopted the costume and etiquette of the Turks but retained the language and ways of life of their own country.

From here going southwest for more than two hundred *li*, I arrived at the City of White Water, which is six or seven *li* in circuit. The native products and climatic conditions are much better than in Taras. Going south for more than two hundred *li*, I reached Gongyu City, which is five or six *li* in circuit. The plains and marshlands are rich and fertile and covered with luxuriant trees. From here going south for forty or fifty *li*, I came to the country of Nujkend.

The country of Nujkend is more than one thousand *li* in circuit, and the soil is fertile, tilled and reaped perfectly. The vegetation is luxuriant and there are profuse flowers and fruits. Grapes are grown in large quantities and are highly valued. There are about a hundred cities and towns, each governed by its own ruler, and they are mutually independent in taking action. Although they have clearly demarcated areas, they are collectively known as the country of Nujkend. From here going westward for over two hundred *li*, I came to the country of Shash (known as the country of Shi in Chinese).

The country of Shash is more than one thousand *li* in circuit, bordering on the She River on the west. It is narrow from east to west and long from south to north. The natural products and climate are the same as in Nujkend. There are several tens of cities and towns, each having its own ruler without a sovereign lord, and all of them are under the control of the Turks. From here proceeding southeast for more than one thousand *li*, I reached the country of Feihan.

The country of Feihan is over four thousand *li* in circuit and is surrounded by mountains on four sides. The land is fertile and the agricultural products are rich. There are plenty of flowers and fruits, and it is fit for rearing sheep and horses. The climate is windy and cold, and the people are stout and brave by nature. Their language is different from those of other countries, and their features are ugly and misshapen. For the last several decades there has been no sovereign ruler in the country; the chieftains compete with one another for power and no one yields to the others. They have delimited the boundaries of their districts by rivers and precipitous mountains. From here going westward for more than one thousand *li*, I reached the country of Sutrūshana.

The country of Sutrūshana is fourteen or fifteen hundred *li* in circuit, bordering on the She River on the east, which has its source in the plateau to the north of the Pamir Range. It is a mighty river of muddy water with rapid currents. The native products and customs are the same as in the country of Shash. In this country there is a king, who is affiliated with the Turks.

From here going toward the northwest, I entered a great desert in which there is absolutely no water or grass. The roads are lost in the vast waste, and its limits are unfathomable. Only by looking at the huge mountains and following the scattered skeletons can one know the direction and find the path. After travelling for over five hundred *li*, I reached the country of Samarkand (known as Kangguo in Chinese).

The country of Samarkand is sixteen or seventeen hundred *li* in circuit, long from east to west and narrow from south to north. The capital city is more than twenty *li* in circuit and is a completely invulnerable stronghold with a large population. Precious goods 871c
of different quarters are mostly centralized in this country. The soil is rich and fertile, and all kinds of crops are cultivated. The trees of the forests are luxuriant and have profuse flowers and fruits. This country yields many good horses, and its skillful craftsmen are the best among various countries. The climate is mild and temperate, but the people are irascible by nature. The various

states of the Hu tribe regard this country as their center, and the people far and near follow the example of this country in social manners and behavior. The king is a valorous man, and the neighboring countries obey his orders. He has a strong military force consisting of a large body of Cakar warriors, and the people of Cakar are courageous by nature, fearless of death, and without rivals in fighting. From here proceeding toward the southeast, one goes to the country of Mimohe (known as Miguo in Chinese).

The country of Mimohe is four or five hundred *li* in circuit, situated in the middle of a plain, narrow from east to west and long from south to north. The native products and customs are the same as in the country of Samarkand. From here proceeding toward the north, one arrives at the country of Kapūtānā (known as Caoguo in Chinese).

The country of Kapūtānā is fourteen or fifteen hundred *li* in circuit, long from east to west and narrow from south to north. The native products and customs are the same as in the country of Samarkand. From this country proceeding westward for more than three hundred *li*, one arrives at the country of Kuṣāṇika (known as Heguo in Chinese).

The country of Kuṣāṇika is fourteen or fifteen hundred *li* in circuit, narrow from east to west and long from south to north. The native products and customs are the same as in the country of Samarkand. From this country proceeding westward for more than two hundred *li*, one reaches the country of Khagan (known as East Anguo in Chinese).

The country of Khagan is more than one thousand *li* in circuit, and the native products and customs are the same as in the country of Samarkand. From this country proceeding westward for more than four hundred *li*, one reaches the country of Bukhārā (known as Middle Anguo in Chinese).

The country of Bukhārā is sixteen or seventeen hundred *li* in circuit, long from east to west and narrow from south to north. The native products and customs are the same as in the country of Samarkand. From this country proceeding westward for more than four hundred *li*, one reaches the country of Betik (known as West Anguo in Chinese).

The country of Betik is more than four hundred *li* in circuit and its native products and customs are the same as in the country of Samarkand. From here proceeding southwest for over five hundred *li*, one reaches the country of Horiṣmīka.

The country of Horiṣmīka, lying along the Oxus River on both banks, is twenty or thirty *li* from east to west and over five hundred *li* from south to north. The native products and customs are the same as in the country of Betik, but the language is slightly different. Going southwest from the country of Samarkand for more than three hundred *li*, I reached the country of Kasanna (known as Shiguo in Chinese).

The country of Kasanna is fourteen or fifteen hundred *li* in circuit, and the native products and customs are the same as in the country of Samarkand. From here going southwest for more than two hundred *li*, I entered a mountainous region, where the 872a
roads are rough and rugged and the narrow path is dangerous. There are no inhabitants and little water and grass. Going southeast among the mountains for over three hundred *li*, I entered the Iron Gate.

On both sides of the Iron Gate there are precipitous rocks. Although there is a narrow path, it is hardly accessible. The rocky walls standing on both sides of the path are of the color of iron. The door-leaves are strengthened with iron and many iron bells are hanging on them. As it is in an impregnable position, it is called by this name.

Going out of the Iron Gate, I arrived at the country of Tukhāra (formerly transcribed incorrectly as the country of Tuhuoluo). This territory is over one thousand *li* from south to north and more than three thousand *li* from east to west. It borders on the Pamir Range in the east, adjoins Persia in the west, touches the Great Snow Mountains in the south, and occupies the Iron Gate in the north, with the great Oxus River flowing westward through the middle of it. For several centuries the royal family had no offspring, and the powerful chieftains competed vigorously with one another, each trying to be the lord of his own district delimited by rivers and strategic positions, and they divided the country into twenty-seven states. Although each of them has his own clearly demarcated territory, they are all under the domination of the Turks. As the climate is temperate, illness and pestilence are rampant. By the end of winter and at the beginning of spring, when there is continuous heavy rain, febrile ailment is prevalent in all the countries south of this territory down to the north of Lampā. The monks commence their summer retreat on the sixteenth day of the twelfth month and end it on the fifteenth day of the third month. It is because this place has so much rain that the dates are thus fixed according to the seasons. The people are timid and cowardly and are bad-looking, but they are in a manner creditable and loyal, and seldom resort to deception. Their language and manners are slightly different from those of other countries. In their alphabet there are twenty-five letters, by which various words are formed to express all things. Their writing is horizontal from left to right, and their records have been gradually increased until they exceed those of Suli in number. They use more cotton than hemp in making clothes. For currency they use golden, silver, and other coins, which are different in shape from those of other countries.

Following the course of the Oxus River northward to the lower reaches, one arrives at the country of Tirmidh.

The country of Tirmidh is more than six hundred *li* from east to west and over four hundred *li* from south to north, its capital city being more than twenty *li* in circuit, long from east to west and narrow from south to north. There are more than ten monasteries with over one thousand monks. The stupas (known in old times as futu, toupo, tapo, sitoubo, or soudoubo, all erroneous) and the venerated images of the Buddha are mostly miraculous and cause spiritual manifestations. To the east of this country is the country of Sahāniyan.

The country of Sahāniyan is more than four hundred *li* from east to west and over five hundred *li* from south to north; its capital city is more than ten *li* in circuit. There are five monasteries with very few monks. To the east of this country is the country of Kharūn.

The country of Kharūn is over one hundred *li* from east to west and more than three hundred *li* from south to north, its capital city being over ten *li* in circuit. The king is a Turk from Xisu. There are two monasteries with over one hundred monks. To the east of this country is the country of Shūmān. 872b

The country of Shūmān is more than four hundred *li* from east to west and over one hundred *li* from south to north, its capital city being sixteen or seventeen *li* in circuit. The king is a Turk from Xisu. There are two monasteries with very few monks. To the southwest along the Oxus River is the country of Kuvāyāna.

The country of Kuvāyāna is more than two hundred *li* from east to west and over three hundred *li* from south to north, its capital city being over ten *li* in circuit. There are three monasteries with over one hundred monks. To the east of this country is the country of Wakhsh.

The country of Wakhsh is more than three hundred *li* from east to west and over five hundred *li* from south to north, its capital city being sixteen or seventeen *li* in circuit. To the east of this country is the country of Khuttalān.

The country of Khuttalān is over one thousand *li* from east to west and more than one thousand *li* from south to north, its capital city being over twenty *li* in circuit. It adjoins the Pamir Range and reaches the country of Komidai in the east.

The country of Komidai is more than two thousand *li* from east to west and over two hundred *li* from south to north, being situated among the mountains of the Pamir Range. The capital city is more than twenty *li* in circuit. It borders on the Oxus River in the southwest and adjoins the country of Śikni in the south. Crossing the Oxus River to the south, it reaches the country of Dharmasthiti, the country of Madakhshān, the country of Yamgān, the country of Kurān, the country of Himatala, the country of Pārghar, the country of Kishm, the country of Rāhula, the country of Ārhan, and the country of Munjān. To the southeast of the country of Warwālīz are the countries of Khost and Andarāb. Accounts of these countries may be found in the descriptions of my return journey. To the southwest of the country of Warwālīz is the country of Baghlan.

The country of Baghlan is more than fifty *li* from east to west and over two hundred *li* from south to north; its capital city is more than ten *li* in circuit. To the south is the country of Hrum-Simingān.

The country of Hrum-Simingān is over one thousand *li* in circuit, and its capital city is fourteen or fifteen *li* in circuit. To the southwest is the country of Khulm.

The country of Khulm is over eight hundred *li* in circuit and its capital city is five or six *li* in circuit. There are more than ten monasteries with over five hundred monks. To the west is the country of Baktra.

872c The country of Baktra is more than eight hundred *li* from east to west and over four hundred *li* from south to north, bordered by the Oxus River on the north. Its capital city, which is more than twenty *li* in circuit, is popularly known as the Smaller Rājagṛha. It is a strongly fortified city but sparsely populated. There are a great many varieties of native products, and the terrestrial and aquatic flowers are too many to be enumerated. There are more than one hundred monasteries with over three thousand monks, all of whom study and practice the Hinayana teachings.

To the southwest outside the city, there is the New Monastery, built by a previous king of this country. This is the only monastery north of the Great Snow Mountains in which various Buddhist commentators have worked continuously without intermission. The Buddha's image is adorned with famous jewels, and the halls are decorated with rare precious substances. For this reason, the rulers of various countries attacked the monastery, in order to capture the valuables. In the monastery there is a statue of the deity Vaiśravaṇa, who is reliable in his spiritual power and serves as a guardian of the monastery in a hidden sense. Recently the Turkish Shehu Khan's son, named Si Shehu Khan, mobilizing all the forces of his tribe and commanding his army, launched a surprise attack on the monastery and attempted to seize the jewels. Not far away from the monastery he camped with his troops. In the night he dreamed of Vaiśravaṇa, who said to him, "What power do you have that you dare to devastate the monastery?" So saying, he thrust his spear through the chest of the Khan. Waking in terror, the Khan felt an acute heartache and told his subordinates about his evil dream. Then he hurriedly sent messengers to invite the monks so that he might confess his wickedness in their presence, but he died before the messengers returned.

In the southern Buddha hall of this monastery, there is a Buddha's bathing pot of about one *dou* (1 decaliter) in capacity. It is of a variegated color and dazzlingly brilliant, and it is difficult to say whether it is made of metal or of stone. There is also a Buddha's tooth relic about one inch long and eight or nine *fen* (1 *fen* = 1/10 of an inch) broad. It is yellowish white in color and bright and clean in texture. There is also a Buddha's broom, made of *kāśa* grass, about two feet long and seven inches around, the handle being adorned with various precious substances. These three articles are always shown on the six fast days to the assembly of monks and lay people, who make offerings to them. When moved by the sincerity of the devotees, these articles may emit a brilliant light. To the north of the monastery there is a stupa over two hundred feet in height, plastered with diamonds and decorated with various precious substances. A piece of relic bone is enshrined in the stupa, which often issues a divine light.

To the southwest of the monastery there is a *vihāra* (temple) that was built many years ago. Numerous learned monks congregated at this monastery from distant places, and it is difficult to number those who were Arhats (saints). Therefore only those Arhats who had manifested supernatural powers at the time of entering Nirvana and had become well known to the monks had stupas built for them. These were a hundred in number, with their bases very close together. Although those monks who had attained sainthood were also numbered by the thousand, no memorials were erected for them as they did not show supernatural powers at death.
Now there are over a hundred monks, who work hard day and 873a
night for spiritual cultivation, but it is difficult to know who is an ordinary monk and who is a saint.

Over fifty *li* to the northwest of the capital is the city of Trapuṣa, and over forty *li* to the north of this city is the city of Bhallika. In each of the two cities there is a stupa more than thirty feet in height.

When the Tathāgata (one who has attained Buddhahood) first realized Buddhahood, he rose from his seat under the Bodhi Tree. When he was about to go to the Deer Park, the two elders [Trapuṣa and Bhallika] met him in his majestic glory and offered him some parched grain and honey out of their travelling provisions. The World-honored One spoke to them on the blessedness acquired by men and heavenly beings, and they were the first to hear the Five Precepts and the Ten Good Deeds. After having heard the instructions on the Dharma, they requested something for them to worship. Then the Tathāgata gave them some of his hair and nail parings to take back home. As they asked about the manner of venerating these relics, the Tathāgata folded his *saṃghāti* (double robe) (incorrectly transcribed as sengqili in olden times) into a square and spread it on the ground, and he did the same with his *uttarāsaṅga* (upper robe) and *saṃkakṣikā* (side-covering vest) (incorrectly transcribed as sengqizhi in olden times). Then he placed his alms bowl inverted on the robes and set up his pewter staff on the bowl to make the shape of a stupa. The two men returned to their respective cities and each built a stupa after the pattern shown by the holy Buddha. This was the prototype of the stupas built by the Buddhists according to the teachings of the Buddha.

More than seventy *li* to the west of the city is a stupa over twenty feet in height, which had been built long ago at the time of Kāśyapa Buddha. Proceeding southwest from the capital city, one enters a nook of the Snow Mountains and reaches the country of Zumathān.

The country of Zumathān is fifty or sixty *li* from east to west and over one hundred *li* from south to north, its capital city being more than ten *li* in circuit. Proceeding southwest one reaches the country of Gūzgānān.

The country of Gūzgānān is more than five hundred *li* from east to west and over one thousand *li* from south to north, its capital city being more than twenty *li* in circuit. This country has many mountains and rivers and produces good horses. Proceeding northwest one reaches the country of Talaqān.

The country of Talaqān is over five hundred *li* from east to west and fifty or sixty *li* from south to north, its capital city being more than ten *li* in circuit. It borders on the country of Persia in the west.

Going south from the country of Baktra for more than one hundred *li*, I arrived at the country of Kacik.

The country of Kacik is more than five hundred *li* from east to west and over three hundred *li* from south to north, its capital city being four or five *li* in circuit. The soil is hard and infertile, with hills and mounds connecting one another. There are few flowers or fruits, but much pulse and wheat. The climate is severely cold, and the people are harsh and fierce by custom. There are more than ten monasteries with over three hundred monks, all of whom study the Sarvāstivāda school of the Hinayana teachings. Proceeding southeast one enters the Great Snow Mountains. The mountains are high and the valleys deep, with peaks and cliffs fraught with danger. Wind and snowfall follow each other, and even in the 873b
height of summer it is cold to the point of freezing. Snow heaps up in the valleys, and the footpath is hard to jog on. Mountain deities and evil ghosts, when enraged, send forth monstrous sprites to create havoc. It is also infested with gangs of brigands, whose business is homicide.

Going for more than six hundred *li*, I came out of the territory of Tukhāra country and reached the country of Bāmīyāna. The country of Bāmīyāna is more than two thousand *li* from east to west and over three hundred *li* from south to north, being situated among the Snow Mountains. The people lived on the slopes of the valleys and gradually became town-dwellers. The capital city lies upon a cliff and stretches across a valley six or seven *li* in length, with a lofty precipice at its back on the north. It produces winter wheat, but few flowers and fruits. It is fit for cattle breeding, and there are many sheep and horses. The climate is severely cold, and the customs are harsh and rude. The people mostly wear fur and hempen clothes, which are suitable for them. The written language, social institutions, and currency are the same as those in the Tukhāra country. The spoken language is slightly different, but their manners and features are generally the same. Their mind of pure faith is far better than that of the neighboring countries. They worship the Triple Gem with the utmost sincerity and venerate all gods down to the various deities. When merchants coming and going happen to witness visions of heavenly deities, whether as good omens or as predictions of disaster, they worship the deities to pray for blessedness. There are several tens of monasteries with several thousand monks, who follow the Hinayana teachings of the Lokottaravāda school.

To the northeast of the royal city, there is at a corner of the mountains a rock statue of the Buddha standing, one hundred forty or fifty feet in height, a dazzling golden color and adorned with brilliant gems. To the east there is a monastery built by a previous king of the country. To the east of the monastery there is a copper statue of the Buddha standing, more than one hundred feet tall. It was cast in separate pieces and then welded together into shape.

In the monastery situated two or three *li* to the east of the city, there is an image of the Buddha recumbent, more than one thousand feet long, in the posture of entering Nirvana. At this place the king often convened the Quinquennial Assembly, in which he offered everything from his queen down to the national treasures as alms to the monks. When the state repository was exhausted, he gave himself up to the monks, and then his officials paid ransom to the monks to redeem the king. This practice has become the king's regular duty.

Going from the monastery of the image of the Buddha recumbent toward the southeast for over two hundred *li*, I crossed the Great Snow Mountains and reached the Small Marshland in the east, where the water of the springs and ponds is as clear and lucid as a mirror, with luxuriant trees of green leaves. There is a monastery in which are preserved a tooth relic of the Buddha and a tooth of a Pratyekabuddha who lived at the beginning of the present kalpa (aeon), more than five inches long and less than four inches broad. There is also a tooth of a Gold Wheel King, three inches long and two inches broad, as well as the iron alms bowl used by the great Arhat Śāṇakavāsa (incorrectly transcribed as Shangnahexiu in olden times), with a capacity of eight or nine *sheng* (liter). These three kinds of relics left by the holy ones are sealed up in golden containers.

There is also preserved a piece of Śāṇakavāsa's *saṃghāti* robe, consisting of nine stripes of a dark red color. It was made of the cloth woven with the fiber of the *śāṇaka* (hemp) plant. Śāṇakavāsa was a disciple of Ānanda. In a former life he presented a piece of 873c
hempen robe to the monks on the last day of the summer retreat. By this meritorious deed, he was born five hundred times always wearing a hempen garment, whether he was in the state of intermediate existence or was born into the human world. In his last birth he was born wrapped in a hempen garment, which became enlarged with the growth of his body. When he was converted by Ānanda to the Buddhist order, his garment turned into a religious robe, and when he received full ordination, it became a *saṃghāti* robe of nine stripes. When he was about to realize Nirvana, he entered the Ultimate Samādhi of Perfection; and by the power of his vow of wisdom, he left his robe to last in the world until the end of the bequeathed teachings of the Buddha. It will decay only after the termination of the Dharma. It is now slightly diminished, and this is evidence for the veracity of the legend. Going from here to the east and after crossing the Black Range, I reached the country of Kāpiśī.

The country of Kāpiśī is more than four thousand *li* in circuit, with the Snow Mountains at its back in the north and the Black Range surrounding the three other sides. It is fit for growing rice and wheat, and there are plenty of fruit trees. It produces good horses and aromatic turmeric. Rare commodities from different places are mostly concentrated in this country. The climate is windy and cold, and the people are rude and rustic by nature. Their language is vulgar and indecent, and they practice mixed marriage. The written language is generally the same as in the country of Tukhāra, but the customs and spoken language and social institutions are quite different. They wear woolen and cotton clothes and also use fur and hemp in making garments. For currency they use golden and silver coins and small coppers, of which the size and shape are different from those of other countries. The king, who belongs to the Suli tribe, is a man of strategics, brave and fiery by nature and feared by neighboring regions; he has more than ten countries under his dominion. He loves and nurtures his subjects and venerates the Triple Gem. Every year he makes a silver image of the Buddha eighteen feet in height. He also holds a Quinquennial Assembly for the distribution of charity to the poor and needy; and he gives alms to widows and widowers. There are over one hundred monasteries with more than six thousand monks, most of whom study the teachings of the Mahayana school. The stupas and monasteries are tall and spacious and are kept clean in a solemn manner. There are over ten deva-temples with more than one thousand heretical believers, either going naked or smearing dust on their bodies; some wear strings of skulls as head ornaments.

Three or four *li* to the east of the great city, there is a large monastery at the foot of the northern mountain with over three hundred monks, all of whom study the teachings of the Hinayana schools. I heard some old people saying that when King Kaniṣka of the country of Gandhāra was on the throne, his prestige extended to the neighboring countries and his influence reached distant regions. He strengthened his military forces and expanded his territory to the east of the Pamir Range. Out of fear of the king's might, the lord of a Chinese vassal state west of the Yellow River sent his son as hostage to the king. Upon receiving the hostage prince, King Kaniṣka treated him with special kindness and courtesy, providing him with different lodgings according to the seasons. In the winter he lodged in various states in India, and in the summer he returned to the country of Kāpiśī, while in the spring and autumn he stayed in the country of Gandhāra. Therefore a monastery was built at each of these places where the hos-
874a tage prince lived in the three different seasons. This monastery was the one built at his summer residence. Thus on the walls of the buildings are painted pictures of the hostage prince, his features and costume being quite the same as those of the Chinese people.

Afterward he was sent back to his own country, but in memory of his old residences, he continued to send offerings to the monasteries without interruption in spite of the obstacles of mountains and rivers. Now the monks of the monastery still perform grand religious functions at the times of commencing and dissolving the summer retreat to pray for blessedness and perform meritorious deeds on behalf of the hostage prince without cease up to the present time.

Under the right foot of the statue of the great deity at the southern side of the east gate of the Buddha hall courtyard of the monastery, there was an underground treasure laid up by the hostage prince with an inscription, reading, "When the monastery is in need of repair, take this treasure for its renovation." Recently the king of a frontier country, who was an avaricious and cruel man, heard that there were plenty of jewels and gems stored in the monastery. When he had expelled the monks and was about to dig up the treasure, the figure of a parrot on the crown of the great deity vigorously flapped its wings and screamed in a terrible manner, causing an earthquake. The king and his soldiers were so frightened that they fainted and fell on the ground, and it was a long time before they came to and returned home apologetically.

On the mountain to the north of the monastery there are several caves in which the hostage prince practiced meditation. A large quantity of miscellaneous valuables was stored in the caves with an inscription placed beside them and guarded by a *yakṣa* (demon). Whenever anyone wished to open the caves to take away the treasure, the *yakṣa* would appear in different forms by his supernatural powers, as a python, as a fierce animal, or as a poisonous insect, all greatly enraged. Therefore nobody dared to capture the valuables by force.

On a great mountain two or three *li* to the west of the caves, there is a statue of Avalokiteśvara Bodhisattva. When anybody earnestly wishes to see the Bodhisattva, he appears out of the statue in a graceful form to comfort the devotee.

Over thirty *li* to the southeast of the great city is the Rāhula Monastery. Beside it there is a stupa more than one hundred feet in height that sometimes emits a brilliant light on fast days. From a crevice on the body of the stupa in the shape of an inverted alms bowl, black aromatic oil oozes out, and on a quiet night one sometimes hears the sound of music. I heard some old people saying that it was built by Rāhula, a minister of this country. When the construction was completed, he dreamed that a man said to him, "In the stupa you have constructed, there is no *śarīra* (relic bone) enshrined. Tomorrow morning someone will offer one to the king. You may as well ask the king for it." Next morning the minister went to court and said to the king, "May I have the imprudence to beg a favor from Your Majesty?" The king said, "What is your desire?" The minister asked, "Will Your Majesty grant me what is first offered to you today?" The king said, "Let it be so!"

Rāhula then waited at the gate of the palace to see who was coming first, and in a moment a man came with a bottle containing a grain of *śarīra*. The minister inquired of the man, "What are you going to offer to the king?" The man said, "A Buddha *śarīra*."
874b The minister said, "I shall watch the *śarīra* for you while you go in to make a report first to the king." Rāhula, fearing that the king might be reluctant to part with the precious *śarīra* and might go back on his promise, quickly went to the monastery and climbed up on the stupa with such a pious mind that the stupa in the shape of an inverted alms bowl, moved by his earnestness, opened by itself so that he could deposit the *śarīra* inside. He then hurriedly came out, and the gusset of his robe was caught by the closing crevice. The king's messenger chased after the relic, but the stone stupa had already closed. Thus black aromatic oil oozed out from the crevice.

More than forty *li* to the south of the city is the City of the Śvetavat Temple. Whenever there is a big earthquake and the mountains and precipices collapse, nothing is shaken within the limits of this city.

More than thirty *li* to the south of the City of the Śvetavat Temple is Aruṇa Mountain with its lofty peaks and cliffs and gloomy valleys stretching far. The top of the mountain increases every year several hundred feet in height, as if to look at Śunāśīra Mountain in the country of Jāguḍa, and then it collapses all at once. I heard the local people saying that when the deity Śunā first came here from a distant place, he wished to stay at this mountain. Being terrified, the mountain god shook the rivulets in the valleys. The deity said, "You do not wish me to take up my lodgings with you, and so you shook the earth. If you had shown me a little hospitality, I should have filled your chest with riches and valuables. Now I am going to the Śunāśīra Mountain in the country of Jāguḍa. Each year at the time when I receive worship and offerings from the king and his ministers, you may just look at me!" Thus Aruṇa Mountain increases to a height and then soon collapses.

More than two hundred *li* to the northwest of the royal city are the Great Snow Mountains, on the top of which there is a lake. Whenever people come here to pray for rain or fine weather, their wishes are always fulfilled. I heard some old people saying that formerly there was an Arhat in Gandhāra, who always received offerings of alms from the Nāga king of this lake. Every day at the time of taking the midday meal he would sit on his folding chair and fly through the air to the lake by supernatural powers. Once his attendant novice hid himself below the folding chair, and the Arhat went to the lake as usual when the time arrived for him to make the journey. Upon reaching the Nāga's palace, he discovered the novice, and so the Nāga king also invited him to the meal. The Nāga king offered heavenly delicious rice to entertain the Arhat, while he fed the novice with food of the human world. When the meal was over, the Arhat preached on the Dharma for the Nāga king, and the novice washed his master's alms bowl as usual. When he discovered some remaining grains of rice in the bowl, he was amazed by the fragrance of the rice, and he immediately cherished a malignant feeling against his master and the Nāga king, saying, "May the power of whatever good deeds I have performed appear to kill this Nāga and let me be the king." The moment when the novice expressed this desire, the Nāga king felt a head- 874c
ache. After listening to the sermons delivered by the Arhat, the Nāga king repented his misdeed and blamed himself, but the novice, deeply resentful, would not make a confession nor accept the

Nāga king's apology. The novice, having returned to the monastery, by his earnest desire and the power of his good deeds, died that night and was reborn as a great Nāga king with majesty and valor. He came to the lake, killed its Nāga king, occupied the Nāga palace, took possession of his subordinates, and became the master of all. Out of his old indignation, he caused a violent storm that uprooted the trees, and he intended to destroy the monastery.

At that time King Kaniṣka, being perplexed by the accident, made inquiries into the matter, and the Arhat told him everything. The king then built a monastery at the foot of the Snow Mountains with a stupa over one hundred feet high for the Nāga. With his old resentment, the Nāga sent forth wind and rain. The king cherished the mind of universal salvation, but the Nāga caused storms six times, out of the malignance of hatred, to destroy the monastery and stupa; but they were built seven times. King Kaniṣka, being ashamed of his failure, intended to fill up the Nāga's lake and demolish his dwellings. He mobilized his troops and came to the foot of the Snow Mountains. Deeply terrified, the Nāga king transformed himself into the form of an old Brahman, halted the king's elephant, and presented a remonstrance to him, saying, "Because, Great King, you have in the past performed good deeds and sowed many superior causes, you are now a king of men, and no one dares to disobey you. Why do you contend with a Nāga today? A Nāga is an animal, and though he is of a base and evil species, he possesses great power not to be subjugated by strength. He can ride on a piece of cloud and fly through the air, or tread upon empty space and walk over water, beyond the control of the power of men. What influence can your anger produce upon him? Now you have mobilized all of the military forces in the whole country to fight with a Nāga. Even if you win in the battle, you will not gain the prestige that you gain when you conquer a distant land; and if you lose the war, you will bring shame on yourself for being unable to defeat your enemy. It is in your own interest to withdraw your troops."

King Kaniṣka did not listen to this remonstrance, and the Nāga returned to his lake and caused a thunderstorm and a hurricane

that uprooted the trees. Sand and stones rained down from the air, clouds and mist darkened the world, and the king's troops and horses were frightened. The king then took refuge in the Triple Gem, begging for protection, saying, "Because I have done many good deeds in the past, I am now a king of men with mighty power to subdue strong enemies and rule over Jambudvīpa. Now I am humiliated by this Nāga animal, which shows that my blessedness is scanty. May whatever power I have gathered from doing good deeds be present at this very moment!" Immediately a huge flame arose from his shoulders, the Nāga retreated, the wind died down, and the mist and clouds dispersed. The king ordered each man of his army to carry a piece of stone to fill up the Nāga lake. The Nāga king resumed the form of a Brahman and said again to the king, "I am the Nāga king of this lake, and out of fear of your puissance, I come to pledge allegiance to you. May the king have pity on me and forgive me for the faults that I have committed. You are a king who nourishes and protects all living beings, so why should you do harm to me alone? If you kill me, both of us will fall into the evil ways of existence, 875a
because you will commit the sin of taking life, while I shall cherish the feeling of hatred and vengeance in my mind. Karmic retribution is apparent, and shows plainly what is good and what is evil."

Then the king concluded an agreement with the Nāga that should the Nāga commit another offense in the future, the king would certainly not pardon him. The Nāga said, "Because of my evil karma done in the past, I am now a Nāga. As a Nāga is violent by nature, I am unable to restrain myself, and in a fit of anger I may forget about the obligation. If you build another monastery, I shall not dare to destroy it again. Please always send a man to watch the peak of the mountain. In case a black cloud arises, he should at once strike an instrument. When I hear the sound I shall quench my evil mind." The king then constructed another monastery together with a stupa, and a man was stationed to watch to see if any black cloud appeared. This is still done without interruption. I heard some old people saying that inside the stupa there was preserved about one *sheng* of bone and flesh relics of the Tathāgata.

Marvelous events are difficult to relate in detail. Once smoke suddenly arose from inside the stupa, and in a moment raging flames burst out of it. The people thought that the stupa must have been consumed by the fire, but after looking at it for a long time, when the smoke and flames had vanished, they saw the relics resembling a streamer of white pearls, winding upwards around an ornamental pillar, up to the clouds and whirling down again.

In Old Royal Monastery on the southern bank of the great river in the northwest of the royal city is a deciduous tooth of Śākyamuni Bodhisattva about one inch long. To the southeast of this monastery there is another one also called Old Royal Monastery, in which is preserved a piece of the Tathāgata's skull bone about one inch broad, yellowish white in color, with distinctive hair pores. There is also a hair of the Tathāgata's head, dark purple in color, curled up rightward about half an inch long, but when extended it measures about one foot. These three objects are worshipped with scattering of flowers by the king and his ministers on the six fast days of every month.

To the southwest of this skull-bone monastery is Old Queen's Monastery, in which there is a gilt copper stupa more than one hundred feet in height. I heard some local people saying that it contained over one *sheng* of the Buddha's relic bones, from which at night on the fifteenth day of every month there issued a round light shining continuously upon the dew basin of the stupa and gradually fading into it at dawn.

To the southwest of the city is Pilusāra (Strong Elephant) Mountain. It is called Strong Elephant because the tutelary deity of the mountain assumed the form of an elephant. Formerly, when the Tathāgata was living in the world, the deity of Strong Elephant Mountain once invited the World-honored One and his twelve hundred great Arhats to the mountain. There was a large flat rock on the top of the mountain, where the Tathāgata took his seat and accepted the alms offered by the deity. Afterward King Aśoka erected a stupa more than one hundred feet high on the rock. This is what the people now call Strong Elephant Stupa, and it is also said that about one *sheng* of the Tathāgata's relic bones is preserved in it.

Below the cliff to the north of Strong Elephant Stupa is a Nāga spring, where the Tathāgata and Arhats washed their mouths by chewing willow twigs after taking the meal offered by the deity. They planted the twigs in the ground, and they took root and grew into the dense wood that it is now. Afterward, people built at this place a monastery called Piṇḍaka (Chewing willow twigs) Monastery. 875b

From here I travelled east for more than six hundred *li* through mountains and valleys connected with each other. The peaks and cliffs are steep and precipitous. After crossing the Black Range, I entered the territory of North India and reached the country of Lampā (in the domain of North India).

End of Fascicle One

Fascicle II

Three Countries, From Lampā to Gandhāra

1. The Country of Lampā
2. The Country of Nagarahāra
3. The Country of Gandhāra

In a careful study we find that Tianzhu is variantly designated, 875b causing much confusion and perplexity. Formerly it was called Shengdu, or Xiandou, but now we should name it Indu (India) according to the right pronunciation. The people of India use different names for their respective countries, while people of distant places with diverse customs generally designate the land that they admire as India. The word Indu means the moon, which has many names, and this is one of them. It means that living beings live and die in the wheel of transmigration ceaselessly in the long night of ignorance without a rooster to announce the advent of the dawn. When the sun has sunk, candles continue to give light in the night. Although the stars are shining in the sky, how can they be as brilliant as the clear moon? It was for this reason that India was compared to the moon. It was because saints and sages emerged one after another in that land to guide living beings and regulate all affairs, just as the moon shines upon all things, that it was called India. In India the people are divided into different castes and clans, among whom the Brahmans are the noblest. Following their good name, tradition has designated the whole land as the Brahmanic country, disregarding the regular lines of demarcation.

As regards the territory, we may say that the whole of India with its five parts is over ninety thousand *li* in circuit, with three sides facing the sea and the Snow Mountains at its back in the north. It is broad in the north and narrow in the south, in the shape of the crescent moon. The land is divided into more than seventy countries. The climate is particularly hot and the soil is
875c mostly humid with many springs. In the north there are many mountains, and the hills are of saline-alkaline soil. In the east the plain is rich and moist, and the cultivated fields are productive. In the south vegetation is luxuriant, while in the west the soil is hard and barren. Such is the general condition told in brief.

For the measurement of space there is the *yojana*. (In olden times it was called youxun, yuzhena, or youyan, all incorrect.) One *yojana* is the distance covered by the ancient royal army in one day's time. Formerly it was said to be forty *li*, or thirty *li* according to Indian usage, while in Buddhist texts it was counted as only sixteen *li*. To divide it down to the infinitesimal, one *yojana* is divided into eight *krośa*s, one *krośa* being the distance within which the mooing of a bull can be heard, one *krośa* into five hundred bows, one bow into four cubits, one cubit into twenty-four fingers, and one finger-joint into seven grains of winter wheat. Then the division goes on by sevens through the louse, the nit, the crevice-dust, the ox-hair, the sheep-wool, the hare-hair, the copper-dust [particle], the water-dust, down to the fine dust, and one fine dust [particle] is divided into seven extremely fine dust [particles]. The extremely fine dust is indivisible, and if divided it becomes emptiness. This is why it is called extremely fine dust.

Although the names of the [periods of] alternation of day and night and the emergence and disappearance of the sun and moon are different [from those used in China], there is no difference in the measurement of time and season. The months are named according to the position of the Big Dipper. The shortest space of time is called a *kṣaṇa*, one hundred twenty *kṣaṇa*s make one *tatkṣaṇa*, sixty *tatkṣaṇa*s make one *lava*, thirty *lava*s make one *muhūrta*, five *muhūrta*s make one *kāla*, and six *kāla*s make one day and one night (three *kālas* in the daytime and three in the night). Secular people divide one day and one night into eight *kālas* (four *kālas* in the daytime and four in the night, each being subdivided into four divisions). From the waxing moon to the full moon is known as the white division, and from the waning moon to the last day of the month is called the black division. The black division has fourteen or fifteen days, as the month may be "small" or "big." The anterior black division and the posterior white division constitute one month, and six months make one year. When the sun moves inside the celestial equator, it is the northern revolution, and when it moves outside the celestial equator, it is the southern revolution. These two revolutions constitute one year. The year is also divided into six seasons, namely, from the sixteenth day of the first month to the fifteenth day of the third month is the season of gradual heat; from the sixteenth day of the third month to the fifteenth day of the fifth month, the season of intense heat; from the sixteenth day of the fifth month to the fifteenth day of the seventh month, the rainy season; from the sixteenth day of the seventh month to the fifteenth day of the ninth month, the season of exuberance; from the sixteenth day of the ninth month to the fifteenth day of the eleventh month, the season of gradual cold; and from the sixteenth day of the eleventh month to the fifteenth day of the first month, the season of severe cold.

According to the holy teachings of the Tathāgata, a year is divided into three seasons, namely, from the sixteenth day of the first month to the fifteenth day of the fifth month is the hot season; from the sixteenth day of the fifth month to the fifteenth day of the ninth month, the rainy season; and from the sixteenth day 876a
of the ninth month to the fifteenth day of the first month, the cold season. Or it is divided into four seasons, namely, spring, summer, autumn, and winter. The three months of spring are called Caitra, Vaiśākha, and Jyeṣṭha, corresponding to the period from the sixteenth day of the first month to the fifteenth day of the fourth month in China. The three months of summer are called Āṣāḍha, Śravaṇa, and Bhādrapada, corresponding to the period

from the sixteenth day of the fourth month to the fifteenth day of the seventh month in China. The three months of autumn are known as Āśvayuja, Kārttika, and Mārgaśīrṣa, corresponding to the period from the sixteenth day of the seventh month to the fifteenth day of the tenth month in China. The three months of winter are named Pauṣa, Māgha, and Phālguna, corresponding to the period from the sixteenth day of the tenth month to the fifteenth day of the first month in China.

Thus according to the holy teachings of the Buddha the monks of India observe the summer retreat during the rainy season, either in the earlier three months or in the later three months. The earlier three months correspond to the period from the sixteenth day of the fifth month to the fifteenth day of the eighth month in China, and the later three months correspond to the period from the sixteenth day of the sixth month to the fifteenth day of the ninth month in China. Former translators of scriptures and Vinaya texts used the terms zuoxia or zuola (to sit for the summer or the annual retreat). This was because they were outlandish people who did not understand the Chinese language correctly, or were not conversant with the dialects, and so committed mistakes in their translations. Moreover, there are divergences in the calculation of the dates of the Buddha's entry into his mother's womb, birth, renunciation, enlightenment, and Nirvana; this point will be discussed later.

As regards the towns and cities, they have square city walls, which are broad and tall. The streets and lanes are narrow and winding, with stores facing the roads and wineshops standing beside the streets. Butchers, fishermen, harlots, actors, executioners, and scavengers mark their houses with banners and are not allowed to live inside the cities. When they come to town, they have to sneak up and down along the left side of the road. Concerning the building of residential houses and the construction of the city walls, they are mostly built with bricks, as the terrain is low and humid, while the walls of houses may be made of wattled bamboo or wood. The roofs of houses, terraces, and pavilions are made of planks, plastered with limestone and covered with bricks or adobe. Some of the lofty buildings are similar in style to those in China. Cottages thatched with cogon grass or ordinary straw are built with bricks or planks, and the walls are adorned with limestone. The floor is purified by smearing it with cow dung, and seasonal flowers are scattered over it. In this matter they differ [from Chinese custom].

The monasteries are constructed in an extremely splendid manner. They have four corner towers and the halls have three tiers. The rafters, eaves, ridgepoles, and roof-beams are carved with 876b
strange figures. The doors, windows, and walls are painted with colored pictures. The houses of the common people are ostentatious inside but plain and simple outside.

The inner chambers and main halls vary in their dimensions, and the structures of terraces in tiers and storied pavilions have no fixed style, but the doors open to the east, and the throne also faces the east. For a seat to take rest on, a rope-bed is used. The royal family, great personages, officials, commoners, and magnates adorn their seats in different ways, but the structure is the same in style. The sovereign's throne is exceedingly high and wide and decorated with pearls. Called the Lion's Seat, it is covered with fine cotton cloth and is mounted by a jewelled footstool. The ordinary officials carve their seats in different decorative patterns according to their fancy and ornament them with rare gems. Both the upper and the under garments, as well as ornamental garbs, need no tailoring. Pure white is the color appreciated, and motley is held in no account. The men wind a piece of cloth round the waist under the armpits and leave the right shoulder uncovered. The women wear a cape that covers both shoulders and hangs down loose. The hair on the top is combed into a small topknot with the rest of the hair falling down. Some men clip their mustaches and have other strange fashions, such as wearing a garland on the head or a necklace on the body. For dressing, they use *kauśeya* and cotton cloth, *kauśeya* being the silk spun by wild silkworms. The *kṣauma* [linen] cloth is made of hemp or similar fibers.

The *kambala* is woven with fine sheep wool, while the *hela* cape [a sort of raincoat?] is woven with the wool of a wild animal. As this wool is fine and soft and can be spun and woven, it is valued for making garments.

In north India, where the climate is bitterly cold, the people wear tight-fitting short jackets, quite similar to those of the Hu people. The costumes of the heretics are various in style and strangely made. They dress in peacock tails, or wear necklaces of skulls, or go naked, or cover their bodies with grass or boards, or pluck their hair and clip their mustaches, or have disheveled hair with a small topknot. Their upper and under garments have no fixed style and the color may be red or white—there is no definite rule.

The monks have only the three regular robes, [the *saṃghāti* and] the *saṃkakṣikā* and the *nivāsana* robes as their religious garments. The different sects have different ways of making the three robes, of which the fringes may be broad or narrow, and the folds may be small or large. The *saṃkakṣikā* (known in Chinese as armpit cover and formerly transcribed as sengqizhi incorrectly) covers the left shoulder and veils both armpits. It is open on the left and closed on the right side, reaching below the waist. Since the *nivāsana* (known in Chinese as skirt and formerly transcribed as niepanseng incorrectly) has no strings for fastening, it is worn by gathering it into pleats, which are tightened with a braid. The pleats are folded in different ways by different sects, and the color is also different, either yellow or red. People of the Kshatriya (military and ruling class) and the Brahman (priestly class) castes are pure and simple in lodging and clean and frugal. The dress and ornaments of the kings and ministers are very ostentatious. Garlands and coronets studded with gems are their headdresses, and rings, bracelets, and necklaces are their bodily ornaments. The wealthy merchants use only bracelets. Most people go barefoot; few wear shoes. They stain their teeth red
876c or black, have closely cropped hair, pierce their earlobes, and have long noses and large eyes. Such are their outward features.

They voluntarily keep themselves pure and clean, not by compulsion. Before taking a meal they must wash their hands. Remnants and leftovers are not to be served again, and food vessels are not passed on from one person to another. Earthenware and wooden utensils must be discarded after use, and golden, silver, copper, or iron vessels are polished each time after use. When the meal is over, they chew willow twigs to cleanse [their mouths], and before washing and rinsing their mouths they do not come into contact with one another. Each time after going to stool or to urinate, they must wash themselves and daub their bodies with a fragrant substance such as sandalwood or turmeric. When the monarch is going to take a bath, the music made by beating drums and playing stringed instruments is performed along with singing. Before offering sacrifices to gods and worshipping at temples they take baths and wash themselves.

It is known that their writing, composed of forty-seven letters, was invented by the deva Brahmā as an original standard for posterity. These letters are combined to indicate objects and used as expressions for events. The original [language] branched as it gradually became widely used, and there are slight modifications of it according to place and people. As a language in general, it did not deviate from the original source. The people of Central India are particularly accurate and correct in speech, and their expressions and tones are harmonious and elegant like the language of the devas. They speak accurately in a clear voice and serve as a standard for other people. The people of neighboring lands and foreign countries became accustomed to speaking in erroneous ways until their mistakes became accepted as correct, and they vied with one another in emulating vulgarities, not sticking to the pure and simple style.

As regards their records of sayings and events, there are separate departments in charge of them. The annals and royal edicts are collectively called *Nīlapiṭa* (Blue collection), in which good and bad events are recorded, and calamities as well as auspicious signs are noted down in detail. To begin the education of their children and induce them to make progress, they first guide them to learn the *Book of Twelve Chapters*; and when the children reach the age of seven, the great treatises of the five knowledges are gradually imparted to them. The first is the knowledge of grammar, which explains the meanings of words and classifies them into different groups. The second is the knowledge of technical skills, which teaches arts and mechanics, the principles of *yin* and *yang* (negativity and positivity), and calendrical computation. The third is the knowledge of medicine, including the application of incantation, exorcism, drugs, stone needles, and moxibustion. The fourth is the knowledge of logic, by which orthodox and heterodox are ascertained, and truth is differentiated from falsehood. The fifth is the inner knowledge, which thoroughly investigates the teachings of the Five Vehicles and the subtle theory of cause and effect.

The Brahmans study the Four Vedic Treatises (formerly transcribed as Pituo incorrectly). The first treatise is on longevity, dealing with the preservation of good health and the readjustment of mentality. The second one is on worship, that is, offering sacrifices and saying prayers. The third one is on equity, concerning ceremonial rituals, divination, military tactics, and battle formation. The fourth one is on practical arts, which teaches unusual abilities, crafts and numeration, incantation, and medical prescriptions.

877a The teachers must be learned in the essence [of these treatises] and thoroughly master the profound mysteries. They expound the cardinal principles [to the pupils] and teach them with succinct but penetrating expressions. The teachers summon up their pupils' energy to study and tactfully induce them to progress. They instruct the inert and encourage the less talented. Those disciples who are intelligent and acute by nature and have sensible views, intending to live in seclusion, confine themselves, and lock the door against the outside until they complete their studies. Just at the age of thirty, they have fixed their minds and gained achievements in learning. After having been appointed to official posts, the first thing they do is to repay the kindness of their teachers.

There are some men who are conversant with ancient lore and fond of classic elegance, living in seclusion to preserve their uprightness. They drift along the course of life without worldly involvement and remain free and unfettered, above human affairs. They are indifferent to honor and humiliation, and their renown spreads far. The rulers, even treating such men with courtesy, cannot win them over to serve at court. But the state honors wise and learned men, and the people respect those who are noble and intelligent, according high praise to them and treating them with perfect etiquette. Therefore men can devote their attention to learning without feeling fatigue, and they travel about seeking knowledge and visiting masters of the Way in order to rely upon the virtuous ones, not counting a thousand *li* as a long journey. Although their families may be rich, such men make up their minds to live wandering about the world, begging for their food wherever they go. They value the acquisition of truth and do not deem poverty a disgrace. Those people who lead a life of amusement and dissipation, eating delicious food and wearing expensive garments, neither have virtue nor study constantly; they incur shame and disgrace upon themselves, and their ill repute spreads far and wide.

The Tathāgata's teachings may be comprehended by each listener according to his own type of mentality, and as we are now far away from the time of the holy Buddha, some of his right Dharma is still pure and some has become defiled. With the faculty of understanding, all people can acquire the enlightenment of wisdom. There are different sects, like peaks, standing against each other and debating various viewpoints as vehemently as crashing waves. They study divergent specific subjects, but they all lead to the same goal. Each of the eighteen sects is expert in argumentation using sharp and incisive words. The manner of living of the Mahayana (Great Vehicle) followers and that of the Hinayana (Small Vehicle) followers differ from each other. They engage themselves in silent meditation, or in walking to and fro, or in standing still. *Samādhi* (intense mental concentration) and *prajñā* (wisdom) are far apart, and noisiness and calmness are quite different. Each community of monks has laid down its own restrictive rules and regulations. All books, whether belonging to the Vinaya (disciplinary rules), the Abhidharma (treatises), or the Sutras (discourses), are scriptures of the Buddha. A monk who can expound one of the books is exempted from routine monastic duties. One who can expound two books is supplied with additional good rooms and daily requisites. One who can expound three is to be served by attendants. One who can expound four is provided with lay servants at his service. One who can expound five is entitled to ride an elephant when going out. One who can expound six has a retinue protecting him.

The honor given to those who have high morality is also extraordinary. Assemblies for discussion are often held to test the intellectual capacity of the monks, in order to distinguish the superior from the inferior, and to reject the dull and promote the bright. Those who can deliberate on the subtle sayings, and glorify the wonderful theories with refined diction and quick eloquence, may ride richly caparisoned elephants with hosts of attendants preceding and following behind them. But those to whom the theories are taught in vain, or who have been defeated in a debate, explaining few principles in a verbose way, or distorting the teachings with language that is merely pleasant to the ear, are daubed with ocher or chalk in the face, while dust is scattered over the body, and are expelled to the wilderness, or discarded into ditches. In this way the good and the evil are distinguished, and the wise and the ignorant disclosed. Thus men may take delight in the Way and study diligently at home. They may either forsake their homes or return to secular life as they please. To those who commit faults or violate the disciplinary rules, the community of monks may mete out punishments. A light offense incurs public reprimand, and the penalty for the offense next in gravity is that the monks do not
877b speak to the offender. One who has committed a grave offense is excommunicated, that is, expelled contemptuously by the community of monks. Once expelled, the offender will have nowhere to take shelter and will suffer the hardships of a vagabond life, or he may return to his former life as a layman.

As far as the different clans are concerned, there are four castes among the people. The first caste is that of the Brahmans, who are pure in conduct, adhere to their doctrines, live in chastity, and preserve their virtue in purity. The second is the caste of Kshatriyas (formerly transcribed wrongly as chali), who are royal descendants and rule the country, taking benevolence and humanity as their objects in life. The third is the caste of Vaisyas (formerly transcribed wrongly as pishe), who are merchants and traders, exchanging goods to meet the needs of one another and gaining profit far and near. The fourth caste is that of Sudras, who are farmers laboring in the fields and toiling in sowing and reaping. These four castes are differentiated by their hereditary purity or defilement. People of a caste marry within the caste, and the conspicuous and the humble do not marry each other. Relatives either on the father's or the mother's side do not intermarry. A woman can marry only once, and she can never remarry. There are numerous miscellaneous clans grouped together according to their [professional] categories, and it is difficult to give a detailed account.

The monarchs and kings of successive generations have only been Kshatriyas. When usurpations and regicides occasionally happened, other families assumed the supreme power. The warriors of the nation are well-chosen men of extraordinary bravery, and as the occupation is hereditary, they become experienced in the art of war. In peacetime they guard the palace buildings, and in times of war they forge ahead courageously as the vanguard. The army is composed of four types of troops, namely, infantry, cavalry, charioteers, and elephant-soldiers. The elephant is covered with strong armor and its tusks are armed with sharp barbs. The general who controls the armed forces rides on it with two soldiers walking on each side to manage the animal. The chariot is drawn by four horses, with the commander-in-chief sitting in it, and arrays of soldiers stay beside the wheels protecting him. The cavalrymen spread open to draw up a defensive formation, or gallop to pursue the defeated enemy. The infantrymen go lightly into battle and are daring men chosen for their boldness. They carry big shields and hold long spears, sabers, or swords, dashing to the front of the battle array. All their weapons are sharp and keen, and they have been drilled in such instruments of war as spear, shield, bow and arrow, saber, sword, battle-ax, hatchet, dagger-ax, long pole, long spear, discus, rope, and the like, which are practiced generation after generation.

Although the people are violent and impetuous by temperament, they are plain and honest in nature. They never accept any wealth without considering the propriety of the action but give others more than what is required by righteousness. They fear the retribution for sins in future lives and make light of the benefits they enjoy at the present time. They do not practice treachery and are creditable in keeping their oaths.

Governmental administration lays stress on simplicity and honesty, and the people are amicable by social custom. There are occasionally criminals and scoundrels who violate the national law or scheme to endanger the sovereign. When the facts are discovered, they are often cast into jail, where they are left to live or die; they are not sentenced to death but are regarded no longer as members of human society. The punishment for those who infringe the ethical code or behave against the principles of loyalty and filial piety is to cut off the nose, or excise an ear, or mutilate a hand, or amputate a foot, or banish the offender to another country or into the wilderness. Other offenses can be expiated by a payment of money.

When a judge hears a case, no torture is inflicted upon the accused to extort a confession. The accused answers whatever questions are put to him, and then a sentence is fairly passed according to facts. There are some who refuse to admit their unlawful activities, being ashamed of their faults, or trying to cover up their
877c mistakes. In order to ascertain the actual facts of a case, ordeals are required to justify a final judgment. There are four ways of doing so, namely, the ordeals by water, fire, weighing, and poison. The ordeal by water is to put the accused man into a sack, while a stone is put into another; the two sacks are connected together and thrown into a deep stream to discriminate the real criminal from the suspect. If the man sinks and the stone floats, the man's guilt is proved, but if the man floats and the stone sinks, he is then judged as having concealed nothing. The ordeal by fire is to make

the accused crouch on a piece of hot iron, and he is required to stamp on it with his feet, to touch it with his hands, and to lick it with his tongue. If the charge against him is false, he will not be hurt, and if he is burned, he is the real culprit. As a weak and feeble man cannot stand the heat of the scorching iron, he is asked to scatter some flower buds over the hot iron. If he is falsely charged, the buds open into flowers, and if he is truly a criminal, the buds are burned. The ordeal by weighing is to weigh the accused on a balance against a stone to see which is heavier. If the charge is false, the man goes down while the stone goes up, and if the charge is true, the stone is weightier than the man. The ordeal by poison is to cut the right hind leg of a black ram and put poison into the leg as a portion for the accused to eat. If the charge is true, the man is poisoned to death, and if the charge is false, the poison is counteracted and the accused may survive. These four ordeals are the ways for the prevention of a hundred misdeeds.

There are nine grades in the manner of paying homage. They are (1) inquiring after one's health, (2) bowing down three times to show respect, (3) bowing with hands raised high, (4) bowing with hands folded before the chest, (5) kneeling on one knee, (6) kneeling on both knees, (7) crouching with hands and knees on the ground, (8) bowing down with hands, elbows, and head to the ground, and (9) prostrating oneself with hands, elbows, and head touching the ground. In all these nine grades, the utmost veneration is expressed by doing only one obeisance. To kneel down and praise the other's virtue is the perfect form of veneration. If one is at a distance [from the venerated person], one just prostrates oneself with folded hands. If one is nearby, one kisses the feet and rubs the heels [of the venerated person]. When one is delivering messages or receiving orders, one should hold up one's robe and kneel down. The honored person who receives veneration must say some kind words in return, or stroke the head or pat the back of the worshipper, giving him good words of admonition to show his affection and kindness. When a homeless monk receives salutation, he only expresses his good wishes in return and never stops the worshipper from paying homage to him. To a great respected master, one often pays reverence by going round him once or thrice, or as many times as one wishes if one has a special request in mind.

When a man is sick, he refrains from eating food for seven days, and in this period he may often recover his health. If he is not cured, then he takes medicine. The medicines are of various properties and have different names, and the physicians differ in medical technique and in methods of diagnosis.

At a funeral ceremony, the relatives of the departed one wail and weep, rend their clothes and tear their hair, strike their foreheads and beat their chests. They do not wear mourning costume and have no fixed period of mourning. There are three kinds of burial service. The first is cremation: a pyre is built, on which the body is consumed. The second is water burial: the corpse is put into a stream to be carried away. The third is wilderness burial: the body is discarded in a forest to feed wild animals.

After the demise of a king, the first function is to enthrone the crown prince, so that he may preside over the funeral ceremony and fix the positions of superiority and inferiority. Meritorious titles are conferred on a king while he is living, and no posthumous ap-
878a pellations are given to him after his death. Nobody goes to take a meal at a house where the people are suffering the pain of bereavement, but when the funeral service is over things go back to normal and there are no taboos. Those who have taken part in a funeral procession are considered unclean, and they all bathe themselves outside the city before entering the city walls.

As regards those who are getting very old, approaching the time of death, suffering from incurable disease, and fearing that life is drawing to an end, they become disgusted with this world, desire to cast off human life, despise mortal existence, and wish to get rid of the ways of the world. Their relatives and friends then play music to hold a farewell party, put them in a boat, and row them to the middle of the Ganges so that they may drown themselves in the river. It is said that they will thus be reborn in the heavens. Out of ten people only one cherishes such ideas, and so far I have not seen it with my own eyes.

According to monastic regulations, homeless monks should not lament over the deaths of their parents but should recite and chant scriptures in memory of their kindness, so as to be in keeping with the funeral rites and impart happiness to the departed souls.

As the government is liberal, official duties are few. There is no census registration and no corvée is imposed upon the people. The royal land is roughly divided into four divisions. The first division is used by the state to defray the expense of offering sacrifices to gods and ancestors, the second division is for bestowing as fiefs to the king's assistants and ministers, the third division is for giving as rewards to prominent and intelligent scholars of high talent, and the fourth division is for making meritorious donations to various heterodox establishments. Therefore taxation is light and forced labor scarcely levied. Everyone keeps to his hereditary occupation, and all people cultivate portions of land allotted to them *per capita*. Those who till the king's fields pay one sixth of the crops as rent. Also, in order to gain profits the merchants and traders travel to and fro to exchange commodities, and they pay light duties at ferries and barriers before passing. For public construction no forced labor is enlisted; the laborers are paid according to the work they have done. Soldiers dispatched to garrison outposts and palace guards are conscripted according to circumstances, and an announcement of a reward is made to obtain applicants. Magistrates and ministers, as well as common government officials and assistants, all have their portions of land, so that they may sustain themselves by the fief granted to them.

As climate and soil vary at different places, the natural products also differ in various districts. There are diverse descriptions of flowers, herbs, fruits, and trees with different names. There are such flowers as *āmra* (mango), *āmla* (tamarind), *madhūka* (licorice), *badara* (jujube), *kapittha* (wood-apple), *āmalaka* (myrobalan), *tinduka* (*Diospyros*), *uḍumbara* (*Ficus glomerata*), *moca* (plantain), *nārikera* (coconut), and *panasa* (jackfruit). It is difficult to give a full list of such fruits, and here I just mention a few of them, which are valued by the people. As regards the date, chestnut, and green and red persimmon, they are unknown in India. Pear, crab apple, peach, apricot, and grape are often alternately grown in Kaśmīra and onward, while pomegranate and sweet orange are planted in all countries.

In the cultivation of fields, such farm work as sowing and reaping, ploughing and weeding, seeding and planting are done according to the seasons, either laboriously or with ease. Among the native products, rice and wheat are particularly abundant. As for vegetables, there are ginger, mustard, melon, calabash, and *kanda* (beet). Onion and garlic are scanty and few people eat them. Those who eat them are driven out of the city.

As to milk, ghee, grease, butter, granulated sugar, rock candy, mustard-seed oil, and various kinds of cakes and parched grains,
878b they are used as common food, and fish, mutton, and venison are occasionally served as delicacies. The meat of such animals as oxen, donkeys, elephants, horses, pigs, dogs, foxes, wolves, lions, monkeys, and apes is not to be eaten as a rule. Those who eat the meat of such animals become despicable and detestable to the public and are expelled to the outskirts of the city; they rarely show themselves among the people.

As regards the different spirits and sweet wines of diverse tastes, drinks made from grapes and sugarcane are for the Kshatriyas, and fermented spirits and unfiltered wines are for the Vaisyas to drink. The Śramaṇas and Brahmans drink grape and sugarcane juice, as they refrain from taking alcoholic beverages. For the low and mixed castes, there are no specific drinks.

As to household implements, there are different articles made of various materials for diverse purposes. Miscellaneous necessities are always sufficiently at hand. Although cauldrons and big pots are used for cooking, the rice steamer is unknown. The cooking utensils are mostly made of earthenware, and few are made of brass. At the time of taking a meal, a man eats from one vessel, in which all ingredients are mixed together. He takes the food with his fingers, never using spoons or chopsticks; but the aged and the sick use copper spoons for eating food.

Gold, silver, brass, white jade, and crystal are local products, which are amassed in large quantities. Precious substances and rare treasures of different descriptions, which are procured from overseas, are commodities for trading. For the exchange of goods, gold and silver coins, cowries, and small pearls are used as the media of exchange.

The territories and boundaries of India have been described above, and the different local conditions have been briefly related here. I have made only a rough statement of what is common in all the regions of the country in a generalized manner. As regards the particular political administrations and social customs of different regions, I shall explain them separately under the heading of each country as follows.

The country of Lampā is over one thousand *li* in circuit, with the Snow Mountains at its back in the north and the Black Range on the other three sides. The capital city is more than ten *li* in circuit. Several hundred years ago the royal family of this country ceased to exist, and powerful families have competed with each other for superiority in the absence of a great monarch. It has recently become a dependency of Kāpiśī. The country produces nonglutinous rice and much sugarcane. There are many trees but few fruits. The climate is temperate, and there is little frost and no snow. The country is a rich and happy land, and the people are fond of singing and chanting but are timid and deceitful by nature. They cheat each other and never respect one another. They are ugly and short in stature and are frivolous and impetuous in behavior. They mostly wear white cotton and are nicely dressed. There are more than ten monasteries with a few monks, most of whom are students of the Mahayana teachings. There are several tens of deva-temples with many heretics.

From here going southeast for over one hundred *li*, I crossed a high mountain and a large river and then arrived in the country of Nagarahāra (in North India). This country is over six hundred *li* from east to west and two hundred fifty or sixty *li* from south to north. It is surrounded by steep and dangerous precipices on all sides. The capital city is more than twenty *li* in circuit. There is no

sovereign king to rule over the country, and it belongs to Kāpiśī as
878c a vassal state. Grain and fruits are produced in abundance, and the climate is moderately warm. The people are simple and honest as well as courageous and valiant. They slight wealth and esteem learning, and venerate the Buddha-dharma, though a few of them have faith in heretical religions. There are many monasteries but few monks. All the stupas are deserted and in dilapidated condition. There are five deva-temples with over one hundred heretics.

Two *li* to the east of the capital city there is a stupa more than three hundred feet high built by King Aśoka with stones piled up, on which there are marvellous sculptures. This was the place where Śākya Bodhisattva [once in a former life] met Dīpaṃkara Buddha, spread a piece of deerskin and his own hair to cover the muddy ground [for the Buddha to tread on], and received the prediction of Buddhahood from him. Although it has passed through a kalpa (aeon) of destruction, this ancient trace remains intact. On fast days showers of various kinds of flowers descend on the spot, and multitudes of the common people vie with one another in making offerings [to the stupa]. In a monastery to the west of the stupa there are a few monks. Further to the south, a small stupa marks the spot where the Bodhisattva covered up the muddy ground in a former life. It was erected by King Aśoka at a secluded place to avoid the highway.

Inside the capital city there are the old foundations of a great stupa. I heard the local people saying that it had formerly contained a tooth relic of the Buddha and that it was originally a tall and magnificent structure. Now there is no more tooth relic but only the old foundations remaining there. Beside them there is a stupa more than thirty feet high, and according to the local tradition its origin is unknown. The people said that it dropped down from the air and took root at the spot. It was not built by human beings, and it manifested many spiritual signs.

Over ten *li* to the southwest of the capital city, there is a stupa that marks the spot where the Tathāgata once alighted during his flight from Central India on his itinerary of edification. Being moved by the event, the people of the country built the base of this spiritual stupa out of admiration. Not far away to the east, there is a stupa marking the place where Śākya Bodhisattva met Dīpaṃkara Buddha in a former life and purchased some flowers [to offer to the Buddha].

More than twenty *li* to the southwest of the capital city, one reaches a small range of rocky hills where there is a monastery with lofty halls and storied pavilions, all constructed with rocks. The buildings were all quiet and silent, and not a single monk was to be found. Within the compound of the monastery, there was a stupa more than two hundred feet high built by King Aśoka.

To the southwest of the monastery is a deep gully with overhanging rocks [on the two sides], from which water falls down the wall-like precipices. On the rocky wall at the east precipice is a 879a
large cave, which was the dwelling place of the Nāga Gopāla. The entrance is small and narrow, and it is dark inside the cave; water drips from the rocks down to the mountain path. Formerly there was a shadow of the Buddha, resembling his true features with all the good physical marks, just as if he were alive. But in recent years it is not visible to everybody, and even those who see it can only perceive an indistinct outline. Those who pray with utmost sincerity may get a spiritual response and see a clear picture, but only for a short moment.

When the Tathāgata was living in the world, the Nāga was a cowherd whose duty was to supply the king with milk and cream. Once, as he failed to fulfill his task properly, he was reprimanded by the king. With a feeling of hatred and malice he purchased some flowers to offer to the stupa of prediction, in the hope that he might be reborn as an evil Nāga to devastate the country and injure the king. Then he went up to the rocky precipice and jumped down to kill himself. Thus he became a Nāga king and lived in this cave. The moment he desired to go out of the cave to carry out his evil wishes, the Tathāgata, with a mind of compassion for the people of the country, who would suffer havoc caused by the Nāga, arrived from Central India by flight with his supernatural powers.

At the sight of the Tathāgata, the Nāga's malignant mind ceased. He accepted the rule of non-killing and wished to protect the right Dharma. So he requested that the Tathāgata dwell in that cave permanently, and he would always offer alms to all his saintly disciples. The Tathāgata said to him, "I shall enter Nirvana, but I shall leave my shadow behind for you, and I shall send five Arhats always to receive your offerings. Even when the right Dharma has disappeared into oblivion, this arrangement will not be altered. In case your malignant mind is agitated, you should look at my shadow, and on account of your compassion and benevolence, your malignant mind will come to an end. During this Bhadrakalpa (Good aeon), all the future World-honored Ones will have pity upon you and leave their shadows behind."

Outside the door of this Shadow Cave there are two square rocks, on one of which is the trace of the Tathāgata's footprint with the wheel-sign dimly visible, and it sometimes emits a light. On either side of the Shadow Cave there are many other caves, which are the places where the saintly disciples of the Tathāgata used to sit in meditation. At a corner to the northwest of the Shadow Cave there is a stupa that marks the place where the Tathāgata once took a walk. Beside it is another stupa, in which are stored the relics of the Tathāgata's hair and nail parings. Not far from here another stupa marks the spot where the Tathāgata preached on the true doctrine of the *skandha*s (five attributes of being), the *āyatana*s (twelve sense-fields), and the *dhātu*s (eighteen spheres, consisting of six sense-organs, six sense objects, and six consciousnesses). To the west of the Shadow Cave, there is a large flat rock on which the Tathāgata once washed his robe, and the traces of the robe left on the rock are still dimly visible.

At more than thirty *li* to the southeast of the city, one reaches the city of Hilo, which is four or five *li* in circuit; [its city wall] is high, precipitous, and impregnable. There are flowers, trees, and pools with pure water as bright as a mirror. The inhabitants of the city are simple and honest, and they believe in the right Dharma. There is a storied pavilion with colorfully painted beams and pillars.

On the second story, there is a small stupa made of the seven precious substances, in which is preserved a piece of the Tathāgata's skull bone twelve inches in circumference with distinct hair pores, 879b
yellowish white in color, contained in a precious casket that has been placed inside the stupa. Those who wish to tell their fortunes may prepare some fragrant plaster to make an impression of the skull bone and read a clear written prediction according to their effects of blessedness. There is another small stupa made of the seven precious substances in which is stored the Tathāgata's cranial bone, which has the shape of a lotus leaf and is of the same color as the skull bone. It is also contained in a precious casket that has been sealed up and placed [in the stupa]. There is another small stupa made of the seven precious substances, in which is preserved an eyeball of the Tathāgata, as large as a crab apple, being brilliant and transparent in and out. It is also contained in a precious casket that has been sealed up and placed [in the stupa]. The Tathāgata's upper robe, made of fine cotton in a yellowish red color, is placed in a precious casket. As it has lasted a long time, it is slightly damaged. The Tathāgata's pewter staff, with rings made of pewter and a sandalwood handle, is stored in a precious tube.

Recently a king heard that these relics belonged to the Tathāgata; and he captured them by force. After returning to his own country, the king kept the relics in his palace, but in less than twelve days the relics were lost. When he searched for them, he found that they had returned to their original places. These five holy objects have shown many spiritual signs. The king of Kāpiśī ordered five attendants to take care of the relics by offering incense and flowers, and worshippers came to pay reverence to them without cease.

The attendants, wishing to spend their time in quietness, and thinking that people would value money more than anything else, made a rule to stop the hubbub caused by the visitors, to the effect that one gold coin should be charged to see the skull bone, and five gold coins for making an impression. This rule was also applicable in different grades to the other relics. Although the charges were high, the number of worshippers increased.

To the northwest of the storied pavilion, there is a stupa that is also very lofty and has shown many marvellous signs. When it is touched with a finger, it shakes down to the basement and its bells ring harmoniously.

From here going toward the southeast among mountains and valleys for over five hundred *li*, I reached the country of Gandhāra (at former times incorrectly transcribed as Qiantuowei, in the domain of North India).

The country of Gandhāra is more than one thousand *li* from east to west and over eight hundred *li* from south to north, with the Indus on the east. The capital city, called Puruṣapura, is more than forty *li* in circuit. The royal family is extinct and the country is now under the domination of Kāpiśī. The towns and villages are desolate and have few inhabitants. In one corner of the palace city there are over one thousand families. They produce abundant cereals and have flowers and fruits in profusion. The country grows much sugarcane and produces sugar candy. The climate is mild and shows scarcely any frost or snow. The people are shy and timid by nature and are fond of literature and the arts. Most of them respect heretical religions and only a few believe in the right Dharma. Since ancient times, masters who wrote commentaries
879c and theoretical treatises in India, such as Nārāyaṇadeva, Asaṅga, Vasubandhu, Dharmatrāta, Manoratha, Pārśva, etc. have been born in this country. There were more than a thousand monasteries, but they are now dilapidated and deserted, and in desolate condition. Most of the stupas are also in ruins. There are about a hundred deva-temples, inhabited by various heretics.

At the northeast inside the royal city, there are the remains of the foundation of a precious terrace on which the Buddha's alms bowl was once placed. After the Tathāgata's decease, the bowl was brought to this country, where it was venerated with formal rituals for several hundred years, and then it was brought to various countries. It is now in Persia. At a distance of eight or nine *li* to the southeast outside the city, there is a pipal tree more than one hundred feet tall with profuse branches and leaves that cast a dense shade on the ground. The four past Buddhas sat under this tree, and now the statues of the four Buddhas are still to be seen. The remaining nine hundred ninety-six Buddhas of the Bhadrakalpa will also sit under it, divinely guarded and protected by gods and deities. When the Śākya Tathāgata was once sitting under this tree with his face toward the south, he told Ānanda, "Four hundred years after my decease, there will be a king named Kaniṣka, who will erect a stupa not far to the south of here. Most of my bodily remains will be collected in it."

To the south of the pipal tree there is a stupa constructed by King Kaniṣka. In the four hundredth year after the demise of the Tathāgata, King Kaniṣka ascended the throne and ruled over Jambudvīpa. He did not [originally] believe in the theory of retribution of good and evil deeds and contemptuously defamed the Buddha-dharma. Once he was hunting in a marsh when a white hare appeared. The king chased after the hare and it suddenly disappeared at this place. He saw in the woods a young cowherd building a small stupa three feet high. The king asked the boy, "What are you doing?" The boy said in reply, "Formerly the Śākya Buddha made a wise prediction; 'A king will build a stupa at this auspicious place, and most of my bodily remains will be collected in it.' Your Majesty's holy virtues were cultivated in your previous lives, and your name coincides with the one mentioned in the prediction. Your divine merits and superior blessedness will be realized at this time. Thus I am here as a preliminary sign to remind you of the prediction." With these words, the cowherd vanished.

Upon hearing these words, the king was overjoyed and was proud to know that his name had been predicted by the Great Sage in his prophecy. Therefore he professed the right faith and deeply believed in the Buddha-dharma. Around the small stupa he built a stone stupa, wishing to encompass the small one, by the power of his merits. But no matter how tall he built the stone stupa, the small one was always three feet higher, until it increased to over four hundred feet tall, standing on a base one and one-half *li* in circuit, with five flights of steps leading up to a height of one

880a hundred fifty feet, so that it could cover the small stupa. The king was delighted, and so he made in addition gilded copper disks arranged in twenty-five tiers on the top. Then he placed one *hu* (hectoliter) of the Tathāgata's relic bones in the stupa, to which he piously made offerings. When he had just completed the construction, he saw the small stupa protruding with half its body sideways at the southeast corner of the great base. The king was enraged and threw it upward, and so it stayed, half appearing in the stone base under the second flight of steps of the stupa; but another small stupa emerged at the original place. The king then gave up and remarked with a sigh, "Human affairs are bewildering, but the merits of deities are insuppressible. What is the use of being angry with it, if it is supported by the gods?" In shame and fear, the king apologized and returned home.

These two stupas are still in existence. Those who are sick and wish to pray for recovery offer incense and flowers to the stupas with pious minds, and can in most cases become cured. On the southern side of the flight of steps at the east of the great stupa, there are two carved stupas, one three and the other five feet high, in the same style and shape as the great stupa. There are also two carved images of the Buddha, one four and the other six feet high, resembling the Buddha sitting cross-legged under the Bodhi Tree. In the sunshine these images are of a dazzling golden color, and when they are gradually covered by shade the lines on the stone become bluish violet in color. Some local old people said that several hundred years ago there were golden colored ants in the crevice of the stone, the big ones being of the size of a fingernail and the small ones of a grain of wheat. They followed one another, gnawing at the surface of the stone, and the lines they made on the stone looked like incised grooves, filled with golden sand to delineate the images, which are still in existence.

On the south side of the flight of steps leading up to the great stupa, there is a painting of the Buddha sixteen feet in height, with two busts above the chest but one body below it. Some old people said that there was formerly a poor man who sustained

himself by working as a laborer. Once he earned one gold coin and wished to make a portrait of the Buddha. He came to the stupa and said to a painter, "I wish to make a portrait of the Tathāgata's excellent features, but I have only one gold coin, which is really insufficient for remuneration. This has been my long-cherished desire, but I am poor and lacking in money." In consideration of the poor man's sincerity, the painter did not argue about the payment and promised to accomplish the job. Another man under the same circumstances came with one gold coin to request the painter to draw a portrait of the Buddha. Thus the painter accepted the money from the two men, and he asked another skillful painter to work together with him in drawing one portrait. When the two men came on the same day to worship the Buddha, the two painters showed them the portrait, pointing at it and saying, "This is the portrait you ordered." The two men looked at each other bewildered, and the painters realized that the two men were doubtful about the matter and said to them, "Why are you pondering over 880b
the matter for so long? Whatever object we undertake to produce is done without the slightest fault. If our words are not false, the portrait will show miracles." As soon as they had uttered these words, the portrait manifested a wonder: the body split into two busts, while the shadows intermingled into one, with the features shining brilliantly. The two men were happily convinced, and delightedly fostered faith.

More than a hundred paces to the southwest of the great stupa there is a standing image of the Buddha made of white stone, eighteen feet high, facing the north. It often worked miracles and frequently emitted light. Sometimes people see it walking at night and going round the great stupa. Recently a band of robbers intended to enter the stupa to steal the contents. The image came out to meet the robbers head-on, and the robbers withdrew in fear. Then the image returned to its original place and stood there as usual. Thence the robbers corrected their errors and made a fresh start in life. They walked in towns and villages and told the event to all people far and near.

At the left and right sides of the great stupa there are hundreds of small stupas as closely arranged as the scales of a fish. The Buddha's images are magnificent, as they are made with perfect craftsmanship. Unusual fragrances and strange sounds are sometimes perceived, and spirits and genii, as well as holy ones, may be seen circumambulating the great stupa. It was predicted by the Tathāgata that when this stupa will have been burned down and rebuilt seven times, the Buddha-dharma will come to an end. Previous sages have recorded that it has been destroyed and reconstructed three times. When I first came to this country, the stupa had just suffered the disaster of conflagration. It is now under repair, and the structure is not yet completed.

To the west of the great stupa there is an old monastery built by King Kaniṣka. The storied pavilion and the houses built on terraces were constructed so that eminent monks could be invited in recognition of their distinguished merits. Although the buildings are dilapidated, they may still be regarded as wonderful constructions. There are a few monks, who study the Hinayana teachings. Since the monastery was constructed, it has produced extraordinary personages from time to time, who were either writers of treatises or men who realized sainthood. The influence of their pure conduct and perfect virtue is still functioning.

On the third story of the pavilion, there is the room used by the Venerable Pārśva (Ribs). It has been in ruins for a long time, but it is indicated with a mark. At first the venerable monk was a Brahmanic teacher; he became a Buddhist monk at the age of eighty. Some young men in the city sneered at him, saying, "You stupid old man, why are you so ignorant? A Buddhist monk has two duties, first to practice meditation and second to recite scriptures. Now you are getting old and feeble and cannot make any more progress. So you are trying to pass yourself off as a monk among the pure mendicants, but you do nothing but eat your fill."

Having heard about this reproach, the Venerable Pārśva apologized to the people and made a vow, saying, "If I do not thoroughly master the teachings of the Tripiṭaka and do not cut off all desires

of the three spheres of the world, so as to realize the six supernatural powers and possess the eight emancipations, I shall not lie down to sleep with my ribs touching the mat." Then he worked hard and always meditated whether he was walking, sitting, or standing still. In the daytime he studied theories and doctrines, and at night he sat quietly in meditation with a concentrated mind. In three years' time, he completely mastered the Tripiṭaka, cut off the desires of the three spheres of the world, and obtained the 880c
wisdom of the three knowledges. As the people respected him, they called him the Venerable Ribs—Pārśva.

To the east of the Venerable Pārśva's chamber, there is an old room in which Vasubandhu Bodhisattva composed the *Abhidharmakośa-śāstra*. Out of respect for him, the people had the room sealed up with a mark.

On the second story of the pavilion, at a place more than fifty paces to the south of the room of Vasubandhu Bodhisattva, is the site where the Śāstra-master Manoratha (As you wish) composed the *Vibhāṣā-śāstra*. The Śāstra-master was born one thousand years after the Nirvana of the Buddha. When he was young, he loved learning and was eloquent in speech. His fame spread far, and both clerical and lay people had faith in him. At that time the influence of King Vikramāditya (Valor sun) of Śrāvastī reached far and brought the various parts of India under his domination. Every day he distributed five lakhs of gold coins as alms to the paupers, the orphans, and the solitary. The state treasurer, fearing that the national treasury might be exhausted, ironically remonstrated with the king, saying, "Your Majesty's strong influence extends to various peoples, and your kindness benefits even insects. Pray spend five more lakhs of gold coins to relieve the poor and needy of the four quarters. When the treasury is exhausted, we can levy more taxes, and repeated taxation will arouse the people's resentment and grievance everywhere, but the monarch above may show off his kindness in bestowing charity upon the people and we subjects below will bear the blame of being disrespectful." The king said, "We collect surplus money to give to those who are short of it, and it is not for ourselves that we squander the national wealth." Thus five lakhs of gold coins were added to the sum of money given to the poor and needy.

Later, in the course of hunting, the king lost the trace of a wild boar, and a man who found the animal was granted a reward of one lakh of gold coins. Now when the Śāstra-master Manoratha once had his hair shaved, he paid the barber one lakh of gold coins, and the state annalist accordingly put the event on record. The king was ashamed to have been surpassed by a monk in lavishing money and intended to insult the Śāstra-master Manoratha in public. Thus he summoned one hundred heretical teachers of high virtue and deep learning, to whom he issued an order, saying, "We wish to glean various views to find out the truth, but different schools have different theories, so that we do not know where to fix our mind. Now we wish to see which of your schools is superior and which is inferior, so that we may know which way we should follow exclusively."

At the time when the discussion was held, the king issued another order, saying, "These heretical Śāstra-masters are brilliant and talented scholars, and the Śramaṇas of the Dharma should master their own theories well. If they win in the debate we shall venerate the Buddha-dharma, otherwise we shall slaughter the Buddhist monks." Then Manoratha debated with the heretics and defeated ninety-nine of the opponents, who fled away in retreat. He slighted the last antagonist with contempt and talked with him fluently. When he came upon the subject of fire and smoke, the king and the heretic said aloud, "The Śāstra-master Manoratha has made a faulty statement. It is common sense that smoke should precede fire." Although Manoratha wished to explain his viewpoint, nobody would listen to his argumentation. Ashamed of being insulted in public, he bit off his tongue and wrote a letter to his disciple
881a Vasubandhu, saying, "Among groups supported by factions, one cannot hold a great principle in competition, and in an assembly of ignorant people there is no way to argue for the right theory." He died after having written these words.

Not long afterward, King Vikramāditya lost his kingdom and was succeeded by another king who adored and respected men of eminence and wisdom. Wishing to rehabilitate his teacher's good name, Vasubandhu Bodhisattva came to the new king and said to him, "Your Majesty rules over the kingdom by your saintly virtues and renders support to all living beings. My late teacher Manoratha was learned in abstruse and profound theories, but the previous king held a grudge against him and had his good name besmirched in public. As I have studied under his instruction, I wish to avenge the wrong done to my teacher."

The king, knowing that Manoratha had been a wise man, and appreciating Vasubandhu's upright character, summoned all the heretics who had debated with Manoratha to a meeting. Vasubandhu then reiterated what his teacher had expounded, and all the heretics were defeated and withdrew.

Going to the northeast for more than fifty *li* from the monastery built by King Kaniṣka, I crossed a large river and reached the city of Puṣkarāvatī, which is fourteen or fifteen *li* in circuit. It is well-populated, and the lanes and alleyways are connected with each other. Outside the west gate of the city there is a deva temple, in which the deva image is austere in appearance and often works miracles. To the east of the city there is a stupa built by King Aśoka. It marks the place where the four past Buddhas preached the Dharma. Ancient saints and sages coming from Central India to subdue divine beings and teach human mortals at this place were very numerous. It was at this place that the Śāstra-master Vasumitra (or Shiyou in Chinese, and formerly transcribed erroneously as Hexumiduo) composed the *Abhidharma-prakaraṇa-pāda-śāstra*.

Four or five *li* to the north of the city, there is an old monastery, of which the buildings are in desolation, with a few resident monks, who are followers of Hinayana teachings. This is the place where the Śāstra-master Dharmatrāta (known as Fajiu in Chinese and erroneously transcribed as Damoduoluo in olden times) composed the *Abhidharmatābhidharma-hṛdaya-śāstra*. Beside the monastery there is a stupa several hundred feet high built by King

Aśoka. The wood carvings and stone sculptures are quite different from work done by human artisans. Formerly, when the Śākya Buddha was a king, he practiced the way of the Bodhisattva at this place and gave alms tirelessly to all living beings according to their wishes. He was the king of this land for one thousand lives, and it was at this auspicious place where he surrendered his eyes in one thousand lives.

Not far east of where he forsook his eyes, there are two stone stupas, both more than one hundred feet high. The one on the right was erected by Brahmā and the one on the left by Indra, and both are beautifully decorated with wonderful jewels and gems. After the demise of the Tathāgata, the gems turned into stone. Although the foundations have sunk, the stupas still stand high and lofty.

More than fifty *li* to the northwest of the stupas built by Brahmā and Indra there is a stupa that marks the place where
881b the Śākya Tathāgata converted the goddess Hārītī to prevent her from doing harm to people. Thus it became the custom of the country to pray to the goddess for offspring.

More than fifty *li* to the north of the place where Hārītī was converted, there is a stupa built at the spot where Śyāmaka Bodhisattva (formerly transcribed incorrectly as Shanmo Bodhisattva) gathered fruits to offer to his blind parents in fulfillment of his filial duty and met the king who was hunting and who accidentally hit him with a poisoned arrow. His mind of sincerity moved Indra, who dressed his wound with medicine, and his virtuous deed inspired the gods, who restored him to life very soon.

Going to the southeast for more than two hundred *li* from the place where Śyāmaka Bodhisattva was injured, I reached the city of Varṣa. To the north of the city there is a stupa built at the place where Prince Sudāna (Good tooth) [*sic*] said farewell to his countrymen at the city gate, when he was banished from the city and apologized to the people for having given his father's elephant as a gift to a Brahman. In the monastery beside the stupa there are more than fifty monks, all of whom are followers of the Hinayana teachings. It was at this place that the Śāstra-master Īśvara (Self-existence) composed the *Abhidharmadīpa-śāstra*.

Outside the east gate of Varṣa city there is a monastery with more than fifty monks, all of whom are followers of the Mahayana teachings. There is a stupa built by King Aśoka. Formerly, when Prince Sudāna was living in exile at the Daṇḍaloka Mountain (formerly known as Tante Mountain erroneously), a Brahman begged for his sons and wife and sold them at this place.

At a place more than twenty *li* to the northeast from Varṣa city, one reaches the Daṇḍaloka Mountain. On the ridge there is a stupa built by King Aśoka to mark the place where Prince Sudāna once lived in seclusion. Not far away from it there is another stupa, built at the spot where the prince forsook his sons and wife to a Brahman. The Brahman beat the prince's sons and wife until their blood ran to the ground and stained the earth. Even now the grass and plants still retain a reddish hue. The cave on the cliff was the place where the prince and his wife practiced meditation. The branches of the trees in the valley droop like curtains, and here the prince used to roam about. Nearby is a stone hermitage, which was the abode of an ancient *ṛṣi* (sagely anchorite).

At more than one hundred *li* to the northwest from the hermitage, one crosses over a small hill and arrives at a big mountain. On the south of the mountain there is a monastery, in which lived a few monks who studied Mahayana teachings. The stupa beside it was built by King Aśoka at the place where the *ṛṣi* Unicorn once lived. This *ṛṣi* was ensnared by a lustful woman and lost his supernatural powers. The lustful woman then rode on his shoulders and returned to the city.

At more than fifty *li* to the northeast from Varṣa, one reaches 881c
a lofty mountain, on which there is a bluish stone image of Bhīmādevī, wife of Maheśvara. The local people said that this image of the goddess existed by nature. It showed many marvels and many people came to give prayers. In all parts of India, the people, noble and mean, who wish to pray for blessedness flock to this place from far and near. Those who wish to see the physical form of the goddess may get a vision of her after fasting for seven days with a sincere and concentrated mind, and their wishes will in most cases

be fulfilled. At the foot of the mountain, there is a temple for Maheśvara in which the ash-smearing heretics perform ceremonies.

Going for one hundred fifty *li* to the southeast from the Bhīmādevī temple, I reached the city of Uḍakhand, which is more than twenty *li* in circuit, bordering on the Indus in the south. The inhabitants are rich and happy, while precious goods pile up high and most of the rare and valuable things of different places are collected here.

Going for more than twenty *li* to the northwest from Uḍakhand, I reached the city of Śalātura, the birthplace of the *ṛṣi* Pāṇini, the author of the *Śabda-vidyā-śāstra*. At the beginning of antiquity, the written language was rich and extensive in vocabulary, but with the passage of the kalpa of destruction, the world became empty, and afterward the long-lived deities descended to the earth to guide human beings. Thereafter, literary documents were produced, and thenceforth the source of literature became a torrential flood. Brahmā and Indra wrote model compositions as the time required, and the *ṛṣi*s of each of the heretical systems formed their own words. The people studied what was taught by their predecessors and learned emulously what was handed down; but the students would waste their effort, because it was difficult for them to master all in detail.

At the time when human life was one hundred years in length, the *ṛṣi* Pāṇini was born with innate knowledge of wide scope. Having pity on the shallowness of learning in his time, and wishing to expunge what was superficial and false and delete what was superfluous, he travelled about to make inquiries into the way of learning. He met with Maheśvara and told the deity about his intention. Maheśvara said, "How grand it is! I shall render you assistance." The *ṛṣi* withdrew after hearing these words and concentrated his mind to ponder over the matter. He collected all words and composed a word book in one thousand stanzas, each stanza consisting of thirty-two syllables. In this book he made a thorough study of the written and spoken language of both ancient and modern times, and he offered it to the king in a sealed envelope.

The king treasured it very much and ordered that all people in the country should learn the book; one who could recite it fluently by heart would be rewarded with one thousand gold coins. Thus this book was transmitted from teacher to pupil and became prevalent at that time. Henceforth the Brahmans in this city are great scholars of high talent with knowledge of wide scope.

In the city of Śalātura there is a stupa built at the place where an Arhat converted a disciple of Pāṇini. Five hundred years after the decease of the Tathāgata, a great Arhat came from Kaśmīra to this place in the course of his journey. When he saw a Brahman teacher beating a schoolboy, he asked the Brahman, "Why are you 882a
chastising the child?" The Brahman said, "I asked him to learn the *Śabda-vidyā-śāstra*, but he has not made progress with the passage of time." The Arhat smiled amiably, and the old Brahman said, "A Śramaṇa should be compassionate and have sympathy with all living beings. But you are now smiling, and I should like to know why." The Arhat said in reply, "It is not easy for me to tell you, for fear that it might cause you a deep doubt. Have you ever heard about the *ṛṣi* Pāṇini, who composed the *Śabda-vidyā-śāstra* for the instruction of posterity?" The Brahman said, "He was a scion of this city. Out of admiration for his virtue, his disciples have made an image of him, which is still in existence." The Arhat said, "Now this son of yours is [a reincarnation of] that *ṛṣi*. On account of his rich knowledge he took delight in studying worldly books, discussing only the heretical theories and never researching into the truth. He wasted his spirit and wisdom and is still involved in the wheel of rebirth. By virtue of his surplus good deeds, he has been born your beloved son. But the study of the diction and language of worldly books simply wasted his energy. How can that be the same as the Tathāgata's holy teachings, which give rise to bliss and wisdom in a mysterious way?

"In olden times there was a decayed tree by the beach of the South Sea, and five hundred bats lived in the holes of the tree. Once a caravan of merchants stayed under the tree. As the season was windy and chilly and the merchants were hungry and cold, they piled up firewood and built a fire under the tree. The smoke and flames gradually began to burn fiercely, and they set the decayed tree on fire. One of the merchants recited the *Abhidharma-piṭaka* after midnight, and the bats, though scorched by the heat, loved to listen to the recitation of the Dharma so much that they would not leave the place; they disregarded the intense heat and died on the tree. According to their karmic force, they were reborn as human beings and renounced their homes to learn and practice [the Buddhist teachings]. As they had heard the recitation of the Dharma, they were clever and intelligent and realized sainthood; thus they became fields of blessedness for the world.

"Recently King Kaniṣka and the Venerable Pārśva summoned five hundred holy persons in Kaśmīra to compile the *Vibhāṣā-śāstra*, and these five hundred holy persons are the five hundred bats that lived on that decayed tree. Although I am an unworthy man, I was one of them. From this we may see that between the superior and the inferior, the virtuous and the vicious, there is such a great difference as between those flying high in the air and those crouching down on the ground. Permit your beloved son to become a monk, for the merits of becoming a monk are indescribable in words."

After having said these words, the Arhat performed miracles and disappeared all of a sudden. The Brahman cherished a deep feeling of awe and faith and exclaimed, "Sādhu," (excellent!) for a long time. He told everything to the people of the neighborhood and permitted his son to become a monk to learn and practice [the Buddhist teachings]. He then gained faith and honored the Triple Gem, and his countrymen have accepted his edification with more and more earnestness up to this day.

Going from Uḍakhand city to the north over mountains and across rivers for more than six hundred *li*, I reached the country of Udyāna. (This means park, as it was a pleasure garden of a previous Wheel King. Formerly it was transcribed as Wuchang or Wutu, both erroneously. It is in the domain of North India.)

End of Fascicle Two

Fascicle III

Eight Countries, From Udyāna to Rājapura

The country of Udyāna is over five thousand *li* in circuit, with 882b mountains and valleys connecting each other and rivers and marshes linking together. Although crops are planted, the yield is poor owing to the infertility of the land. There are many grape vines, but sugarcane is scanty. The country produces gold and iron, and the soil is suitable for growing saffron. The woods are exuberant and flowers and fruits abundant. The climate is mild with timely wind and rain. The people are timid and overcautious by nature, and the practice of fraudulence is the common custom. They enjoy learning but do not make profound studies, and they take the recitation of spells as their profession. They mostly wear white cotton and have few other garments. Although they speak a different dialect, it is roughly the same as that spoken in India, and their written language and etiquette are closely related to those of India. They hold Buddhism in high esteem and reverently believe in the Mahayana teachings. Along the two sides of the Śubhavastu River, there were formerly one thousand four hundred monasteries, but most of them are now in desolation. In the old days there were eighteen thousand monks, but now the number has gradually decreased. They all study Mahayana teachings and spend their time in silent meditation. They can recite their books well, but they do not make researches into the deep meanings. They are pure in observing the disciplinary rules and are specially adept in reciting incantations. There are five traditions of the Vinaya rules, namely, the Dharmaguptaka, the Mahīśāsaka, the Kāśyapīya, the Sarvāstivāda, and the Mahāsāṃghika. There are more than ten deva-temples with heretics living together. There are four or five fortified cities, and the king mostly rules over the country from the city of Maṅgala, which is sixteen or seventeen *li* in circuit and is well populated.

Four or five *li* to the east of Maṅgala city there is a stupa that has shown a great number of spiritual signs. This was the spot where the Buddha, once being the *ṛṣi* Patience in a previous life, had his limbs mutilated by King Kali (Fighting, formerly transcribed as Geli erroneously).

Going to the northeast for two hundred fifty or sixty *li* from Maṅgala city, I came to a great mountain and reached the Apalāla Dragon Spring, which is the source of the Śubhavastu River and has a tributary flowing to the southwest. In the morning and
882c evening, the white spray falls like snowflakes with all the colors of the rainbow, shining upon all sides. At the time of the Kāśyapa Buddha, this dragon was born a human being named Jingqi; he was an expert in the art of exorcism and thus restrained a malicious dragon from causing rainstorms. It was because of his help that the people of the country could have surplus grain to store at home. Out of gratitude for the exorcist's virtuous deeds, each household of the inhabitants contributed one *dou* (ten liters) of grain as gift to him. As time passed, some people neglected their duty, and Jingqi became angry and wished to become a malignant dragon and cause storms to spoil the seedlings of the crops. After his death he was reborn a dragon at this place and caused white water flowing from the spring to damage the fertility of the soil. When the Śākya Tathāgata came to guide the world with a mind of great

pity, he had sympathy with the people of this country, who alone suffered from the disaster, and sent a deity to the place to convert the ferocious dragon. The deity Vajrapāṇi struck the mountain cliffs with his *vajra* (thunderbolt), and the shock terrified the dragon king, who came out and took refuge in the Buddha. After hearing the Buddha preaching the Dharma for him, the dragon purified his mind and had faith in enlightenment. The Tathāgata then forbade him to destroy agricultural products. The dragon said, "Whatever food I eat is collected from the fields cultivated by men. Under your holy teachings, I fear that I could not sustain my life. I hope that I may be allowed to collect grain for storage once every twelve years." The Tathāgata tolerated the dragon's request and consented with compassion. Thus the country suffers this white water calamity once every twelve years.

More than thirty *li* to the southwest of the Apalāla Dragon Spring and on the northern bank of the river, there is a huge rock with a footprint of the Tathāgata, which varies in size according to the power of the merits of the measurer. It was left by the Tathāgata when he was going away after having converted the dragon. Afterwards, people built a stone chamber on the rock, and worshippers came here from far and near to offer flowers and incense. Going downstream for more than thirty *li*, one reaches the rock on which the Tathāgata washed his robe. The lines of the robe are still clearly visible, as if they were carved on the rock.

More than four hundred *li* to the south of Maṅgala city, one reaches Hiḍḍa Mountain, where the stream in the valley flows westward. As one goes up to the east against the current of the stream, there are various kinds of flowers and strange fruits, covering the gully and climbing the steeps. The peaks and cliffs are precipitous, and the brooks and ravines wind and meander. The sound of loud talking and the echo of music are sometimes heard. Lying linked together in the valley, there are square rocks resembling bedsteads made by craftsmen. This was the place where the Tathāgata once in a former life, forsook his life to hear half a stanza of the Dharma. (The word "stanza" was formerly transcribed as 883a jie, an abbreviation of the original Sanskrit, or as jieta, a mispronunciation of the Sanskrit word. The correct reading should be *gāthā*, meaning a "verse" consisting of thirty-two syllables.)

More than two hundred *li* to the south of Maṅgala city is Mahāvana (Great forest) Monastery located beside a mountain. This was the place where the Tathāgata—when he was practicing the way of the Bodhisattva in one of his previous lives as a king named Sarvadatta (All-giving)—came incognito after having abandoned his kingdom to avoid an enemy. He met a poor Brahman coming to beg for alms. Since the king had lost his kingdom, he had nothing to give as alms. So he asked the Brahman to bind him, send him to the enemy king, and claim a reward, so that he might give the reward as alms to the Brahman.

Going down the mountain for thirty or forty *li* from the northwest of Mahāvana Monastery, one reaches Mayū (Bean) Monastery. There is a stupa over one hundred feet high, beside which is a big square rock with a footprint of the Tathāgata. In one of his previous lives, the Buddha stood on the rock and emitted millions of rays of light to illumine Mahāvana Monastery, while he related the Jātaka stories to human and divine beings. Below the base of the stupa, there is a stone, yellowish white in color and always exuding a greasy substance. This was the place where the Tathāgata, when practicing the way of the Bodhisattva, wrote down scriptures with a splinter of his bone in order to hear the right Dharma.

Sixty or seventy *li* to the west of Mayū Monastery is a stupa built by King Aśoka. This was the place where the Tathāgata once in a former life, as a king named Śivaka (Giving, formerly transcribed as Shipi erroneously), sliced his body to ransom a dove from a hawk, in order to acquire Buddhahood when he was practicing the way of the Bodhisattva.

More than two hundred *li* to the northwest of the place where the dove was ransomed, one enters the Sanirāja valley and reaches Sarpauṣadhi (Serpent medicine) Monastery, where there is a stupa over eighty feet high. This was the place where a famine occurred with a pestilence when the Tathāgata was Indra in a former life. Medical treatment failed to cure the people, who died one after another on the road. With a mind of pity, Indra wished to save them, and so he transformed himself into a huge python lying dead in the valley, and an announcement echoed in the air. Those who heard about it were glad to rush to the spot to cut off pieces of flesh, which were at once replaced, to satisfy their hunger and cure their disease. Not far away, there is the great Sūma Stupa, which was the place where the Tathāgata, as Indra in a year of famine in one of his former lives, pitied the suffering people. He changed himself into a large *sūma* (water) serpent, and all those who ate its flesh were cured.

Beside the cliff at the north of the Sanirāja River, there is a stupa that often cures sick people who come to pray for the recovery of their health. When the Tathāgata was a peacock king in a former life, he came here with his flock. As it was the hot season, the peacocks were thirsty, but they could not find any water to drink. The peacock king then pecked the cliff to let water flow out 883b
of the rock. Now a pond has been formed, the water of which is effective for healing illness. There are traces of the peacocks still visible on the stone.

More than sixty or seventy *li* southwest from Maṅgala city, there is a stupa over sixty feet high built by King Uttarasena at the east side of a great river. When the Tathāgata was about to enter Nirvana, he told the assembly of monks: "After my Nirvana, King Uttarasena of Udyāna should be given a portion of my relic bones." The various other kings wished to share the relics equally among themselves, and as King Uttarasena arrived later, he was despised by the other kings. At that time all men, heavenly beings, and monks reiterated the Tathāgata's last words. Thus the king [Uttarasena] took part in sharing the relics and carried his portion back to his own country, where he reverently constructed a stupa.

On the bank beside the great river, there is a huge rock in the shape of an elephant. Formerly when King Uttarasena used his great white elephant to carry the relics home, it suddenly fell down and died at this place; it was transformed into a rock, and so a stupa was erected beside it.

More than fifty *li* to the west of Maṅgala city and across a great river, one reaches the Rohitaka (Red) Stupa, which is over fifty feet in height and was built by King Aśoka. Formerly when the Tathāgata was practicing the way of the Bodhisattva as a king named Maitrībala, he drew blood from his body to feed five *yakṣa*s (formerly transcribed as yecha erroneously).

More than thirty *li* to the northwest of Maṅgala city, one reaches the Adbhuta (Marvellous) stone Stupa, which is over forty feet in height. Formerly the Tathāgata preached the Dharma to instruct men and heavenly beings at this place. When the Tathāgata had left the place, this stupa emerged from the ground, to which the people offered incense and flowers reverently and without cease.

Crossing the great river at the west of the stone stupa and going for thirty or forty *li*, I reached a *vihāra* (temple) in which is enshrined an image of Avalokiteśvara Bodhisattva (known as Guanzizai in Chinese. When it is pronounced in connected syllables, it reads as the above-mentioned Sanskrit form, and when it is read separately, it is divided into *avalokita*, translated as *guan* or "observe," and *īśvara*, translated as *zizai* or "master." Formerly it was translated as Guangshiyin, or Guanshiyin, or Guanshizizai, all erroneously). Its protective spiritual influence is latent, but its divine manifestations are apparent. Both monks and lay people come here one after another to make offerings to it without cease.

Going northwest for one hundred forty or fifty *li* from the image of Avalokiteśvara Bodhisattva, I reached Lanpolu Mountain, on the top of which is a dragon lake more than thirty *li* in circuit, a vast expanse of green water as pure as a brilliant mirror. Formerly when King Virūḍhaka went to attack the Śākyas, four men of the Śākya clan resisted the [invading] army, and their relatives were exiled to different places. One of the four men came out of the capital city and, feeling tired during the trudge, stopped midway.
883c At this time a wild goose came before him, and as the bird was docile and friendly, the man rode on its back. The goose flew up and alighted beside the lake. The Śākya man, having travelled through the air and arrived in a distant and strange land, lost his way and took a nap under the shade of a tree.

The young daughter of the dragon in the lake was enjoying the scenery at the lakeside when she suddenly saw the Śākya refugee. Fearing that her shape was unfit [to appear before a stranger], she changed herself into a human being and stroked him. The Śākya was startled, and he asked her, "I am a poor traveler; why are you so intimate with me?" Then he tried to be affectionate with the girl and attempted to have illicit intercourse with her. The girl said, "If I had the permission of my parents, I should be glad to comply with your wishes. Although you show me favor, [I cannot accept it] without my parents' consent." The Śākya said, "In this wilderness of mountains and valleys, where is your home?" The girl said, "I am the daughter of the dragon in this lake. I have heard that people of your noble clan have become destitute and homeless in the course of fleeing from calamity. I am lucky to have this opportunity to comfort you in your fatigue while I am making an excursion here. You ask me to have intimacy with you, but I have not received instructions from my parents. Moreover, it is due to my evil deeds done in past lives that I have been born in the shape of a dragon. A man and an animal are beings of different ways, and [their union] is unheard-of." The Śākya said, "Once I get your consent, my mind will be satisfied." The dragon girl said, "Then I shall accept your orders and shall do whatever you wish me to do."

The Śākya man then made an oath in his mind; "I shall render the whole body of this dragon girl [permanently] transformed into a human being by the power of whatever blessedness and virtue I have accumulated." Thus the dragon girl actually changed her form by the power of the man's blessedness. Having assumed the form of a human being, the girl was overjoyed, and she thanked the Śākya, saying, "Due to my past evil deeds, I was born in the wheel of the evil ways of existence. I am lucky that your power of blessedness has transformed my wicked body, in which I was born for many kalpas in the past, into a human figure in a moment. I am so grateful to you that even if I smashed my body into pieces, it would not be sufficient to express my thanks. I am willing to be together with you, but I fear criticism from the people. I wish to tell my parents to arrange the rites in the proper way."

The dragon girl returned to the lake and said to her parents, "Today when I was making an excursion, I met a Śākya man, who by the power of his blessedness transformed me into a human being. As we wish to get married, I venture to inform you of the fact." The dragon king was pleased with human beings and had respect for the holy clan, so he consented to his daughter's request and came out of the lake to express his thanks to the Śākya, saying, "You condescend to marry my daughter despite her station as a nonhuman being. Please come to my home and let her serve you."

At the invitation of the dragon king, the Śākya man came in and stayed in his abode. He lived in the dragon palace together [with the dragon girl] after performing due ceremonies, and the two of them lived a happy conjugal life with great pleasure. But the Śākya man always feared and loathed the sight of dragons, and so he desired to beg leave to depart. The dragon king stopped him, saying, "Please do not go far away but stay near us as neighbors. I shall cause you to possess territory and have the grand title of king; you will have ministers and subjects under your control and rule over the country for a long time." The Śākya declined, saying, "What you have said is not my wish."

The dragon king then put a sword into a small chest and covered it with a piece of the best white cotton. He said to the Śākya, "Hold up this white cotton and present it to the king. He will certainly accept the gift with his own hands from a man coming from
884a afar. At this moment you can kill the king, and wouldn't it be good to seize the kingdom in such a way?"

Thus at the instigation of the dragon, the Śākya went to offer the gift. While the King of Udyāna personally took up the white cotton, the Śākya got hold of his sleeve and stabbed him. The king's attendants and guards were thrown into a hubbub of confusion at the flight of steps leading up to the audience hall. The Śākya wielding the sword said to them, "This sword in my hand was given to me by a divine dragon to kill those who surrender after the others or who refuse to serve me." Fearing his divine martial power, they all supported him in his ascent to the throne. Then he rectified the abuses of the government and implemented new policies, eulogizing the sages and sympathizing with those who were in trouble. He mobilized his retinue and rode in a carriage to return to the dragon palace to make a report on his mission, as well as to welcome the dragon girl to the capital.

As the influence of the dragon girl's evil deeds done in the past was not completely wiped out, she often appeared with nine dragon heads when she was in her private chamber. The Śākya man feared and abhorred the sight and did not know what to do about it. He waited for a time when the girl was asleep and came up to cut off her heads with a sharp knife. The dragon girl was startled from sleep and said, "This will not be advantageous to our offspring. Not only am I slightly injured, but your descendants will also suffer from headache." Thus the clansmen of this country often suffer from this ailment. Although it is not continuously painful, it recurs from time to time.

After the death of the Śākya man, his son succeeded to the throne as King Uttarasena (Superior army).

After King Uttarasena had ascended the throne, his mother lost her sight. When the Tathāgata had subdued the Apalāla dragon and was on his return journey, he descended from the air and alighted at the palace at a time when King Uttarasena was out hunting. Then the Tathāgata briefly preached the Dharma to [Uttarasena's] mother. Having met the Holy One and heard the Dharma, she regained her sight. The Tathāgata asked her, "Your son is a clansman of mine. Where is he now?" The king's mother said, "He went out in the morning on a hunting excursion. He is about to come back." When the Tathāgata and his retinue of monks were about to resume their journey, the king's mother said, "I am fortunate to have given birth to a son of the holy clan; and you have had pity on us so that you condescended to visit us in person. My son will come back soon, so please stay and wait for a moment." The World-honored One said, "As this person is a clansman of mine, he can become enlightened upon hearing of my teachings, so it is needless for him to receive my personal instruction for the development of his mind. I am going now. You may tell him on his return that the Tathāgata has gone to Kuśinagara to enter Nirvana between the Śāla trees. He can obtain some of my relic bones for his private worship." The Tathāgata and his assembly of monks rose into the air and went away.

When King Uttarasena was hunting, he saw from afar that his palace was shining brightly, and he suspected that a fire might have occurred. He stopped hunting and returned to find that his mother had regained her sight. He asked delightedly, "What auspicious event has happened during my brief absence that my kind mother's eyesight has been restored?" His mother said, "When you were out, the Tathāgata came here. After hearing the Buddha's
844b Dharma I regained my sight. The Tathāgata has gone from here to Kuśinagara to enter Nirvana between the Śāla trees. He suggested that you go promptly to obtain a portion of his relic bones."

Upon hearing these words, the king wailed piteously and fainted, and he recovered himself only after a long time. He got into his carriage and hurried to the Śāla trees, but the Buddha had already entered Nirvana. The other kings despised him as a king from a vulgar borderland, and as they valued the relic bones, they did not wish to share them with him. At this time the assembly of gods and men repeated the Buddha's last words. Only when the kings heard the Buddha's words did they share with him an equal portion of the relics.

Climbing over mountains and crossing valleys to the northwest from Maṅgala city, and going upstream along the Indus River, the road is perilous and goes through gloomy gullies, which are linked either by thick ropes or by iron chains, with viaducts and bridges constructed at the precipices and wooden pegs installed on the rocks as steps for climbers to set foot on. After a journey of over one thousand *li*, I reached the plain of Darada, the old capital of Udyāna, where gold and saffron are produced in abundance. Beside the great monastery at Darada there is a wooden statue of Maitreya Bodhisattva more than one hundred feet tall, of golden hue and latent spiritual power. It was made by the Arhat Madhyāntika (formerly transcribed as Motiendi erroneously and abridged). With his supernatural powers, the Arhat brought a craftsman up to the Tuṣita Heaven (formerly transcribed as Doushuaita or Doushuta erroneously) three times to observe the fine features of the Bodhisattva, and then he completed the task. The Dharma has been transmitted to the East since the time when this statue was made.

From here going to the east across mountains and valleys upstream of the Indus River, and over flying bridges and viaducts through perilous regions for more than five hundred *li*, I reached the country of Balūra (in the domain of North India).

The country of Balūra is more than four thousand *li* in circuit. Situated among the Great Snow Mountains, it is long from east to west and narrow from south to north. It yields much wheat and pulse and produces gold and silver. Having the advantage of gold resources, the country has ample means for state expenditure. The climate is bitterly cold, and the people are rude by nature, lacking in kindness and righteousness and knowing nothing of politeness. They are ugly in features and wear coarse woolen garments. Their writing is roughly the same as that of India, but their spoken language diverges from those of other countries. There are several hundred monasteries with several thousand monks, who do not study the theories of any one specific school, and they are mostly defective in observing the Vinaya rules.

From here I went back to Uḍakhand city and crossed the Indus River to the south. Flowing southwest, the river is three or four *li* broad, with pure and limpid water moving rapidly. Poisonous dragons and evil animals make their dens in the river, and they often overturn the boats of those who carry precious objects, seeds of rare flowers and fruits, or the Buddha's relic bones across the river. After crossing the river, I reached the country of Takṣaśilā (in the domain of North India).

The country of Takṣaśilā is more than two thousand *li* in circuit, and its capital city is over ten *li* in circuit. The regional chieftains have competed with each other for sovereignty, the royal family being extinct. Formerly it belonged to the country of Kāpiśī,

884c but recently it became a dependency of the country of Kaśmīra. The soil is fertile and the crops are rich, with many springs and luxuriant vegetation. The climate is mild and the people are reckless and brave by custom, and they venerate the Triple Gem. There are many monasteries, but most of them are in desolation. There are a few monks, all of whom study Mahayana teachings.

More than seventy *li* to the northwest of the capital city is the pond of Elāpattra the dragon king, which is about one hundred paces in circuit. The water is lucid and has lotus flowers of different colors growing in it. This dragon was a monk who injured an *elāpattra* tree at the time of Kāśyapa Buddha. Therefore, when the people of this land went up to the dragon to pray for rain or fine weather, they had to invite a monk to go with them to the pond. When the monk snapped his fingers to comfort the dragon, the people's wishes would surely be fulfilled.

Going southeast for more than thirty *li*, I entered a spot between two mountains where there is a stupa more than one hundred feet high built by King Aśoka. This was the place where the Śākya Tathāgata predicted that when Maitreya would appear in the world as a Buddha, four great treasures would naturally come into existence. This auspicious spot is one of the four places. I heard the local people saying that at the time of an earthquake, all the mountains would shake, but about one hundred paces around this treasure place, the earth would not even quiver a bit. Some foolish people once vainly attempted to excavate the treasure, but the earth quaked and all the people toppled over onto the ground. Beside this spot is a monastery, which is in a very much deserted condition, having had no monks living in it for quite a long time.

Twelve or thirteen *li* to the north of the city is a stupa built by King Aśoka. On fast days it sometimes emits a light amid divine flowers and heavenly music. I heard the local people saying that recently a woman suffering from malignant leprosy secretly came to this stupa to make self-reproach and repentance [of evil deeds she had done in her past lives]. When she saw that the compound was in a filthy condition, she removed the dirt, swept the place clean, smeared incense paste and scattered flowers on the ground, and plucked some blue lotus flowers to scatter on the road. By doing so, she was cured of her malignant disease and became beautiful in appearance, and a sweet smell as fragrant as blue lotus issued from her body.

This was also the place where the Tathāgata, while practicing the Dharma in a former life as a great king named Candraprabha (Moonlight), cut off his head for alms-giving in the course of acquiring enlightenment. He performed such alms-giving a thousand times in past lives.

Beside this stupa where the head was forsaken, there is a desolate monastery with a few monks. Formerly Kumāralāta (known 885a
as Tongshou in Chinese), a Śāstra-master of the Sautrāntika school, wrote treatises at this monastery.

Outside the city to the southeast, at the northern side of South Hill, is a stupa over one hundred feet high built by King Aśoka at the place where his son, Prince Kuṇāla, had his eyes torn out by the calumny of his stepmother. Blind people prayed at this place, and most of them recovered their eyesight.

This prince, who was borne by the chief queen, was a handsome man and well-known for his kindness. After the death of the chief queen, his stepmother, a lascivious woman, out of immorality tried to force the prince to have illicit relations with her; but the prince, shedding tears, blamed himself for his refusal and withdrew with an apology. Having been rejected by the prince, she was shamed into anger, and after waiting for a chance, she said to the king coolly, "As Takṣaśilā is in a strategic position, who else but a royal descendant can be depended on for its guard? Now the prince is a man well-known for his kindness and filial piety. Because you do not employ sagacious persons, the people are critical of you." Being deluded by these words, the king was pleased with the intrigue. Thus he ordered the prince, saying, "I succeeded to the throne handed down by our ancestors to rule over the country, and I fear to lose it—our forerunners would be disappointed. As Takṣaśilā is a strategic place, I now appoint you to garrison that country. State affairs are important, and human relationships are treacherous. You must not move about at will so as to jeopardize the foundation of the state. Whenever there is a [written] summons from me, you should verify it by my teeth marks. My teeth are in my mouth, so nobody can make a forgery."

Thus the prince went to the garrison post by order of the king, and although time passed, his stepmother became all the more angry with him. She issued a false order in the name of the king, sealed it with purple clay, and had it marked with the king's teeth at a moment when he was asleep. It was then dispatched to the prince for his reprimand. His assistants knelt down to read the order, and they looked at each other, not knowing what to do. The prince inquired, "What is it that makes you look so miserable?" They said, "The great king has issued an order to reprimand Your Highness, stating that your eyes should be torn out and that you should be exiled to the valleys among mountains and left there to live or die with your wife. Nevertheless, the order may be fraudulent, and it is better for you to see the king face to face and hear his personal verdict." The prince said, "How can I disobey my father's order, even if he asked me to die? There is no mistake, as the order is sealed with his teeth marks."

The prince then asked a *caṇḍāla* (outcaste) to tear out his eyes, and after having lost his eyesight he lived as a beggar, wandering from place to place until he came to his father's capital city. His wife told him, "This is the royal city, in which we are now suffering from hunger and cold. Formerly you were a prince, but now you are a beggar! I wish to report the matter to the king, and ask him to reconsider the reprimand." Then through some trick they slipped into the royal stable, where they shed tears in the cool breeze, late in the night, and sang piteously to the accompaniment of a *konghou* (a sort of harp).

On a lofty pavilion, the king heard the melodious singing of melancholy and sorrowful words, and feeling it strange, he asked, "The voice of the singing accompanied by a *konghou* sounds like that
885b of my son. Why has he come here?" He inquired of the stableman as

to who was singing in the stable. So the man brought the blind singer into the presence of the king. Upon seeing the prince, the king felt sorrowful and asked him, "Who disfigured you into such a disastrous condition? Not even knowing that my beloved son had lost his eyesight, how can I [claim to] see into the affairs of my people? Good Heavens! Oh, good Heavens! How is it that my virtue has corrupted to such an extent?" The prince wept piteously and said in reply with an apology, "It is due to my unfilialness that I incurred the blame of Heaven. On such-and-such a day, I suddenly received your compassionate edict. I had no way to speak to you, nor did I dare to evade my responsibility [to implement your edict]." Finding out that it was all done illegally by his second wife, the king inflicted capital punishment upon her without further investigation.

At that time there was at the monastery near the Bodhi Tree a great Arhat named Ghoṣa (Wonderful voice), who possessed the four kinds of unhindered eloquence and was complete with the three insights. The king told him what his blind son had said and wished him to be so kind as to restore his son's eyesight. At the request of the king, the Arhat then made an announcement on that day to the people of the country, saying, "On the day after tomorrow, I shall speak on the sublime doctrine. You may come to listen to the Dharma, and each of you should bring a vessel with you to hold tears." Thus men and women coming from far and near flocked to the place. At that time, the Arhat spoke on the Twelvefold Causation. None of those who heard the Dharma did not shed tears, and they collected their tears in the vessels. When the preaching was over, the tears of the whole assembly were collected in a golden basin. The Arhat then made a pledge, saying, "All that I have said is the Buddha's ultimate truth. If it is untrue, and if I have spoken wrongly, I shall have nothing more to say. Otherwise, I wish to wash the blind man's eyes to restore his eyesight to what it was before." Having said this, he used the tears to wash the eyes of the prince, whose eyesight was thus restored.

The king then reproached his ministers and denounced his assistants at court, who were dismissed, or banished, or relegated, or executed, and many powerful and wealthy families were deported to the desert to the northeast of the Snow Mountains.

From here going to the southeast across mountains and valleys for over seven hundred *li*, I reached the country of Siṃhapura (in the domain of North India).

The country of Siṃhapura is over three thousand five hundred or six hundred *li* in circuit, bordering on the Indus River on the west. The capital city of the country is fourteen or fifteen *li* in circuit, and since it was built with a range of hills at the back, it is an impregnable stronghold. The farmers exert little effort but gain much profit from the land. The climate is cold, and the people are rude by nature. They are valiant but deceitful by custom. There is no king ruling over the country, and it is a dependency of the country of Kaśmīra.

Not far to the south of the city is a stupa built by King Aśoka. Although its decorations have become incomplete, it continues to be effective in showing spiritual manifestations. Beside it there is a monastery devoid of monks.

Forty or fifty *li* to the southeast of the city there is a stone
885c stupa more than two hundred feet high built by King Aśoka. There are about ten ponds around the stupa. The banks of the ponds are built with rocks carved in various strange shapes, and clear water brawls into the ponds giving off spray. Dragons, fish, and other aquatics move about in the grottoes under the water. Lotus flowers of the four colors cover the surfaces of the clear ponds, and all kinds of fruit trees blossom luxuriantly in different hues. With the woods reflected in the ponds, this place is truly a pleasure garden. There is a monastery nearby, but it has been deserted of monks for a long time.

Not far from the stupa is where the founder of the white-clothed [Jains] realized the principles he was seeking and first preached his doctrine. Now there is a memorial of the event, and beside it is a deva-temple. His disciples practice austerities perseveringly day and night without leisure to take rest. The doctrine preached by the founder was mostly taken from the tenets of the Buddhist scriptures, and he taught them according to the different inclinations of people and laid down disciplinary rules. The senior disciples are called *bhikṣus* and the junior ones *śrāmaṇeras*. Their manner of living and code of deportment are quite similar to those of the Buddhist monks, except that they keep a tuft of hair on the head, and [some] go naked. If they put on any dress, the special color is white, which is a mark to differentiate them from other sects. The statues of the founder are made, without authority, in the same posture as the images of the Tathāgata. The only difference is in the costume; the good features are exactly the same.

From here I returned to the northern part of the country of Takṣaśilā, where I crossed the Indus River, and after going southeast for more than two hundred *li*, I came across a great rocky pass. Formerly the Prince Mahāsattva sacrificed his body at this place to feed a starving tigress. About one hundred forty or fifty paces to the south is a stone stupa, built at the spot where the Mahāsattva had pity on the enfeebled tigress. When he came here, he pricked himself with a dry bamboo splinter so as to feed the tigress with his blood. Then the animal [gained enough strength and] devoured him. The soil and plants of this place are dark reddish in color, as if they have been stained by the blood. When people come to this spot, they feel nervous and uneasy, as if they had prickles hurting their backs, and whether they believe it or doubt it, they are moved to pity.

To the north of this stupa of the sacrifice of the body, there is a stone stupa more than two hundred feet high built by King Aśoka. It is decorated with marvellous engravings, and it sometimes emits a divine light. Smaller stupas and stone niches, counted by the hundreds, surround the sepulchral ground. Those who are suffering from illness circumambulate this place and most of them are cured.

To the east of the stone stupa there is a monastery with more than one hundred monks, all of whom study Mahayana teachings. From here going east for more than fifty *li*, I reached an isolated hill where there is a monastery with over two hundred monks, all of whom study Mahayana teachings. There are luxuriant flowers and fruit trees with ponds of spring water as lucid as a mirror. Beside it is a stupa over two hundred feet high, built at the spot where the Tathāgata in a former life converted an evil *yakṣa* (demon) and taught him not to eat meat. From here going southeast for more than five hundred *li*, I reached the country of Uraśā (in the domain of North India).

886a The country of Uraśā is more than two thousand *li* in circuit, with mountains and hills connected together, rendering the cultivated fields narrow and small. The capital city of the country is seven or eight *li* in circuit; it is without a sovereign king, and the country is a dependency of the country of Kaśmīra. The soil is suitable for growing cereals, and the country has few flowers and fruits. The climate is mild and there is not much frost or snow. The people are rough and deceitful and without the custom of observing the proprieties, and they do not believe in Buddhism. About four or five *li* to the southwest of the capital city there is a stupa more than two hundred feet high built by King Aśoka. Beside it is a monastery with few monks, all of whom study Mahayana teachings. From here going southeast for more than one thousand *li* over mountains, along dangerous paths, and across iron bridges, I reached the country of Kaśmīra (formerly transcribed erroneously as Jibin, in the domain of North India).

The country of Kaśmīra is more than seven thousand *li* in circuit, with precipitous mountains surrounding it on all sides. Although there are passes, the passages are very narrow. Since ancient times no hostile neighboring countries could invade this country. The capital city, with a great river on its west, is twelve or thirteen *li* from south to north and four or five *li* from east to west. The soil is suitable for growing cereals, and there are plenty of flowers and fruits. It produces horses of the dragon breed and also yields saffron, fire-pearls, and medicinal herbs.

The climate is bitterly cold and there is much snow but little wind. The people wear woolen or cotton clothes. They are frivolous by custom and mostly timid. As the country is protected by a dragon, the people hold sway over the neighboring regions. Their features are handsome, but they are of a deceitful disposition. They are fond of learning and have a wide scope of knowledge, believing in both heretical and the right teachings. There are over one hundred monasteries with more than five thousand monks. There are four stupas, all built by King Aśoka, each containing about one *sheng* of the Tathāgata's relic bones.

In the *National Record* it is said that this country was originally a dragon lake. Formerly, when the Buddha, the World-honored One, had subdued an evil god in the country of Udyāna and was flying over this country on his way back to Central India, he said to Ānanda, "After my Nirvana the Arhat Madhyāntika will at this place establish a country, settle people, and propagate the Buddha-dharma." In the fiftieth year after the Tathāgata's Nirvana, Ānanda's disciple, the Arhat Madhyāntika, who possessed the six supernatural powers and attained the eight emancipations, heard about the Buddha's prediction with a feeling of rejoicing. Then he came here and sat down in a wood on a great mountain, showing great supernatural powers. Upon seeing him, the dragon had deep faith in him and asked him what he wanted. The Arhat said, "I want you to give me space to keep [just] my knees in the lake." Thereupon the dragon king withdrew water from the lake to offer [dry land] to the monk. But the Arhat enlarged his body by his miraculous powers, and the dragon did his utmost to draw away the water from the lake until it was completely exhausted, so that the dragon had to ask for some place for himself. The Arhat reserved a lake more than one hundred *li* in circuit in the northwest for the 886b
dragon, while the dragon's relatives dwelt separately in a small lake.

The dragon king said, "Now that I have presented all the land of the lake to you, please always accept my offerings." Madhyāntika said, "As I shall enter Parinirvana (complete Nirvana) very soon, how shall I be able always to accept your offerings, though I would like to?" The dragon then requested that five hundred Arhats should always accept his offerings until the extinction of the Dharma, and that after the extinction of the Dharma he should then retake this country as his dwelling lake. Madhyāntika assented to this request.

After having obtained the land, the Arhat established five hundred monasteries with his great supernatural powers and bought slaves from different countries to serve the monks. When Madhyāntika had entered extinction, the slaves made themselves rulers. The neighboring countries despise them as low-born people and do not interact with them, calling them the Krīta (the Bought). Now spring water is overflowing at many places.

King Aśoka of Magadha ascended the throne in the hundredth year after the Tathāgata's Nirvana and exerted his influence upon distant lands. He deeply believed in the Triple Gem and fostered all creatures of the four forms of birth. There were then five hundred Arhat monks and five hundred ordinary ones, whom the king respected and treated with equal hospitality. There was one ordinary monk named Mahādeva (Great deity), a man of extensive learning and great wisdom, who had made profound studies of the categories of name and reality. He wrote an elaborate treatise in exposition of theories contrary to the holy teachings [of the Buddha], and all his friends and acquaintances followed his heterodox views. Being unable to discern the Arhats from the ordinary monks, King Aśoka had sympathy with those whom he liked and supported those who were on intimate terms with him. He summoned the monks to the Ganges, intending to sink them into the deep water to kill them all. The Arhats, realizing that their lives were at stake, employed their supernatural powers and flew through the air to this country [Kaśmīra], where they lived on the mountains and in the valleys. Upon hearing this, King Aśoka was afraid and repented; he came in person to apologize and invited the Arhats to return to his country, but the Arhats flatly refused the invitation. Thus King Aśoka built five hundred monasteries for the Arhats and offered the whole country as alms to the community of monks.

King Kaniṣka of the country of Gandhāra ascended the throne in the four hundredth year after the Tathāgata's Nirvana; his influence reached far and distant lands, which then became affiliated with him. In his leisure hours he always studied Buddhist scriptures, and each day he invited a monk to preach the Dharma in his

palace. As the monks belonged to different schools, their views were at variance with each other, and so the king was very much puzzled and could not get rid of his delusions. At that time the Venerable Pārśva said, "In the long lapse of time since the Tathāgata passed away, his disciples have adhered to different schools, and the masters have held various views, each grasping his own opinions and giving rise to contradictions." The king was quite moved to hear this, and after brooding in a sorrowful mood for a long time, he said to the venerable monk, "By the remnant blessedness of my ancestors I am lucky enough to have succeeded to 886c
the exploits of my predecessors. Although I am far away from the time of the Buddha, I am still fortunate. I venture to forget my vulgarity and incompetence and wish to propagate the Dharma by expounding the whole Tripiṭaka according to the tenets of different schools." The Venerable Pārśva said, "Your Majesty has planted the root of good deeds in the past and has accumulated much blessing. It is my wish that Your Majesty should pay attention to the Buddha-dharma."

Then the king issued an order to summon holy and learned monks throughout the country far and near. Thus brilliant scholars and wise monks flocked to the assembly from great distances in the four quarters, to be entertained with the four requisites of a monk for seven days. Since it was for the discussion of the great Dharma, too many participants would be too boisterous for the meeting. Thus the king respectfully said to the monks, "Those who have attained saintship may stay, while those who are still under the bondage of rebirth may go back." As the remaining number was still too numerous, the king declared again, "Those who have completed their learning may stay, while those who are still in the course of learning may go back." The remaining number was still too numerous, and so he ordered again, "Those who possess the three insights and have the six supernatural powers may stay, while the rest may go back." But as the remaining number was still too numerous, he again issued an order, saying, "Only those who are well-versed in the Tripiṭaka with its supramundane theories and who thoroughly understand the five mundane branches of knowledge may remain, while the others may go back." Thereupon four hundred ninety-nine persons were selected.

The king wished [to hold the convention] in his own country, but his country was too hot and humid for the purpose. He also wished to go to the cave at Rājagṛha, where Mahākāśyapa had convened his assembly. The Venerable Pārśva and others discussed the matter and said, "No! There are [at Rājagṛha] many heretics who engage themselves in debate, holding divergent heterodox views. We would get involved with them in disputations, and then how could we have time to write our treatises?" Thus the monks in the meeting all favored this country [Kaśmīra].

As this country was surrounded by mountains on the four sides and was strongly guarded by *yakṣa*s, and had fertile soil and rich products, it was a place where sages and saints met and took up their lodgings, and it was frequented by spirits and genii. The monks discussed this place and all said that it was an appropriate venue [for the meeting]. The king and the Arhats then came from their country [Gandhāra] to this country [Kaśmīra] and constructed a monastery to collect and compile the Tripiṭaka with the intention of composing a *Vibhāṣā-śāstra*.

At that time the Venerable Vasumitra, dressed in a monk's patched robe, was outside the door, when the Arhats said to him, "You have not got rid of the bondage of the passions, and your arguments are absurd and erroneous. You should go far away and not stay here." Vasumitra said, "You sagacious monks have no doubts about the Dharma, and you are spreading the Buddha's teachings in his place. You are collecting the great doctrines with the intention of writing a standard treatise. Although I am unintelligent, I do know something of the subtle teachings. I have made profound studies of the abstruse texts of the Tripiṭaka and the sublime principles of the five branches of knowledge, and I have mastered their essences." The Arhats said, "You must not speak in this manner. You should live in seclusion and attain Arhatship quickly. Then it will not be too late for you to come and join us at the meeting." Vasumitra said, "I deem the attainment of Arhatship to be as insignificant as spittle. My ambition is to gain Buddhahood, and I do not wish to go by the small path. But I can still attain the holy fruit of Arhatship before a ball of thread falls down to the ground after I have thrown it up into the air."

The Arhats again reproached him, saying, "You are truly an arrogant man. As Arhatship is what all the Buddhas have praised, you should quickly realize it, so as to remove the doubts of the 887a
monks." Then Vasumitra threw a ball of thread up into the air, but the devas took hold of it and made an appeal to him, saying, "You should now attain Buddhahood and become the successor to Maitreya in the future, to be specially honored by all the three realms and be someone that all beings of the four forms of birth can depend on. Why should you wish to realize the small fruit here and now?" Upon seeing this event, the Arhats apologized [to Vasumitra] and elected him to be the elder of the meeting, and all dubious points were settled by him.

At first the five hundred saintly and holy monks composed the *Upadeśa-śāstra* (formerly transcribed wrongly as Youpotishelun) in one hundred thousand stanzas for the exposition of the *Sūtra-piṭaka* (formerly transcribed wrongly as Xiuduoluozang). Then they wrote the *Vinaya-vibhāṣā-śāstra* in one hundred thousand stanzas for the exposition of the *Vinaya-piṭaka* (formerly transcribed wrongly as Pinayezang). Lastly they compiled the *Abhidharma-vibhāṣā-śāstra* in one hundred thousand stanzas for the exposition of the *Abhidharma-piṭaka* (known as Apitanzang in abbreviation). There are altogether three hundred thousand stanzas with nine million six hundred thousand words for the full explanation of the Tripiṭaka, to be studied for all ages to come. They probe into all branches and ramifications whether shallow or deep. The general meanings are repeatedly clarified and the subtle sayings made apparent. They are widely circulated for the guidance of posterity.

King Kaniṣka had these treatises incised on red copper plates and kept them in stone cases, and a stupa was constructed for their preservation. He ordered the *yakṣa* deities to be on guard all around the country to prevent heretics from taking the treatises out of the country. Those who wished to study them might do so inside the country. After having completed the task, the king returned to his own capital with his army, and when he had come out of the western gate of the capital city of this country [Kaśmīra], he knelt down facing the east to offer the whole country as alms to the monks. After the death of Kaniṣka, the Krīta tribe resumed kingship, expelled the monks, and demolished the Buddha-dharma.

The king of Himatala (meaning Below the Snow Mountains) in the country of Tokhāra, a descendant of the Śākya clan, fully occupied his territory and ascended the throne in the six hundredth year after the Tathāgata's Nirvana. He planted his mind in the earth of the Buddha and poured his sentiments into the sea of the Dharma. When he heard that the Krīta tribesmen were destroying the Buddha-dharma, he mustered three thousand brave warriors of his country and put them in the guise of merchants; they carried with them a large quantity of valuable goods, keeping weapons secretly among the merchandise, and came to this country. The lord of this country treated them with special courtesy. From among the [disguised] merchants, five hundred men of bravery and stratagem were selected, each equipped with a sharp dagger secretly kept in his sleeves; they carried rare valuables to present to the lord in person. At that moment the king of Himatala took off the hat of the lord and occupied his throne. The king of the Krīta tribe was taken aback by the surprise attack and was beheaded right away. [The king of Himatala] declared to the people, "I am the king of Himatala in the country of Tokhāra. I was enraged by this low-born tribesman, who openly carried out cruel policies. I
887b have put him to death because he was guilty. You innocent people are guiltless." But the chief ministers of the court were banished to a foreign land. When order was restored in the country, the monks were invited back, and monasteries were built as peacefully as before. The king again knelt down outside the western gate of the capital city with his face turned to the east to offer this country as alms to the monks.

As the Krīta tribesmen had lost power on account of monks on several occasions, they bore them a grudge for generations and hated the Buddha-dharma. After a long lapse of time, they resumed the kingship once again. Therefore Buddhism is not much believed in by the people of the country, while deva-temples enjoy much attention.

More than ten *li* to the southeast of the new city, and at the south side of a great mountain to the north of the old city is a monastery with over three hundred monks. In the stupa of the monastery there is a Buddha's tooth relic, about one and a half inches long, yellowish white in color. On fast days it sometimes issues a light.

Formerly when the Krīta tribesmen persecuted the Buddha-dharma, the monks scattered to various places and lived separately. One of the Śramaṇas went to India to visit and worship the sacred sites with utmost sincerity. Later, when he heard that order had been restored in his country, he started on his return journey, and on the way he met a herd of elephants running amok in the marsh, trumpeting and rampaging wildly. At the sight of the elephants, the Śramaṇa climbed up a tree to avoid them. At that moment, the elephants rushed to a pond to get water to soak the root of the tree, while they pushed the tree until it fell down.

Having got hold of the Śramaṇa, the elephants carried him to a big forest, where a sick elephant was lying with a painful sore. They put the monk's hand on the painful spot, and he found that it was wounded by a bamboo prickle. After plucking out the bamboo prickle and applying medicine to the wound, the Śramaṇa tore off a piece of his robe to dress the sick elephant's wounded foot. One of the elephants took a golden casket to the sick elephant, and the sick elephant handed it over to the Śramaṇa. Upon opening the casket, the Śramaṇa saw a Buddha's tooth relic in it. As the monk was surrounded by the elephants, he could not get away from them. At mealtime on the following day, they brought him strange fruits for his midday meal. After the meal was over, they carried the monk out of the forest, and having carried him for several hundred *li*, they let him get down and knelt on the ground to worship him before they dispersed.

When the Śramaṇa reached the western boundary of the country, he boarded a ferryboat to cross a rapid river, and in midstream the boat was almost overturned. The other passengers in the boat said among themselves, "This Śramaṇa must be the cause of our trouble—almost getting drowned in the river. He must have carried with him some relic bones of the Tathāgata, which the dragons highly value." The boatman searched the passengers and in fact discovered the Buddha's tooth relic. The Śramaṇa then held the tooth relic high and lowered his head to say to the dragon [in the river], "Now I hand this over to you for safekeeping, but I shall come soon to take it back." He did not cross the river but disembarked, and looking at the river he said regretfully, "As I did not learn the craft of subduing dragons, I am now bullied by this beast of a dragon!" So he went again to India to learn the magical craft of suppressing dragons. After three years, he started again on his return journey, and when he reached the bank of the river and was preparing an altar [for performing the rites], the dragon
887c handed over the casket containing the Buddha's tooth relic to the Śramaṇa, who took it back and enshrined it at this monastery.

Fourteen or fifteen *li* to the south of the monastery [of the tooth relic], there is a small monastery in which is enshrined a standing statue of Avalokiteśvara Bodhisattva. If a worshipper decides to starve himself to death, in case he cannot fulfill his wish to see the Bodhisattva in person, the Bodhisattva appears in his marvellous corporeal body out of the statue.

Over thirty *li* to the southeast of the small monastery, I arrived at a great mountain on which was an old monastery built on a magnificent scale, but it is now mostly in ruins. There is only one small storied pavilion at a corner of the monastery, with more than thirty monks, who study Mahayana teachings. Formerly the Śāstra-master Saṃghabhadra (known as Zhongxian in Chinese) composed the *Abhidharma-nyāyānusāra-śāstra* here. On the left and right sides of the monastery there are stupas containing relic bones of great Arhats. Monkeys and other wild animals pluck flowers as offerings at all times of the year without interruption, as if they were performing a duty under instruction. There are many strange traces on this mountain, such as rocky walls being split across, or hoofprints of horses left on the tops of the peaks. All these traces have strange shapes. Arhats who were *śrāmaṇera*s (not fully ordained monks) drew them with their fingers while they were riding to and fro on pleasure trips. Such traces are so numerous that it is difficult to give a full account.

Over ten *li* to the east of the Buddha Tooth Monastery on the steep side of a northern mountain, there is a small monastery where the great Śāstra-master Skandhila composed the *Abhidharma-prakaraṇa-pāda-śāstra* in former times.

In the small monastery there is a stone stupa more than fifty feet high containing the relic bones of an Arhat. Formerly there was an Arhat who was a big and tall man with the appetite of an elephant. The people of the time sneered at him, saying, "You just know how to satiate yourself and have no sense of right and wrong!" When the Arhat was about to enter Nirvana, he told the people, "I shall soon take up complete extinction. I wish to tell you the wonderful Dharma I have personally realized." Upon hearing this, the people jeered at him all the more, and they all assembled to see what would happen. The Arhat then said to the people, "Now I shall tell you my personal karmic conditions. Before my present existence, I was born an elephant, and lived in the royal stable of a king of East India. There was then in this country [Kaśmīra] a Śramaṇa who was taking a long journey in India in search of sacred scriptures and commentaries. The king presented me as a gift to the Śramaṇa to carry the Buddhist scriptures for him to this country. Soon afterwards I died, and by the merit of having carried scriptures I was born a human being, and with the surplus blessedness I was able to become a monk at an early age. I worked 888a
hard to find liberation from the circle of rebirth, without spending a single moment in idleness, until I attained the six supernatural powers and cut off the passions of the three realms. But my old habit of eating was still as usual, though I restricted myself to eating only one-third of my regular amount of food."

Although he said this the people did not believe him, so he rose into the air and entered the Samādhi (concentrated trance) of Fire-light; flames and smoke came from his body, and he entered extinction, while his remains dropped down, over which a stupa was built.

Going northwest from the royal city for over two hundred *li*, I reached the Vikrītavana Monastery, where the Śāstra-master Pūrṇa (known as Yuanman in Chinese) composed the *Exposition of the Abhidharma-śāstra*.

Going west from the city for one hundred forty or fifty *li*, I reached the north of a great river at the south side of a mountain and came to a monastery of the Mahāsāṃghika school with more than one hundred monks. This was the place where the Śāstra-master Bodhila composed the *Tattvasaṃcaya-śāstra* of the Mahāsāṃghika school.

Going southwest from here for more than seven hundred *li* over mountains and across dangerous rivers, I reached the country of Parṇotsa (in the domain of North India).

The country of Parṇotsa is more than two thousand *li* in circuit and has many mountains and rivers; it has narrow strips of cultivated land. The crops are sown in season, and flowers and fruits are luxuriant. There is plenty of sugarcane but no grapes. Trees bearing such fruits as *āmra* (mango), *uḍumbara* (fig), *moca* (plantain), etc. are planted by householders in woods near their dwelling places, because the people enjoy their tastes. The climate is humid and hot, and the people are bold and fiery by custom. Their garments are mostly made of cotton cloth. They are simple and straightforward by nature and believe in the Triple Gem. There are five monasteries, mostly in ruins. The country has no ruler and is a dependency of Kaśmīra. In the monastery to the north of the city, there are a few monks. To the north of the monastery, there is a stone stupa that often shows miracles. From here going southeast for more than four hundred *li*, I reached the country of Rājapura (in the domain of North India).

The country of Rājapura is over four thousand *li* in circuit; the capital city, which is more than ten *li* in circuit and has many hills and mounds around it, is a strong fortress. The valleys and plains are narrow, and the soil is not productive. The native products and climate are the same as those of Parṇotsa. The people are bold and fiery by custom and are brave and valiant by nature. The country has no ruler and is a dependency of Kaśmīra. There are ten monasteries with few monks. There is one deva-temple with many heretics.

From the country of Lampā up to this land, the inhabitants are coarse and vulgar in appearance and rustic and violent by nature. They speak unrefined dialects, have little courtesy, and are lacking in the sense of righteousness. Their lands do not belong to India proper but are uncivilized frontier regions.

From here proceeding southeast, descending from a mountain and crossing a river, and going for more than seven hundred *li*, I reached the country of Ṭakka (in the domain of North India).

End of Fascicle Three

Fascicle IV

Fifteen Countries, From Ṭakka to Kapitha

1. The Country of Ṭakka
2. The Country of Cīnabhukti
3. The Country of Jālaṃdhara
4. The Country of Kulūta
5. The Country of Śatadru
6. The Country of Pāriyātra
7. The Country of Mathurā
8. The Country of Sthāneśvara
9. The Country of Śrughna
10. The Country of Matipura
11. The Country of Brahmapura
12. The Country of Goviṣāṇa
13. The Country of Ahicchattra
14. The Country of Vilaśāṇa
15. The Country of Kapitha

The country of Ṭakka is more than ten thousand *li* in circuit with 888b
the Vipāśā River at its east and the Indus River at its west, and the capital city is over twenty *li* in circuit. The soil is good for growing nonglutinous rice, and there is plenty of winter wheat. The country produces gold, silver, brass, copper, and iron. The climate is hot and there is much violent wind. The people are rude and ill-tempered, and their language is base and vulgar. They dress in white garments known as *kauśeya* (wild silk) clothes and "morning glow" (fine cotton) costume. Few of them believe in the Buddha-dharma, and most of them serve the deities. There are ten monasteries and several hundred deva-temples. In this country there were formerly many alms houses to render help to the poor and needy, or give them free food and medicine, and provide travellers with meals so that they might dispel their fatigue.

Going fourteen or fifteen *li* to the southwest from the capital city, I reached the old city of Śākala. The city wall is dilapidated, but the foundations are still tough and strong. It is over twenty *li* in circuit, inside which there is a smaller city, six or seven *li* in circuit, with rich and prosperous inhabitants. This was the original capital city of the country.

Several hundred years ago, there was a king named Mahirakula (known as Dazu, or Great clan, in Chinese), who reigned in this city over all parts of India. He was a man of talent and intelligence with a bold and furious nature, and all the neighboring countries were his vassal states. Wishing to learn the Buddha-dharma in his leisure time, he ordered the monks to recommend a learned monk of virtue [to be his teacher]. But none of the monks dared to accept the offer, as they had few desires in their inactive lives and did not seek fame or eminence, while those who were erudite and prominent feared his majesty.

888c At that time there was a man who had been a servant of the royal household but had been a monk for a long time. Being a man of refined speech and skillful in discussion, he was chosen by the monks to accept the king's appointment. The king said, "Out of respect for the Buddha-dharma, I tried to seek a monk of renown, and now you recommend a slave to hold discussions with me. I thought that there were many brilliant scholars in the community of monks, and now I have come to know the actual condition. What is there for me to respect?" Then he issued an order to all the five parts of India to destroy whatever was connected with Buddhism and to expel all monks and not allow a single one to remain behind.

Now in the country of Magadha, King Bālāditya (known as Youri, or Morning sun, in Chinese) respected the Buddha-dharma and loved his subjects, and as King Mahirakula employed cruel punishment and practiced tyranny, Bālāditya defended his own territory and refused to pay tribute to King Mahirakula as his subordinate. When King Mahirakula mobilized his troops to punish Bālāditya, Bālāditya got news of the invasion and said to his ministers, "I have heard that the invaders are coming, but I do not have the heart to injure the soldiers. May you officials and commoners spare me of guilt and allow my humble self to hide in the grassy marshland." Having said so, he left the palace and went to the mountainous wilderness, and several myriads of his admirers and followers accompanied him to take refuge on an island.

King Mahirakula then handed over his troops to his younger brother and sailed across the sea to attack the island. King Bālāditya guarded the strategic points and sent his light cavalrymen to lure the enemy to war. Amidst the clamor of gongs and drums, Bālāditya's soldiers lying in ambush suddenly appeared in all quarters and captured Mahirakula alive, who was then granted the favor of an audience. Being ashamed of his misbehavior, King Mahirakula covered his face with his robes. King Bālāditya, crouching on his lion seat and surrounded by his officials, ordered his attendants to tell Mahirakula, "Uncover your face, as I wish to speak to you." Mahirakula said in reply, "The vassal and the lord have changed positions. We are now facing each other in grudges and enmity, and since we are not on friendly terms, what is the use of having a face-to-face talk?" In spite of repeated exhortation, he would not accept the advice. Then it was ordered to enumerate his faults. "The Triple Gem being the Field of Blessedness, it is that which all creatures of the four forms of birth can depend on. If I had allowed you to act as a jackal or a wolf, you would have completely destroyed the causes of superior deeds. Good luck is not on your side, and so you are captured by me. Your crimes are unpardonable, and you must be sentenced to death."

When the mother of King Bālāditya, who was a woman of erudition and good memory and an expert physiognomist, heard that Mahirakula was to be executed, she promptly told King Bālāditya, "I have heard that Mahirakula is a man of marvellous features and great wisdom. I wish to have a look at him." King Bālāditya then had Mahirakula led to his mother's palace. The queen mother said, "Alas, Mahirakula! You need not feel ashamed. The world is impermanent, and honor and disgrace replace each other alternately. I am just as your mother and you, my son. You should remove the covering on your face, so that we may talk face to face." Mahirakula said, "I was the lord of a country hostile to you, but I

am now a captive at your court. I have demolished the achievements of my forerunners and brought extinction to my ancestral lineage. Not only I am ashamed to face my forefathers but also I
889a feel remorseful to my subjects. As I am ashamed to see heaven and earth, I have regretfully covered up my face with my clothes." The king's mother said, "The rise and fall of a nation depends on circumstances, and existence or extinction is predestined by fate. If your mind looks at things with a view of equality, then both gain and loss are forgotten. If your mind is controlled by things, there will then arise the feelings of calumny and commendation. You should believe in karmic retribution and change with the change of time. If you remove your covering and speak to me face to face, you may perhaps be able to keep your life."

Mahirakula said gratefully, "I am a man of no talent, who attained the throne by mere chance. Through my malpractice in political administration, my royal lineage was brought to an end. Although I am under arrest, I still cling to my life even for a short while. For your great courtesy I thank you face to face with profuse gratitude." Then he removed his robes from his face. The king's mother said to him, "Take good care of yourself and you will live to the natural end of your life."

Then she told King Bālāditya, "It is laid down in the code of our ancestors that we should forgive other people's faults and be kind to living beings. Although King Mahirakula has done evils for a long time, his personal blessedness has not been exhausted. If you kill this man, we shall suffer famine for twelve years. He has prognostic signs of reinstatement, but he will not be the king of a great country; he will occupy and possess a small country in the north." Under the admonition of his compassionate mother, King Bālāditya took pity on the lord who had lost his kingdom; he married his young daughter to him and treated him with special hospitality. His defeated soldiers were enrolled to reinforce his guards before he was sent out of the island.

But King Mahirakula's younger brother had returned to his own country and established himself as king, and so Mahirakula had lost the throne and had to flee and hide himself in the mountainous wilderness. Then he went north to seek refuge in the country of Kaśmīra, and the king of Kaśmīra accorded him deep courtesy and conferred feudal estates upon him.

After the lapse of some years, [Mahirakula], commanding the people of his fiefdom, killed the king of Kaśmīra on some pretext and proclaimed himself king. With the prestige of his success in the war, he then attacked the country of Gandhāra in the west, and by having his troops lie in ambush, he killed the king. The members of the royal clan and all the ministers were slaughtered, and one thousand six hundred stupas and monasteries were demolished. Apart from those killed in the war, there were nine *koṭis* of people who remained alive, and he intended to kill them all and not allow a single one to survive. At that time his assistants at court admonished him, saying, "Your Majesty's prestige awed the strong enemies so much that their chiefs were executed even before the soldiers exchanged blows. What guilt have the common people committed? We wish to substitute our humble lives for their deaths." The king said, "You believe in the Buddha-dharma and think highly of future blessedness. Because you desire to achieve Buddhahood, you widely propagate the Jātaka stories. Do you intend to hand down my evil repute to posterity? Go back to your seats and say no more!"

Then three *koṭis* of people of the upper class were taken to the bank of the Indus River and put to death, three *koṭis* of people of the middle class were drowned in the river, and three *koṭis* of people of the lower class were granted to the soldiers [as slaves]. After that, he carried the booty he had taken from the conquered country and marched home in triumph. But in less than a year's time, he died a sudden death, when clouds and mist darkened the sky, and the earth 889b
quaked with a violent wind blowing vehemently. At that time someone who had realized sainthood had pity on him and remarked with a sigh of regret, "You unjustly killed innocent people and destroyed the Buddha-dharma. You will fall into the deepest hell of incessant suffering and rotate [in the wheel of rebirth] without end."

In the old city of Śākala there is a monastery with more than one hundred monks, all of whom study Hinayana teachings. Formerly Vasubandhu Bodhisattva composed the *Paramārtha-satya-śāstra* at this monastery. Beside it is a stupa over two hundred feet high built at a place where the four past Buddhas preached the Dharma. There are also the ruins of a place where the four Buddhas used to walk up and down. Five or six *li* to the northwest of the monastery there is another stupa over two hundred feet high built by King Aśoka at a place where the four past Buddhas had preached the Dharma.

Going for more than ten *li* to the northeast of the new capital city, I reached a stone stupa over two hundred feet high built by King Aśoka at a place where the Tathāgata had once halted halfway on his evangelical journey to the north. It is said in the *Record of India* that there are many relic bones preserved in the stupa and on fast days they often emit a light. From here going eastward for more than five hundred *li*, I reached the country of Cīnabhukti (in the domain of North India).

The country of Cīnabhukti is more than two thousand *li* in circuit, and its capital city is fourteen or fifteen *li* in circuit. It is abundant in cereals, but fruit trees are scarce. The inhabitants are enrolled in household registrations, and they live in peace and contentment. The state treasury has rich and profuse resources. The climate is temperate and warm, and the people are timid and weak by custom. They study the theories of both the transcendental and the conventional truth in a comprehensive way and believe in heterodoxy as well as orthodoxy. There are ten monasteries and eight deva-temples.

When King Kaniṣka was on the throne, his fame reached the neighboring countries, and his prestige covered distant lands with dissimilar customs. In fear of his influence, a vassal state to the west of the Yellow River [in China] sent a hostage to him. King Kaniṣka received the hostage with munificent hospitality, providing him with three residences for the three seasons of the year and appointing the four divisions of soldiers to be his guards. As the winter residence of the hostage was in this district, it was called Cīnabhukti (known as Hanfeng, or China fief, in Chinese), which was also the name of the country where he had sojourned.

In this district and beyond it in the various parts of India, there had been no pears or peaches; it was the hostage who first planted them. Thus peaches are called *cīnanī* (brought from China), and pears are called *cīnarājaputra* (Chinese prince). Therefore the people of this country have a deep respect for the East Land, and pointing at me, they often said to one another, "This is a man from the land of our former king."

Going to the northeast for more than five hundred *li* from the capital city, I reached Tamasāvana-saṃghārāma (known as Anlin, or Dark forest, in Chinese), where there are more than three hundred monks, who study the teachings of the Sarvāstivāda school. They behave in a solemn and respectful manner with pure and high 889c
virtues. They are particularly learned in the doctrines of the Hinayana schools. All the thousand Buddhas of the Bhadrakalpa will hold meetings of heavenly and human beings at this place to speak on the profound and marvelous Dharma. In the three hundredth year after the Nirvana of the Śākya Tathāgata, the Śāstra-master Kātyāyana (wrongly transcribed as Jiazhanyan in olden times) composed the *Abhidharma-jñāna-prasthāna-śāstra* at this monastery.

Inside the Dark Forest Monastery there is a stupa more than two hundred feet high built by King Aśoka. Beside it are the ruins of places where the four past Buddhas used to sit and walk up and down. Small stupas and large caves, of which the number is unknown, lie close together. They were built since the beginning of the present kalpa when Arhats of different stages passed away at this place, of which I cannot give a full description, and their holy tooth relics are still kept there. The range of hills that encircles the monastery is over twenty *li* in circuit. There are hundreds and thousands of stupas containing the Buddha's relic bones, which are built so close that their shadows touch one another. Going northeast from here for more than one hundred forty or fifty *li*, I reached the country of Jālaṃdhara (in the domain of North India).

The country of Jālaṃdhara is over one thousand *li* from east to west and more than eight hundred *li* from south to north, the capital city being twelve or thirteen *li* in circuit. It yields cereals and has plenty of nonglutinous rice. The trees in the forests are luxuriant, and flowers and fruits are abundant. The climate is temperate and warm, and the people are violent and indomitable by custom and ugly in appearance, but all their households are wealthy. There are over fifty monasteries with more than two thousand monks, who have specialized knowledge of both Mahayana and Hinayana teachings. There are three deva-temples with over five hundred heretics, who all smear their bodies with ashes.

A previous king of this country had venerated heretics, but later he met an Arhat from whom he heard the Dharma, and he came to understand and believe in it. The king of Central India, appreciating his sincere faith, empowered him to be the sole controller over all affairs connected with the Triple Gem in all the five parts of India. [The king of Jālaṃdhara] made no distinction between different regions, and forgetting his personal likes and dislikes he supervised all the monks, skillfully pointing out even the minutest of their good and evil deeds. Therefore virtuous monks of good repute were highly respected, while those who violated the disciplinary rules were denounced and punished. At all sacred sites he erected memorial buildings, either stupas or monasteries, which were found everywhere in India.

Going from here to the northeast for more than seven hundred *li* over precipitous ranges, through deep valleys, and along perilous paths, and trudging on dangerous tracks, I reached the country of Kulūta (in the domain of North India).

The country of Kulūta is more than three thousand *li* in circuit, surrounded by mountains, and the capital city is fourteen or fifteen *li* in circuit. The soil is fertile, and cereals are sown and planted in season. Flowers and fruits are abundant, and various kinds of grasses and trees are luxuriant. As it is bordering on the Snow Mountains, it is rich in precious medicinal herbs. It yields
890a gold, silver, red copper, crystal, and brass. The climate is somewhat

cold but there is little snow or frost. The people are ugly in features and suffer from goiter as well as edema. They are violent and furious by nature and uphold the spirit of bravery. There are more than twenty monasteries with over one thousand monks, most of whom study Mahayana teachings; but a few of them practice the tenets of various [Hinayana] schools. There are fifteen deva-temples with heretics living together. On the steep mountains there are caves situated in connection with one another, which were either the lodgings of Arhats or the abodes of *ṛṣis*.

In this country there is a stupa built by King Aśoka in memory of the event of the Tathāgata coming to this place in olden times to preach the Dharma for the conversion of the people.

From here the road, leading to the north for one thousand eight hundred or nine hundred *li* by perilous paths and over mountains and valleys, takes one to the country of Lāhul. Going further to the north over two thousand *li* along a route full of difficulties and obstacles, in cold winds and wafting snowflakes, one could reach the country of Marsa (also known as the country of Sanbohe). From the country of Kulūta going south for more than seven hundred *li* over a great mountain across a big river, I reached the country of Śatadru (in the domain of North India).

The country of Śatadru is more than two thousand *li* in circuit, bordering on a big river in the west. The capital city is seventeen or eighteen *li* in circuit. Cereals are grown in abundance and fruits are plentiful. It produces much gold and silver and also yields pearls. The people's dress and utensils are bright and clean, and their clothes are extravagant and gorgeous. The climate is hot, and the people are honest and amiable by custom. Their disposition is kind and gentle, and the superior and inferior are in proper order. They earnestly believe in the Buddha-dharma with a true attitude of respect. In and outside the royal city, there are ten monasteries, which are in desolation and have few monks. Three or four *li* to the southeast of the city, there is a stupa over two hundred feet high built by King Aśoka. Beside it are the ruins of places where the four past Buddhas used to sit and walk up and down. Going from here to the southwest for over eight hundred *li*, I reached the country of Pāriyātra (in the domain of Central India).

The country of Pāriyātra is more than three thousand *li* in circuit, the capital city being fourteen or fifteen *li* in circuit. It yields cereals and winter wheat in abundance and has a particular species of rice that is ready for harvest after sixty days of planting. It has plenty of cattle and sheep, but flowers and fruits are scarce. The climate is hot, and the people are violent and furious by custom. They do not esteem learning, and they profess false teachings. The king, a descendant of the Vaisya caste, is a man of courage and military skills. There are eight monasteries, standing in an extremely ruinous condition, with few monks who study the teachings of the Hinayana schools. There are over ten deva-temples with more than one thousand devotees. Going from here to the east for more than five hundred *li*, I reached the country of Mathurā (in the domain of Central India).

The country of Mathurā is more than five thousand *li* in circuit, the capital city being over twenty *li* in circuit. The land is fertile, and agriculture is the main occupation. Mango trees are grown by the people in their homesteads. There are two species of
890b this fruit, one being small and turning yellow when ripe, the other large and always remaining green. The country produces fine kapok cloth and gold. The climate is hot, and the people are good and genial by custom. They like to work for the happiness of the dead, they respect the virtuous, and they advocate learning. There are over twenty monasteries with more than two thousand monks who study the teachings of both the Mahayana and the Hinayana schools. There are five deva-temples, where heretics live together. There are three stupas, all built by King Aśoka, and numerous traces left by the four past Buddhas.

There are also stupas containing the relic bones of the holy disciples of the Śākya Tathāgata, such as Śāriputra (formerly known as Shelizi or Shelifu in wrongly abbreviated forms), Maudgalyāyana (formerly known as Mujianlian erroneously), Pūrṇamaitrāyaṇīputra (known as Mancizi, or Full compassion son, in

Chinese, and formerly transcribed in a wrongly abbreviated form as Midouluonizi), Upāli, Ānanda, and Rāhula (formerly known as Luohou or Louyun, both being erroneous and abbreviated forms); and there are stupas for such Bodhisattvas as Mañjuśrī (known as Miaojixiang, or Wonderful auspices, in Chinese, and formerly known as Rushou, or Wenshushili, or Manshushili, and wrongly translated as Wonderful virtue), etc. In the three fast months of the year and on each of the six fast days of the month, the monks would vie with their friends and acquaintances in carrying utensils of worship and many rare and strange articles to offer to the images of their particular patrons. Those who study the Abhidharma make offerings to Śāriputra, those who practice meditation to Maudgalyāyana, the sutra reciters to Pūrṇamaitrāyaṇīputra, the Vinaya students to Upāli, the *bhikṣuṇīs* to Ānanda, the *śrāmaṇeras* to Rāhula, and the Mahayana students to the various Bodhisattvas. On such a day offerings are made in competition to the various stupas, and pearled banners are displayed and gemmed canopies arranged in rows; the smoke of incense pervades the air like clouds, and flowers are scattered in showers that obscure the sun and the moon and cause great tumult in the valleys. The king and his ministers perform good deeds as their bounden duty.

Going east for five or six *li* from the city, I came to a hill monastery, of which the chambers are carved on the precipice of a mountain, with an entrance facing the valley. It was built by the Venerable Upagupta (known as Jinhu, or Near protection, in Chinese). In the monastery is a stupa preserving the fingernails of the Tathāgata.

On the steep rock to the north of the [hill] monastery, there is a cave more than twenty feet in height and over thirty feet in breadth. Fine chips four inches long [used as counters] are accumulated in the cave. When the Ven. Upagupta was preaching the Dharma to convert the people, every married couple that attained Arhatship put down a counter here, but single members of a family were not counted, though they had become Arhats.

Going twenty-four or five *li* to the southeast from the cave, I came to a large dried-up pond with a stupa beside it. Formerly when 890c the Tathāgata was once going across this place, a monkey offered him some honey. The Buddha had it mixed with water and distributed the beverage to the assembly of monks. The monkey was so delighted that it gamboled with joy, fell into a pit, and died. By the merits of this offering, it was reborn as a human being.

Not far away to the north of the [dried-up] pond there is a large wood in which are traces left by the four past Buddhas when they walked up and down. Beside it are the places where the one thousand two hundred and fifty great Arhats, Śāriputra, Maudgalyāyana, etc., practiced meditation, and stupas have been built to mark the traces. When the Tathāgata was living in the world, he frequently visited this country, and at the places where he preached the Dharma trees have been planted. From here going to the northeast for more than five hundred *li*, I reached the country of Sthāneśvara (in the domain of Central India).

The country of Sthāneśvara is more than seven thousand *li* in circuit, the capital city being over twenty *li* in circuit. The land is fertile and crops grow in abundance. The climate is hot and the people are unkind and ignoble by custom. The householders are wealthy and vie with each other in showing extravagance. The people are learned in art of magic, and they highly esteem unusual capabilities. Most of them engage in trade in pursuit of profits, and few of them are farmers. Exceptional goods of various places are collected in this country. There are three monasteries with over seven hundred monks, all of whom study the teachings of the Hinayana schools. Deva-temples amount to over one hundred and have numerous heretics.

Around the great city within a radius of two hundred *li*, the district is called by the people of the country the Land of Blessedness. I heard some old people saying that the five parts of India were formerly ruled separately by two kings. As their territories were adjacent to each other, the two kings carried out mutual invasions in endless wars. Then the two of them agreed to fight a final battle to see who was to be the master, so as to give peace to their subjects. But all the common subjects bore a grudge against war and would not obey the orders of their kings. Thinking that it was difficult to discuss the matter with his subjects, the king [of Sthāneśvara] considered that the gods might be able to arouse his people and that power might help him achieve his exploit. There was then a Brahman who was known for his high talents. [The king] secretly sent him a roll of silk and invited him to the back chambers of the palace to compose a Dharma book, which was then hidden in a rock cave. After a long lapse of years, trees overgrowing at the place covered up the cave.

One day at an audience in the morning, the king said to his ministers, "As a man of no virtue, I have unworthily occupied the throne. The Lord of Heaven has favored me with a dream in which he granted me a spiritual book, which is now hidden under a certain peak at a certain mountain." Then he gave orders to seek for the book, and to the delight of the ministers, as well as to the pleasure of the common people, the book was found in a forest on a mountain. The contents of the book were made known to all people far and near, and they read briefly as follows:

> The [wheel of] life and death is endless, and it rotates incessantly without limit. Those who are submerged in the sea of rebirth cannot save themselves. I have a wonderful device to release you from all kinds of suffering. The region two hundred *li* wide around the royal city is the Land of Blessedness handed down by former kings from generation to generation, but in the long lapse of time the inscriptions 891a
> have become obliterated. As the people are not aware of the fact, they are sunk in the sea of suffering. What would people say if we failed to rescue those who are being drowned? You people will be reborn among men if you die in fighting your enemies, and if you slaughter many innocent people, you will enjoy happiness in heaven. Obedient grandsons and filial sons serving their parents in touring this region will gain infinite blessedness. Why should you lose the chance to obtain much blessedness by performing a small meritorious deed? Once the human body is lost, you will suffer in

> the darkness of the three evil states of rebirth. Therefore every one of you should cultivate good karma.

Thus all the people practiced military arts and looked upon death as going home.

The king then ordered that brave and high-spirited warriors be enrolled, and in the war that took place between the two counties numerous corpses of those killed on the battlefield were piled up high, and even now the skeletons are scattered about in the wilderness. Because this happened in ancient times, the bodies of the fighters were very large in size. This region is known as the Land of Blessedness by tradition of the country.

Four or five *li* to the northwest of the city is a stupa more than two hundred feet high built by King Aśoka. The bricks are all yellowish red in color, very lustrous and clean. It contains one *sheng* of the Tathāgata's relic bones, which often emit a light with many divine manifestations.

Going south for over one hundred *li* from the city, I came to the Govinda Monastery, which consists of storied pavilions with the ridges of the roofs connected together, and terraces of many tiers standing one higher than another. The monks lead a pure and strict life and comport themselves in a calm and refined manner. From here going northeast for more than four hundred *li*, I reached the country of Śrughna (in the domain of Central India).

The country of Śrughna is more than six thousand *li* in circuit, with the Ganges River bordering on the east, big mountains lying at its back in the north, and the Yamunā River flowing through the middle of its territory. The capital city, which is over twenty *li* in circuit, borders on the Yamunā River on the east. Although the city is in a desolate condition, the foundations are still strong. The native products and customs and habits are the same as in the country of Sthāneśvara. The people are honest by nature and believe in heretical theories. They esteem the learning of arts and crafts and advocate the cultivation of blessedness and wisdom. There are five monasteries with over one thousand monks, most of whom study Hinayana teachings, but a few learn the tenets of other schools. They discuss the subtle teachings and deliberate on the abstruse doctrines. Talented scholars of different places come to them to hold discussions in order to solve their doubts. There are one hundred deva-temples with numerous heretics.

To the southeast of the great city and outside the eastern gate of a big monastery at the west of the Yamunā River, there is a stupa built by King Aśoka at a place where the Tathāgata once preached the Dharma to convert the people in olden times. Beside it another stupa contains hair and fingernail relics of the Tathāgata. Hair and fingernail relics of Śāriputra, Maudgalyāyana, and other Arhats are preserved in several tens of stupas built around here. After the Nirvana of the Tathāgata, the country was led astray by heretics, and the people abandoned the right views. The five monasteries now in existence were built by foreign Śāstra-masters who 891b
had defeated the heretics and Brahmans in debates at the places where the monasteries were consequently built.

Going east from the Yamunā River for over eight hundred *li*, I came to the Ganges River, the source of which is three or four *li* wide flowing southeast to the sea; it is over ten *li* at its mouth. The water is dark blue in color with great waves rising in it. Although there are many strange monsters [in the river], they do people no harm. The water is sweet, and fine grains of sand come down with the current. According to the local popular records, this river is known as the Water of Blessedness. One's accumulated sins can be expiated by taking a bath in it. Those who drown themselves in the river will be reborn in heaven to enjoy happiness, and one whose corpse is thrown into the river will not fall into the evil states of existence in his next birth. By raising waves and blockading the current, the souls of the dead will be saved.

Deva Bodhisattva of the country of Siṃhala was a man learned in the theory of reality; he understood the nature of all Dharmas. Having pity upon ignorant people, he came here to enlighten them. At the time when the people, male and female, old and young, assembled at the banks of the river, raised waves, and blockaded the current, Deva Bodhisattva mingled with them to draw up the water and lowered his head to push the current in a reverse way, dissimilar to that of the people. A heretic said to him, "Why are you doing it in a strange way?" Deva Bodhisattva said, "My parents and other kinsfolk are in the country of Siṃhala, and as I fear that they may be suffering from hunger and thirst, I am trying to send this water from afar to save them." The heretic said, "You are mistaken. You did not consider the matter well and behaved erroneously. Your home country is far away, separated [from here] by big mountains and rivers. To agitate the water here with the hope of saving those who are hungry there is like someone going backward in order to advance. This is something unheard-of !" Deva Bodhisattva said, "If sinners in the nether world can be benefitted by this water, why does it not save the people separated [from here] by mountains and rivers?" The heretics then realized their fault and acknowledged defeat. They renounced their erroneous views, accepted the right Dharma, corrected their mistakes, and made a fresh start by wishing to listen to the instructions [of Deva Bodhisattva]. Crossing the river to the east bank, I reached the country of Matipura (in the domain of Central India).

The country of Matipura is more than six thousand *li* in circuit, and its capital city is over twenty *li* in circuit. It yields rice and wheat and has plenty of flowers and fruits. The climate is temperate and the people are honest by custom. They esteem the learning of arts and crafts and are learned in the art of sorcery. Half of the population believes in heterodox religions and the other half in the right teachings [of Buddhism]. The king is a Sudra by caste who does not believe in the Buddha-dharma but worships the devas. There are over ten monasteries with more than eight hundred monks, most of whom study the teachings of the Sarvāstivāda school of Hinayana Buddhism. There are over fifty deva-temples where heretics live together.

Four or five *li* to the south of the great city is a small monastery with over fifty monks. Formerly the Śāstra-master Guṇaprabha (known as Deguang, or Virtue light, in Chinese) composed at this place the *Tattva-satya-śāstra* and other treatises, totaling over one hundred books. The Śāstra-master was eminently smart when he

was young, and when he had grown up he became intelligent and vastly learned, a versatile scholar of good memory and erudite 891c
learning. At first he studied Mahayana teachings, but before he could thoroughly understand these profound teachings he came upon the *Vibhāṣā-śāstra*, and thus he changed his course of study and devoted himself to learning Hinayana theories. He wrote several tens of treatises in refutation of the principles of Mahayana teachings and for the grasping of Hinayana theories. He also wrote several tens of secular books to denounce the classical works written by his predecessors. He pondered over the Buddhist scriptures and found more than ten dubious points that he could not solve, and in spite of his studies for a long time, his doubts were not removed.

There was then the Arhat Devasena (known as Tianjun, or Heavenly army, in Chinese), who used to frequent the Tuṣita Heaven [where Maitreya Bodhisattva resided]. Guṇaprabha wished to see Maitreya to seek instructions for the solution of his doubts, and Devasena brought him to the heavenly palace by his supernatural powers. Upon seeing Maitreya, [Guṇaprabha] would not salute him in the proper way, and Devasena said to him, "As Maitreya Bodhisattva is next only to the Buddha in position, why are you so conceited as not to worship him? Since you desire to study under his guidance, how can you be so unruly toward him?" Guṇaprabha said in reply, "What you, Venerable Sir, have said is truly a good admonition, but I am a fully ordained *bhikṣu*, a homeless disciple, while Maitreya Bodhisattva is enjoying the bliss of heaven and is not a homeless monk. I am afraid it is unfitting for me to worship him." The Bodhisattva, knowing that his conceited mind was so stubborn that he was not a competent person to hear the Dharma, would not solve his doubts, though he came up to heaven three times. [Guṇaprabha] said to Devasena that he wished to see the Bodhisattva once more so as to worship him, but Devasena detested his conceit and contemptuously ignored his request. Having not satisfied his wish, Guṇaprabha retired to a forest, holding a grudge, to practice meditation for the development of supernatural powers, but as he did not eliminate his conceit, he could not attain sainthood.

Three or four *li* to the north of Guṇaprabha's monastery, there is a big monastery with more than two hundred monks, all of whom study Hinayana teachings. This is the place where the Śāstra-master Saṃghabhadra passed away. The Śāstra-master, a native of the country of Kaśmīra, was an intelligent and learned man who had had a good reputation since he was a youth and had made a profound study of the *Vibhāṣā-śāstra* of the Sarvāstivāda school.

There was then the Bodhisattva Vasubandhu, whose mind was fixed on the abstruse Way and on seeking implications that were beyond words. In order to refute the *Vibhāṣā* masters, he composed the *Abhidharma-kośa-śāstra*, a work written in fine and dexterous diction, explaining the meanings in a pure and sublime manner. When Saṃghabhadra read this work, he made up his mind to probe into the contents of it. After making a profound study of the work for twelve years, he composed the *Kośa-karakā-śāstra* in twenty-five thousand stanzas and eight hundred thousand words. It was a book consisting of words of far-reaching import, searching into the depths of abstruse and subtle theories. He said to his disciples, "With my outstanding competence and correct reasoning, go and refute Vasubandhu to frustrate his sharpness and break the old man's monopoly on eminent fame." Thus three or four of his prominent disciples took his treatise and went to visit Vasubandhu.

At that time Vasubandhu was at Śākula city in the country of Ṭakka, when tidings arrived that Saṃghabhadra was coming.
892a Upon hearing this news, Vasubandhu packed up his things. His bewildered disciples came forward to remonstrate with him, saying, "Great Master, your virtue surpasses that of former sages, and your unique fame spreads far in the present world. All scholars far and near have great esteem for you. Why are you so alarmed at the news of Saṃghabhadra's arrival? Even should he come to humiliate us, we would face him with boldness." Vasubandhu said, "It is not because I wish to avoid this man that I am going far away. Looking around this country, I find no one skillful and competent enough to decide the case. Saṃghabhadra is a young man, eloquent in debate, while I am advanced in years and could not

hold a discussion with him. I wish to defeat his heterodox views with one word, and I intend to lure him to Central India to meet old and learned scholars who can discern truth from falsehood and find out right and wrong." Before long, he asked his companion to carry his bookcase for him and started on a long journey.

Śāstra-master Saṃghabhadra arrived at this monastery one day after [the departure of Vasubandhu], and he suddenly found himself feeble in breath. So he wrote a letter of apology to Vasubandhu, in which he said, "After the Nirvana of the Tathāgata, his disciples split into different sects and schools, each propagating his own theories in specific ways. They defended those who belonged to their own sects and hated those who were affiliated with other groups. Being an ignorant man of shallow learning, I had the opportunity to pursue knowledge under my teachers and read the *Abhidharma-kośa-śāstra* composed by you for the refutation of the principles of the *Vibhāṣā* masters. I overrated my abilities and worked for many years on this treatise [the *Kośa-karakā-śāstra*] with the intention of making it a book for the support of the correct theories. My scheme was great but my wisdom too small, and the time of my death is approaching. You, being a Bodhisattva, expound the subtle sayings and propagate the supreme truth. I should be happy if you would not deny what opinions I hold, so that my treatise might be preserved. Then I can die without regret."

He selected some of his disciples who were eloquent in debate and said to them, "I am really a man of the younger generation and despised the sages of older times. What can I do, if such is my fate? I shall be dying soon. You should take this letter together with my treatise to apologize to that Bodhisattva and show repentance on my behalf." As soon as he finished these words, he passed away.

His disciples took the letter and went to the place of Vasubandhu, to whom they said, "Our teacher Saṃghabhadra has passed away. He left word for us to send this letter to express his self-reproach and to apologize to you for his mistakes, hoping that you would not bring down his reputation; though this may be beyond our expectation."

Vasubandhu Bodhisattva read the letter and glanced over the treatise for a long while before he spoke to the disciples, saying, "Śāstra-master Samghabhadra was a young scholar of intelligence. In his treatise the theories are not sufficiently elucidated, but his phraseology is sharp enough. If I wish to confute his treatise, it would be as easy as pointing at my palm. Considering his request made on his deathbed, and having noticed the words he spoke after realizing the difficulties in his attempt, I shall comply, out of the principle of righteousness, with his long-cherished ambition; moreover, in his treatise the views of my school are also expounded." Then he changed the title of the treatise to *Nyāyānusāra-śāstra*.

[Vasubandhu's] disciples remonstrated with him, saying, "Before the death of Saṃghabadra, you, a great teacher, went far away from him, and now after having obtained his treatise, you changed its title for him. How can any of your disciples have the face to bear the shame?" In order to clear up their doubt, Vasubandhu Bodhisattva uttered the following stanza:

When a king of lions
892b Runs away from a pig,
The wise should know
Which is winner in strength.

After Saṃghabhadra's death, his body was cremated and his ashes were preserved in a stupa built in a mango grove over two hundred paces to the northwest of the monastery, and it is still in existence.

Beside the mango grove there is a stupa containing the remains of the Śāstra-master Vimalamitra (known as Wugouyou, or Stainless friend, in Chinese). This Śāstra-master was a native of the country of Kaśmīra and became a monk of the Sarvāstivāda school. He was widely learned in various scriptures and studied the treatises of diverse sects, and he travelled in all the five parts of India to learn the abstruse texts of the Tripiṭaka. After he had gained fame and completed his studies, he started on his homeward journey, and on his way he came across the stupa of Saṃghabhadra. He patted the stupa and said with a sigh, "You, Śāstra-master, were a man of magnanimity and eminence and extolled the great teachings. Why did you live such a short life and die at the time when you were just about to defeat the heterodox schools and establish your own sect? I, Vimalamitra, am a man of shallow learning, and although we have lived at different times, I admire your righteousness and have always remembered your virtue for many years. Vasubandhu is dead, but his theories are still in vogue. I shall exhaust my knowledge to write treatises for all the scholars in Jambudvīpa to efface the fame of the Mahayana teachings and the name of Vasubandhu. This will be an unending task, but I shall do my best for its fulfillment."

After having said these words, [Vimalamitra] became delirious at once, and five tongues stuck out of his mouth and hot blood oozed from it. Knowing that he was sure to die, he wrote a letter of repentance, saying, "The Mahayana doctrines are the ultimate truth of the Buddha-dharma, which is beyond the scope of both conception and substance and has deep and abstruse principles. I have been so imprudent as to denounce an advanced teacher with my ignorance. Karmic retribution is apparent, and it is just and right that I should lose my life. I venture to advise my fellow students to consider me as an example. Be careful in making your aspirations and cherish no more doubt."

At the moment of his death the earth quaked, and a pit was formed at the place where he died. His travelling companions cremated his corpse and collected the ashes, over which a memorial was built. At that time an Arhat witnessed the event, and said with a sigh, "What a pity, and how sorrowful it is! This Śāstra-master waywardly grasped his own views and vilified the Mahayana doctrines, and thus he fell into the hell of unintermitted suffering."

In the northwest of this country [Matipura] and on the east bank of the Ganges is the city of Mayūra, which is more than twenty *li* in circuit and has a dense population; it has many watercourses interflowing with one another. It produces brass, crystal, and valuable articles. Not far away from the city on the bank of the Ganges there is a great deva-temple with many miraculous manifestations.

Inside the compound of the shrine is a pond, of which the banks are inlaid with slabs of stone. Water is led from the Ganges to replenish the pond. People of all the five parts of India call it the Gate of the Ganges, as it is a place to perform meritorious deeds and expiate sins. There are always hundreds and thousands of people flocking from afar to bathe themselves in the pond. Philanthropic kings
892c have constructed almshouses to provide isolated, solitary, and helpless people with free food and medical service. From here going northward for more than three hundred *li*, I reached the country of Brahmapura (in the domain of North India).

The country of Brahmapura, which is over four thousand *li* in circuit, is surrounded by mountains on all four sides, and the capital city is more than twenty *li* in circuit. It is densely populated, and the inhabitants are rich and prosperous. The land is fertile, and crops are sown and reaped in good time. It yields brass and crystal, and the climate is somewhat cold. The people are rude and violent by custom, and few of them learn arts and crafts; the majority engages in business to gain profits. They believe in both heterodox and orthodox teachings. There are five monasteries with few monks, and more than ten deva-temples with heretics living together.

In the Great Snow Mountains to the north of this country is the country of Suvarṇagotra (known as Jinshi, or Gold clan, in Chinese). It produces gold of the best quality, hence the name of the country. It is long from east to west and narrow from south to north. This is what is known as the Eastern Woman's Country, as it is ruled from generation to generation by a woman. Her husband is king, but he does not administer state affairs. The men's duty is only to serve in the army and to cultivate the fields. The soil is good for growing winter wheat, and many sheep and horses are reared. The climate is severely cold, and the people are violent by nature. In the east it borders on the country of Tubo, in the north it adjoins the country of Khotan, and in the west it abuts on the country of Sanbohe. Going from Matipura to the southeast for more than four hundred *li*, I reached the country of Goviṣāṇa (in the domain of Central India).

The country of Goviṣāṇa is over two thousand *li* in circuit, and the capital city is fourteen or fifteen *li* in circuit. Lofty mountains serve as impregnable barriers to the city, and the inhabitants are rich and prosperous. Flowery woods and ponds and pools are to be seen everywhere one after the other. The climate and natural products are the same as in the country of Matipura. The people are sincere and honest by custom, and they are assiduous in learning and are fond of doing meritorious works. Most of them believe in heterodox teachings, seeking happiness for the present life. There are two monasteries with over one hundred monks, all of whom study the Hinayana teachings. There are more than thirty deva-temples where heretics live together.

In an old monastery beside the capital city, there is a stupa more than two hundred feet high built by King Aśoka. Formerly the Tathāgata once preached on the various principles of the Dharma at this place for one month. Beside it, there are traces where the four past Buddhas used to sit and walk up and down. Alongside the traces, there are two stupas, each over ten feet high, containing hair and fingernail relics of the Tathāgata. Going from here to the southeast for more than four hundred *li*, I reached the country of Ahicchattra (in the domain of Central India).

The country of Ahicchattra is more than three thousand *li* in circuit, and the capital city, which is built upon strongly fortified positions, is seventeen or eighteen *li* in circuit. The country produces rice and wheat and has many woods and springs. The climate is mild and pleasant, while the people are sincere and honest by custom. They take delight in studying the Way and are diligent in learning, and they possess much talent and extensive knowledge. There are over ten monasteries with more than one thousand monks, who study the teachings of the Saṃmitīya sect of the 893a
Hinayana school. There are nine deva-temples with more than three hundred followers who are worshippers of Īśvara and smear themselves with ashes.

Beside a dragon pond outside the city there is a stupa built by King Aśoka. Formerly the Tathāgata preached the Dharma for the dragon at this place for seven days. Beside it there are four smaller stupas built at spots where the four past Buddhas sat and walked up and down. From here going east for two hundred sixty or seventy *li* and crossing the Ganges to the south, I reached the country of Vilaśāṇa (in the domain of Central India).

The country of Vilaśāṇa is more than two thousand *li* in circuit, its capital city being over ten *li* in circuit. The climate and natural products are the same as in the country of Ahicchattra. The people are fierce and violent by custom, but they have an inclination for learning. They believe in heretical theories; and only a few of them venerate the Buddha-dharma. There are two monasteries with three hundred monks, all of whom study Mahayana teachings. There are five deva-temples, and heretics live together.

In an old monastery inside the capital city there is a stupa of which the base, though dilapidated, remains over one hundred feet in height. It was built by King Aśoka at the spot where the Tathāgata preached the *Skandha-dhātu-āyatana-sūtra* for seven days. Beside it are traces where the four past Buddhas used to sit and walk up and down. From here going southeast for more than two hundred *li*, I reached the country of Kapitha (formerly known as the country of Sengjiashe, in the domain of Central India).

The country of Kapitha is more than two thousand *li* in circuit, and the capital city is over twenty *li* in circuit. The climate and natural products are the same as in the country of Vilaśāṇa. The people are honest and amiable by custom, and most of them learn handicrafts. There are four monasteries with over one thousand monks, all of whom study the teachings of the Sammitīya sect of the Hinayana school. There are ten deva-temples where heretics live together; all of them serve and worship Īśvara.

Over twenty *li* to the west of the city there is a great and beautifully constructed monastery consisting of many lofty and spacious buildings adorned with exquisite carvings. The holy images and statues are made in a most stately manner. There are several hundred monks who study the teachings of the Sammitīya sect; several myriads of lay people, who are attendants of the monks, live in their houses beside the monastery.

Inside the great wall of the monastery, there are three precious stairways standing in a row from south to north and sloping down to the east. This was the place where the Tathāgata descended from

the Trayastriṃśa Heaven and returned to earth. Formerly the Tathāgata set out from the Jetavana Garden and ascended to Devapura (the residence of Indra); he stayed in the Hall of the Good Dharma, where he preached the Dharma for his mother. At the end of three months, when he desired to descend, Indra employed his divine power to construct the stairways. The middle flight of stairs was made of gold, the left one of crystal, and the right one of silver. The Tathāgata started from the Hall of the Good Dharma, and accompanied by a multitude of heavenly beings he walked down the middle flight of stairs; Brahmā holding a white chowri walked down the silver stairs, attending the Buddha 893b
at his right, while Indra carrying a precious canopy walked down the crystal stairs, attending the Buddha at his left. The multitude of heavenly beings flying high in the air scattered flowers and praised the virtues of the Buddha.

A few hundred years ago, the stairs were still there, but they have now completely sunk down. The kings of various countries, regretting that they had not seen the holy structures, piled up bricks and stones on the old base with ornaments of gems and jewels to the height of seventy feet to imitate the original precious stairways. A shrine room was built on the top with a stone image of the Buddha installed in it, while on the left and right flights of stairs there are the statues of Indra and Brahmā respectively, made after the original postures, as if they were walking down. Beside the stairs is a stone pillar more than seventy feet high erected by King Aśoka. Being dark purple in color, it is made of lustrous hard stone with a fine grain, and on its top is a carved lion crouching and facing toward the stairs. On the surface all around the pillar there are engraved various kinds of strange figures, which appear in a shadowy way to viewers according to their good or bad deeds.

Not far away from the precious stairs is a stupa built at a place where the four past Buddhas sat and walked up and down, and another stupa beside it was built at a place where the Tathāgata bathed. The temple beside the stupa was at a place where the Tathāgata sat in meditation. Beside the temple there is a great stone terrace fifty paces long and seven feet high at a place where the Tathāgata walked up and down. The footprints have the shapes of lotus flowers. On the left and right sides of the terrace there are two small stupas, one built by Indra and the other by Brahmā.

In front of the stupas built by Indra and Brahmā is the place where the *bhikṣuṇī* Utpalavarṇā, wishing to be the first to see the Buddha, appeared in the form of a universal monarch. When the Tathāgata returned from Devapura to Jambudvīpa, Subhūti (known as Shanxian, or Good manifestation, in Chinese, formerly transcribed as Xufuti or Xuputi, and translated as Good auspices, all erroneously) was sitting in meditation in a cave. He reflected, "Now the Buddha attended by human and heavenly beings is returning to earth. Being such as I am, what should I do? I have heard the Buddha saying that knowing the voidness of all things and understanding the nature of all things are to see the Buddha's spiritual body with the eye of wisdom."

At that time the *bhikṣuṇī* Utpalavarṇā, wishing to be the first to see the Buddha, appeared in the form of a universal monarch accompanied by attendants holding the seven kinds of precious objects and guarded by the four divisions of troops. When she came to the place of the Tathāgata, she resumed the form of a *bhikṣuṇī*. The Tathāgata told her, "You are not the first person to see me, because Subhūti, who has insight into the voidness of all things, has seen my spiritual body [before you]."

Within the enclosure of the holy traces, divine manifestations occurred in succession. To the southeast of the great stupa there is a pond in which a dragon always protected the holy traces, and under its divine protection they were not easily violated. They became dilapidated through erosion over time, but no human effort could destroy them. From here going southeast for less than two hundred *li*, I reached the country of Kanyākubja (known as Qunüchengguo, or the Country of hunchbacked maidens, in the domain of Central India).

End of Fascicle Four

Fascicle V

Six Countries, From Kanyākubja to Viṣaka

The country of Kanyākubja is more than four thousand *li* in circuit, and the capital city, with the Ganges at the west, is over twenty *li* in length and four or five *li* in breadth. The city wall and moat are strongly built, and terraces and pavilions are to be seen everywhere. Flowery woods are brilliant in color, and the ponds are filled with transparent water like a mirror. Rare goods of different places are collected here; the inhabitants live happily in abundance, and their families are rich and prosperous. There are many kinds of flowers and fruits, and crops are sown and reaped in good time. The climate is mild and pleasant, and the people are simple and honest by custom. Their features are handsome and graceful, and their clothes and adornments are bright and resplendent. They earnestly study arts and literature and talk in a lucid and far-sighted manner. Heterodoxy and orthodoxy are followed each by half of the population, and both the Mahayana and Hinayana teachings are studied by the people. There are more than two hundred deva-temples with several thousand heretics. 893c

In the age when human life was very long, the old capital city of the country of Kanyākubja was called Kusumapura (known as Huagong, or Flowery palace, in Chinese). The king, named Brahmadatta, was a man endowed with both bliss and wisdom; he was well-versed in literature and the arts of war. His prestige kept Jambudvīpa in awe of him, and his renown spread to the neighboring countries. He had one thousand sons, who possessed the qualities of wisdom and bravery as well as magnanimity and resoluteness. He also had one thousand daughters, who were beautiful in features and refined in manners.

There was then a *ṛṣi* (sage) who lived by the side of the Ganges; he concentrated his mind in meditation for several myriads of years, and his form became like that of a dried-up tree. Some migratory birds alighted upon him and dropped a fruit of the *nyagrodha* (banyan) tree on his shoulder. With the passage of many hot and cold seasons, the fruit grew into a big tree with branches growing downward to form a vault. After many years, he rose from his meditation and wished to shake off the tree, but he feared that he might overturn the nests of the birds. The people appreciated his virtue and called him the Ṛṣi of the Big Tree.

One day while the *ṛṣi* enjoyed the view of the riverside, he made a pleasure trip into the dense wood, where he saw the king's daughters playing and frolicking merrily. Thus his sexual passion was aroused and his mind became stained. So he went to the Kusumapura to ask for the hand of one of the king's daughters. Upon hearing of the *ṛṣi*'s arrival, the king received him in person and greeted him, saying, "As Your Reverence lives outside the scope
894a of the human world, why do you condescend to pay me a visit?" The *ṛṣi* said, "I have lived in the woods and near the lakes for many long years. When I came out of the state of meditation, I made a pleasure trip and saw your daughters, for whom a mind of contamination has arisen in me. I have come from afar to propose marriage." After hearing these words, the king did not know what to do, and he said to the *ṛṣi*, "Now return to your place and wait for an auspicious time." Upon hearing the king's order, the *ṛṣi* went back to the woods.

The king then consulted with his daughters about the matter, but none of them would consent to accept the offer. He feared the *ṛṣi*'s divine power and became heavy-hearted and weighed down with worry. One day when the king was at leisure, his youngest daughter calmly asked him, "Father, you have a thousand sons and you are admired by all countries. Why do you look so worried, as if you had a fear in your mind?" The king said, "The Ṛṣi of the Big Tree has come to propose marriage, but none of your sisters would consent to be married to him. The *ṛṣi* has divine power and could cause either disaster or bliss. If I cannot fulfill his desire, he will certainly be angry with me and destroy our country and terminate our ancestral line, causing insult to our forefathers. This is why I am deeply worried; this is really my fear." The king's youngest daughter said apologetically, "It is our sin to have caused you such deep worry. I wish to offer my humble self to lengthen the transmission of the royal line." The king was delighted to hear this, and he ordered a carriage so that he might take his youngest daughter to her [new] home.

Upon arriving at the *ṛṣi*'s hermitage, the king apologized to the *ṛṣi*, saying, "You, Great Ṛṣi, comply with supramundane sentiments, and you also stoop to care for worldly affection. I venture to offer you my youngest daughter to be at your service." The *ṛṣi* was displeased at the sight of the girl, and he said to the king, "You despise me as an old man to give me such an ill-looking girl in marriage." The king said, "I have asked all my other daughters, but none of them would obey my order. Only this youngest one consented to serve you." The *ṛṣi* was thus enraged, and he called down evil upon the king's other daughters, saying, "Let all ninety-nine [*sic*] girls immediately become hunchbacked, and with their shapes disfigured let them be unmarried their whole lives long!" The king's messenger went back to check the efficacy of the curse and found that the girls had actually become hunchbacked. Henceforward the place was called the City of Hunchbacked Maidens.

The present king, named Harṣavardhana (known as Xizeng, or Increment of happiness), is a descendant of the Vaisya caste. His family had three kings ruling over the country in two generations. His father was named Prabhākaravardhana (known as Guangzeng, or Increment of light) and his elder brother, Rājyavardhana (known as Wangzeng, or Increment of the kingdom). As Rājyavardhana was the senior prince, he succeeded to the throne and administered state affairs in a virtuous manner. At that time, King Śaśāṅka (known as Yue, or Moon, in Chinese) of the country of Karṇasuvarṇa (known as Jiner, or Golden ear, in Chinese) in East India often said to his ministers, "A sagacious king in a neighboring country might be the cause of disaster to our own country." Thus he lured Rājyavardhana to his country and murdered him. Since the people lost their lord, the country [Kanyākubja] fell into a chaotic condition.

At that time, the minister Bhaṇḍi, a man of high position and good repute, said to his colleagues, "Today we should make a decision about a matter of fundamental importance for the nation. The son of the former king and younger brother of the late monarch is a man of kindness and benevolence, having filial piety toward his parents and an affectionate mind; he respects the sages and treats his subordinates with equality. I wish to propose him for the throne. What do you think of it? Please state your views." They all admired the virtue of the late king's younger brother and
894b had no objection to him. Thus the assistant ministers and other officials exhorted him to be king, saying, "May the prince listen to us. By accumulating merits and cultivating virtues, the former king possessed the throne and ruled over the country extensively. When the throne was handed down to Rājyavardhana, he should have lived to a ripe age, but due to the incapability of his assistant ministers, he was killed by the hands of his enemy. This is a great shame to our country, and it is also the fault of the humble ministers. Current public opinion and folk rhymes are saying that you, who are a sagacious prince, should succeed to the throne in order to avenge your deceased brother and wipe out the national humiliation, as well as to glorify the deeds of your father. This is really a great exploit, so we hope you will not decline the offer."

The prince said, "From ancient times up to the present, it has always been an important affair for one to succeed to the throne, and we should be prudent in establishing a man in the position of a monarch. I am, indeed, poor in virtue, and both my father and my elder brother have departed. Although you recommend me to succeed to the throne, do you think I am a competent candidate for the vacancy? In spite of public opinion, I dare not forget my own unsubstantiality and shallowness. Now on the bank of the Ganges there is an image of Avalokiteśvara Bodhisattva, which has shown many spiritual manifestations. I wish to go there to consult the oracle of the Bodhisattva." So he went to the image of the Bodhisattva and prayed before it after having observed the appropriate fast. Being moved by his sincerity, the Bodhisattva revealed his true features and inquired of him, "For what are you seeking with such sincerity and earnestness?" The prince said, "It was my accumulated ill fortune that caused the death of my father, and the murder of my elder brother was a heavy punishment inflicted upon me. I am aware of my own lack of virtue, but the people wish to elect me to succeed to the throne to glorify the deeds of my departed father. Being ignorant of what to do, I hope to hear your holy mandate." The Bodhisattva told him, "In your previous life you were a forest-dwelling *bhikṣu* in this wood and practiced the Way diligently. By the power of this meritorious action, you are now a prince in this life. Since the king of the country of Karṇasuvarṇa destroyed the Buddha-dharma, you should ascend the throne to work for its revival. With a mind of great compassion, and having sympathy for the people, you will soon become king of all the five parts of India. If you wish to prolong the sovereignty of your country, you should follow my advice, and then you will be blessed by the gods and have no powerful enemy in neighboring countries. You should not ascend the Lion Seat, nor should you assume the title of king." With this instruction the prince left the image and ascended the throne with the appellation of Prince and the name of Śīlāditya (known as Jieri, or Sun of morality).

Then he said to his ministers, "So long as my elder brother is not avenged and the neighboring countries have not pledged allegiance to me, I shall not take food with my right hand. I hope you officials at court will work together with one heart." Then he took command of his troops in the whole country and trained the fighters, who consisted of five thousand elephant soldiers, twenty thousand cavalrymen, and fifty thousand infantrymen. He marched from west to east to attack those who refused to acknowledge allegiance to him. With his elephants unreleased and his men fully armed for six years, he subjugated all the five parts of India. He not only expanded his territory but also enlarged his military forces, having increased his elephant corps to sixty thousand men and his cavalrymen to one hundred thousand strong.

Then for thirty years no weapon was raised for fighting, and he administered the country in peace and practiced frugality. He sought after blessedness and performed good deeds so sedulously that he forgot about eating and sleeping. He ordered that within the five parts of India nobody was allowed to eat meat, and if a man killed any living creature, the culprit would be executed with-
894c out pardon. Alongside the Ganges, he built several thousand stupas, each over one hundred feet high. Temples were constructed in towns and villages and at thoroughfares and crossroads in the five parts of India, where food and drink were stored and medicines laid in to be distributed as alms to wayfarers and the poor without negligence. At sacred sites, monasteries were constructed, and once every five years a great congregation was convened, in which everything in the royal treasury, except weapons, was given away as alms. Every year Śramaṇas of different countries were invited to attend a meeting for twenty-one days, during which time they were provided with the four monastic requisites, and seats were prepared on well-decorated mats so that they might carry out debates and arguments about the teachings of Buddhism, to see who was superior and who inferior in learning. The good ones were praised and the bad ones censured, while the ignorant ones were dismissed and the brilliant ones promoted. Those who strictly observed the disciplinary rules and were pure in morality were selected to ascend the Lion Seat, and the king received the Dharma from them in person. Those who were pure in observing the disciplinary rules but lacked learning were merely saluted to show respect to them. Those who violated the disciplinary rules and whose immorality was obvious were banished from the country, never to be seen or heard of again.

If the lords and their assistant ministers of the small neighboring countries performed meritorious deeds tirelessly and sought after goodness without weariness, the king would take them by the hand to sit together with him and call them "good friends." He never spoke to those kings who were different in character, and if a negotiation was required to settle a matter, an envoy was sent to deal with it. Whenever he went on an inspection tour, he would not stay at any one place but would have a hut made for his lodging wherever he stopped on the way. During the three months of the rainy season, he would not travel about, because of the rain. At his temporary residence he always had delicious food prepared to feed one thousand monks of different schools and five hundred Brahmans every day. He always divided a day into three periods, of which one was spent in attending to state affairs and two were devoted to performing meritorious deeds and doing good work. He lived assiduously, and the day was too short for him.

At first I was invited by King Kumāra to proceed from the country of Magadha to the country of Kāmarūpa. At that time King Śīlāditya was making an inspection tour in the country of Kajuṅghira, and he sent an order to King Kumāra, saying, "It befits you to come promptly with the Śramaṇa, a guest from a distant land, to Nālandā, to attend an assembly." Thus I went together with King Kumāra to meet him. After exchanging greetings, King Śīlāditya inquired of me, "Which country do you come from? What is the purpose of your journey?" I said in reply, "I come from the country of Great Tang to seek the Buddha-dharma." The king said, "Where is the country of Great Tang situated, by what route did you travel, and how far is it from here?" I replied, "It is situated to the northeast at a distance of several myriads of *li*, and it is the country known in India as Mahācīna."

The king remarked, "I have heard that in the country of Mahācīna, the Prince of Qin has been an intelligent man since his youth, and that now that he has grown up he is a man of unusual bravery. The generation before his was a time of chaos, and the country had disintegrated. Wars were waged one after another, 895a causing the people to suffer bitterly. But the Prince of Qin, who was far-sighted at an early age, cherished the mind of great compassion to save living beings, and he restored order in his country. His moral influence spread widely, and his beneficence extended far. People of different localities and regions admire him and serve him as his subjects. Out of gratitude for his edification and maintenance, all the common people chant the *Music of Prince Qin's Victory* in praise of him. It has been a long time since we heard this elegant eulogy bestowed on him. Is the good repute heaped on him for his great virtue true to the facts? Is such the actual condition of the country of Great Tang?" I said in reply, "Yes. Cīna is the name of the country [now and] during the reign of the former king, while Great Tang is the national title of the reigning sovereign. Before his accession to the throne he was called the Prince of Qin, and having mounted the throne he is now entitled the Son of Heaven. When the fortune of the previous monarch came to an end, the people lost their lord, and the country fell into a chaotic condition caused by war and inflicting cruel harm and injuries upon the people. The Prince of Qin, being endowed with innate ambition, had the mind of compassion, and by exerting the influence of his prestige he annihilated all his enemies. Peace prevailed over all the eight quarters, and tributes were presented by different countries. He loves and tends creatures of the four kinds of birth, and he respects the Triple Gem with veneration. He has reduced taxation and mitigated penalties, but he has surplus funds in the state treasury, and nobody attempts to violate the law. Concerning his moral influence and his profound edification of the people it is difficult for me to narrate in detail." King Śīlāditya remarked, "How grand it is! The people of that land have performed good deeds that caused them to have a saintly lord."

When King Śīlāditya was about to return to the city of Kanyākubja to convoke a religious assembly, hundreds of thousands of his followers flocked on the southern bank of the Ganges, while King Kumāra, followed by a multitude of tens of thousands of men, was on the northern bank of the river. Divided by the stream, the two retinue groups proceeded both by land and by water simultaneously, with the two kings leading their four divisions of troops, who were sailing in boats and riding on elephants, beating drums and blowing conches, plucking strings and playing pipes. After travelling for ninety days, they reached the city of Kanyākubja. In a great flowery wood to the west of the Ganges, more than twenty kings of various countries, who had been informed beforehand, came with intelligent Śramaṇas and Brahmans as well as officials and soldiers of their respective countries to attend the great assembly.

The king [Śīlāditya] had previously constructed a large monastery on the west bank of the river, with a precious terrace erected at the east to the height of over one hundred feet, on which was placed a golden image of the Buddha of the same size as the king. At the south of the terrace was erected a precious altar, which was the place for bathing the Buddha's image. At a distance of fourteen or fifteen *li* to the northeast from here, a temporary palace was built. It was in the second month of spring, and from the first day up to the twenty-first of the month, the Śramaṇas and Brah- 895b
mans were feted with delicious food. From the temporary palace up to the monastery, pavilions adorned with countless jewels were erected along the road on both sides, and musicians standing motionless performed elegant music uninterruptedly. From the temporary palace the king, with a concentrated mind, took out a dimly visible golden image that was more than three feet tall. It was carried by a big elephant and screened by a precious curtain. King Śīlāditya dressed as Indra held a precious canopy and attended on the left side, while King Kumāra attired as Brahmā carried a white chowri and attended on the right side. On each side there were five hundred elephant soldiers, clad in armor and guarding the Buddha image before and behind, and on each side there were one hundred elephants that carried musicians to perform music. As he walked on, King Śīlāditya scattered pearls and miscellaneous jewels, as well as pieces of gold and silver and flowers, as offerings to the Triple Gem. He first bathed the image with perfumed water on the precious altar. The king personally carried the image to the

west terrace and offered to it hundreds and thousands of jewels and gems and pieces of *kauśeya* cloth. At that time there were only about twenty Śramaṇas participating in the function with the king, while the kings of other countries acted as attendant guards. After the meal was over, the monks of different schools assembled to discuss the subtle theories and deliberate on the ultimate truth. When the sun was about to set, the king returned to the temporary palace. In this manner the golden image was taken out every day with the same procession as on the first day, till the dispersal of the convocation.

The great terrace suddenly caught fire, and the monastery and its entrance arch were set ablaze. The king said, "I have spent all the valuables of the national treasury to construct this monastery in the name of my late father in order to glorify his superior deeds. Owing to my lack of virtue, I could not invite spiritual protection but caused this calamity. Unlucky man that I am, what is the use for me to live any longer?" Then he burned incense to worship [the Buddha] and made a pledge, saying, "It was due to my good deeds in the past that I could be a king ruling over all parts of India. May the power of my blessedness extinguish this disastrous conflagration. If no spiritual response arises, I shall give up my life right now." While saying so, he jumped down and lighted on the doorsill. Then the fire immediately went out, as if someone had put it out, and the smoke vanished. The various kings, having seen this strange event, gained increased awe and respect for him. Without changing his countenance, and speaking in his normal tone, he inquired of the various kings, "What would you think if this disaster had actually consumed all that I had achieved?" The kings prostrated themselves on the ground and said while shedding tears piteously, "We expected that this superior site achieved by you would be handed down to posterity. If it had been consumed all at once, nothing else would have been memorable. Only the heretics would have felt delighted and rejoiced over the disaster." The king said, "In view of this accident, what the Tathāgata has taught is true. The heretical and heterodox schools persist in the view of permanence, but our great teacher alone inculcated the theory of impermanence. I have given in alms what I could afford, to the satisfaction of my mind. But this is transient and destructible, and it proves the truth as taught by the Tathāgata. [The accident] is a great beneficence, for which there is no reason to be deeply regretful."

Then he followed the various kings and went up to the great stupa in the east to have a view of the scenery. When he was coming down the steps after having viewed the environs, a stranger 895c
suddenly appeared and attempted to attack him with a knife. The king, cornered by the assailant, retreated to a higher step, and bending down his back he got hold of the man and handed him over to his officials. At that time the officials were so alarmed with fright that they forgot to come to the rescue of the king. The various kings demanded that the man be put to death, but King Śīlāditya, without any resentment, ordered that he not be killed, and he personally interrogated him, asking, "What wrong did I do to you that you attempted to commit such a violent atrocity?" The man said in reply, "Your Majesty's virtuous benevolence is impartial, and all people both in your country and abroad are recipients of your benefits. I am a wild idiot, not knowing what is of great importance. At the instigation of one word of the heretics, I acted as an assassin and attempted to murder you." The king said, "Why did the heretics cherish such an evil intention?" In reply, the man said, "Your Majesty assembled [the Śramaṇas] of different countries, emptied the treasury for their maintenance, and cast images of the Buddha, while the heretics summoned from distant places were not properly cared for. Thus they felt ashamed and ordered me, a wild idiot, to commit this malicious act in a deceitful way." Through a further investigation into the heretical adherents, it was found that five hundred Brahmans and other men of high talents who were assembled under the order of the king were envious of the hospitality and veneration enjoyed by the Śramaṇas and shot a burning arrow to set fire to the precious terrace in the hopes of murdering the great king amid the turmoil of people trying

to put out the fire. As they did not have such an opportunity, they hired this man to carry out the assassination at a strategic point. At that time the various kings and ministers proposed to put the heretics to death, but the king punished only the chief criminals, while the rest of the party were pardoned, and the five hundred Brahmans were banished from the domain of India. After that the king returned to his capital city.

The stupa at the northwest of the city was constructed by King Aśoka at the site where the Tathāgata had once spoken on various wonderful doctrines for seven days. Beside it were sites where the four past Buddhas used to sit and walk up and down. There is also a small stupa containing hair and nail relics of the Tathāgata. The stupa built at the place where the Tathāgata preached the Dharma faces the Ganges on the south. There are three monasteries built in one enclosure with separate entrances. The images of the Buddha are magnificent and beautiful, and the monks are quiet and austere. There are several thousand families of monastic servitors. In a precious casket in the temple there is a tooth relic of the Buddha about one and a half inches long, with a special luster that changes color between morning and evening. Hundreds and thousands of people, both officials and commoners, come every day from far and near to see it and pay homage to it. Its guardians, who did not like the din and hubbub caused by the crowd, started demanding a heavy entrance fee from the worshippers, and they announced far and near that those who wished to see the Buddha's tooth relic would pay a large amount of money. Worshippers were displeased with these monks, thinking that they took pleasure in collecting money in the form of the entrance fee. On each fast day, the relic was exposed on a high cushion, and hundreds and thousands of people burned incense and scattered flowers. However many the flowers that were piled up high, the relic casket was never covered. At each side and in front of the monasteries, there is a temple more than one hundred feet high built with brick on stone bases. Therein the Buddha images, cast either in gold and
896a silver or in brass, were adorned with various kinds of gems. In front of each of the two temples there is a small monastery.

Not far to the southeast of the monasteries there is a large temple more than two hundred feet high built with brick on stone bases, housing a standing statue of the Buddha over thirty feet tall, which was cast in brass and adorned with various kinds of gems. On the stone walls of the temple, there are carvings depicting in full detail the acts of the Tathāgata when he was practicing the Way of a Bodhisattva. Not far to the south of the stone temple there is a temple of Sūrya (the Sun god), and not far further to the south there is another temple dedicated to Maheśvara (Śiva), both of which were built with bluestone fully carved with sculptures. Their size is the same as that of the Buddhist temple, and each has one thousand families to serve as scavengers to keep the place clean. Music of drums and voices is performed day and night without cease.

At a distance of six or seven *li* to the southeast of the great city there is a stupa over two hundred feet high built by King Aśoka at the site where the Tathāgata once preached on the doctrine that the physical body is impermanent, sorrowful, void, and impure. Beside it is a site where the four past Buddhas used to sit and walk up and down. There is also a small stupa containing hair and nail relics of the Tathāgata. When a man suffers from an illness, he can surely be cured and benefitted if he goes round the stupa with a pious mind.

Going southeast from the great city for more than one hundred *li*, I reached the city of Navadevakula, which is situated on the eastern bank of the Ganges and is over twenty *li* in circuit, with flowery woods and pure ponds that reflect one upon the other. To the northwest of the city of Navadevakula at the east of the Ganges is a deva-temple consisting of storied pavilions and multitiered terraces, which were exquisitely constructed. Five *li* to the east of the city there are three monasteries built in one enclosure but with separate gates. There are over five hundred monks, all of whom study the teachings of the Hinayana Sarvāstivāda school. More than two hundred paces in front of the monasteries there is a stupa built by King Aśoka. Although the foundations have sunk, the structure still remains more than one hundred feet high. It was built at the site where the Tathāgata preached the Dharma for seven days. In the monasteries there is a piece of *śarīra* that emits a light from time to time. Beside them there are places where the four past Buddhas used to sit and walk up and down. Three or four *li* to the north of the monasteries and on the bank of the Ganges, there is a stupa more than two hundred feet high that was built by King Aśoka at the site where the Tathāgata preached the Dharma for seven days. Five hundred hungry ghosts then came to the Buddha and became awakened after hearing the Dharma; being released from the realm of ghosts, they were reborn in the heavens.

Beside the stupa at the place where the Buddha preached the
896b Dharma is a site where the four past Buddhas used to sit and walk up and down. Beside it is a stupa containing the Tathāgata's hair and nail relics.

From here going to the southeast for over six hundred *li*, I crossed the Ganges to the south and reached the country of Ayodhyā (in the domain of Central India). The country of Ayodhyā is more than five thousand *li* in circuit, and its capital city is over twenty *li* in circuit. This country abounds in cereal crops and has plenty of flowers and fruits. The climate is mild and the people are benignant by custom. They have an inclination for performing meritorious deeds and are diligent in learning the arts and crafts. There are more than one hundred monasteries with over three thousand monks, who study both Mahayana and Hinayana doctrines. There are ten deva-temples with a few heretics. In the great city there is an old monastery that was the place where Vasubandhu Bodhisattva (known as Shiqin in Chinese, and formerly called Poshubandu, which was wrongly translated as Heavenly kinsman) spent several decades in composing various treatises on both Mahayana and Hinayana doctrines. The old foundations beside it are the ruins of a hall in which Vasubandhu Bodhisattva expounded the Buddhist theories and spoke on the Dharma for the kings of different countries, as well as for prominent Śramaṇas and Brahmans coming from the four quarters.

Four or five *li* to the north of the city, in a great monastery on the bank of the Ganges, there is a stupa over two hundred feet high built by King Aśoka, marking the place where the Tathāgata spoke on the various wonderful doctrines to heavenly and human beings for three months. The stupa beside it marks a place where the four past Buddhas used to sit and walk up and down. Four or five *li* to the west of the monastery is a stupa containing the Tathāgata's hair and nail relics. To the north of the stupa containing hair and nail relics are the ruins of a monastery in which the Śāstra-master Śrīlabdha (known as Shengshou, or Received in victory, in Chinese) of yore composed the *Vibhāṣā-śāstra* of the Sautrāntika school.

In a great mango grove five or six *li* to the southwest of the city, there is an old monastery where Asaṅga Bodhisattva (known as Wushuo, or No attachment, in Chinese) received instructions and guided the common people. At night he went up to the place of Maitreya Bodhisattva in the [Tuṣita] Heaven to learn the *Yogācāra-bhūmi-śāstra*, the *Mahāyāna-sūtrālaṃkāra-śāstra*, the *Madhyānta-vibhāga-śāstra*, etc.; in the daytime, he lectured on the marvellous principles to a great audience. More than one hundred paces to the northwest of the mango grove is a stupa containing hair and nail relics of the Tathāgata. The old foundations beside it mark the place on which Vasubandhu Bodhisattva descended from the Tuṣita Heaven to see Asaṅga Bodhisattva.

Asaṅga Bodhisattva, a native of the country of Gandhāra, was born a man of virtue one thousand years after the demise of the Buddha and realized the Way after receiving edification. He became a monk of the Mahīśāsaka school to learn its teachings, but soon afterward he turned his mind toward the Mahayana doctrines. His younger brother, Vasubandhu Bodhisattva, became a monk of the Sarvāstivāda school to receive an education. He was a man of wide learning and had a retentive memory, and he possessed com- 896c
prehensive knowledge and probed into its essence. Asaṅga's disciple Buddhasiṃha (known as Shizijue, or Buddha lion) was a monk who observed the disciplinary rules immaculately and was well known for his high talents. These two or three sagely persons often said among themselves that since the purpose of their spiritual cultivation was to see Maitreya in person [in their next birth], any one of them who should die first and fulfill his long-cherished wish should come back to inform the others where he had been reborn.

Afterward Buddhasiṃha died first, but he did not come back to report his whereabouts for three years. Later on, Vasubandhu also passed away, and he too did not report back after six months. Then the heretics sneered at them, deeming that Vasubandhu Bodhisattva and Buddhasiṃha had been reborn in an evil state, so that they could not show any spiritual response.

Afterward when Asaṅga Bodhisattva was instructing his disciples in the methods of practicing meditation, at the beginning of one night, the lamplight suddenly faded out and a great brightness appeared in the sky. A heavenly being descended from the air and entered the courtyard to worship Asaṅga, who asked him, "Why do you come so late? What is your name now?" [The heavenly being] said in reply, "After my death here I repaired to the Tuṣita Heaven, where I was born from a lotus flower in the inner department of the heaven. When the lotus flower opened, Maitreya said to me with praise, 'Welcome, Guanghui (Vast wisdom)! Welcome, Guanghui!' As soon as I had just finished going round him once, I came down to report it to you." Asaṅga Bodhisattva asked, "Where is Buddhasiṃha now?" The reply was, "When I was going round [Maitreya], I saw Buddhasiṃha in the outer department indulging himself in sensual pleasures, and he was so busy that he had scarcely any time to look at me, not to say to come down to make a report to you!" Asaṅga Bodhisattva said, "Let it be so. Now what does Maitreya look like? What Dharma is he preaching?" The reply was, "His features are so beautiful that they are beyond description. He preached on the wonderful Dharma, of which the purports were the same as you have explained here. But the Bodhisattva has a melodious voice, which is so fluent and elegant that the hearers forget about tiredness, and his students never feel bored."

More than forty *li* to the northwest of the old foundations of Asaṅga's lecture hall, I came to an old monastery with the Ganges at its north, in which is a brick stupa over one hundred feet high. This was the place where Vasubandhu Bodhisattva began to cherish a mind to accept the Mahayana teachings. When he came here from North India, Asaṅga Bodhisattva sent a disciple to greet him midway, and it was at this monastery that they met each other.

Asaṅga's disciple stayed outside the house, and late in the night he recited the *Daśabhūmi-sūtra*. Upon hearing the recitation, Vasubandhu became awakened and repented that he had not heard the very profound and wonderful Dharma before. Thinking that the source of the fault of slandering is the tongue, he intended to cut it off. When he had grasped a scraping knife to slice his tongue, he saw Asaṅga appearing before him and telling him, "The system of Mahayana teachings is the ultimate truth, praised by all the Buddhas and regarded as the orthodox school by various saints. I intended to admonish you, but now you have become awakened by 897a
yourself. Nothing is better than a timely awakening. According to the teachings of the Buddhas, cutting off one's tongue is not a way of repentance. In the bygone days you calumniated the Mahayana teachings with your tongue, so it is better for you to amend your ways by praising Mahayana teachings, also with your tongue. What is the benefit of becoming mute?" After having said so, [the illusion] disappeared. Following its advice, Vasubandhu did not cut off his tongue and proceeded to Asaṅga to study Mahayana teachings with him. Thus he engaged himself in careful learning with profound speculation, and he wrote more than a hundred treatises on Mahayana theories, all of which are very popular works.

From here going to the east for more than three hundred *li*, I crossed the Ganges to the north and reached the country of Ayamukha (in the domain of Central India).

The country of Ayamukha is two thousand four hundred or five hundred *li* in circuit. The capital city borders on the Ganges and is more than twenty *li* in circuit. The climate and local products of this country are the same as in the country of Ayodhyā. The people are honest and their custom is plain and simple. They are diligent in learning and like to perform meritorious deeds. There are five monasteries with over one thousand monks who study the Hinayana teachings of the Saṃmitīya school. There are more than ten deva-temples, where heretics live together.

Not far away to the southwest of the city, there is a stupa at the bank of the Ganges. Built by King Aśoka, it is two hundred feet high, marking the place where in olden times the Tathāgata preached the Dharma for three months. Beside it there is a place where the four past Buddhas used to sit and walk up and down, and there is also a stupa containing the Tathāgata's hair and nail relics. In the monastery beside the stupa, there live over two hundred monks. The Buddha's image is well adorned and has an austere appearance, as if he were still alive. The terraces and pavilions of the monastery are grand and beautifully built in a special style, rising high up into the air. This was the place where in olden times the Śāstra-master Buddhadāsa (known as Jueshi, or Buddha servant) composed the *Mahā-vibhāṣā-śāstra* of the Sarvāstivāda school.

From here going to the southeast for more than seven hundred *li*, I crossed the Ganges to the south and reached the country of Prayāga, north of the Jumna River (in the domain of Central India).

The country of Prayāga is more than five thousand *li* in circuit, and its capital city, situated at the confluence of the two rivers, is over twenty *li* in circuit. It abounds in cereal crops, and fruit trees are luxuriant. The climate is temperate, and the people are kind and agreeable by custom. They take pleasure in learning arts and crafts and believe in heretical religions. There are two monasteries with few monks, all of whom study Hinayana teachings. Deva-temples amount to several hundreds, and they have a large number of heretics.

In the wood of *champaka* flowers to the south of the great city, there is a stupa built by King Aśoka, which is still more than one hundred feet high though the foundations have sunk down. Formerly the Tathāgata subdued heretics at this place. Beside it is a stupa containing hair and nail relics, and there is also a site where
897b he used to walk up and down. Beside the stupa of hair and nail relics is an old monastery where Deva (known as Tian, or God) Bodhisattva composed the *Śata-śāstra-vaipulya* to frustrate the Hinayana adherents and conquer the heretics.

At the beginning, when Deva Bodhisattva came to this monastery from South India, there was in the city a heretical Brahman who was a learned debater, eloquent in discussion without impediment. He insisted on the identification of names and facts, and he would refute his opponents to their wits' end. Knowing that Deva was widely learned in profound doctrines, and wishing to break his spirit, the Brahman started the conversation by inquiring his name, saying, "What is your name?" Deva said, "Deva." The heretic said, "Who is Deva?" Deva said, "I am." The heretic said, "Who is I?" Deva said, "A dog." The heretic said, "Who is the dog?" Deva said, "You." The heretic said, "Who are you?" Deva said, "Deva." The heretic said, "Who is Deva?" "I am." The heretic said, "Who is I?" Deva said, "A dog." The heretic said, "Who is the dog?" Deva said, "You." The heretic said, "Who are you?" Deva said, "Deva." In this manner they argued in a circle, and then the heretic began to understand [that Deva was irrefutable]. Since then he deeply respected Deva's moralizing edification.

In the city there is a deva-temple consisting of many lofty and beautifully decorated buildings, which showed spiritual signs in various ways. According to the records of the temple, this is the best place for people to plant meritorious seeds. The merit of donating one coin at this temple is greater than that of giving one thousand pieces of gold in alms at other places, and one who kills oneself and dies in this temple can enjoy eternal bliss in the heavens. In front of the temple there is a big tree with luxuriant branches and leaves that cast a dark shadow on the ground. A man-eating ghost made his abode on the tree, and so skeletons were scattered at its left and right sides. People coming to this temple are liable to give up their lives, as they are both frightened by the horrible tradition and allured by the evil spirits. This absurd practice has been carried out without alteration from ancient times up to the present.

Recently there was a young man of the Brahman caste who was intelligent and magnanimous in character and endowed with brilliant wisdom and high talent. He came to the temple and said to the people, "Crooked customs and corrupt desires are hard to mend by dissuasion and guidance. I must practice the same in order to correct them." He climbed up the tree and said to his friends below it, "I am going to die to testify to the truth of what is deceitful. Heavenly maidens and musicians are in the air to greet me. I

shall forsake this humble body of mine at the best place for doing so." When he was about to throw himself down to end his life, his relatives and friends tried to dissuade him from doing so, but he would not change his mind. They spread their garments on the ground below the tree and saved his life when he dropped to the ground. After a long while, he came to his senses and said, "I only saw some evil spirits in the air beckoning to me, and there was
897c nothing of heavenly bliss."

To the east of the great city and at the junction of the two rivers, there is a dune more than ten *li* wide, dry and covered with fine sand. From ancient times up to now, the various kings and men of great wealth have always come here whenever they wished to give alms. This is called the Grand Place of Alms-giving, where gifts are distributed without counting.

At present, King Śīlāditya follows the example of his predecessors in practicing alms-giving. He spends all the wealth he has accumulated in five years on alms-giving in a single day and piles up precious things at the Place of Alms-giving. Once on the first day he installed a large image of the Buddha adorned with various gems, to which he offered the best rare jewels. Next he gave offerings to the resident monks, next to those who were present in the assembly, next to the highly talented, learned, erudite, and versatile scholars, next to the heretical students, hermits, and recluses, and next to the kinless and the poor. To all of them various kinds of precious objects and the best delicious food were distributed in a perfect manner according to grades and ranks. When the treasury was emptied and clothes and other objects were exhausted, the lustrous pearl in his topknot and the necklace on his body were given away one after the other without the least reluctance. When he had done the alms-giving, he said, "How happy I am! I have placed all I had in the adamantine and indestructible storehouse!" After that the lords and kings of various countries offered him precious jewels and garments, and in less than ten days, his treasury was replenished.

At the confluence of the two rivers to the east of the Grand Place of Alms-giving, several hundred people drown themselves every day. It is the custom of the people to believe that in order to be reborn in the heavens, they should starve and sink into the river at this spot. They take a bath at midstream to wash away their sins and defilements. Thus people of different countries come together to this place from distant regions to starve for seven days and die. Even mountain apes and wild monkeys come in groups to the riverside. Some of them take a bath and go back, and some starve themselves to death. When King Śīlāditya was performing the great alms-giving, a monkey stayed alone under a tree at the riverside and fasted without going anywhere. In a few days it died of starvation. Some heretical ascetics plant long poles in the river, and at dawn they climb up the poles and stand with one hand holding the top of the pole and one foot on a peg, while the other hand and foot stretch out in the air. With their necks craned out and eyes widely open, they gaze at the sun moving to the right and do not come down until dusk. There are several scores of such ascetics, who hope to get out of the wheel of rebirth by practicing such rigorous austerities, and some of them have never relaxed their self-mortification in several decades.

From here I entered a great forest in the southwest, where ferocious animals and wild elephants in groups attack wayfarers. Unless one goes with a large number of companions, it is difficult for a traveller to traverse this region alone. After going for more than five hundred *li*, I came to the country of Kauśāmbī (formerly known as Jushanmi erroneously, in the domain of Central India).

The country of Kauśāmbī is over six thousand *li* in circuit, and 898a
its capital city is more than thirty *li* in circuit. The land is fertile and good for agricultural production. The country abounds in non-glutinous rice and yields plenty of sugarcane. The climate is hot, and the people are bold and furious by custom. They love to learn classical texts and arts and advocate the performance of good and meritorious deeds. There are about ten monasteries lying in a dilapidated and deserted condition, with more than three hundred monks who study the Hinayana teachings. There are over fifty deva-temples with numerous heretics.

In the old palace in the city there is a great temple more than sixty feet in height that houses an image of the Buddha carved in sandalwood, with a stone canopy suspended over it. It was made by King Udayana (known as Chuai, or Release from passion and formerly mistranslated as King Youtian). It often shows spiritual signs and emits a divine light from time to time. The kings of various countries, relying upon their might, wished to lift it up, but they could not move it, although a large number of people were employed to do so. Then they had pictures of the image produced for worship, and each of them claimed that his picture was true to life. Speaking about the origin of the image, it is said that when the Tathāgata, after having realized full enlightenment, went up to the Trayastriṃśa Heaven to preach the Dharma to his mother, the king was eager to see him and wished to make a likeness of him. Then he requested the Venerable Maudgalyāyana to transport by supernatural power an artisan to the heavenly palace to observe the fine features of the Buddha, and the artisan carved an image of him in sandalwood. When the Tathāgata returned to earth from the heaven, the sandalwood image stood up to greet the World-honored One, who said to it sympathetically, "Are you tired from teaching the people? You are what we hope will enlighten the people at the last period of the Buddha-dharma."

More than a hundred paces to the east of the temple are sites where the four past Buddhas used to sit and walk up and down. Not far away are a well and bathhouse used by the Tathāgata. The well still supplies water, but the bathhouse has fallen into ruins. At the southeast corner inside the city are the ruins of the old residence of the Elder Ghoṣila (formerly transcribed as Jushiluo incorrectly), where stand a Buddhist temple and a stupa containing [the Buddha's] hair and nail relics. Another old foundation is that of the Buddha's bathhouse.

Not far to the southeast of the city is an old monastery built in the garden of the Elder Ghoṣila in which is a stupa more than two hundred feet high built by King Aśoka. The Tathāgata stayed here preaching the Dharma for several years. Beside it are sites where

the four past Buddhas used to sit and walk up and down. There are also stupas containing the Tathāgata's hair and nail relics. On the storied pavilion to the southeast of the monastery there is an old brick chamber in which Vasubandhu Bodhisattva stayed and composed the *Vijñapti-mātratā-siddhi-śāstra* to refute Hinayana teachings and defeat the heretics. In a mango grove to the east of the monastery is an old foundation of a house, in which Asaṅga 898b
Bodhisattva composed the *Prakaraṇāryavācā-śāstra*.

Eight or nine *li* to the southwest of the city is the cave of a venomous dragon. Formerly the Tathāgata subdued this dragon and left his own shadow in the cave. Although this is recorded in books, nothing more is to be seen now. Beside the cave is a stupa more than two hundred feet high built by King Aśoka. At its side are sites where the Tathāgata used to sit and walk up and down, and a stupa containing his hair and nail relics. Those who are suffering from illness come here to pray for health, and most of them are cured. As this will be the country where Śākyamuni's Dharma will finally come to an end, all people from the kings down to the common subjects naturally feel sad when they come into this land and shed tears before going back with sighs of regret.

Going for more than seven hundred *li* through a great forest to the northeast of the dragon's cave, I crossed the Ganges to the north and reached the city of Kāśapura. It is over ten *li* in circuit, and the inhabitants are rich and happy. Beside it there are the ruins of a monastery, in which Dharmapāla Bodhisattva subdued the heretics in the old days. A previous king of this country who supported heterodox views intended to destroy the Buddha-dharma so as to uphold the heretics. He invited from among them a Śāstra-master, who was intelligent, had great talent, and understood subtle theories, to compose a fallacious book of one thousand stanzas with thirty-two thousand words to denounce the Buddha-dharma and make his own sect the orthodox one. Then the king summoned the monks to hold a debate on the condition that should the heretical Śāstra-master win the contest, the Buddha-dharma would be destroyed, and if the monks were not defeated, the Śāstra-master would cut off his tongue.

At that time the monks, fearing that they might be defeated, assembled to discuss the matter, saying, "The Sun of Wisdom has sunk, and the Bridge of the Dharma is about to be destroyed. How can we rival the heretics who have the king standing by their side? Under such circumstances, what should we do?" The assembly remained silent, and nobody ventured to raise a proposal. Dharmapāla Bodhisattva, who was then at a youthful age, who was eloquent, intelligent, and learned, and who had a widespread reputation, declared in the assembly, "Although I am an ignorant person, I venture to make a brief statement. It would truly befit you to send me promptly to answer the king's order. If I win the debate, it will be due to spiritual protection, and if I fail, my youthful age can be blamed. In this way we can give an explanation in either case, and no censure will be incurred upon the Dharma or the community of monks." The whole assembly consented to his proposal, and according to his suggestion he was sent to answer the king's order.

He mounted the seat of discussion, and the heretic [Śāstra-master] recited his book in a rhythmic voice, brought out all the essentials of his work, and waited for a refutation. Dharmapāla, listened to his recitation and said with a smile, "I have won. Shall I recite your book backwards, or shall I recite it with the phrases transposed in order?" The heretic was dismayed and said, "You should not be self-important. One who can fully understand the
898c meanings of my book is the winner. First recite it in its proper sequence and then give an explanation of the text." Dharmapāla then imitated his rhythmic voice, recited the text, and expounded the meanings of its contents, with no fault either in phraseology or in principles, nor was there any deviation in the intonation. After hearing this, the heretic was ready to cut off his tongue. Dharmapāla said to him, "Cutting off your tongue is not a way to amend yourself. Real repentance is to correct your [wrongly] grasped opinions." He preached the Dharma to the heretic, who began to have faith in it and understand its meanings. The king gave up the erroneous way and embraced the Dharma in adoration.

Beside the place where Dharmapāla subdued the heretic there is a stupa built by King Aśoka. Though the foundations have sunk, it is still more than two hundred feet high. Formerly the Tathāgata preached the Dharma for six months at this place. Beside it are a site where [he] walked up and down and a stupa containing his hair and nail relics. Going northward from here for one hundred seventy or eighty *li*, I reached the country of Viṣaka (in the domain of Central India).

The country of Viṣaka is more than four thousand *li* in circuit, and its capital city is sixteen *li* in circuit. It abounds in cereal crops and yields plenty of flowers and fruits. The climate is moderate, and the people are sincere and honest by custom. They are fond of learning without feeling tired and never regress in performing good deeds. There are more than twenty monasteries with over three thousand monks, all of whom study the teachings of the Saṃmitīya sect of the Hinayana school. There are over fifty deva-temples with a great many heretics.

To the south of the city, there is a large monastery on the left side of the road in which the Arhat Devaśarman composed the *Vijñānakāya-śāstra* to advocate the theory of non-ego in the human body, while the Arhat Gopa wrote the *Treatise on the Essential Truth of the Holy Teachings (Sheng-jiao-yao-shi-lun)* to maintain the doctrine of the existence of the ego in the human body. These incompatible views about the Dharma caused much controversy. It was also in this monastery that Dharmapāla Bodhisattva subdued one hundred Hinayana Śāstra-masters in seven days. Beside the monastery there is a stupa more than two hundred feet high built by King Aśoka. Formerly the Tathāgata preached the Dharma for six years at this place to edify the people. There is a marvellous tree, about six or seven feet tall, which neither sprouts in the spring nor withers in the autumn season. Formerly the Tathāgata cast down a tooth twig he had used for cleaning his teeth, and it took root and grew into the luxuriant tree it is now. People holding heterodox views and heretics have tried to cut it down, but it grows as usual. Not far away from the tree there are sites where the four past Buddhas used to sit and walk up and down, and there is also a stupa containing the Tathāgata's hair and nail relics. The foundations of the holy sites are connected with one another in a wood with ponds, in which the shadows of the trees are reflected. Going from here to the northeast for over five hundred *li*, I reached the country of Śrāvastī (formerly known as Shewei erroneously, in the domain of Central India).

End of Fascicle Five

Fascicle VI

Four Countries, From Śrāvastī to Kuśinagara

1. The Country of Śrāvastī
2. The Country of Kapilavastu
3. The Country of Rāma[grāma]
4. The Country of Kuśinagara

The country of Śrāvastī is over six thousand *li* in circuit. Its capital 899a
city is in desolation, and there is nothing to mark its boundaries. The old foundations of the palace city are more than twenty *li* in circuit. Although it is mostly in ruins, it is still inhabited. It abounds in cereal crops, and the climate is temperate. The people are sincere and honest by custom and are diligent in study and like to perform meritorious deeds. There are several hundred monasteries, most of which are dilapidated, with few monks who are followers of the Saṃmitīya school. Deva-temples amount to a hundred, and they have many heretics. This was the capital of the country ruled by King Prasenajit (known as Shengjun, or Victorious army, and formerly called Bosini erroneously in abbreviation) when the Tathāgata was living in the world. The old foundations in the palace city are the remnant bases of King Prasenajit's palace. Not far to the east, there is another old foundation, on which a small stupa has been built to mark the site of the Great Dharma Hall constructed by King Prasenajit for the Tathāgata in olden times. Not far from the Dharma Hall a stupa was built on the old foundations of the temple of the Buddha's maternal aunt, Bhikṣuṇī Prajāpatī (known as Shengzhu, or Protectress of creatures, and formerly mistranscribed as Boshe-boti), constructed for her by King Prasenajit. Next to the east, a stupa marks the site of the old residence of Sudatta (known as Shanshi, or Good alms-giver, and formerly mistranscribed as Xuda).

Beside the residence of Sudatta, there is a great stupa built at the spot where Aṅgulimāla (known as Zhiman, or Chaplet of finger bones, and formerly mistranscribed as Yangjuemoluo) gave up his evil practice. Aṅgulimāla was a wicked man of Śrāvastī who did harm to living beings and committed atrocities in the city and country. He murdered people to collect their finger bones to make a chaplet. When he attempted to kill his mother to get her finger bone to make up the number of bones required for the chaplet, the World-honored One with a mind of compassion was making a tour of edification. Upon seeing the World-honored One at a distance, Aṅgulimāla was glad in his mind, saying, "I am sure to be reborn in the heavens, as my late teacher has taught me that one who hurts the Buddha and kills one's own mother will be reborn in the Brahmā Heaven." Then he said to his mother, "Old lady, you may stay here for a while. I shall go to kill that great Śramaṇa first." Saying so, he held a sword and went to meet the World-honored One. The Tathāgata retreated slowly, but the wicked Aṅgulimāla could not catch up, though he walked very fast. The World-honored
899b One said to him, "Why do you stick to your ignoble ideas? You have abandoned the root of goodness and aroused the source of wickedness." Upon hearing this admonition, Aṅgulimāla became aware that his behavior was wrong. Hence he took refuge [in the Buddha] and sought to learn the Dharma. As he studied diligently, he attained Arhatship.

Five or six *li* to the south of the city is the Jetavana (known as Shenglin, or Victor's wood, and formerly mistranscribed as Qituo), which was the garden of Anāthapiṇḍika, where King Prasenajit's minister Sudatta constructed a temple for the Buddha. In the old days it was a monastery, but now it lies in ruins. There are two stone pillars over seventy feet high, one at each side of the east gate. On the top of the left pillar there is carved the wheel sign, and a figure of a bull is engraved on the top of the right one. Both pillars were erected by King Aśoka. The buildings are dilapidated, having only the remains of old foundations, with the exception of a brick chamber standing there in lonely solitude. In the chamber there is an image of the Buddha. After the Tathāgata preached the Dharma for his mother in the Trāyastriṃśa Heaven, King Prasenajit made this image upon hearing that King Udayana had carved an image of the Buddha in sandalwood.

The Elder Sudatta was a kind and intelligent man who knew how to accumulate wealth and how to spend money in helping the poor and needy and in giving alms to kinless and aged people. In praise of his virtue, the people of his time called him Anāthapiṇḍika (Giver of alms to the poor and helpless). Upon hearing about the Buddha's virtues, he cherished a deep adoration for him and wished to build a temple to which to invite the Buddha. The World-honored One sent Śāriputra to go [with Sudatta] to make a survey of the location, and they found that only Prince Jeta's garden was a suitable high and dry site. They went to see the prince and told him their intention. The prince said in jest, "I shall sell my garden for as many pieces of gold as it takes fully to cover the ground!"

Upon hearing this, Sudatta was exhilarated, and he took out gold coins from his treasury to pave the ground of the garden as suggested. When only a small portion of the land was uncovered, the prince begged to retain it for himself, saying, "The Buddha is really like a plot of good land, and I also should sow good seeds in it." Thus he built a temple on the uncovered portion of the ground. Then the World-honored One went there and said to Ānanda, "As the ground of the garden has been purchased by Sudatta and the trees have been given by Prince Jeta, the two of them having the same purpose in mind, their merits should be esteemed alike, and henceforward this place should be called the Garden of Jetavana-Anāthapiṇḍika."

To the northeast of the Garden of Anāthapiṇḍika is a stupa at the place where the Tathāgata once bathed a sick *bhikṣu*. When the Tathāgata was living in the world, a sick *bhikṣu* suffering from pain lived alone in solitude. Upon seeing him, the World-honored One asked him, "What is your malady and why are you living alone?" The *bhikṣu* said in reply, "I am indolent by nature and cannot endure medical treatment. That is why I am sick and without anyone

to attend me." With a mind of pity, the Tathāgata said to him, "Good man, now I am here to attend you." Saying so, he stroked the sick *bhikṣu* with his hand, and he thus completely cured him and helped him go out of the door; he changed his bedding, bathed him, and dressed him in new clothes. The Buddha said to the *bhikṣu*, "You should always be diligent and exert yourself." Upon
899c hearing this instruction, the *bhikṣu* felt grateful and was happy in mind and comfortable in body.

To the northwest of the Garden of Anāthapiṇḍika is a small stupa at the place where Maudgalyāyana could not lift by his supernatural powers the belt of Śāriputra's robe. Once the Buddha was at the Anavatapta Lake with a congregation of men and heavenly beings. Śāriputra alone was absent from the meeting, and the Buddha asked Maudgalyāyana to summon him to the congregation. When Maudgalyāyana came by the order of the Buddha to the place of Śāriputra, the latter was mending his clerical robe. Maudgalyāyana said to him, "The World-honored One is now at the Anavatapta Lake and has ordered me to summon you." Śāriputra said, "Wait a moment. When I have finished mending my robe, I shall go with you." Maudgalyāyana said, "If you do not go with me immediately, I shall exercise my supernatural powers to carry you and your rock chamber to the congregation!" Śāriputra then untied his belt and put it on the ground, saying, "If you can pick up my belt, I shall start with you." Maudgalyāyana exercised his great supernatural powers, but he could not pick the belt up, even though his strength caused an earthquake. Then he returned to the Buddha through the air by the power of his magic feet and found that Śāriputra was already seated in the congregation. Maudgalyāyana remarked with a sigh, "Now I have realized that the power of divine capabilities is inferior to that of transcendental wisdom."

Not far from the stupa of belt-lifting is a well from which water was drawn for the use of the Tathāgata when he was living in the world. Beside it is another stupa built by King Aśoka, in which are preserved the relics of the Tathāgata. At the sites where he walked up and down and preached the Dharma, indicative emblems were raised and stupas constructed. All these places are protected by deities, who occasionally show spiritual manifestations in the form of celestial music or divine fragrance. Other auspicious signs of great blessedness are difficult for me to relate in detail.

Not far behind the monastery is the place where some young Brahmanic students killed a prostitute to slander the Buddha. The Tathāgata was in possession of the Ten Powers as well as fearlessness and omniscient wisdom and was honored by men and heavenly beings and respected by saints and sages. The heretics discussed the matter together, saying, "We should contrive a crafty scheme to slander and insult him in public." Then they hired a prostitute to pretend to be a hearer of the Dharma. When she became known as such to all, the heretics killed her in secret, buried the corpse beside a tree, and appealed to the king for redress. The king ordered an investigation and discovered the corpse in the Jetavana Garden. The heretics exclaimed, "The great Śramaṇa Gautama often preached disciplinary rules and endurance. But now he has had illicit intercourse with this woman and killed her in order to shut up her mouth. He has violated the rules against unchastity and murder. What disciplinary rules and endurance has he practiced?" At that moment, heavenly beings in the air cried out, "The wicked heretics are merely making up a slander!"

More than a hundred paces to the east of the monastery, there is a large and deep pit, which was the place where Devadatta, who
intended to poison the Buddha, fell into hell alive. Devadatta (known 900a
as Tianshou, or Given by heaven) was the son of King Droṇodana. Through twelve years' study with zealous perseverance, he mastered all the eighty thousand Dharma-piṭakas. Afterward he sought to learn supernatural powers for the sake of gaining material advantage, and he associated with evil friends, to whom he said in a discussion, "I have as many as thirty physical marks of a great man, almost as many as the Buddha [who had thirty-two], and I also have a great following surrounding me. What is the difference between me and the Tathāgata?" With this thought in mind, he caused a schism in the community of monks. By order of the Buddha

and with the aid of his spiritual power, Śāriputra and Maudgalyāyana preached the Dharma and exhorted those monks who had gone astray to return to harmony in the community of monks. But Devadatta did not relinquish his evil mind and put poison in his fingernails, intending to injure the Buddha at the time of paying homage to him. To carry out his plot, he came from a great distance, and when he reached this spot the earth cracked and he fell into hell alive.

To the south of this pit, there is another one, which was the place where Bhikṣu Kokālika fell into hell alive, because he slandered the Buddha.

More than eight hundred paces to the south of the pit of Kokālika, there is another large and deep pit, which was the place where the Brahman woman Ciñcā fell into hell alive because she slandered the Buddha. Once the Buddha was preaching the essentials of the Dharma to men and heavenly beings, when a [woman] disciple of a heretical religion saw him at a distance in an assembly of respectful people. [The woman] thought, "Today I must insult Gautama to spoil his fame, so as to let my teacher alone enjoy a high reputation." Then she hid a wooden basin inside her clothes and came to the Anāthapiṇḍika Garden, where she declared aloud in the assembly, "This preacher had illicit intercourse with me, and the child in my womb is a Śākya!" The heretics believed in her words, but the staunch followers of the Buddha knew that she was committing slander. At that moment Indra, wishing to clear up the doubts, transformed himself into a white rat and gnawed through the cord that bound the basin, which dropped down with a thud and startled the assembly. All those who witnessed this event were greatly delighted, and a man in the assembly picked up the wooden basin and showed it to the woman, saying, "Is this your child?" At that time the earth cracked and the woman fell alive into the hell of uninterrupted pains to suffer retribution.

All these three pits are bottomless, and during the autumn and summer seasons, when torrential rains inundate the ditches and pools, water never collects in these pits.

Sixty or seventy paces to the east of the monastery is a temple over sixty feet high, in which there is an image of the Buddha sitting with its face toward the east. The Tathāgata once held a discussion with the heretics at this place. Further to the east is a deva-temple, which is of the same size as the Buddhist temple. At sunrise the shadow of the deva-temple does not fall on the Buddhist temple, but at sunset the shadow of the Buddhist temple covers the deva-temple.

Three or four *li* to the east of the overshadowing temple is a 900b
stupa built at the place where the Venerable Śāriputra had a discussion with the heretics. When the Elder Sudatta first purchased Prince Jeta's garden with the intention of building a temple for the Tathāgata, the Venerable Śāriputra went together with the Elder to make a survey of the plot, and the teachers of the six heretical schools challenged him to a contest in demonstrating supernatural powers. Acting according to circumstances in carrying out edification, Śāriputra subdued the heretics in conformity with their propensities. In front of the temple and beside the [Śāriputra] stupa, there is another stupa built at the spot where the Tathāgata defeated various heretics [in debate] and also accepted the invitation of Mother Viśākhā.

To the south of the stupa of accepting the invitation is the place where King Virūḍhaka (formerly known as the Lord of Piliuli erroneously), on his way to invade the Śākyas, saw the Buddha and turned back with his army. After ascending the throne, King Virūḍhaka raised an army and mobilized his people to avenge a former insult. When his troops were deployed, he ordered them to march. A *bhikṣu* got wind of this and informed the Buddha about it. The World-honored One then went to sit under a withered tree. When King Virūḍhaka saw the World-honored One at a distance, he dismounted to worship him and stood aside, saying, "Why do you not sit under a tree with luxuriant branches and rich foliage but stay under this tree with dead branches and withered sprouts?" The World-honored One said in reply, "My clansmen are branches and leaves to me. Now that they are in danger, where can I get any more shelter?" The king remarked, "The World-honored One is speaking for his clansmen. I should go back." He looked at the Buddha, and moved by his compassion he called his army back home.

Near the place of withdrawing troops is a stupa marking the spot where the Śākyan maidens were slaughtered. When King Virūḍhaka won the battle against the Śākyas, he selected five hundred Śākyan maidens for his harem. The Śākyan maidens were so indignant that they uttered words of resentment and insolently abused the king as the son of a slave. When the king heard about it, he was enraged and ordered the slaughter of the Śākyan maidens. By order of the king, the executioners mutilated their hands and feet and threw them into a pit. The Śākyan maidens, suffering from bitter pain, called on the Buddha. The World-honored One saw the sad plight of the maidens with his eye of discernment, and while ordering a *bhikṣu* to send some clothes to the maidens, he went to preach the wonderful Dharma to them, namely, the bondage of the five desires, the three ways of transmigration, and the long and distant course of rebirth with the pain of separation from one's beloved. Upon hearing the Buddha's teachings, the Śākyan maidens got rid of defilements and gained the Pure Eye of the Dharma. They all died at the same time and were reborn in heaven. Indra appeared as a Brahman and had their bodies collected and cremated. People of later times put this event down in record.

Not far from the stupa of the slaughter of the Śākyan maidens is
900c a big dried-up pool where King Virūḍhaka fell into hell. After visiting the Śākyan maidens, the World-honored One returned to the Anāthapiṇḍika Garden and told the *bhikṣu*s, "Now King Virūḍhaka will be burned to death after seven days." Upon hearing the Buddha's prediction, the king was very much frightened. [But] on the seventh day the king was as happy as ever and had no [feeling of] danger. To celebrate he ordered the ladies of his harem to go with him to the riverside for merry-making. As he still feared that a fire might occur, he sailed in a boat and drifted with the waves of the river. But a blazing fire suddenly broke out and burned the light boat; the king was thrown alive into the hell of uninterrupted torture.

Going three or four *li* to the northwest of the monastery, I reached the Wood of Regaining Eyes. There are sites where the Tathāgata walked up and down and various saints practiced meditation, and stupas were built to mark the places.

Once there was a band of five hundred brigands in this country, who ran amok in the villages and plundered the cities. King Prasenajit arrested them, extracted their eyes, and threw them into a great forest. Under the painful torture of this punishment, the bandits sorrowfully called on the Buddha. The Tathāgata was at the Jetavana Temple and heard their pitiful voices and had compassion on them. A cooling breeze blew mildly and wafted some medicine down from the Snow Mountains, which filled their eyes, and they recovered their eyesight. On seeing the World-honored One standing before them, they cherished the mind of Bodhi (enlightenment), worshipped him with happiness, and departed after throwing down their staves, which then took root on the ground.

More than sixty *li* to the northwest of the great city is an ancient city that was the birthplace of Kāśyapa Buddha, who was born at the time when human life was twenty thousand years long in the Bhadrakalpa (the period of virtue). To the south of the city is a stupa marking the spot where he first met his father after having realized full enlightenment. The stupa to the north of the city contains the whole body of Kāśyapa Buddha, and all these stupas were erected by King Aśoka. Going from here to the southeast for over five hundred *li*, I reached the country of Kapilavastu (formerly mistranscribed as Jialuowei, in the domain of Central India).

The country of Kapilavastu is more than four thousand *li* in circuit, and there are two palace cities, which are wholly deserted. The wall of the royal city is dilapidated, and its circumference is unknown. The inner palace city is fourteen or fifteen *li* in circuit, and its wall is built of bricks; the foundation is thick and strong. The country has been deserted for a long time and has a sparse population. There is no grand ruler, and each city has its own lord. The soil is rich, and crops are sown and reaped in season. The climate is never abnormal, and the people are genial by custom. There are more than one thousand ruined foundations of old monasteries, and beside the palace city there is a monastery inhabited by over three thousand monks, who study the Hinayana teachings of the Saṃmitīya school. There are two deva-temples, with heretics living together.

901a Inside the palace city there is the old foundation of the main audience hall of King Śuddhodana. A statue of the king is placed in a shrine built on the old foundation. Not far from it is the old foundation of Lady Mahāmāyā's bedchamber. In a shrine built on the old foundation is kept a statue of the lady. Beside it is another shrine, marking the place where Śākya Bodhisattva's spirit descended to become incarnate in his mother's womb, and in this shrine is a likeness depicting the Bodhisattva's spirit [entering his mother's womb]. According to the tradition of the Sthavira sect, the Bodhisattva's spirit entered his mother's womb on the night of the thirtieth day of the month of Uttarā-Āṣāḍhā, corresponding to the fifteenth day of the fifth month in our country, while the tradition of the other sects holds that it took place on the night of the twenty-third day of that month, corresponding to the eighth day of the fifth month in our land.

To the northeast of the place of the descent of the Bodhisattva's spirit, there is a stupa marking the place where the *ṛṣi* Asita read the prince's physiognomy. On the day when the Bodhisattva was born, many lucky and auspicious signs appeared simultaneously. King Śuddhodana summoned various physiognomists and said to them, "Now a son is born to me. What is his future, good or evil? You should tell me straight in plain words." They said, "According to the records of ancient sages and the appearance of good signs, the prince will be a universal monarch if he remains at home, and if he renounces his home he will become a fully enlightened person." At that time the *ṛṣi* Asita came from a distance and knocked at the door, asking for an audience. The king, greatly delighted, greeted the *ṛṣi* and paid him due salutation. He invited the *ṛṣi* to sit on a precious seat and said to him, "I did not expect that you,

Great Ṛṣi, would condescend to favor me with your presence today." The *ṛṣi* said, "When I was sitting at ease in the heavenly palace, I suddenly saw the heavenly beings dancing for joy. I asked them why they were so much exhilarated. They said, 'We should inform you, Great Ṛṣi, that the first lady of King Śuddhodana of the Śākya clan in Jambudvīpa has given birth to a son today, who will attain perfect enlightenment and omniscient wisdom.' Because I have heard this information, I have come to see him. But I am sorry that I am getting old, and I shall not be able to hear his holy teachings."

At the south gate of the city there is a stupa marking the place where the prince wrestled with other Śākyas in a contest and threw an elephant [over the city moat]. Being a versatile youth, the prince was peerless and had no rival. When King Śuddhodana was on his way back home in a cheerful mood, his mahout drove an elephant out of the city to greet him. Devadatta, who always boasted of his strength, was coming into the city and asked the mahout, "You have caparisoned the elephant nicely; who is going to ride on it?" The mahout said, "As the prince is coming home, I am going out to serve him." Devadatta, being irritated by these words, drew up to the elephant, struck its forehead, and kicked its abdomen. The animal fell to the ground and obstructed the road, becoming a hindrance in the way, but nobody could remove it. Later, Nanda came and inquired, "Who killed this elephant?" "Devadatta," was the reply. Then he pulled the dead elephant aside to a corner of the road. When the prince arrived, he also asked, "Who is so wicked as
to have killed this elephant?" "It was Devadatta who killed this 901b
elephant to blockade the city gate, and Nanda pulled it aside to open the way." The prince then lifted up the dead elephant and flung it across the moat. When the corpse of the elephant fell to the ground, it made a great pit, and this is called by tradition the Pit of the Falling Elephant. In the shrine beside the pit is a statue of the prince. Another shrine beside it marks the site of the bedchamber of the prince's consort, where statues of Yaśodharā and Rāhula are kept. In the shrine beside the palace is a statue [of the prince] in the posture of learning; this was the old site of the prince's schoolroom.

At the southeast corner of the city there is a shrine in which is a picture of the prince riding on a white horse galloping in the air. This is the place where he went out over the city wall. Outside the four gates of the city, there are four shrines, separately keeping the statues of an aged man, a sick man, a dead man, and a Śramaṇa. These were the places where the prince witnessed on a pleasure trip the sorrowful sights by which he was moved to disgust at worldly life, at which awakening he ordered the driver to turn his carriage back and head for home.

Going southward for more than fifty *li* from the city, I reached an old city with a stupa. This was the natal city of Krakucchanda Buddha at the time of the Bhadrakalpa when human life was sixty thousand years long. Not far to the south is a stupa marking the place where this Buddha met his father after attaining full enlightenment. Inside the stupa at the southeast of the city the remains of that Tathāgata are contained, and in front of the stupa is a stone pillar over thirty feet high with the carving of a lion on its top; the events of his Nirvana are inscribed on its sides. This pillar was erected by King Aśoka.

Going northeast for more than thirty *li* from the city of Krakucchanda Buddha, I reached a great ancient city with a stupa. This was the natal city of Kanakamuni Buddha at the time of the Bhadrakalpa when human life was forty thousand years long. Not far to the northeast is a stupa marking the place where this Buddha converted his father after attaining full enlightenment. Further to the north is a stupa containing the remains of that Tathāgata. In front of the stupa is a stone pillar over twenty feet high with the carving of a lion on its top; the events of his Nirvana are inscribed on its sides. This pillar was erected by King Aśoka.

More than forty *li* to the northeast of the city is a stupa that marks the spot where the prince [Siddhārtha] once sat under the shade of a tree, watching farmers plowing the land, and practiced meditation, by which he became free of passions. King Śuddhodana saw the prince sitting in meditation under the shade of a tree, and that the shadow of the tree did not move, though the sunlight had changed the direction of its shining. Reminded that the prince was a saintly person, the king treasured and respected him all the more.

In the northwest of the city, there are hundreds and thousands of stupas built at the place where the Śākyas were slaughtered. After overcoming the Śākyas, King Virūḍhaka captured ninety-nine million nine hundred thousand Śākyan people and had them all massacred. The corpses were piled up like haystacks and blood flowed into a pool. Amid the panic of heavenly beings and the ter- 901c
ror in human minds, the corpses were collected and buried.

To the southwest of the place where the Śākyas were slaughtered, there are four small stupas built at the spots where four Śākyas resisted the [invading] army. At first when King Prasenajit succeeded to the throne, he sought a matrimonial alliance with the Śākyan clan. The Śākyas despised him as a man not of the same caste, and they deceitfully gave him a slave girl to be his bride with pompous ceremony. King Prasenajit made this girl his chief queen, and the son she bore was King Virūḍhaka. Virūḍhaka wished to pursue his studies under the guidance of his maternal uncle. When he came to the south of the city, he saw a new lecture hall and went in to take a rest. Upon hearing this, the Śākyas chased him out with abuse. "How dare you, son of a slave woman, stay in this hall?" It was built by the Śākyas for the use of the Buddha. After his accession to the throne, Virūḍhaka made up his mind to avenge the previous insult and stationed an army at this place. Four Śākyan men, who were plowing the land, offered resistance and dispersed the invading army. Then the four of them entered the city, but their clansmen thought that they, being descendants of a universal monarch and the offspring of a Dharmarāja, should not have dared to commit violence and so complacently kill others. As they had blemished the good name of the clan, they were expelled from the clan and banished far away. The four men were exiled to the Snow Mountains in the north, where one of them became the King of Udyāna, one the King of Bāmīyāna, one the King of Himatala, and one the King of Shangmi. They handed down their dominions to their descendants from generation to generation without interruption.

Three or four *li* to the south of the city, in a banyan wood, is a stupa built by King Aśoka. This was the place where the Śākya Tathāgata, on his way back home after having gained full enlightenment, saw his father and preached the Dharma for him. Knowing that the Tathāgata had subdued the army of Māra, the Evil One, and was travelling around to edify the people, King Śuddhodana was eager to see him and pay homage to him. So he dispatched a messenger to invite the Tathāgata with the words: "Formerly you promised to return to your native country after becoming a Buddha. Your words are still ringing in my ears, and it is time now for you to turn your steps toward home." The messenger came to the presence of the Buddha and informed him of the king's words. The Tathāgata told him, "After seven days I shall return to my natal country." The messenger returned and reported this message to the king. So King Śuddhodana ordered his ministers and people to sprinkle water and sweep the roads and streets and prepare flowers and incense ready for use. Together with his ministers, he went out to a distance of forty *li* to wait for his arrival.

At that time the Tathāgata and his retinue of disciples, protected by the eight Diamond Guardians, with the four Heavenly Kings as vanguards, with Indra and the celestial beings of the Kāmadhātu (the realm of sensual desires) attending on his left and Brahmā and the celestial beings of the Rūpadhātu (the realm of pure form) attending on his right, and with all the *bhikṣus* following behind, walked in the air to his natal country. In the assembly the Buddha was like the moon among the stars; his austerity moved all the three spheres of the world, and his radiance surpassed
902a the light of the seven luminaries. When the king and his ministers had worshipped the Buddha, they returned together to the capital city, and the Buddha stayed at the Banyan Monastery.

Not far from the monastery is a stupa marking the place where the Tathāgata once sat facing the east under a big tree and accepted the gift of a robe sewn with golden thread offered by his aunt. The next stupa was built at the place where the Tathāgata converted eight princes and five hundred Śākyan clansmen.

Inside the east gate of the city, on the left side of the road, is a stupa at the place where Prince Siddhārtha practiced various skills and attainments. Outside the gate is an Īśvara deva-temple, in which is enshrined a stone image of Īśvara in the posture of trying to stand up. This was the temple that the prince entered when he was in his swaddling clothes. When King Śuddhodana brought the prince home from Lumbinī, he passed by this temple on the way and said, "This deva-temple often manifests spiritual responses and is sure to answer the prayers of Śākyan children. The prince should be sent in to worship the deva." Then the nurse brought the prince into the temple, but the stone image of the deva stood up to greet him, and when the prince left the deva image resumed its seat.

Outside the south gate of the city, on the left side of the road is a stupa at the place where the prince competed with other Śākyas in the arts of war, and shot at iron drums. At a distance of more than thirty *li* away to the southeast from here is a small stupa, beside which is a spring with a flow of clear water. When the prince was competing with other Śākyas in the skill of archery he drew his bow, and as the arrow left the string it struck through the surface of the drums and reached the ground with its feathers fully sinking into the earth; a spring of pure water was thus formed. By tradition it is called the Arrow Spring. When people are sick they drink the water or bathe in it, and in most cases they are cured. People from distant places bring home the clay of the spring and make it into a paste to apply it on the forehead whenever they have any ailment. As the clay is protected by spirits and deities, it has a healing effect in most cases.

Going northeast from the Arrow Spring for eighty or ninety *li*, I reached the Lumbinī Wood, where there is a bathing pool full of transparent water, with flowers of different descriptions spreading all over the place. Twenty-four or twenty-five paces to the north of the pool is an *aśoka* tree, which is now withered; this was the place where the Bodhisattva was born into the world. The Bodhisattva was born on the eighth day of the second half of the month of Vaiśākha, corresponding to the eighth day of the third month in

our calendar, but the Sthavira sect holds that it was on the fifteenth day of the second half of the month of Vaiśākha, corresponding to the fifteenth day of the third month in our calendar. Further east is a stupa built by King Aśoka at the place where two dragons bathed the [newborn] prince. When he had been born, the Bodhisattva walked seven steps unaided to each of the four quarters, while he announced, "In the heavens above and on the earth below, I am the sole Honored One! From now onwards I shall have no more rebirth." Under each step a big lotus flower sprang up from the earth. Two dragons appeared in the air, one emitting cool
902b water and the other one warm water to bathe him.

To the east of the stupa of bathing the prince are two lucid springs, beside which are two stupas built at the place where the two dragons emerged from the earth. After the Bodhisattva was born, his relatives and clansmen hurried up to get the water to wash themselves, and so, before the lady, two springs, one cold and one hot, gushed out water for them to take a bath. A stupa at the south marks the place where Indra received the Bodhisattva with both hands when the Bodhisattva was born. Indra knelt down to receive him in a piece of wondrous celestial cloth. Next are four stupas marking the place where the four Heavenly Kings carried the Bodhisattva. When the Bodhisattva was born from the right side of his mother, the four Heavenly Kings got hold of him with a piece of golden-colored fine cotton and placed him on a small gold table, which they carried into the presence of his mother, saying "It is truly a joyous event for celebration that Your Ladyship has given birth to such a blessed son. Even the heavenly beings are delighted, let alone the human beings of the earth."

Not far from the stupa where the four Heavenly Kings carried the prince, there used to be a great stone pillar erected by King Aśoka, with the figure of a horse on the top. Later, it was broken in the middle by a thunderbolt caused by an evil dragon, and half of it fell on the ground. Beside it is a rivulet flowing toward the east; it is called the Oil River by the local people. When Lady Mahāmāyā had given birth [to the prince], the heavenly beings produced a pool of lucent and pure water at this place for the lady to bathe herself, so as to wash off soil and dust. It has now become [a stream of] water, but it is greasy. From here going eastward for more than two hundred *li* through a wild jungle, I reached the country of Rāma (in the domain of Central India).

The country of Rāma has been deserted for many years, and it has no boundary marks. The towns and villages are in ruins and have a sparse population. On the southeast of the old capital city is a brick stupa less than one hundred feet high that was built by a former king of this country. When the Tathāgata had entered Nirvana, the king of this country obtained a portion of his relic bones, which he brought back to his own country; he built this stupa for paying homage to his share of the relics. It shows spiritual manifestations from time to time and often emits a divine light.

Beside the stupa is a clear pool from which a dragon often emerges in the shape of a snake to worship the stupa by circumambulating it from left to right. Wild elephants come in groups to pick flowers and scatter them on the stupa, and it has been under spiritual protection without intermission. When King Aśoka was constructing more stupas for the dissemination of the Buddha's relic bones, he opened up the stupas formerly built in seven countries to take out the relic bones [for redistribution]. When he came to this country and was about to start working [on the stupa of this country], the dragon of the pool, fearing that he might be deprived of the relics, appeared as a Brahman and halted the king's elephant, saying, "Your Majesty's goodwill extends to the Buddha-dharma, and you have widely cultivated the field of blessedness. I venture to invite you to deign to visit my abode." The king said, "Where is 902c
your home? Is it far away or nearby?" The Brahman said, "I am the dragon king of this pool. As Your Majesty wishes to perform superior deeds of blessedness, I have ventured to come and beg for an interview." At his invitation, the king entered the dragon's palace, and after sitting for a while the dragon said, "Due to my past evil deeds, I have been born in the shape of a dragon. I make offerings to the Buddha's relics in the hope that I may eliminate my

sins and faults. I wish you to come to see and worship the relics in person." Upon seeing the dragon's paraphernalia for worshipping the relics, the king was awed by the splendor of the articles, and he said, "These utensils for making offerings are not to be seen in the human world." The dragon said, "If that is so, I pray that you not demolish them." Thinking that he was not equal to the dragon in power, King Aśoka relinquished the idea of opening up the stupa. At the place where he came out of the pool there is a mound to mark the spot.

Not far from the stupa is a monastery with few monks. It is a quiet and clean place under the management of a *śrāmaṇera*. When monks come from distant places, they are well received with hospitality and are invited to stay for three days to receive offerings of the four monastic requisites. It is said by the local people that once a *bhikṣu* came with some fellow monks from a distant place to worship the stupa and saw a group of elephants bustling about weeding grass with their tusks and sprinkling water with their trunks, each of them holding different kinds of flowers to make offerings. At this sight the monks were deeply moved and sighed with pity. One of the *bhikṣu*s forsook his position as a fully ordained monk and wished to stay behind [as a *śrāmaṇera*] to attend the stupa. He made his farewells to the other monks, saying, "I am lucky to have become a member, though an incompetent one, of the community of monks. Through the passage of time, I have made no achievement in my spiritual practice. As this stupa contains the Buddha's relics, the elephants are inspired by his holy virtues to come to keep the place clean. I am willing to stay here to work in company with them. If I can spend the rest of my life here, I shall be very fortunate indeed." The other monks told him, "It is a good idea, and we are so ignorant as not to have thought of it. Please take care of yourself and do not fail in your superior deed."

Having parted from his companions, he repeated his sincere vow and lived alone happily with the intention of living in this manner to the end of his life. He built a thatched hut and channelled water to form a tank. He plucked seasonal flowers [as offerings] and kept the locality clean by sprinkling water and sweeping the ground for many years in succession without changing his mind. The kings of the neighboring countries heard about him [and felt] deep respect; they vied with one another in donating wealth and valuables for the construction of a monastery and invited the *śrāmaṇera* to be kind enough to supervise the monastic affairs. Since then the abbot of this monastery has always been a *śrāmaṇera* in memory of the original institution.

Going east from the Śrāmaṇera Monastery for more than one hundred *li* through a big forest, I reached a great stupa built by King Aśoka at the place where the prince halted after he had gone out over the city wall, taken off his precious garments, untied his 903a
necklace, and asked his servant to go back. The prince went over the city wall at midnight and reached here at daybreak, and having fulfilled his cherished desire he said to himself, "This is the place where I go out of prison, unfasten the fetters, and unyoke myself at last!" From his crown he removed the *maṇi* pearl and said to his servant, "Take this pearl and go home to inform my father the king that my present retirement to a distant place is not an inconsiderate departure from home; it is because I wish to cut off what is impermanent and abandon all that causes pain and distress." Chandaka (formerly called Cheli by mistake) said, "How can I have the mind to drive the empty carriage home?" The prince consoled the servant with good words, and the latter became awakened and returned home.

On the east of the stupa where the carriage was sent home, there is a *jambu* tree (*Eugenia jumbolana*), of which the branches and leaves have withered, but the decayed trunk is still there. Beside the tree is a small stupa that was the place where the prince changed his remaining precious garments for a deerskin robe. Although he had cut off his hair and changed his clothes, and had taken off his pearl necklace, he still had his royal robe with him. He said, "This robe is too luxurious; what shall I do for a change [of clothes]?" At that moment a heavenly being of Śuddhavāsa (the Heaven of Pure Abode) appeared as a hunter, wearing a deerskin robe, holding a bow and carrying some arrows. The prince, holding his robe, said to the hunter, "I wish to change this for yours. Will you kindly consent?" The hunter said, "Good." The prince then took off his upper garment and handed it to the hunter, who resumed his heavenly form and went away through the air with the garment he had bartered.

Not far away from the place where the prince changed his clothes is a stupa built by King Aśoka at the spot where the prince had his hair shaved off. The prince asked for a razor from Chandaka and cut off his own locks, which Indra received and brought to his heavenly palace for worship. At that time a celestial being of the Heaven of Pure Abode appeared as a barber, coming slowly with a razor in his hand. The prince asked him, "Can you shave my hair? Please tonsure my head for me." Accordingly the transformed figure shaved his head.

The time of the prince's leaving home by going over the city wall to become a monk is uncertain. Some say that it was when the Bodhisattva was nineteen, or as some others say, twenty-nine years old. And it is said that he renounced his home on the eighth day of the second half of the month of Vaiśākha, corresponding to the eighth day of the third month of our calendar; or that it was on the fifteenth day of the second half of the month of Vaiśākha, corresponding to the fifteenth day of the third month of our calendar.

From the stupa where the prince had his hair shaved, going northeast for one hundred eighty or ninety *li* through a wilderness, I reached a banyan grove in which there is a stupa over thirty feet high. When the Tathāgata entered Nirvana and his relics were distributed, the Brahmans who had not obtained a share of the relics collected the ashes and charcoal from the ground of the *niṣṭapana* (meaning "burning," and formerly known as "shewei" by mistake) and brought them home; they built this holy reliquary for worship. Since then it has manifested many a miracle and re-
903b sponded to most of the sick people who have prayed for recovery.

In the old monastery beside the ash and charcoal stupa there are sites where the four past Buddhas sat and walked up and down.

On both sides of the old monastery are several hundred stupas, among which a large one was built by King Aśoka. Although its lofty foundation has sunk, its height is still over one hundred feet.

From here going northeast, I proceeded through a great forest, in which the road was rough and dangerous with perilous obstacles all along the way. Mountain oxen, wild elephants, brigands, and hunters watched for travellers and did harm to them incessantly. Coming out of this forest, I reached the country of Kuśinagara (in the domain of Central India).

The city wall of the capital of the country of Kuśinagara is in ruins, and the towns and villages are deserted. The brick foundations of the city wall are more than ten *li* in circuit and there are very few inhabitants; the streets and lanes are in desolation. At the northeast corner of the original city is a stupa built by King Aśoka at the old residence of Cunda (formerly mistranscribed as Xuntuo). In the residence there is a well, which was dug at the time when a meal was prepared for the Buddha. Although the well has been there for many long years, the water is still clear and sweet.

At a place three or four *li* to the northwest of the city, I crossed the Ajitavatī River (meaning Unsurpassed, which is the name in common use and is mistaken for the Airāvatī River in olden times; in the texts it is known as Hiraṇyavatī River, meaning Possessing gold). Not far from the west bank of the river is the Śāla Grove. The *śāla* tree is similar to the oak with a greenish-white bark and very glossy leaves. Four of the trees in the grove are unusually tall, and this was the place where the Tathāgata entered Nirvana. In a large brick temple is a statue of the Tathāgata in the posture of entering Nirvana, lying down with his head toward the north. Beside the temple is a stupa built by King Aśoka. Although the foundation has sunk, it is still over two hundred feet high. In front of it is a stone pillar with a record of the event of the Tathāgata's Nirvana inscribed on it, but no date is mentioned in the record. It is said, however, in previous records that the Buddha entered Parinirvana (entire cessation of rebirth) at the age of eighty on the fifteenth day of the second half of the month of Vaiśākha, corresponding to the fifteenth day of the third month in our calendar. But according to the tradition of the Sarvāstivāda school, the Buddha entered Parinirvana on the eighth day of the second half of the month of Kārttika, corresponding to the eighth day of the ninth month in our calendar. The different schools hold variant views concerning the time elapsed after the Buddha's Nirvana, some saying it has been more than one thousand two hundred years, or one thousand three hundred, or one thousand five hundred, or exceeding nine hundred but less than one thousand.

Not far from the temple is a stupa marking the place where the Tathāgata put out a fire when he was born in a previous life as a pheasant in the course of cultivating the Bodhisattva deeds. For-
903c merly there was a great forest at this place, where the beasts and birds lived in caves and nests. One day a gale blew hard when a fire broke out and burned fiercely. Then a pheasant, having pity on the creatures, flapped its wings in a stream and flew up into the air to sprinkle water over the fire. At that moment Indra lowered his head and said to the pheasant, "Why are you so foolish as to work so hard with your wings to no avail? The great fire has just broken out and has set the whole forest ablaze. How can you put it out with the effort of your feeble body?" The pheasant said, "Who is it that is speaking to me?" Indra said, "I am Indra." The pheasant said, "If you are Indra, a being possessing great power of blessedness, you may achieve anything you wish. To relieve creatures from disaster and to rescue those who are in trouble are as easy for you as looking at the palm of your hand, but now you say that I am laboring without effect. Whoever is to be blamed? The fire is burning fiercely; I cannot talk with you any more!" The bird then flew vigorously to the stream to fetch water. Thus Indra scooped water with his hands and sprinkled it over the forest. The fire was then quenched, the smoke vanished, and the creatures were saved from the flames. Therefore it is called the stupa of fire fighting.

Not far from the place where the pheasant put out a fire is a stupa marking the spot where the Tathāgata saved creatures when he was born as a deer in the course of cultivating the Bodhisattva deeds. In the remote past there was a great forest at this locality. Once a conflagration spread in the wilderness, and the birds and beasts were confined in a dangerous plight, as there were the impediments of a rapid stream in front and a violent fire pressing hard at the back. Few of them were not drowned in the stream and escaped death. A deer, having pity on the creatures, strained itself to stretch across the stream in order to save others from drowning, in spite of the pain caused by its injured skin and broken bones, until the last one, a lame hare, had come and been rescued, while the deer endured fatigue and pains. Having exhausted itself, it fell into the stream and was drowned. The heavenly beings collected its carcass and built a stupa for it.

Not far to the west of the place where the deer rescued creatures from drowning is a stupa marking the spot where Subhadra (known as Shanxian, or Good sage, and formerly mistranscribed as Subatuoluo) entered Nirvana. Subhadra was originally a Brahmanic teacher, a wise man one hundred twenty years old. When he heard that the Buddha was about to enter Nirvana he came to the Twin Trees and asked Ānanda, "As the Buddha, the World-honored One, is about to enter Nirvana, may I ask him to solve the doubts I have in my mind?" Ānanda said, "The Buddha is about to enter Nirvana; please do not disturb him." [Subhadra] said, "I have heard that we seldom have a chance to be born at a time when a Buddha is living in the world, and that we cannot often hear the right Dharma. I am afraid I shall have nobody else to solve my deep doubts." Subhadra then came to the presence of the Buddha and first asked him, "There are different groups of self-styled teachers who have variant Dharmas to guide the world here below. Do you know them all, Gautama (formerly known as Qutan in an erroneous and abridged form)?" The Buddha said, "I have made a profound study of them all." And then he gave a description [of the different doctrines]. After having heard the Buddha's words, Subhadra purified his mind with faith and understanding and asked for permission to become a fully ordained Buddhist monk. The Tathāgata asked him, "Can you be a Buddhist monk? Those heterodox

disciples who wish to lead the life of purity have to go through probation for four years for the observation of their demeanor and character. If they are found to be quiet in behavior and honest in
904a speech, they can be admitted into my Order to lead a life of purity. But it all depends on one's effort, and there is no difficulty." Subhadra said, "World-honored One, you are so kind and sympathetic that you are impartial in saving living beings. Through four years' probation, one's three sorts of deeds (relating to body, speech, and mind) may be straightened into good order." The Buddha said, "As I have already said, it all depends on one's effort."

Subhadra then became a monk and received full ordination. He diligently cultivated himself for both mental and physical strength. A moment later he cleared his mind of doubts concerning the Dharma and tried to achieve personal realization. Shortly after dusk, he actually attained Arhatship with all passions extirpated and pure life established. As he could not bear seeing the Buddha entering Mahanirvana, he entered the *samādhi* (trance) of the element of fire and manifested supernatural powers before he entered Nirvana prior to the Buddha. He became the last disciple of the Tathāgata, but he died before him. He was the lame hare in a previous life that was the last to be rescued.

Beside the spot where Subhadra entered Nirvana there is a stupa at the place where Vajrapāṇi (Holder of the diamond club) fell into a swoon. The great sympathetic World-honored One, having completed his task of edifying the living beings according to their capacities and for their benefit, entered the blissful state of Nirvana at the Twin Trees, lying down with his head toward the north. The deity Vajrapāṇi, (alias) the warrior Guhyapati (Lord of the mysteries), having seen the Buddha entering Nirvana, cried sorrowfully, "The Tathāgata has forsaken me and entered Mahanirvana. I shall have nowhere to take refuge and no one to protect me. It is just as if a poisoned arrow had deeply struck me; and a fire of distress is fiercely burning me." He dropped his diamond club and fell into a swoon. After a long while he stood up and said to the others, "In the great sea of birth and death, who will be our boat and oars? In the long night of ignorance, who will be our lamp and torch?"

Beside the spot where Vajrapāṇi fell into a swoon, there is a stupa at the place where [the remains of] the Tathāgata were venerated for seven days after his Nirvana. When the Tathāgata was about to enter Nirvana, a bright light shone everywhere, and men and heavenly beings gathered together with grief. They said to one another, "The great enlightened World-honored One is now about to enter Nirvana. Living beings will come to the end of blessedness, and the world will have no one to depend upon." The Tathāgata, lying on his right side on a Lion Bed, told the gathering, "Do not say that the Tathāgata has eventually entered Nirvana, as the Dharma-body [of a Buddha] is immutable and free from all changes. You should ward off indolence and try to gain liberation at an early time." The *bhikṣus* and others sobbed sadly.

At that time Aniruddha (formerly mistranscribed as Anilü) told the *bhikṣus*, "Stop, stop! Grieve no more! The heavenly beings will reproach you and sneer at you!" When the Malla people had made offerings to the remains, they wished to carry the golden coffin to the burning ghat. Aniruddha said to them, "Wait a moment! The heavenly beings wish to keep it here for seven days for them to make offerings to it." Then the heavenly beings, holding exquisite celestial flowers, came through the air and chanted praise of the Buddha's holy virtues. Every one of them worked with utmost sincerity to make offerings [to the Buddha's remains].

Beside the place where the coffin was lodged, there is a stupa at the spot where Lady Mahāmāyā lamented over the death of the Buddha. When the Tathāgata had entered Nirvana and his re- 904b
mains had been laid in the coffin, Aniruddha ascended to the heaven to inform Lady Mahāmāyā, saying, "The great holy King of the Dharma has entered Nirvana." Upon hearing this news, Mahāmāyā was choked with sobs and fainted away. [When she had recovered her consciousness], she went with the heavenly beings to the Twin Trees, where she saw [the Buddha's] *saṃghāṭi* (double robe), alms bowl and pewter staff. She stroked these articles while weeping piteously until she fainted away, and when she regained her voice, she said, "Men and heavenly beings have come to the end of their blessedness, and the Eye of the World has disappeared.

Now these things are without an owner!" By the saintly power of the Tathāgata, the coffin opened itself. The Buddha emitted a bright light and sat up with his hands put palm to palm, and he consoled his compassionate mother for having come down from a far distance [to see him], saying, "Such is the law of all things. Please do not be overwhelmed by excessive grief." With a sorrowful mind, Ānanda asked the Buddha, "What shall I say if people in the future ask me about today's happening?" "You may say that after the Buddha's Nirvana, his compassionate mother came down from the heavenly palace to the Twin Trees. As a lesson to unfilial people, the Tathāgata sat up in the golden coffin and preached the Dharma [for his mother] with his hands joined palm to palm."

More than three hundred paces across the river at the north of the city, there was a stupa at the place where the Tathāgata's body was cremated. The earth is dark yellowish in color and the soil is mixed with ashes and charcoal. If one prays earnestly, one may obtain *śarīras* (relic bones) at this place. When the Tathāgata had entered Nirvana, men and heavenly beings, lamenting sorrowfully, made a coffin with the seven precious substances and enshrouded the body in one thousand layers of cotton cloth. Holding incense and flowers, as well as banners and canopies, the Mallas pulled the hearse in a procession, going at the front and following behind the coffin, to the north of the Gold River. With sufficient fragrant oil and sweet-scented wood, they prepared a pyre and set fire to it. Two layers of the shroud, the inmost one next to the body and the outmost one covering the outside, were not burned. When the people distributed the *śarīras*, they found that the hair and nails were neatly intact.

Beside the place of cremation is the spot where the Tathāgata showed his feet to Mahākāśyapa. When the Tathāgata's coffin had been laid down, and the pyre of fragrant wood had already been piled up, it could not be kindled, which astonished the assembly. Aniruddha said, "It is merely waiting for Kāśyapa." At that moment, Mahākāśyapa and his five hundred disciples came from the mountains to the city of Kuśinagara, and he asked Ānanda, "May

I have a look at the World-honored One?" Ānanda said, "His body is wrapped in one thousand layers of cotton cloth and laid in the double coffin, and fragrant wood has been piled up ready for the cremation." At that time, [the body of] the Tathāgata lying in the coffin stretched out its feet. When Kāśyapa noticed that the wheel sign on the soles of the Buddha's feet had a strange color, he asked Ānanda, "Why is it so?" [Ānanda] said, "At the moment when the Buddha entered Nirvana, men and heavenly beings wept piteously, and their tears dyed his soles this strange color." Then Kāśyapa paid homage to the coffin by walking round it and chanting praises [of the Buddha], and the fragrant wood spontaneously burst into great flames. Thus after his Nirvana the Tathāgata appeared thrice from his coffin. First, he stretched his arm to ask Ānanda to repair the road; second, he sat up to preach the Dharma for his mother; 904c
and last, he showed his feet to Mahākāśyapa.

Beside the spot where he showed his feet is a stupa built by King Aśoka at the place where the eight kings shared the relics. In front of the stupa there is a stone pillar on which [a description of] the event is inscribed. When the Buddha's body was cremated after his Nirvana, the kings of eight countries arrived with their four divisions of troops and dispatched the Straight-natured Brahman to tell the Mallas of Kuśinagara, "As the teacher of men and heavenly beings has entered Nirvana in this country, we have come here from afar to share his relics." The Mallas said, "As the Tathāgata was in our country when we were bereaved of the Guide of the World and lost the father of living beings, we should naturally keep the relics of the Tathāgata for worship. You will get nothing in spite of the weariness you have suffered in your journey." Since the kings' solicitation was not granted, they said again, "If you do not comply with our polite request, the application of force will be under consideration." The Straight-natured Brahman said in warning, "Just think it over! The great sympathetic World-honored One patiently cultivated blessedness and good deeds for numerous kalpas in the past. I think that all of you have heard this. It is inappropriate for you to fight against each other. Since the relics are in this country, they should be divided into eight equal portions, so that each of you can have a share for worship. What is the use of resorting to force?" The Mallas listened to his words, and when they were about to divide the relics into eight equal portions, Indra said to the kings, "The heavenly beings also have a right to share a portion of the relics. Do not compete for a share on the strength of your might." Then the Nāga kings Anavatapta, Mucilinda, and Elāpattra made a proposal, saying, "Do not forget about us. As far as strength is concerned, none of you is our rival!" The Straight-natured Brahman said, "Do not quarrel! We should share the relics together." Then the relics were divided into three portions, one portion for the heavenly beings, one for the Nāgas, and one for the human world, and the third portion was subdivided into eight parts allotted to the eight kings. The heavenly beings, Nāgas, and kings were all deeply moved.

Going southwest for more than two hundred *li* from the stupa of the division of relics, I reached a great town. There was a Brahman of enormous wealth, and being definitely different from other Brahmans, he was learned in the five *vidyās* (knowledges) and venerated the Triple Gem. Beside his residence he constructed a monastery, which was provided with all sorts of daily requisites and decorated with various kinds of jewels. When monks travelled by way of this monastery, he always earnestly invited them to stay in it to receive offerings for one night or up to seven days. Later, when King Śaśāṅka persecuted the Buddha-dharma, no company of monks came this way for many years, and the Brahman regretfully cherished the memory of them.

One day when he was taking a walk, he saw a Śrāmaṇa with heavy eyebrows and white hair, coming with a pewter staff in hand. He hurried up to greet the monk and inquired whence he came and whither he was going, and he invited him to the monastery to
905a receive various kinds of offerings. The following morning he offered the monk some gruel cooked in pure milk. As soon as the monk tasted the gruel, he put down the bowl and heaved a long sigh. The Brahman who was serving the monk with food knelt down

and said, "You grant benefit to the people according to circumstances and have come to favor me with your presence. Did you not sleep well last night? Or is the gruel unpalatable?" The monk said with regret, "I am sorry that the blessedness of living beings is on the decrease. Let us not talk about it now. I shall tell you something after the meal." When the breakfast was over, the monk tidied his robe and was ready to take leave. The Brahman said, "You promised that you would say something. Why do you not say it now?" The monk told him, "I did not forget about it, but it is not easy for me to say it. It might cause suspicion. If you insist on hearing it, I shall tell you in brief. I just sighed, but not because I disliked the gruel. For several hundred years I have not tasted such a flavor. When the Tathāgata was living in the world, I used to follow him as an attendant at the Jetavana temple in the city of Rājagṛha to wash his eating bowl in a pure stream. I also took baths and rinsed my mouth and washed my hands and head [in the stream]. What a pity that the pure milk of today is less tasty than the plain water of yore! This is because the blessedness of men and heavenly beings is on the decrease." The Brahman said, "In that case, great virtuous one, you must have seen the Buddha in person." The monk said, "Yes. Did you not hear about Rāhula, the son of the Buddha? I am Rāhula. In order to protect the right Dharma, I did not enter Nirvana." Having said so, the monk disappeared all of a sudden.

The Brahman then daubed the room in which the monk had spent the night with incense and swept it clean. An image of the monk was installed in the room in a solemn manner, and it was worshipped just as if the monk were there.

Going through a great forest for more than five hundred *li*, I reached the country of Bārāṇasī (formerly called the country of Boluonai by mistake, in the domain of Central India).

End of Fascicle Six

Fascicle VII

Five Countries, From Bārāṇasī to Nepāla

The country of Bārāṇasī is more than four thousand *li* in circuit, and the capital city, with the Ganges on the west, is eighteen or 905b
nineteen *li* long and five or six *li* broad. The houses in the lanes and streets of the city are close together, and it is densely populated. The inhabitants are enormously rich, and their houses are full of valuable goods. The people are mild and courteous in nature and esteem learning by custom. Most of them believe in heretical theories, and few people venerate the Buddha-dharma. The climate is temperate and the cereal crops are abundant. The fruit trees grow luxuriantly and the vegetation is rich. There are over thirty monasteries with more than three thousand monks, all of whom study the teachings of the Hinayanist Saṃmitīya school. There are more than one hundred deva-temples with over ten thousand heretical followers. Most of them worship Maheśvara, and some of them cut their hair while the others keep it in a topknot. They go naked without any dress and smear their bodies with ash. They are strenuous in practicing austerities, seeking freedom from birth and death.

Inside the great city there are twenty deva-temples, of which the sanctuaries are built with carved stone and ornamental wood on terraces arranged in tiers. Luxuriant trees cast shade over each other, and clear streams flow crosswise. There is a brass statue of the deity, less than one hundred feet tall, in a solemn manner with a stately appearance, as if it were alive.

To the northeast of the great city and on the west bank of the Varaṇā River, there is a stupa more than one hundred feet high, built by King Aśoka. In front of it is a pillar of green stone as smooth as a mirror, and on the lustrous surface, the Tathāgata's portrait is often visible.

Going to the northeast of the Varaṇā River for more than ten *li*, I reached the Deer Park Monastery, which consists of eight divisions, all included in one enclosing wall. There are lofty halls and storied pavilions most splendidly constructed, with one thousand five hundred monks, all of whom study the teachings of the Hinayanist Saṃmitīya school. Within the great enclosure, there is a temple over two hundred feet high with a gilt *āmra* (mango) fruit carved in relief on the top. The foundation and steps are made of stone, while the niches arranged in rows are brickwork. Around the niches there are one hundred steps, and in each niche there is enshrined a gilt image of the Buddha. Inside the temple is a life-size brass image of the Buddha in the posture of turning the Wheel of the Dharma.

To the northeast of the temple is a stone stupa built by King Aśoka. Although the foundation has sunk, the remaining trunk is still one hundred feet high. In front of it is erected a stone pillar more than seventy feet tall, which is as smooth as jade and as reflective as a mirror. With earnest prayer, one may see various shadowy pictures in the surface, and sometimes one can also see good or evil omens. This was the place where the Tathāgata, after having attained full enlightenment, first turned the Wheel of the Dharma. Not far from it, a stupa marks the spot where Ājñāta-Kauṇḍinya and the others went when they saw the Bodhisattva giving up the practice of austerities and refused to be his attendants and guards. So they came here to practice meditation by themselves. The stupa beside it was the place where five hundred Pratyekabuddhas entered Nirvana together. There are also three other stupas marking sites where the three past Buddhas sat and walked up and down.

The stupa located beside the place where the three past Bud- 905c
dhas walked up and down marks the spot where Maitreya (being a surname, meaning Compassion in Chinese, formerly called Mile in erroneous abbreviation) Bodhisattva received the prediction of his attainment of Buddhahood. Once on the Vulture Peak near the city of Rājagṛha, the Tathāgata told the *bhikṣus*, "In the future, when human life will be eighty thousand years long, there will be on this flat land of Jambudvīpa a son of a Brahman of the Maitreya family, whose body will be of golden color shining brightly. He will relinquish his home to achieve full enlightenment and preach the Dharma widely for the living beings in three assemblies. Those who will be saved by him are beings who have cultivated the deeds of blessedness according to the teachings I shall have left to them. As they deeply venerate the Triple Gem with a whole heart, they will receive edification and guidance and attain sainthood and emancipation, irrespective of whether they are laymen or monks and whether they observe or infringe the disciplinary rules. In the three preaching assemblies, those who have followed my bequeathed Dharma will be saved first, and then good friends who have the cause to be saved will be edified."

Then when Maitreya Bodhisattva heard what the Buddha had said, he stood up from his seat and said to the Buddha, "I wish to be that Maitreya, the World-honored One!" The Tathāgata told him, "As you have said, you will achieve that fruit. What I have said above is after the manner of your edification."

To the west of the place where Maitreya Bodhisattva received his prediction is a stupa marking the spot where Śākya Bodhisattva received his prophecy. At the time when human life was twenty thousand years long in the Bhadrakalpa, Kāśyapa Buddha emerged in the world and turned the wonderful Wheel of the Dharma to edify living beings. He prophesied the future of Prabhāpāla Bodhisattva, saying, "This Bodhisattva will become a Buddha with the name of Śākyamuni in the future when human life is one hundred years long."

Not far to the south of the place where Śākya Bodhisattva received his prediction is a site where the four past Buddhas walked up and down. It is over fifty paces long and about seven feet high, built by piling up bluestone, on which is made an image of the Tathāgata in the posture of walking. It is unusually exquisite with an appearance of solemnity and with a tuft of hair specially growing on the fleshy protuberance. Its spiritual features are apparent and its divine manifestation is testified. Inside the enclosure there are really many sacred sites, and the temples and stupas number several hundreds. I have just cited two or three of them, and it is difficult for me to give a detailed description.

To the west of the enclosure of the monastery is a pond of pure water more than two hundred paces in circuit in which the Tathāgata often bathed. Further to the west is another big pond, one hundred eighty paces in circuit, where the Tathāgata used to wash his alms bowl. Further to the north is a pond one hundred fifty paces in circuit where the Tathāgata used to wash his robes. There are dragons staying in all these three ponds. The water is deep and tastes sweet. It is clear and limpid, neither increasing nor decreasing. If one washes in these ponds with a mind of arrogance,
906a one will usually be harmed by a *kumbhīra* (crocodile), but it is safe for one to use the water with a mind of deep respect. Beside the pond for washing robes is a big square rock on which are the traces of the Tathāgata's robes, the lines being distinct just like carvings. Pure believers often come here to make offerings. When heretics and evil people stamp contemptuously on the rock, the dragon king in the pond raises a storm.

Not far from the pond is a stupa at the place where the Tathāgata, in the course of practicing the deeds of a Bodhisattva, was a six-tusked elephant king. A hunter who wished to obtain its tusks disguised himself in a monk's robe and drew his bow to catch the elephant. Out of respect for the robe, the elephant king extracted its tusks and gave them to the hunter.

Not far from the place of the tusk extraction is a stupa at the place where the Tathāgata, in the course of practicing the deeds of a Bodhisattva, manifested as a bird. In pity for the lack of politeness in the world, he discussed with a monkey and a white elephant which of them was the first to see the banyan tree [under which they were sitting]. Each of them gave an account, and according to their statements a sense of seniority and juniority was established. Their influence gradually spread far and near, and the people began to know the order of superiority and inferiority, and both monks and laymen followed their example.

Not far away is a great forest in which there is a stupa at the spot where in the past the Tathāgata and Devadatta, both as deer kings, settled a dispute. Formerly there were two flocks of deer, each flock having more than five hundred animals, in this great forest. Once the king of this country came to hunt in the plain and marshland. The Bodhisattva deer king came forward and said to the king, "Your Majesty is hunting with stout dogs in the plain, while using burning torches and flying arrows. All my followers will lose their lives this morning, and in a few days they will become putrid and stinking and unfit for food. I wish to supply you with a live deer every day by rotation, so that you may have fresh venison, while my followers may lengthen their lives to some extent." The king was pleased with these words and turned back his carriage. Thus each of the two flocks provided the king with a deer on alternate days.

Now in the flock of Devadatta there was a doe big with young. When it was her turn to be killed, she said to the king of her flock, "Although it is my turn to die, my child has nothing to do with it." The deer king said angrily, "Who does not value his life?" The doe remarked with a sigh, "Our king is not kindly and I may die at any moment." So she asked for emergency help from the Bodhisattva deer king. The Bodhisattva said, "How pitiful is the mind of a benign mother, showing kindness to her child that has not yet taken shape! I shall go in place of you." Then he went to the gate of the king's palace, and the people in the street exclaimed, "The great deer king has entered the town!" The officials and common people in the capital rushed out to have a look. When the king heard about it, he thought it was not true, but when the doorkeeper informed the king, he then believed it to be true, and said, "Why do

you, deer king, come so abruptly?" The deer said, "A doe was going to die by turn, but as she is about to give birth to a fawn, I cannot bear the sight of her death. I venture to substitute for her." Upon
906b hearing these words, the king said with a sigh, "I am a human being in form, but I behave like a deer, and you are a deer, yet you have the heart of a man!" Thus the king set free all the deer and asked no more sacrifices from them. The forest was allotted as a preserve for the deer. Therefore it was called the Forest Given to the Deer; hence the name Deer Park.

Two or three *li* to the southwest of the monastery is a stupa more than three hundred feet high. The base of the stupa is broad and high, and it is adorned with rare and brilliant valuables. There are no niches arranged in rows, but a dome in the shape of an inverted alms bowl was constructed instead of them on the base. Although a stone emblematic pillar was erected, it has no decorative wheels or bells. Beside it is a small stupa built at the place where the five persons, Ājñāta-Kauṇḍinya and the others, gave up their restraint and greeted the Buddha. When Prince Sarvārthasiddha (known as Yiqieyicheng, or Accomplishment of all purposes in Chinese, and formerly called Xidaduo in erroneous abbreviation) went across the city wall to live in seclusion in the mountains and valleys, forgetting about himself to seek for the Dharma, King Śuddhodana gave orders to three clansmen and two relatives, saying, "My son Sarvārthasiddha has left home to pursue his studies and is travelling alone in the mountains and marshlands, sojourning solitarily in woods and forests. Thus I order you to follow him so as to know where he is staying. Inwardly you are his paternal and maternal uncles, but outwardly he is your lord and you are his subjects. You should know what to do in whatever circumstances."

Under the order of the king, the five men watched the prince as his guards, and consequently they also sought the Way of Emancipation. They often discussed among themselves whether they should cultivate the Way to attain liberation by practicing asceticism or by living in a pleasant manner. Two of them said that one should cultivate the Way in comfort, while the other three held that one should cultivate the Way in an arduous ascetic fashion. They argued about the matter without coming to a clear decision. The prince pondered over the ultimate truth, and in order to convince the heretics who led a life of severe hardship, he took only gruel to sustain his life. On seeing this, the two men said, "What the prince is doing is not the true Dharma. The Way is something that should be realized in a comfortable manner. He is not of our group, as he has taken to asceticism." So they deserted the prince and fled far away with the intention of attaining the fruit of sainthood.

After practicing asceticism for six years, the prince did not achieve enlightenment, and wishing to prove that asceticism was not the true method, he accepted milk gruel and attained the fruit of sainthood. Upon hearing this, the three men said with a sigh, "At the last moment to gain success, he has retrogressed. All the efforts he has put forth in practicing asceticism for six years are abandoned in a single day." Then they went together to visit the two men [who had left before]. When they saw one another, and having seated themselves, they started to talk bombastically, saying, "Formerly we saw that Prince Sarvārthasiddha left the palace and went to the wilds; he took off his precious garments and put on a deer skin, working hard and perseveringly to seek for the deep and wonderful Dharma wholeheartedly and painstakingly in order to win the supreme fruit of sainthood. But now he has accepted milk gruel offered by some milkmaids and is morally ruined, contrary to his original intention. We know it all, but we could do nothing." The two men said, "How is it that you see it so late? He is merely a capricious man. When he was living in the palace with honor and dignity, he could not keep his mind in peace but went far away to the forests, and he forsook his position of a univer- 906c
sal monarch to lead the life of a low and vulgar man. Why should we remember him? The mention of him merely makes us distressed."

After having bathed himself in the Nairañjanā River, the Tathāgata sat under the Bodhi Tree and attained full enlightenment and the title of Teacher of Devas and Men. He sat quietly, meditating on who should be converted by him, saying, "That Udraka Rāmaputra who has achieved the mental state of Naivasaṃjñāsaṃjñānā-yatana (the state of no thinking and no not-thinking) is competent to receive the wonderful Dharma." The heavenly beings in the air said in reply, "Udraka Rāmaputra passed away seven days ago." The Tathāgata regretted that he could not meet that man who had died suddenly and could not hear the wonderful Dharma. He again observed the world in search of a suitable man and recollected Ārāḍakālāma, who had achieved the mental state of Ākiñcanyāyatana (the state of nothingness), to whom he should impart the ultimate truth. The heavenly beings again said, "He has been dead five days." The Tathāgata regretted once more and had pity on that man for not having had the good luck to hear the Dharma. He again pondered over the matter as to whom he should impart his teachings, and found that nobody but the five men at the Deer Park might be taught first.

At that time the Tathāgata rose from his seat under the Bodhi Tree and repaired to the Deer Park. His deportment was quiet and calm, and he gave off a dazzling divine light. His white eyebrows had the luster of jade, and his body was of the color of genuine gold. He proceeded with composure in order to instruct the five men. When they saw the Tathāgata coming at a distance, they said among themselves, "The man who is coming is Sarvārthasiddha. Through the passage of a long time, he did not achieve the fruit of sainthood. He must have given up what he expected in his mind, and so he has come to look for us. We should remain silent and not stand up to greet or salute him." As the Tathāgata approached them, his divine influence affected them all, and the five men forgot about their restraint, saluted him with greetings, and waited upon him according to etiquette. The Tathāgata gradually taught them the ultimate truth, and at the conclusion of the summer retreat during the rainy season, they attained the fruit of sainthood.

Going to the east of the Deer Park for two or three *li*, I came to a stupa, beside which was a dried-up pond more than eighty paces in circumference with the name of Life-saving or Hero's Pond. I heard the local people saying that several hundred years ago, there

was a hermit living in seclusion in a hut beside the pond. He was learned in arts and crafts and thoroughly mastered the divine principles, being able to turn rubble into gems and interchange the forms of men and animals. But he could not ride on wind and clouds to accompany the fairies, and so he searched into ancient books for the art of becoming a fairy. It was said in the method, "The art of the fairies is the art of longevity. One who wishes to learn it should first of all make up one's mind. An altar should be built more than ten feet in circumference. Ask a hero of outstanding truthfulness and bravery to hold a long knife and stand at a corner of the altar, holding his breath and keeping silence from dusk to the next morning. One who seeks to be a fairy should sit at the center of the altar, while putting his hand on a long knife and repeating an incantation with a concentrated mind, neither seeing nor hearing anything. Before dawn he will become a fairy and the sharp knife will turn into a precious sword. He will be able to walk in the air to rule over the fairies. Wielding his sword as a 907a
commander, he will obtain whatever he desires and never become old or feeble nor suffer illness or death."

After having acquired the method of becoming a fairy, the hermit started to look for a hero, but for a year he could not find a suitable man to his satisfaction. Later, he met a man in the town wailing piteously as he walked along the road. Upon seeing him, the hermit was pleased with his features and asked him sympathetically why he was so sorrowful. The man said, "As I am a poor man, I worked as a servant to sustain myself. My employer was appreciative of my ability and had confidence in me. He promised to pay me good wages should I serve him for five years. Thus I toiled diligently and ignored hardships. But when the term of five years was nearly concluded, I committed a fault, for which not only was I shamefully flogged, but also I lost my pay. This is why I feel so sorry and painful; and no one shows me sympathy."

The hermit asked the man to come with him to the hut and produced delicious food by magical power [to entertain him], and after that he invited him to take a bath in the pond and clothed him with new garments. Then he presented him with five hundred gold coins and said to him, "When you have spent all the money, come again to get more. Please don't make a stranger of yourself." He presented rich gifts to the man on several occasions, with the unspoken intention of winning his heart. The hero repeatedly offered to render a service to the hermit as a repayment for his kindness. The hermit said, "I sought after a hero for a year, and I am lucky to have met you, as your features answer the description of the ancient books. I shall not trouble you with anything else, but I do request that you keep silence for one night." The hero said, "I am not afraid even of death, to say nothing of keeping silence."

Then an altar was prepared for the performance of the rite of becoming a fairy. They acted in accordance with the method and sat down to wait for dusk. After dusk, each of them did his duty, the hermit repeating the incantation while the hero held a sharp knife. At the approach of dawn, [the hero] suddenly shrieked aloud, and consequently a fire fell from the air and smoke and flames covered the place like a cloud. The hermit hastily led the man to seek refuge in the pond and then asked him, "I told you to keep silence, so why did you make such a shrill noise?" The hero said, "After receiving your instructions, I had a nightmare at midnight, in which many strange things appeared. I saw my former employer coming to make a personal apology to me, and out of my deep gratitude to you, I refrained from speaking to him. Being enraged, that man killed me, and then I existed in the *antarābhava* (intermediate state of existence between death and reincarnation). I looked back at my own corpse with a sigh of regret, and by way of repaying your deep kindness, I decided not to speak a word in my future life. Then I saw I was reborn to a great Brahman family in South India, and I never uttered a sound in the course of conception and birth and other painful experiences, always bearing in mind your benefit and kindness extended to me. When I reached the age of schooling, became an adult, got married, lost my parents, and begat a son, I always remembered your kindness and refrained from speaking. All my clansmen and relatives wondered

at me. When I was over sixty-five years old, my wife said to me, 'You should speak now, otherwise I shall kill your son!' Considering that I was getting old in my second life and had only one child, 907b
I stopped my wife from killing him, and thus I uttered that sound." The hermit said, "It is my fault, and it is a mischief caused by a demon." With a feeling of gratitude and being regretful for the failure of the event, the hero died of chagrin. Because the pond prevented the calamity of a conflagration, it is called the Life-saving Pond, and as the hero died there, it is also called the Hero's Pond.

To the west of the Hero's Pond is a stupa built in memory of three animals at the spot where the Tathāgata in the course of practicing the deeds of a Bodhisattva burned himself. At the beginning of the present kalpa, there were three animals, a fox, a hare, and an ape, living harmoniously together in this wild forest. At that time Indra wished to test the one who was cultivating the Bodhisattva deeds and transformed himself into an old man. He said to the three animals, "Are the three of you living in peace and without fear?" The animals said, "We tread on rich grass and frolic in the luxuriant wood. Although we are of different species, we enjoy ourselves in both safety and happiness." The old man said, "I have heard that the three of you are good friends and on terms of intimacy, and so I have come from afar to look for you despite my old age and fatigue. Now I am hungry, and what can you give me for food?" The animals said, "Please wait a moment. We shall go to get something for you."

So they modestly went away on different roads with the same purpose of seeking for some edibles. The fox caught a carp by the riverside, while the ape plucked some strange flowers and fruits in the wood. They came back together to offer their findings to the old man, but the hare returned empty-handed, frisking about him.

The old man said, "As far as I can see, you are not living in harmony. The ape and fox had the same purpose and worked with one mind, but the hare came back empty-handed and has nothing to give me. From this I can understand the situation." Having heard the derisive remark, the hare said to the fox and ape, "Gather a large amount of firewood; I am going to do something." The fox and ape went speedily to gather hay and haul wood, and when they had piled up a huge heap of fuel, it was ignited into raging flames. The hare said, "Kind sir, I am a lower creature and could not get what I wished for. I venture to offer my humble body to be served as a meal to you." Having said so, the hare jumped into the fire and died in the flames.

At that time the old man resumed his form as Indra and collected the ashes of the hare from among the embers with a long sigh of regret. Then he said to the fox and ape, "Since the event has turned out as it has, I am deeply moved by the hare's goodheartedness, and I shall perpetuate its good deed by sending it to the moon to be known to posterity." Therefore the local people say that since then a hare has appeared in the moon. People of later times built a stupa at this place. From here going east along the Ganges for more than three hundred *li*, I reached the country of Garjanapati (in the domain of Central India).

Garjanapati is more than two thousand *li* in circuit, and its capital city, which borders on the Ganges, is more than ten *li* in circuit. The inhabitants are rich and happy, and the towns and villages neighbor on one another. The soil is fertile, and farming is done in accordance with the seasons. The climate is temperate, and the people are simple and honest by social custom and rustic and intrepid by nature. They believe in both the wrong and the right religions.
907c There are over ten monasteries with less than one thousand monks, all of whom follow the Hinayana teachings. Deva-temples amount to twenty, and followers of the different faiths live together.

In a monastery to the northwest of the great city there is a stupa built by King Aśoka. It is said in the *Record of India* that one liter of the Tathāgata's relic bones is preserved in this stupa. In olden times the Tathāgata preached the wonderful Dharma to an assembly of devas and men for seven days at this place. Beside it are sites where the three past Buddhas sat and walked up and down. In the neighborhood of these sites is a statue of Maitreya Bodhisattva. Although it is small in size, its divine power is manifest. It has latent spirituality and works miracles from time to time.

Going eastward from the great city for more than two hundred *li*, I reached Aviddhakarṇa (known as Buchuaner, or Unpierced ears, in Chinese) Monastery. The surrounding wall is not extensive, but the decorative sculptures are very exquisite. The flowers are reflected in the ponds, and the terraces and the ridges of the pavilions are close to one another. The monks are quiet and solemn in deportment, and the community lives in an orderly manner. I heard some elderly people say that formerly in the country of Tukhāra at the north of the Himalaya Mountains, there were two or three Śramaṇas who took delight in learning and often talked together at leisure times after having done religious service and recitation, saying, "The wonderful principles and abstruse theories cannot be thoroughly mastered through empty words, but the holy sites are obvious and discernible and can be visited by making the journey on foot. We should inquire of some bosom friends about the matter and go to visit the holy sites in person." So the two or three friends, holding their pewter staves in hand, started the journey together. When they arrived in India they looked for lodgings in a monastery, but the local monks despised them as frontiersmen and refused to give them accommodation. As they had to stay in the open air, tired and hungry, they became thin and pallid and looked haggard. At that time the king of that country, who was making a pleasure trip in the suburbs, saw the guest-monks. He asked them with amazement, "Mendicants, from where and why did you come here? Your ears are not pierced, and you are dressed in such dirty and shabby robes." The Śramaṇas said in reply, "We are from the country of Tukhāra. We respectfully follow the teachings of the Buddha and left the world [to live as monks]. By our common wish we have come to pay homage to the holy sites. But it is regrettable to say that due to our deficiency in blessedness the Indian monks do not attend to us wayfarers. We wish to return to our native land, but as we have not completed our pilgrimage, we shall endure hardships and go home after our desire is fulfilled."

Upon hearing these words, the king felt pity for the travellers and constructed a monastery at this superior place. He wrote down a rule on a piece of white cotton, saying, "It is due to the spiritual protection of the Triple Gem that I am the most honored person in the world and the noblest in rank among all men. Since I am a king of men and the Buddha has entrusted me [to take care of the religion], I shall extend help to all monks in distress. This monastery is constructed exclusively for the entertainment of travelling monks, and no monks with pierced ears shall stay in this monastery of mine in the future." It is on account of this event that this monastery is called what it is.

908a Going southeast for more than one hundred *li* from Aviddhakarṇa Monastery and crossing the Ganges to the south, I reached the town of Mahāśāla. All the inhabitants are Brahmans by caste, who do not follow the Buddha-dharma. But when they meet Buddhist monks, they inquire about the latters' learning, and if they find that the monks are learned, they salute them with deep respect.

At the north of the Ganges there is a Nārāyaṇa temple consisting of storied pavilions and terraces arranged in tiers, all beautifully decorated. The statues of various devas are carved out of stone with most exquisite craftsmanship, and their spiritual effectiveness is difficult for me to describe in full.

More than thirty *li* to the east of the Nārāyaṇa temple is a stupa built by King Aśoka. A large part of it has sunk into the ground, and in front of it is erected a stone pillar more than twenty feet high with the figure of a lion on its top. Inscribed on the pillar is a record of the event of subduing demons. Formerly there were some demons of the wilderness at this place, who depending upon their strength ate human flesh and blood, doing harm to living creatures in a most evil and monstrous manner. Out of pity for the living beings who would die violent deaths, the Tathāgata induced the demons by his supernatural powers to take refuge [under the Triple Gem] with veneration and taught them to observe the precept of non-killing. The demons accepted the Buddha's teachings and walked around him with respect. Then they raised a rock for the Buddha to sit on, and wished to hear the right Dharma, which they protected wholeheartedly. Afterwards, people who did not believe in the Buddha-dharma tried to push and remove the rock seat set up by the demons, but they could not move it, even though they were counted by the thousands. Around the base of the rock there are luxuriant trees and ponds of clear water, and one who comes near it cannot but feel awe.

Not far from [the stupa of] subduing demons, there are several monasteries. Although they are mostly in dilapidation, there are still monks [living in them], all of whom study and follow the Mahayana teachings.

Going from here to the southeast for over one hundred *li*, I came to a stupa of which the base has slanted and sunk to one side; the remaining part of it is a few scores of feet in height. When the Tathāgata entered Nirvana and the great kings of eight countries divided his relics, the Brahman who measured the relics smeared the inside of the measuring bottle with honey, from which he made allotments for the kings. The Brahman went back with the bottle, and having obtained the relics that stuck to the inside of the measuring bottle he built this stupa and enshrined the bottle in it. Hence it is called by the name [of Relic Bottle Stupa]. Afterwards King Aśoka opened the stupa and took out the relic bottle, for which he constructed a great stupa. On fast days it often emits a brilliant light.

Crossing the Ganges at the northeast of this place and going for one hundred forty or fifty *li*, I reached the country of Vaiśālī (formerly mistranscribed as Pisheli, in the domain of Central India).

The country of Vaiśālī is more than five thousand *li* in circuit. The soil is fertile and there is an abundance of flowers and fruits; mangoes and plantains are plentiful and valuable. The climate is temperate, and the people are simple and honest by social custom. 908b
They take delight in doing good works and attach importance to learning, and they believe in both heterodox and orthodox doctrines. There are several hundred monasteries, most of which are in ruins, with the exception of three to five that remain intact and house a few monks. There are several tens of deva-temples, and the heretics live together. The sect that is in full flourish is that of the naked adherents.

The city wall of the capital of Vaiśālī has badly collapsed, and the original base of the wall is sixty or seventy *li* in circuit, while the palace city is four or five *li* in circuit; there are few inhabitants. Five or six *li* to the northwest of the palace city is a monastery with very few monks, who study the teachings of the Hinayanist Saṃmitīya school. Beside the monastery is a stupa at the place where the Tathāgata delivered the *Vimalakīrti-nirdeśa-sūtra* and Ratnākāra, the son of an Elder, and others offered a sunshade to him. To the east is a stupa at the place where Śāriputra and others attained Arhatship.

To the southeast of the stupa where Śāriputra attained Arhatship is another stupa constructed by the King of Vaiśālī. After the Nirvana of the Buddha, a former king of this country obtained a portion of the Buddha's relic bones for which he respectfully constructed this stupa. It is said in the *Record of India* that there was originally one *hu* of the Tathāgata's relics preserved in this stupa, but King Aśoka opened it and took out nine *dou* of the relics, leaving only one *dou* to be kept in the stupa. Later, another king wished to open the stupa again to get some of the relics, but when he had just started to do the work, the earth quaked, and so he dared not open the stupa.

To its northwest is another stupa built by King Aśoka, and beside it is a stone pillar fifty or sixty feet tall with the figure of a lion on the top. To the south of the stone pillar is a tank that was dug by a group of monkeys for the Buddha, as he once lived at this place in the old days. Not far to the west of the tank is a stupa at the place where the monkeys took the Tathāgata's alms bowl and climbed up a tree to gather honey. Not far to the south of the tank is a stupa at the place where the monkeys offered the honey to the Buddha. At the northwest corner of the tank, some figures of monkeys are still preserved.

Three or four *li* to the northeast of the monastery is a stupa built on the foundation of the old residence of Vimalakīrti (known as Stainless reputation in Chinese and formerly translated as Pure name. But "pure" means "stainless" and "name" is equivalent to "reputation." Although the meaning is the same, the name is translated in different ways. Formerly it was wrongly transcribed as Weimojie). The stupa often reveals spiritual manifestations. Not far from here is a deity's house, which appears to be piled up out of bricks, but according to tradition it was made with stones. This was the place where Vimalakīrti pretended to be sick and preached the Dharma. Not far from here is a stupa built at the place of the old house of Ratnākāra, the son of an Elder. Not far from here is a stupa built at the place of the old house of the woman Āmra[pālī]. The Buddha's aunt and other *bhikṣuṇīs* realized Nirvana at this place.

Three or four *li* to the north of the monastery is a stupa at the 908c
place where human and nonhuman beings stood and waited in the course of following the Tathāgata, who was proceeding to the country of Kuśinagara to enter Parinirvana. Next, not far to the northwest, is another stupa at the place where the Buddha took a last look at the city of Vaiśālī. Not far to the south of this stupa is a temple in front of which is a stupa at the place where the woman Āmra[pālī] offered her garden to the Buddha.

Beside the Āmra[pālī] Garden is a stupa at the place where the Tathāgata announced the time of his Nirvana. Formerly the Buddha told Ānanda at this place, "One who has achieved the four constituent parts of supernatural power can live for one kalpa. Now how long should the Tathāgata live?" He repeated the question three times, but Ānanda, being stupefied by Māra, remained silent, and rising from his seat he went to sit quietly in the wood. At this moment Māra came to the Buddha and said to him, "The Tathāgata has been edifying the people in the world for a long time, and those who have been saved by you from the round of rebirth are as many as the grains of dust and sand. It is now the time for you to enjoy the bliss of Nirvana." The World-honored One then took up a pinch of soil with his nail and said to Māra, "Which is more, the soil on the earth, or that on my nail?" Māra said in reply, "The soil on the earth is more." The Buddha said, "Those I have converted may be compared to the amount of soil on my nail, while those not yet converted to the amount of soil of the great earth. But I shall enter Nirvana in three months." Having heard this, Māra was pleased and retired.

In the wood Ānanda had a strange dream, and he came to tell the Buddha, saying, "In the wood I dreamt that a big tree with luxuriant branches and leaves, casting a dense shade, suddenly fell down in a gale. Does it indicate that the World-honored One intends to enter Nirvana? As my heart is full of fear, I have come to make an inquiry." The Buddha said to Ānanda, "I have told you before, but as you were stupefied by Māra, you did not promptly invite me to stay [in the world]. Māra urged me to enter Nirvana at an early time, and I have given him the date. That is what your dream presaged."

Not far from the place where the Buddha announced the time of his entering Nirvana is a stupa at the spot where one thousand sons saw their parents. Formerly a *ṛṣi* lived in seclusion in a rocky valley. One day in the middle of spring when he was rowing a boat in a clear stream, a doe followed him to drink water; and through inspiration the doe gave birth to a girl, exceedingly beautiful but with feet similar to those of a doe. Upon seeing the girl, the *ṛṣi* took her in and brought her up. Afterward when she was asked to get some live coals from another *ṛṣi*'s hermitage, her steps left traces of lotus flowers on the ground. That *ṛṣi* was deeply surprised at the sight and asked the girl to walk around his hermitage before she was allowed to get the fire. The deer girl did accordingly and obtained the fire and then returned home. At that time King Brahmānanda was making a hunting expedition and saw the flower traces, and following the traces, he found the girl.
909a Being pleased with her unusual appearance, the king carried her back in his carriage. A physiognomist foretold that she would give birth to one thousand sons. When the other ladies [in the harem] heard the prediction, they contrived to take action against her. At the end of her period of gestation, she gave birth to a lotus flower with one thousand leaves and one son sitting on each of the leaves. The other ladies criticized her, saying that it was an inauspicious object, and threw it into the Ganges to be carried away by the

waves. King Ujjayana was making a sightseeing trip at the lower reaches of the river when he saw a yellow canopy, embroidered with a pattern of clouds, flowing down with the waves. He took it up and found one thousand sons wrapped in it. He fed them with milk and brought them up into men of great strength. With the help of these one thousand sons, the king expanded his kingdom to the four quarters, and with his triumphant army he was about to encroach on this country. When King Brahmānanda heard this news, he was shocked and fearful, as his troops were not strong enough to offer resistance, and he was at his wits' end.

At that time the deer woman, knowing that the invaders were her sons, said to the king [Brahmānanda], "Now the invaders are approaching our territory and have caused disunity among ourselves. I, your unworthy wife, with a mind of loyalty, can defeat these strong enemies." The king did not believe her, and she was deeply worried and fearful. Then the deer woman went up to the tower of the city gate to wait for the arrival of the invaders. Her one thousand sons, commanding their troops, besieged the city. The deer woman told them, "Do not do unfilial things! I am your mother, and you are my sons." The one thousand sons said, "How absurd your words are!" But the deer woman pressed her breasts, and milk flowed out, forking into one thousand streams, and owing to the ties of consanguinity, the milk dropped into the mouths of the one thousand sons. So they took off their armor and recognized their mother, and after disbanding their troops, they returned to their own tribe. The two countries restored friendly relations and the people lived in peace and happiness.

Not far from the place where the one thousand sons recognized their mother is a stupa at the old site where the Tathāgata walked up and down, while he pointed at the place and told the assembly, "Formerly at this place, I recognized my mother. If you wish to know who the thousand sons were, they are the one thousand Buddhas of the Bhadrakalpa."

To the east of the place where [the Buddha] related his past life is an old foundation on which is built a stupa that often emits a brilliant light and sometimes answers the entreaties of prayers. This is the remnant site of the storied lecture hall in which the Tathāgata delivered the *Samanta-mukha-dhāraṇī* and other sutras.

Not far from the lecture hall is a stupa in which are preserved the remains of half of Ānanda's body. Not far from this stupa, there are several hundred stupas of which the exact number is unknown; this is the place where one thousand Pratyekabuddhas entered Nirvana. There are numerous holy sites in and around the city of Vaiśālī, and it is difficult to describe them in detail. The old ruins at commanding positions stand with each other like the scales of a fish, but through the passage of time and the change of hot and cold seasons, the woods have withered away and the ponds dried up, leaving behind decayed trees to bear testimony [to past glories].

Going to the northwest for fifty or sixty *li* from the great city, I
909b reached a great stupa at the place where the Licchavis (formerly mistranscribed as Lichezi) bade farewell to the Tathāgata. When the Tathāgata was proceeding to the country of Kuśinagara from the city of Vaiśālī, the Licchavis, having heard that the Buddha was about to enter Nirvana, went to see him off while wailing piteously. Upon seeing that their sorrow was so deep as to be inconsolable by words, the World-honored One produced, by his supernatural powers, a big river with steep banks and a rapid current, so that the Licchavis, crying bitterly, were prevented from following him any further. The Tathāgata left his alms bowl as a memento for them.

Less than two hundred *li* to the northwest of the city of Vaiśālī is an old city that has been lying waste for many years and has few inhabitants. In the city there is a stupa at the place where the Buddha told an assembly of various Bodhisattvas and men and heavenly beings about his past events of cultivating Bodhisattva deeds. He was once a universal monarch, named Mahādeva (known as Datian, or Great deity, in Chinese), in this city, possessing the seven treasures and being competent to rule over the four continents of the world. But as he witnessed the phenomenon of changeability and realized the principle of impermanence, he cherished a high ambition and forgot about the throne. He renounced his country to become a monk and donned the dyed robe to pursue learning.

Going southeast for fourteen or fifteen *li* from the city, I reached a great stupa at the place where seven hundred sages and saints convened the Second Council. One hundred ten years after the Buddha's Nirvana, some *bhikṣus* in the city of Vaiśālī deviated from the Buddha-dharma and observed the disciplinary rules in an erroneous way. At that time the Elder Yaśoda was residing in the country of Kosala, the Elder Sambhoga in the country of Mathurā, the Elder Revata in the country of Hanruo, the Elder Sālha in the country of Vaiśālī, and the Elder Kubjaśobhita in the country of Pāṭaliputra. All these great Arhats had gained mental liberation, mastered the Tripiṭaka, and possessed the three clear insights; they had great reputations and were well known to all as disciples of the Venerable Ānanda. At that time Yaśoda sent a messenger to invite various sages and saints to meet at the city of Vaiśālī. The attendance at the meeting amounted to seven hundred less one. Kubjaśobhita then saw with his clairvoyance that various sages and saints were assembled to discuss matters concerning the Dharma, and he came to the assembly by his supernatural power of ubiquity. Sambhoga, with his right shoulder uncovered and kneeling on the ground, said to the council, "Be quiet! Consider with respect! Although the great holy King of the Dharma entered Nirvana as an expedient many years ago, his oral teachings still exist. Some negligent *bhikṣus* in the city of Vaiśālī are erroneous in their observance of the disciplinary rules and have raised ten points that are contrary to the teachings of the Buddha who possessed the ten powers. Now you sages are conversant with the observance and the violation of the disciplinary rules, and all of you have studied under the instruction of Bhadanta Ānanda. For the sake of repaying the Buddha's kindness, you should reiterate his holy decrees." None of the great saints was not moved to tears. They summoned the faulty *bhikṣus*, and in accordance with the Vinaya 909c
regulations they reprobated them and stopped their misdeeds. Thus the wrong practices were stopped and the holy teachings clarified.

Going south for eighty or ninety *li* from the place where the seven hundred sages and saints held a meeting, I came to Śvetapura Monastery, which consisted of many lofty buildings and magnificent pavilions. The monks are pure and solemn in manner, and all of them study Mahayana teachings. Beside it are old sites where the four past Buddhas sat and walked up and down. The stupa beside it was built by King Aśoka at the place where the Tathāgata halted to take rest, on his way to the country of Magadha in the south, and looked back at the city of Vaiśālī in the north.

More than thirty *li* away to the south of Śvetapura Monastery, there are two stupas, one built on the southern bank and the other on the northern bank of the Ganges. This was the place where the Venerable Ānanda divided his bodily relics for two countries. Ānanda was a cousin of the Tathāgata, and he was a man of wide learning and comprehensive intelligence who had an extensive range of knowledge and a retentive memory. After the decease of the Buddha, he succeeded Mahākāśyapa in upholding the right Dharma and guiding the learners. Once when he was taking a walk in a wood in the country of Magadha, he saw a novice reciting the scriptures wrongly, with passages and sentences in disorder and the wording in confusion. Having heard the recitation, Ānanda recalled the Buddha with a deep feeling of sorrow, and went slowly to the novice to point out his mistakes. The novice said with a smile, "Great Virtuous One, you have become senile and your saying is wrong. My teacher is a wise man in the prime of life. I have personally learned from him, and there is no mistake in his instructions."

Ānanda withdrew quietly with a sigh, saying, "Although I am getting old, I still wish to live longer to uphold the right Dharma for the benefit of living beings. But as living beings are laden with defilement, they are difficult to admonish. It is useless for me to live any longer. I shall quickly enter Nirvana." Then he left the country of Magadha for the city of Vaiśālī. While Ānanda was crossing the Ganges in a boat, sailing in the midstream, the king of Magadha heard that Ānanda was going away, and out of deep affection and in admiration of his virtue, he urgently dispatched his military carriages to go quickly in pursuit of him. Hundreds and thousands of troops camped on the southern bank. [At the same time] the king of Vaiśālī felt both grief and joy at the news that Ānanda was coming [to his country to enter Nirvana], and he also sent his troops to march speedily to welcome him. Hundreds and thousands of soldiers were stationed on the northern bank. The two armies faced each other and their flags obscured the sun. Fearing that they might start a war and kill each other, Ānanda ascended into the air from his boat and entered Nirvana amid the manifestation of supernatural powers. A fire burned his body, which fell down in two portions, one dropping on the southern bank and the other one on the northern bank. So each of the two kings obtained one portion of the relics, with their armies weeping sorrowfully. After returning to their respective countries, they erected stupas to pay homage to the relics. Going from here to the northeast for more than five hundred *li*, I reached the country of Vṛji (called by the northerners the country of Saṃvṛji, in the domain of North India).

The country of Vṛji is more than four thousand *li* in circuit, 910a
long from east to west and narrow from south to north. The soil is fertile and abounds in flowers and fruits. The climate is somewhat cold, and the people are impetuous by nature. Most of them venerate the heretics and a few believe in the Buddha-dharma. There are over ten monasteries with less than a thousand monks, who study both the Mahayana and Hinayana teachings. There are several tens of deva-temples with a great number of heretics. The capital city of the country is called Cañśuma, of which the greater part is in ruins. Inside the old palace city there are still more than three thousand families of inhabitants living together like a village or town.

To the northeast of a big river there is a monastery with a few monks, who are pure and lofty in learning. West of here there is a stupa more than thirty feet high by the side of the river, which flows like a belt in the south. This was the place where the Buddha with his great compassion once converted some fishermen. Far back in the past at the time of the Buddha, there were five hundred fishermen who worked in groups to catch fish, and one day they caught in this river a large fish with eighteen heads, each having two eyes. When the fishermen were ready to kill the fish, the Tathāgata in the country of Vaiśālī saw it with his divine eye and had pity on it. He intended to take this opportunity to edify the fish and to enlighten the fishermen at the same time. He told the assembly of monks, "In the country of Vṛji there is a big fish, which I intend to convert, so as to enlighten the fishermen. You should know that it is time now to do so."

Then the Buddha, surrounded by the assembly of monks, ascended into the air by his power of divine feet and flew to the riverside. He laid down his sitting cloth as usual and said to the fishermen, "Do not kill the fish!" With his supernatural power and in an expedient way, he endowed the big fish with the faculties of knowing its previous life, speaking human language, and understanding human sentiment. Then the Tathāgata purposely asked the fish, though he knew the answer, "What sins did you commit in your previous life, so that you are now in an evil state of rebirth with such a bad shape?" The fish said, "By the effect of good deeds I had done in a former life, I was born to a noble family, and I was known as the great Brahman Kapittha in my previous life. Depending upon the influence of my caste, I despised and bullied other people, and considering myself learned I scorned the scriptures and the Dharma. Disrespectfully I slandered the Buddhas and reproached the monks with abusive language, comparing them to camels, donkeys, elephants, horses, and other ugly animals. Owing to these evil deeds, I am now suffering in this bad shape. But as I did some good deeds in one of my former lives, I have been born at a time when a Buddha is in the world, and I have seen the holy Buddha himself with my own eyes and have heard his holy teachings." Then [the fish] made a confession and repented his evil deeds done in the past.

The Tathāgata taught the fish in accordance with its capacity and enlightened it as was suitable to the occasion. After hearing the Dharma, the fish died and was reborn in heaven by the power of its good deeds. Then he looked at his own celestial body and won-
910b dered why he had been born in heaven. After knowing his past life, he remembered the Buddha with gratitude and came together

with other heavenly beings to see him. Having worshipped the Buddha, he walked around him and stood aside to offer him valuables and fragrant flowers brought from heaven. The World-honored One told the anecdote to the fishermen while pointing at the heavenly beings and preached the wonderful Dharma to them. They were then moved and awakened [from ignorance] and sincerely worshipped the Buddha with repentance, tore up their fishing nets, and burned their boats. They turned their minds to truth and embraced the Dharma. After donning the dyed robes of monks and having heard the ultimate teachings, all of them got rid of defilement and attained the fruit of sainthood.

More than one hundred *li* to the northeast of the place where the fishermen were converted, there is a stupa over one hundred feet high built by King Aśoka at the west of an old city. This was the place where the Buddha once preached the Dharma for six months to convert celestial and human beings. At a distance of one hundred forty or fifty paces to the north of this stupa, there is a smaller stupa marking the place where the Tathāgata laid down the disciplinary rules for the *bhikṣu*s. Next, not far to the west, is another stupa, in which are enshrined the Tathāgata's hair and nail relics. People coming far and near converge at this place to burn incense, scatter flowers, and light lamps and candles without interruption. Going from here to the northwest for one thousand four hundred or five hundred *li*, crossing over mountains and passing through valleys, I reached the country of Nepāla (in the domain of Central India).

The country of Nepāla is over four thousand *li* in circuit, and it is situated among the Snow Mountains. The capital city of the country is more than twenty *li* in circuit, and there are hills and valleys in close connection. The soil is suitable for growing cereals and yields many flowers and fruits. The country produces red copper, yaks, and *jīvaṃjīva*s (birds with two heads). Red copper coins are used as the medium of exchange. The climate is piercingly cold. The people are sinister and iniquitous by social custom, and they are rude and unrestrained by nature and disparage good faith and righteousness. They have no learning but are skillful in craftsmanship. They are ugly in appearance and believe in both wrong and right doctrines. The monasteries and deva-temples are so close together that they touch each other, and there are more than two thousand monks, who study both Mahayana and Hinayana teachings, while the number of heretics is unknown. The king, being a Licchavi of the Kshatriya caste, is an upright man with good learning and is a pure Buddhist. In recent years there was a king named Aṃśuvarman (known Guangzhou, or Brilliant helmet, in Chinese) who as a learned scholar of intelligence and sagacity wrote a treatise on *Śabda-vidyā* (Sanskrit grammar). He esteemed learning and honored the virtuous, and his fame spread far and near.

To the southeast of the capital city, there is a small pool. When fire is thrown into it, the water burns, and when more things are cast into it, they also become fiery.

From here I returned to the country of Vaiśālī, and crossing the Ganges to the south, I reached the country of Magadha (formerly mistranscribed as Mojiatuo or Mojieti, in the domain of Central India).

End of Fascicle Seven

Fascicle VIII

The Country of Magadha (1)

The country of Magadha is more than five thousand *li* in circuit, and the capital city is sparsely populated, while in the towns there are many registered families. The soil is fertile and good for farming. There is a special kind of rice of large grain with an unusual fragrance, and the luster and color are extraordinary. The people call it the rice for great personages. The land is low and humid, and the towns are located on tablelands. After the beginning of summer and before mid-autumn, the plains are flooded and boats can be used. The people are simple and honest by social custom, and the climate is moderately hot. The inhabitants esteem learning and revere the Buddha-dharma. There are over fifty monasteries with more than ten thousand monks, most of whom study Mahayana teachings. There are several tens of deva-temples, and the heretics are truly numerous. 910c

To the south of the Ganges there is an old city over seventy *li* in circuit. Although it has been deserted for a long time, the old foundations are still there. In the past, when human life was innumerable years long, this city was called Kusumapura (known as Xianghuagongcheng, or the Palace city of fragrant flowers, in Chinese). The royal city was full of flowers, hence the name of the city. Later on, when human life was several thousand years long, the name was changed to the city of Pāṭaliputra (formerly mistranscribed as the city of Balianfu).

At the beginning, there was a learned Brahman of high talent who had several thousand disciples studying under him. Once some of the disciples went out together to make a pleasure trip. One of them paced up and down in a melancholy mood, and his companions asked him why he was so sad. He said, "I am in the prime of life, yet I am still a vagabond, having only my shadow to accompany me, and moreover though a long time has passed, I have not made any achievement in learning. On account of this, my mind is heavily laden with sorrow." His schoolmates said to him in jest, "In that case we shall now arrange a ceremony for you to get married." Then they chose two persons to act as the parents of the bridegroom, and two persons as the parents of the bride. The young man was then made to sit under a *pāṭalī* tree, which was thus called the Tree of the Son-in-Law. Seasonal fruits were gathered and pure water was served as wine to make a wedding feast to celebrate the nuptials. The mock father of the imaginary bride broke off a branch of the tree and handed it to the young scholar, saying, "This is your good spouse. I hope you will not refuse the offer." The scholar was happy and satisfied. When it was time for the party to return home at dusk, the young man did not wish to leave the place and wanted to stay behind. The other disciples said to him, "'We were merely making a mock ceremony. Please go home with us now, lest the fierce beasts in the wood hurt you."

911a But the scholar lingered at the place and walked about the tree. After sunset a strange light shone brightly in the wilderness, and elegant music of wind and stringed instruments was heard and a row of tents pitched. In a moment an old man holding a staff came to extend greetings to him. There was also an old woman coming with a maiden, followed by a large number of splendidly dressed attendants amid the sound of music. The old man said to him while pointing at the maiden, "This is your wife." The wedding festivities lasted seven days.

The other disciples suspected that he might be killed by wild animals and came to look for him. Then they saw him sitting alone under the shade of the tree, as if he were accompanying some guests of honor. They asked him to return with them, but he refused to accept their advice. Some time later, he entered the city by himself to see his relatives and friends and told them what had happened to him. Those who heard the story were amazed. His friends went with him to the wood, where they saw a great mansion at the place of the flowering tree, with servants and slaves walking to and fro busily. The old man received them politely and prepared a feast with the performance of music to entertain them according to the etiquette between hosts and guests. When they returned to the city, they told everything to people far and near.

After a year a son was born to the couple, and the young scholar said to his wife, "I wish to go home, but I cannot bear leaving you behind, but if I remain here, I shall always make my lodging in the open wilderness." Having heard this, his wife told it to her father, the old man, who said to the young scholar, "For the enjoyment of life, one need not go back to one's native place. I shall build you a palace. Do not think otherwise." Through the labor of spirits, the palace was promptly completed. The old City of Fragrant Flowers was shifted to this place, and as the city was constructed by spirits for the [infant] son, it was called the city of the Son of Pāṭali.

To the north of the old royal city there is a stone pillar several tens of feet in height, erected at the place where King Aśoka made a hell. In the one hundredth year after the Nirvana of the Śākya Tathāgata, King Aśoka (known as Wuyou, or Not feeling sorrow, in Chinese, formerly mistranscribed as Ayu), the great-grandson of King Bimbisāra (known as Yingjian, or Hard shadow, in Chinese, formerly mistranscribed as Pinpisuo), removed his capital from the city of Rājagṛha to Pāṭaliputra. After a long passage of time, only some old foundations still survive. Of the monasteries, deva-temples, and stupas, there are several hundred remnant sites lying in ruins; only two or three remain intact. Only in a small city situated to the north of the old palace and alongside the Ganges are there over one thousand households.

At first when King Aśoka succeeded to the throne, he was cruel and practiced tyranny. He established a hell to torture people. It was surrounded by lofty walls with watchtowers at the corners. Great furnaces of fierce fire and cutters with sharp points and keen edges, as well as other instruments of torture, were prepared in

imitation of the hells, and a savage and cruel man was appointed to be the jailer. At first it was used for punishing all sorts of criminals of the country, regardless of the nature of their misdeeds. But later on, all casual passersby were captured and put to death, and all who had entered the hell were killed to prevent the secret from
911b leaking out.

Once a newly admitted Śramaṇa came to the gate of the hell in the course of making his round of alms-begging. The cruel jailer caught him and intended to kill him. Being terror-stricken, the Śramaṇa asked permission to perform a confessional ceremony [before death]. In a moment he saw a man who was bound and sent into the hell and was dismembered and cut into pieces. Presently the broken body became rotten and decayed. The Śramaṇa was deeply touched by the sight, and he gained the insight of impermanence and realized Arhatship. The jailer said to him, "It is time now for you to die." Having achieved the fruit of sainthood, the Śramaṇa had no discrimination between life and death. Although he was thrown into a cauldron of boiling water, he was just as if in a pond of cool water, and a huge lotus flower sprang up for his seat. The jailer was surprised by the unusual spectacle and hurried to inform the king, who came to see the sight for himself and highly praised the spiritual protection. Then the jailer said, "Your Majesty must die." "Why?" said the king. The jailer replied, "Your Majesty has previously issued an order as a rule of the hell that whoever has entered the enclosure of the hell must be killed, and it did not say that the king should be excepted from the regulation." The king said, "Once a law is adopted, it should not be altered. But did I make an exception of you when I laid down the rule? It was my fault that you should have lived up to now." Then he ordered the lictors to cast the jailer into the big furnace, and after the death of the jailer, the king came out of the hell. He demolished the walls, filled up the trenches, abolished the hell, and showed leniency thereafter toward criminals.

Not far to the south of the hell there is a stupa of which the foundation has sunk to one side; it has the shape of an overturned alms bowl. It is decorated with gems and has stone balustrades. Being one of the eighty-four thousand stupas built by King Aśoka, this one was constructed by human labor in his palace. Inside it is preserved one *dou* of the Tathāgata's relic bones, which occasionally show spiritual manifestations and issue a divine light from time to time.

After having abolished the hell, King Aśoka met the great Arhat Upagupta, who instructed him according to his capacity in an appropriate way. The king said to the Arhat, "I am lucky to be a lord of men as a result of good deeds I have done in the past, but owing to my spiritual hindrances, I am sorry that I did not receive edification from the Buddha. Now I wish to construct stupas for the veneration of the Tathāgata's relic bones." The Arhat said, "With your power of bliss and virtue, you can command various deities to work for you. It is my wish that you should protect the Triple Gem with great determination. Now is the time for you to do so." Then the Arhat told the king in detail about the latter's cause of offering a handful of earth [to the Buddha in a previous life], and about the merits of building stupas as predicted by the Tathāgata.

King Aśoka was pleased to hear the prediction. He summoned the spirits and deities, to whom he issued an order, saying, "The King of the Dharma has instructed living beings for their happiness, and due to my good deeds done in the past, I am now the most honored person among mankind. In order to venerate the Tathāgata's relic bones, stupas must be constructed. You spirits and deities should work with one heart to construct stupas for the Buddha's relics at all places in Jambudvīpa, which is inhabited by a full *koṭi* of families. Although the project is initiated by me, it depends upon you for its successful completion, and I have no intention of monopolizing the advantages of performing such superior good deeds. Each of you should go to start the construction work and wait for further instructions." Having received the edict, 911c
the spirits and deities went away to start the construction work at their different places, and when the work was completed, they all came to ask for further instructions.

After having opened the stupas built in eight countries and distributed the relic bones [taken out from them] to the spirits and deities, King Aśoka said to the Arhat, "My wish is to enshrine the relic bones in the various stupas at the same time. I hope to do so, but I do not know how to fulfill my wish." The Arhat said, "Your Majesty can order the deities and spirits to enshrine the relics at one moment on the appointed date when they see that the sun is eclipsed by an object in the shape of a hand." The king imparted the instruction to the spirits and deities. On the appointed date King Aśoka observed the sun, and at midday the Arhat stretched his arm to cover up the sun with his hand by supernatural power. At all the places where the stupas were being constructed, the eclipse was seen by all, and at that moment they did the work simultaneously.

Not far from the stupa is a temple containing a big stone on which the Tathāgata once stood, and the traces of his footprints are still in existence. The two footprints have the wheel-signs, and the ten toes have floral ornaments. The fish patterns are visible, and they sometimes issue a bright light. In olden times, when the Tathāgata was about to enter Nirvana, he proceeded northward to the city of Kuśinagara and looked back at the country of Magadha in the south. He was standing on this stone when he told Ānanda, "I leave my last footprints here, while I am going to enter Nirvana and looking back at Magadha. One hundred years afterward there will be a King Aśoka, who will rule over the world and establish his capital at this place. He will protect the Triple Gem and command all kinds of deities to do him service." When King Aśoka succeeded to the throne, he shifted his capital to this place and built a city here, and protected the footprint stone with a shelter. As it was near the palace city, he always came in person to make offerings to it.

Afterward various kings vied with one another in trying to bring the stone home. Although it was not very big, they could not move it. Recently King Śaśāṅka persecuted the Buddha-dharma and went to the place of the stone intending to destroy the holy object. He erased the footprints with a chisel, but they reappeared with the same traces and patterns. Then he threw the stone into the Ganges, but it returned to its original place at once. The stupa beside the stone marks the place where the four past Buddhas sat and walked up and down in olden times.

Not far from the temple of the Buddha's footprints there is a huge stone pillar more than thirty feet tall. The inscription on it has become incomplete, saying roughly that King Aśoka was a staunch believer who offered Jambudvīpa to the Triple Gem thrice and redeemed it thrice with valuable pearls and gems. Such are the fragmentary words still legible.

To the north of the palace city there is a great rock chamber with the appearance of a lofty hill and a space several tens of feet wide inside. It was constructed by the labor of deities and spirits by order of King Aśoka for his younger brother, who was a monk.
At first King Aśoka had a uterine younger brother by the name of 912a
Mahendra (known as Dadi, or Great ruler, in Chinese). As he was born in a royal family, he presumptuously put on the king's robe and led a luxurious and dissolute life, treating people cruelly until they bore a grudge against him. The prime minister and other senior officials exhorted the king, saying, "Your younger brother has gone too far in riding roughshod over the people. As the saying goes, when the government is impartial, the country will be in good order, and when the people are living in harmony, the ruler will be in peace. This precept is handed down from ancient times. We hope that the code of the country will be maintained and that he will be put on trial according to the law."

King Aśoka said in tears to his younger brother, "Since I succeeded to the throne, I have put all living beings under my protection. As you are my brother of the same mother, how can I neglect to benefit you? But I did not guard and guide you in time, so you have incurred the punishment for criminals. I am in fear of my ancestors above and forced by public criticism from below."

Mahendra bowed to the king apologetically and said, "I am so imprudent as to have infringed the law. I hope you will grant me seven days' respite." He was then confined in a dark chamber under strict custody but was provided with the best delicacies without negligence. [At the end of the first day] the guardian announced, "One day has passed and there are six days more." When the sixth day had passed, Mahendra, being deeply worried and fearful, made vigorous efforts both physically and mentally [in spiritual cultivation], and thereupon he gained the fruit of sainthood, ascended into the air, and manifested miracles. Before long he left the world and went far away to live in a rocky valley. King Aśoka went personally to see him and said, "As I was bound by the law of the country, I had to inflict a severe penalty upon you. I did not think that you would elevate yourself and realize the fruit of sainthood. You are now free from trouble, and you may return to our country." His younger brother said, "Formerly I was caught in the net of passions and my mind was stuck to women and song. As I am now free from the city of perils, I take delight in staying in the mountains and valleys. I wish to relinquish the human world and always remain in the hills and vales." The king said, "If you wish to engage yourself in quiet meditation, it is not necessary for you to lodge in secluded mountains. But in compliance with your wish, I shall build a cave for you."

The king then summoned the spirits and deities and said to them, "I shall prepare a grand banquet of delicacies on the day after tomorrow. You may all come to attend the feast, but each of you should bring a big rock as seat for himself." By order of the king, the deities came at the appointed time, and when the feast was over, the king told the deities, "As the stone seats are in a mess, you should pile them up in proper order. I mean to make use of your labor to build a hollow chamber." Under the instruction of the king, the deities completed the work in a few days' time. King Aśoka then went to invite [his younger brother] to stay in the hill-like cave.

To the north of the old palace and at the south of the hell, there is a large trough made by divine labor under the command of King Aśoka for storing comestibles at the time of offering food to the monks.

To the southwest of the old palace, there is a rocky hill around which there are several tens of caves excavated on the steeps by divine labor under the command of King Aśoka for Upagupta and other Arhats. There used to be a lofty terrace beside the hill, but it has collapsed, leaving only a pile of stones as the remnant foundation. In a pond there is rippling water as clear and reflective as a mirror. It is regarded as holy water by the people of neighboring and distant countries. If one drinks or bathes in the water, one's soil will be washed away and one's sins expiated. 912b

To the southwest of the hill, there are five stupas, of which the lofty foundations have sunk down, but the remnant portions are still high. When looked at from a distance, they seem to be verdurous hillocks. Each side of the stupas has a space several hundred paces wide. People of later times constructed small stupas upon the big ones. It is said in the *Record of India* that in the old days when King Aśoka had built eighty-four thousand stupas, he still had five *dou* of [the Buddha's] relics. Therefore he constructed five more stupas in a style different from that of other places. Miracles occurred from time to time to testify to the fivefold spiritual body of the Tathāgata. Some impious people discussed the matter in private, saying that these stupas were constructed by King Nanda of yore to store his seven kinds of treasures. Afterward a king of little faith heard about the rumor, and being covetous of the treasures he sent his troops under his personal supervision to excavate the stupas. But the earth quaked, the mountains collapsed, the clouds enshrouded the sun, the stupas issued a loud sound of thunder, the soldiers fell dead, and the elephants and horses fled in fear. Since then nobody has dared any attempt on the stupas. Some people have said that there were different accounts of this matter, but they were mostly unascertainable. By following the records of ancient books, we may get the true facts.

To the southeast of the old city is Kukkuṭārāma Monastery (known as Jiyuan, or Cock garden, in Chinese), which was built by way of performing good deeds with veneration by King Aśoka when he first had faith in the Buddha-dharma. He summoned one thousand monks, both ordinary persons and saints [to this monastery], offered them the four kinds of monastic requisites, and provided them with other articles for daily use. The monastery has been in ruins for a long time, and only the foundations are still in existence. Beside this monastery is a great stupa called Āmalaka (Emblic myrobalan), which is the name of a sort of medicinal fruit of India.

When King Aśoka was ill on his deathbed, he knew that he was incurable and intended to give up his gems and jewels for the performance of good deeds. But his influential ministers had seized power and would not allow him to do what he desired. Afterward he kept an *āmalaka* fruit from his meal and played with it until it was half spoiled. Holding the fruit in his hand, he said to his ministers with a long sigh, "Who is now the lord of Jambudvīpa?" The ministers said in reply, "Your Majesty is the sole lord of Jambudvīpa." The king said, "No! I am not the lord now! I have sovereign power only over this half a fruit. What a pity! Worldly wealth and nobility are more easily extinguishable than a candle burning in the wind. My position entitled me to control the whole country and my title is the highest of all designations, but I am poor on my deathbed, being under the compulsion of forceful ministers. Although I have lost the empire, I still possess half a fruit." Then he ordered his attending official, "Take this half a fruit to Kukkuṭārāma Monastery and offer it to the monks with the following message: 'I, the former lord of the whole of Jambudvīpa, now the king of half an *āmalaka* fruit, beg to pay homage in front of the monks of great virtues. I hope that you will accept my last alms. I have
912c lost all I had before, except this half a fruit, which is somehow at my disposal. Please have pity on my poverty and let my seeds of blessedness grow and increase.'" The senior monk of the community said, "King Aśoka used to be generous in alms-giving, but now he is suffering from a serious illness, and treacherous ministers have usurped his power. His accumulated valuables are no more his own property, and he has only half a fruit to give as alms. By order of the king, we shall distribute the fruit to all the monks." So the senior monk instructed the steward monk to cook the fruit in a thick soup, and collected the kernel, for which a stupa was built. Since they received the king's great beneficence, it was fitting that they should realize his last wish.

In an old monastery to the northwest of the Āmalaka Stupa, there is a stupa known as Bell Striking. Formerly there were about one hundred monasteries in this city, and the monks were solemn and respectful and had great learning, and the heretical scholars were silenced by them [in debate]. Afterward the monks gradually died, and their successors failed to maintain the tradition of learning. But the heretical teachers taught their students to become perfect in knowledge, and then they summoned their schoolmates, thousands and myriads in number, to assemble at the monastic buildings, shouting aloud, "Strike the bell to call up all your scholars!" Groups of ignorant monks came together and wantonly sounded the bell, and they reported to the king, requesting him to be the judge of the contest. The heretical teachers were highly talented scholars of good learning, and although the monks were numerous, their arguments were shallow and superficial. The heretics announced, "We are the winners in the debate. From now onward no monastery should strike the bell to call assemblies." The king sanctioned the request according to the precedent regulations of debate. Having been put to shame, the monks withdrew in disgrace, and for twelve years they did not strike the bell.

At that time, Nāgārjuna Bodhisattva (known as Longmeng, or Dragon valor, in Chinese, and formerly mistranslated as Longshu, or Dragon tree) of South India had a good reputation from his youth, and when he had grown up he enjoyed unique fame. He renounced the world of lust and love and became a monk to cultivate his learning. He made a profound study of the wonderful principles and attained the first stage [of Bodhisattvaship]. He had a great disciple named Deva, a man of wisdom and cleverness with wits and good understanding. He said to his teacher, "The scholars of Pāṭaliputra were defeated in debate by the heretics, and time passes so quickly that twelve years have elapsed since they stopped striking the bell. I would venture to demolish the hill of erroneous views and light the Torch of the Dharma." Nāgārjuna said, "As the heretics of Pāṭaliputra are erudite scholars, you are not a match for them. I must go in person." Deva said, "To cut off rotten grass, is it necessary to overturn the whole mountain? Under your instruction, I venture to refute the heterodox scholars. May you, my great teacher, raise an argument in favor of the heretical theories and let me analyze the points against them, and we shall see who will be the winner before we plan our action." Then Nāgārjuna proposed a thesis of the heretical theories, while Deva refuted his teacher as the latter tried to maintain his viewpoints. At the end of seven days, Nāgārjuna failed to uphold his proposition. He said with a sigh, "Erroneous views can be easily refuted, and it is difficult to defend wrong theories. Now you may go; you can surely defeat them."

Deva Bodhisattva had always been a man of high renown, and
913a when the heretics of Pāṭaliputra heard about his arrival, they assembled and hurriedly went to report to the king, saying, "Your Majesty has formerly condescended to hear our suggestion that a rule be made to prevent the monks from striking the bell. We pray that a decree be issued to order the guardians of the city gates not to allow a foreign monk from a neighboring country to enter the city lest he conspire to alter the former rule recklessly." The king consented to their proposal and ordered the guardians to keep strict watch. Thus when Deva arrived he could not enter the city. Upon hearing the restriction he changed his clothes, folded his *saṃghāṭi* robe, and wrapped it in a bundle of straw. Holding the front piece of his long gown in hand, he hastily went into the city with the straw bundle carried on his head. After entering the city and having cast away the straw, he put on his religious robe and came to this monastery to ask for lodging. But as he had no acquaintance there, nobody would provide him with a room. So he spent the night at the terrace of the bell, and early next morning, he struck the bell loudly. When the monks heard the sound of the bell, they came out to see and found that it was the travelling monk [who had struck the bell], while the other monasteries did the same in response to the call of this monastery. The king, having heard the sound, inquired into the matter but could not find out who was the first to strike the bell. When the king's man came to this monastery, the monks pointed out Deva, who said, "A bell is sounded for assembling the monks. If you do not strike it, what is the use of

hanging it there?" The king's man said, "Formerly the monks were defeated in a debate, so twelve years ago a rule was laid down to prohibit them from striking the bell." Deva said, "Is that so? I wish to beat the drum of the Dharma again today."

The messenger reported to the king, saying, "A foreign Śramaṇa wishes to avenge a former shame." The king then summoned the scholars and made a rule that one who loses an argument should pay with his life for the failure. Then the heretics displayed their flags, set out their drums, and boisterously talked on different theories, showing off their talent for eloquence. Having sat on the seat of discussion, Deva listened to their disputations, and aiming at their different views he refuted them through analysis. In less than twelve days he vanquished all the heretics, to the delight of the king and his ministers, who built this spiritual stupa in memory of Deva's supreme virtue.

To the north of the Bell Striking Stupa is the old site of the dwelling place of the demon-eloquent Brahman. Formerly there was a Brahman of the city [of Pāṭaliputra] who lived in a thatched hut at a desolate place, dissociating himself from the world. He worshipped demons to beseech them for blessedness, and he had converse with evil spirits. He had brilliant ideas, talked volubly, and answered questions with elegant words. When people held a hot debate with him, he always retorted from behind a curtain. None of the learned scholars with high talents could excel him, and the common people unanimously respected him as a saint.

There was a Bodhisattva named Aśvaghoṣa (known as Maming, or Horse-neighing, in Chinese), whose wisdom comprehended everything, and whose Way extended to the Three Vehicles. He often remarked on the matter, saying, "This Brahman has no teacher to teach him, and his arts are groundless and without ancient basis. He lives in seclusion, enjoying a high renown all by himself. If he does not depend on deities and ghosts and is not obsessed by evil spirits, how could he be what he is? One whose ability of eloquence is endowed by a demon cannot speak face to 913b
face with another man, and he cannot reiterate what he has said

once. I must go there to see how he will behave." So he repaired to the [Brahman's] hut and said to him, "I have heard of your great fame with admiration for quite a long time. I hope you will lift the curtain so that I may express what is on my mind." But the Brahman remained arrogant, talking behind his curtain, and would not speak face to face [with his visitor]. Aśvaghoṣa realized that it was the demon who was so self-conceited. After the conversation was over, he retired and told the people, "I have come to know what is what, and I am sure to defeat him." Then he went to see the king and asked for permission to hold a sharp debate with the hermit. The king was surprised to hear this, and said, "What sort of man are you? If you have not gained the three clear insights or obtained the six supernatural powers, how can you contest with him?" Nevertheless, he ordered that his carriage be prepared and went in person to see the details of the controversy.

At that time Aśvaghoṣa Bodhisattva discussed the subtle words of the Tripiṭaka and elucidated the general meanings of the five branches of knowledge. He talked eloquently and with great ease, and his brilliant views were lucid and far-sighted. When the Brahman had stated his opinion, Aśvaghoṣa said, "In your statement you lost the gist of my argument. Please repeat what you have said." But the Brahman remained silent and became tongue-tied. Aśvaghoṣa rebuked him, saying, "Why do you not solve my interrogation? The demon you serve should hasten to give you words." While saying so, he hurriedly lifted the curtain, trying to get a look at the demon, but the Brahman said in a flurried and fearful manner, "Stop! Stop!" Aśvaghoṣa withdrew and remarked, "That fellow has lost his fame this morning. As the saying goes, false fame cannot last long." The king said, "If it were not for your great virtue, who could have seen through his sinister fraudulence? According to the regular tradition of the country, a man who has an unprecedented and unique capability of discernment should be commended for his perspicacity."

More than two hundred *li* away from the southwest corner of the city, there are the remnant foundations of a monastery, beside which is a stupa that often issues a divine light and manifests spiritual signs. People come here from far and near to say prayers. This was a site where the four past Buddhas sat and walked up and down in ancient times.

Going southwest for more than one hundred *li* from the old monastery, I reached Tilaḍhāka Monastery. It consists of four courts, three-storied pavilions, lofty terraces, and gates that open widely, leading from one to another. All these were built by the last descendant of King Bimbisāra. He selectively invited men of high talents and widely summoned people of great virtue. Scholars of foreign countries and wise men from distant lands, one following another, came in groups of the same caliber and stayed [in this monastery]. There are thousands of monks, all of whom study Mahayana teachings. At the end of the path, facing the middle gate, there are three shrines, which are adorned with wheel-signs on the roofs and have bells and chimes suspended in the air. On the terrace below, there are spacious balustrades made all around. The doors, windows, beams, outer walls, and stairs are embellished with gilt or copper ornaments in relief. In the middle shrine, the standing statue of the Buddha is thirty feet in height, while in the left one is a statue of Tārā Bodhisattva, and in the right one a statue of Avalokiteśvara Bodhisattva. All three statues, cast in brass, are austere in appearance, and spread far-reaching divine 913c
precepts. In each of the three shrines, there is one *sheng* of [the Buddha's] relic bones, which sometimes emit a divine light and show signs of unusual auspiciousness from time to time.

At a distance of over ninety *li* to the southwest of Tilaḍhāka Monastery, I reached a great mountain, where spirits and immortals dwell among the dense clouds and rocks lying in seclusion, venomous snakes and violent dragons lurk in the hollows of the marshes, fierce beasts hide in the woods, and birds of prey perch on the trees. On the summit of the mountain is a large flat rock on which is built a stupa over ten feet high. This was a place where the Buddha had once sat in *samādhi*.

Formerly the Tathāgata once came here by supernatural power and sat on this rock in the Samādhi of Complete Cessation for a whole night. The devas, spiritual beings, and saints made offerings to him, performed celestial music, and rained heavenly flowers. When the Tathāgata had emerged from the state of *samādhi*, the heavenly beings, out of feelings of respect and admiration, constructed a stupa with gems, gold, and silver, but in the lapse of time the precious substances turned into stone. Since ancient times, nobody has ever visited the stupa. Looking from afar at the high mountain, one could see strange beings, long snakes, and fierce beasts circumambulating to the right around the stupa, and devas, immortals, spirits, and saints coming one after the other to sing praise. On a hillock to the east of the mountain is a stupa built at the place where the Tathāgata once walked and stood to look at the country of Magadha.

At a spur of a hill over thirty *li* to the northwest of the mountain, there is a monastery built on an elevated place backed by a ridge, with lofty pavilions excavated on the precipices. There are more than fifty monks, all of whom study the Mahayana teachings. This was the place where Guṇamati (known as Dehui, or Virtue-wisdom, in Chinese) Bodhisattva subdued the heretics.

At first there was at this mountain a Brahman named Mādhava, who was a follower of the theories of the Sāṃkhya school and practiced the same accordingly. He was an expert in both Buddhist and heretical doctrines and could talk well on the principles of nonexistence and existence. His fame excelled that of his predecessors, and his virtue won the respect of his contemporaries. The king esteemed him as national treasure, and the ministers and common people honored him as their private teacher. Scholars of neighboring countries accepted his style of learning, respected him for his virtue, and regarded him as a pioneer. He was indeed a learned and erudite man. He lived on the fief of two cities in an abode surrounded by feudal lands.

At that time Guṇamati Bodhisattva of South India had been a man of intelligence since his childhood. He had been exquisite in learning in his early days, had thoroughly mastered the Tripiṭaka, and perfectly understood the Four Noble Truths. When he heard that Mādhava's theories were most profound and abstruse, he decided to frustrate his vainglory. He sent a disciple to the Brahman with the following message, "I respectfully inquire after the health of Mādhava and hope you live in peace and happiness. It befits you to forget about tiredness and make a good review of your old learning. In three years I shall put an end to your good repute." In the second and third years, he repeated the message to the Brahman. When he was about to start the journey [to see the Brahman] he wrote another letter to him, saying, "The time is drawing to an end. How is the progress of your studies? You should know that I am coming soon." Greatly worried with fear, Mādhava warned his disciples and feudal tenants that from then onward they should not take in any Śramaṇa or heathen and told them to pass the notice to all others and not to infringe the admonition.

At that time Guṇamati Bodhisattva came with his pewter staff 914a
to the fief of Mādhava, and the tenants, in keeping with the prearrangement, refused to give him lodgement. The Brahman reproached him, saying, "With a tonsured poll and dressed in a queer costume, what a strange figure you are! It befits you to go away quickly and not stay here!" As Guṇamati wished to defeat the Brahman, he desired to stay in the latter's feudal land, and said in polite words with a mind of compassion, "You people are pure ascetics following the worldly truth, while I am a pure ascetic practicing the superior truth. Since we all are pure ascetics, why do you reject me?" The Brahman would not speak with him but simply drove him away. Being driven out of the feudal land, Guṇamati entered a great forest in which fierce beasts made havoc in groups.

A pure believer, who feared that Guṇamati might be hurt by the beasts, came with a torch and a staff in hand and said to the Bodhisattva, "A Guṇamati Bodhisattva of South India whose fame has spread far is coming to hold a debate. Thus the lord of the fief, fearing that his good name might be lost in the polemic, issued a strict order to his men not to take in any Śramaṇa for the night. For fear that he may be harmed by wild beasts, I have come here to help him. He may go his way in safety without worry." Guṇamati said, "I may tell you, pure believer, that I am Guṇamati." Having heard these words, the pure believer showed still deeper respect to Guṇamati and said to him, "If that is the case, you should leave here in haste." So they came out of the dense forest and halted at an open marsh where the pure believer built a fire. Holding a bow in his hand, he walked round about. When the night had passed, he said to Guṇamati, "You may go now lest people should get wind of you and come to injure you." Guṇamati said with thanks, "I shall never forget your kindness."

Then he went to the palace and said to the gatekeeper, "A Śramaṇa coming from a great distance wishes to obtain the permission of the king to hold a debate with Mādhava." Having heard this announcement, the king was amazed and said, "This man must be crazy!" Then he ordered a messenger to go to the place of Mādhava to declare his edict, saying, "A strange Śramaṇa has come and begged to hold a debate [with you]. The ground for the argumentation has been swept clean and an announcement has been sent to places far and near. I hope you will kindly attend the meeting with your gracious presence." Mādhava asked the messenger, "Is the man the Śāstra-master Guṇamati of South India?" The messenger said, "Yes." Mādhava was very much displeased to hear it, but he could not decline the invitation and so he repaired to the venue of contention. The king and his ministers, as well as scholars, the common people, and the nobles, gathered at the meeting, wishing to listen to the learned discussion.

Guṇamati put forward his proposition first, but up to sunset Mādhava refused to offer a retort on the excuse that owing to his senility he could not give a prompt reply and that he had to go back to ponder over the question in quiet before coming to give his refutation. For every new point [raised by his opponent], he always said that he must go back before making a reply. The next morning, when he had taken his seat in the discussion, he could not utter a word in refutation, and on the sixth day he died vomiting blood. On his deathbed he said to his wife, "You are a woman of great talent, and you must not forget the shame I have suffered."
914b Mādhava's death was kept secret, and his wife, attired in gorgeous dress, came to the meeting. The people in the assembly made a hubbub and said among themselves, "Mādhava is self-conceited

and is too shy to face Guṇamati, and so he has sent his wife to come to the meeting. It is apparent who is superior and who is inferior." Guṇamati Bodhisattva said to Mādhava's wife, "The one who can subjugate you has been subjugated by me." The woman then beat a retreat in the face of difficulties.

The king said [to Guṇamati], "What secret words did you say that made the woman go away in silence?" Guṇamati said, "What a pity! Mādhava is dead! His wife came with the intention of holding the debate with me." The king said, "How did you know it? Please tell me." Guṇamati said in reply, "When she came she wore a sorrowful look of mourning and her voice betrayed her feeling of grief and sadness. That is how I knew that Mādhava was dead. By saying 'the one who can subjugate you,' I referred to her husband." The king then sent a man to see what had happened, and found that things were truly as had been said. The king said in self-reproach, "The Buddha-dharma is abstruse and wonderful and has brilliant sages coming forth in succession; nonaction is the Way that benefits living beings. According to the original institutions and regulations of our country, I shall praise and honor men of virtue in the regular manner." Guṇamati said, "Stupid as I am, I practice the Way and abide by chastity, and I observe the precepts of contentment and self-restraint and study the means of helping others. Whenever I attempt to induce a man [to the right path], I always suppress his arrogance first and then convert him in an appropriate way. Now it is time for me to request Your Majesty to assign all the tenants of the fiefs of Mādhava to be men of the monastery for innumerable generations, so as to leave an example for people in the future and transmit the fame of these good deeds forever. As to the pure believer who rendered me protection, I hope he will live blissfully in the world and enjoy the same provisions that are given to the monks, so as to persuade people to have pure faith, as well as to exalt his profound goodness." Thus this monastery was constructed for the glorification of this superior event.

At first, when Mādhava had been frustrated in the debate, some tens of Brahmans fled to take refuge in a neighboring country and informed the Brahmans of that land about the shameful

affair. They recruited brilliant scholars and returned home to seek vengeance for the former insult. As the king respected Guṇamati, he went in person to invite the latter, saying, "The heretics who overrate their own abilities have organized a party, formed cliques, and ventured to sound the drum to demand the holding of a debate. I hope you, Venerable Sir, will crush the heretics." Guṇamati said, "The debaters may be called to an assembly." The heretical scholars were delighted to hear this and said among themselves in consolation, "We shall certainly win the case today!" Then the heretics expounded their theoretical principles. Guṇamati Bodhisattva said, "These heretics here have taken refuge in a distant land, and according to the king's former ordinance, they have become contemptible. How can I debate with them face to face?" Now Guṇamati had a page to serve him as a seat carrier, who always heard his master's supererogatory disputations and had become adept in discussing the gists of subtle teachings. As he was standing by the side of his master, listening to his eloquent talk, Guṇamati clapped his seat and said, "Seat carrier, you may debate with them." All the people in the assembly were surprised by his order. Then the page started to raise questions. His words of deep meaning gushed like a spring, and his clear eloquence echoed in the air. In three rounds the heretics were vanquished in the disputation, the sharpness of their tongues being blunted and the shafts of the feathers of their wings broken. Since they were defeated in
914c the debate, they were made feudal tenants of the monastery.

More than twenty *li* to the southwest of Guṇamati Monastery is an isolated hill, with a monastery built by the Śāstra-master Śīlabhadra (known as Jiexian, or Precept-virtue, in Chinese) with the revenue of a city, donated to him as a reward for a successful discussion. The isolated hill resembled a stupa in shape for the preservation of the Buddha's relics. The Śāstra-master, being a Brahman by caste, was a scion of the royal family of the country of Samataṭa. When he was young he was fond of learning and had a good character. He travelled to various parts of India in search of men of wisdom. When he came to Nālandā Monastery in this country, he met with Dharmapāla Bodhisattva, from whom he heard about the Dharma with faith and understanding, and under whose guidance he donned the dyed robe of a monk. He inquired into the consummate principles and sought the way of emancipation. He mastered both the ultimate truth and the subtle theories. He was well-known in his own time, and his fame was high in foreign regions.

There was then in South India a heretic who searched into profound teachings and delved into what was kept secret, having a thorough comprehension of abstruse knowledge and a keen insight into subtle tenets. Upon hearing of the high repute of Dharmapāla, he became deeply jealous and prideful. In spite of the obstacles of mountains and rivers he came to beat the drum and demanded to hold a discussion with him. He said [to the king], "I am a man from South India. I have heard that in your kingdom there is a great Śāstra-master. Although I am not clever, I wish to have a full discussion with him." The king said, "Yes, we have one as you say." Then he sent a messenger to invite Dharmapāla, saying, "A heretic of South India has come from a distance of no less than one thousand *li*, wishing to hold a competitive discussion with you. I hope you will condescend to come to the debating ground."

Having heard this message, Dharmapāla tidied his robe and was ready to go, when his disciple Śīlabhadra, an outstanding young man, stepped forward and said, "Why are you going in such a hurry?" Dharmapāla said, "Since the Sun of Wisdom ceased shining and the Lamp of Transmitting the Dharma became extinct, the heretics have swarmed like ants, and heterodox views have spread like wasps flying in groups. Therefore I must go to crush that debater." Śīlabhadra said, "I have heard with respect your supererogatory discussions, with which I dare to crush the heterodox follower." Knowing that he was a man of outstanding talent, Dharmapāla gave his consent to the request. As Śīlabhadra was then just thirty years old, the assembly slighted him as being too young and feared that it would be difficult for him to combat his opponent by himself alone. Knowing that the assembly was not content with the choice, Dharmapāla said in explanation, "What is valued in a man is his good learning and intelligence, and not his age. In view of the present situation, [Śīlabadhra] is sure to defeat the heretic." On the day of the discussion, young and old people coming from far and near gathered together. The heretic widely expounded his theories to the utmost extent, while Śīlabhadra refuted him by reasoning in a most profound and abstruse way. Having exhausted his words, the heretic retired in shame.

As a reward for [Śīlabhadra's] virtue, the king wished to give him this city as a fief. The Śāstra-master declined the offer, saying, "As I am a monk dressed in the dyed robe, living with contentment and keeping myself in purity, what is the use of a fief for me?" The king said, "The King of the Dharma has disappeared and the Boats of Wisdom have sunk one after another. If there is no distinction [made to the worthy ones], how can we encourage scholars of the younger generation? In order to spread the right Dharma, I hope you will kindly accept the gift." As he could not decline the offer, the Śāstra-master accepted the city as his fief.
915a He constructed a monastery according to the regulations, and provided daily necessities for the monks with the revenue of the city.

Going southwest for forty or fifty *li* from Śīlabhadra Monastery, I crossed the Nairañjanā River and reached the city of Gayā. This city is strongly built but only sparsely populated, having only some one thousand Brahmanic families, the descendants of a great *ṛṣi*. The king did not make them his subjects, and the people honor them respectfully. More than thirty *li* to the north of the city is a clear spring, which is regarded by Indian tradition as holy water, and when one drinks the water or washes in it, one's sinful defilements are purified. Five or six *li* to the southwest of the city is Gayā Mountain, which has deep valleys and far-reaching streams among steep peaks and high cliffs. In India it is traditionally called Spiritual Mountain. Since ancient times when the kings and monarchs ascended the throne, exerted influence upon distant peoples, and excelled their predecessors in virtue, they all came up to this mountain to make an announcement of their achievements. On the top of the mountain is a stone stupa more than one hundred feet high built by King Aśoka. It has latent spiritual power and emits a divine light from time to time. This is the place where the Tathāgata formerly preached the *Ratna-megha-sūtra* and other scriptures.

To the southeast of Gayā Mountain is a stupa built at the birthplace of Kāśyapa, and to its south are two stupas built at the places where Gayākāśyapa and Nadīkāśyapa worshipped fire. At the place where Gayākāśyapa worshipped fire, crossing a big river to the east, one reaches the Prāgbodhi Mountain (known as Qianzhengjueshan, or Preenlightenment mountain, in Chinese, as the Tathāgata ascended this mountain prior to his realization of perfect enlightenment). Having striven hard for six years, he did not gain perfect enlightenment; then he gave up austerities and accepted milk gruel. When he came from the northeast to this mountain, he saw that it was a quiet place and wished to gain enlightenment there. From the northeast ridge he climbed up to the summit of the mountain, when the earth quaked and the mountain trembled. As the mountain god was frightened, he told the Bodhisattva, "This mountain is not a blessed place for you to achieve enlightenment. If you stay here and enter the Diamond Samādhi, the earth will sink and the mountain topple down." The Bodhisattva came down by the southwest side of the mountain. Halfway down the mountain there was a large cave with its back to the crag and its mouth opening on a brook in front. The Bodhisattva went in and sat cross-legged. The earth quaked again and the mountain trembled for a second time. At that time beings of the Pure Abode Heaven chanted in the air, "This is not the place for the Tathāgata to achieve enlightenment. Fourteen or fifteen *li* southwest from here and not far away from the place where you practiced austerities, there is a pipal tree, under which is a Diamond Seat. It is on this seat that all the Buddhas of the past and future sit to achieve perfect enlightenment. Please go there!" But the dragon of the cave said, "This cave is a 915b
quiet and suitable place for you to attain sainthood. May you have compassion and not relinquish it." Knowing that this was not the place for him to realize Buddhahood, the Bodhisattva left his shadow in the cave to satisfy the dragon's wishes and went away.

(This shadow was formerly visible to both the wise and the ignorant, but now only some people are able to see it.) Being preceded by the heavenly beings, the Bodhisattva went to the Bodhi Tree. Later, when King Aśoka rose to power, he built monuments and stupas at the sites where the Bodhisattva ascended and descended the mountain. Though these monuments are different in size, they are the same in showing spiritual signs, either raining celestial flowers or emitting a light to illumine the deep valleys. Every year at the end of the summer retreat, monks and laymen of different places come here to make offerings and spend two nights before going home.

Going southwest from Prāgbodhi Mountain for fourteen or fifteen *li*, I reached the Bodhi Tree. The surrounding walls are built high and strong with brick, and they are long from east to west and narrow from south to north, being about five hundred paces in circuit. There are exotic trees and famous flowers, casting continuous shade on the ground, and fine sand and strange plants cover the earth with a green quilt. The main gate opens east toward the Nairañjanā River, and the southern gate is close to a large flower pool. The west side is an inaccessible natural barrier, while the northern gate leads to a big monastery. Inside the enclosure the sacred sites are connected with one another. The stupas or shrines were all built by monarchs, ministerial officials, and nobles of various countries of Jambudvīpa as memorials to their acceptance of the bequeathed teachings of the Buddha.

At the center of the enclosure of the Bodhi Tree is the Diamond Seat, which came into existence together with the great earth at the beginning of the Bhadrakalpa. It is in the middle of the Three Thousand Great Chiliocosm, reaching down to the golden wheel below the surface of the earth. It is made of diamond and is over one hundred paces in circuit. As the one thousand Buddhas of the Bhadrakalpa all sit on it to enter the Diamond Samādhi, it is called the Diamond Seat, and because it is the place for realizing the Sacred Way, it is also called the *Bodhimaṇḍa* (Seat for realizing Buddhahood). When the earth quakes, this spot alone remains stable. Thus when the Tathāgata was about to attain enlightenment, all the places where he went at the four corners of this seat trembled, and when he came here, it was calm and quiet, without agitation. Since the commencement of the period of decline at the end of the kalpa when the right Dharma started to decline, this site was covered by sand and earth and became lost to sight. After the Buddha's Nirvana, the monarchs of various countries set up two sitting statues of Avalokiteśvara facing the east at the southern and northern limits of the enclosure according to the Buddha's description as they had heard from the tradition. Some old people said that when the statues of the Bodhisattva disappear and become invisible, the Buddha-dharma will come to an end, and now the statue at the south corner has already sunk down up to the chest.

The Bodhi Tree at the Diamond Seat is a pipal tree, which was several hundred feet tall at the time of the Buddha, and although it has been cut down or damaged several times, it still remains forty or fifty feet high. As the Buddha attained full enlightenment while sitting under this tree, it is called the Bodhi Tree (Tree of enlightenment). The trunk of the tree is yellowish white in color, 915c
and its branches and leaves are always green; they never wither away nor change their luster, whether in the winter or in the summer. Each year on the day of the Tathāgata's Nirvana, the leaves fade and fall; but they grow out again very soon. On that day the monarchs of various countries and monks and laymen of different places, thousands and myriads in number, gather here by their own will to irrigate and bathe the tree with scented water and milk to the accompaniment of music; with arrays of fragrant flowers and lamps burning uninterruptedly the devotees vie with each other in making offerings to the tree.

After the decease of the Tathāgata, when King Aśoka had just ascended the throne, he believed in heretical doctrines and destroyed the sites left by the Buddha. He sent his troops and went in person to cut the tree. He chopped the roots, stalks, branches, and leaves into small pieces and had them heaped up at a spot a few tens of paces to the west, where fire-worshipping Brahmans were ordered to burn the pile as a sacrifice to their god. But before the smoke and flames had vanished, two trees grew out of the furious fire with luxuriant and verdurous leaves; these trees were thus called Ash Bodhi Trees. Upon seeing this strange sight, King Aśoka repented his misdeeds and irrigated the remnant roots with sweet milk. When it was nearly dawn, the tree grew up as before. The king was highly exhilarated to have seen this spiritual wonder and made offerings to the tree in person with so much delight that he forgot to go back home. The queen, being a heretical believer, secretly sent a man to fell the tree after nightfall. When King Aśoka went to worship the tree at dawn, he was very sad to see only the stump of the tree. He prayed earnestly and irrigated the stump with sweet milk, and in a few days the tree grew up once again. With deep respect and astonishment, the king built a stone enclosure to the height of more than ten feet around the tree, which is still in existence. Recently King Śaśāṅka, being a heretical believer, denounced the Buddha-dharma out of jealousy, destroyed monasteries, and cut down the Bodhi Tree. When he dug the ground so deep as to have reached spring water and could not get at the ends of the roots, he set fire to burn it and soaked it with sugarcane juice with the intention of making it rotten, so as to prevent it from sprouting. Several months later, King Pūrṇavarman (known as Manzhou, or Full armor, in Chinese) of Magadha, the last descendant of King Aśoka, heard about the event and said with a sigh of regret, "The Sun of Wisdom has sunk, and only the Buddha's tree remained in the world; now that the tree has been destroyed, what else is there for living beings to see?" He prostrated himself on the ground and wept touchingly. He irrigated the tree with milk obtained from several thousand cows, and it grew up to some ten feet high in one night. Fearing that people of later times might cut it down, he surrounded it with a stone enclosure to the height of twenty-four feet. Thus the Bodhi Tree at present is behind the stone wall, with over ten feet of its branches growing out above the wall.

To the east of the Bodhi Tree is a shrine one hundred sixty or seventy feet high built on a base of which the front is more than twenty paces broad. It was built with brick and plastered with lime. In all the niches arranged in tiers, there are golden images,

and on the four walls there are marvellous carvings in the shapes of strings of pearls or figures of fairies. On the top there is installed a gilded copper *āmalaka* fruit (it is also said to be a precious bottle or a precious pot). It is connected with a storied pavilion 916a
at the east, of which the eaves are in three layers, while the rafters, pillars, ridgepoles, beams, doors, and windows are adorned with gold and silver carvings and studded with pearls and jade in a mixed way. The innermost chamber of the shrine has three doors connecting with the other parts of the structure. On each side of the outer door there is a niche containing an image of Avalokiteśvara Bodhisattva on the left side and that of Maitreya Bodhisattva on the right side, both cast in silver and more than ten feet in height.

Formerly King Aśoka had built a small shrine at the site of the [present] shrine, and later a Brahman extended it. At first there was a Brahman who did not believe in the Buddha-dharma but worshipped the deity Maheśvara. He heard that the deity was living in the Snow Mountains, and so he went with his younger brother to seek the fulfillment of his wishes from the deity. The deity said, "Your wishes can be fulfilled only when you have done meritorious deeds. It is not that you can get things by saying prayers, nor can I make you satisfied." The Brahman said, "What meritorious deed should I do so that my mind can be satisfied?" The deity said, "If you wish to plant the seed of goodness, you should find the Field of Blessedness. As the Bodhi Tree is the place where the Buddha attained Buddhahood, you should quickly go back to the Bodhi Tree to build a great shrine, dig out a large pond, and make various offerings, and then your wishes will be fulfilled." Under the injunction of the deity, the Brahman cherished a mind of great faith and returned with his younger brother. The elder one built the shrine and the younger one excavated a pond. Then they made rich offerings to seek the fulfillment of their wishes. Finally they realized their wishes and became cabinet ministers to the king. Whatever emoluments or rewards they received they gave away as alms.

When the shrine was completed, artists were invited to make an image of the Tathāgata as he was at the time of attaining Buddhahood. But for a long time, nobody answered the call for the job.

At last a Brahman came and said to the monks, "I am good at making fine images of the Tathāgata." The monks said, "What do you need for making the image?" The Brahman said, "I only need some scented clay and a lamp to be placed inside the shrine. When I have entered the shrine, the door should be tightly closed and opened after six months." The monks did as they were told. But when it was four days short of six months, they opened the door out of curiosity to see [what was going on]. They saw that the image inside the shrine was in the posture of sitting cross-legged facing the east, with the right foot upon [the left thigh]; the left hand was drawn back, and the right one pointed downward. It was just as if it were alive. The pedestal was four feet two inches high and twelve feet five inches wide, while the image was eleven feet five inches tall, the two knees being eight feet eight inches apart, and the breadth from one shoulder to another measured six feet two inches. All the auspicious physical symbols of a Buddha were complete, and its features of compassion were true to reality, except that a little spot above the right breast was unfinished. As they saw nobody in the shrine, they realized that there was a divine hand at work, and all the monks were filled with amazement and eagerly wished to know about the affair. One of the Śramaṇas, a man of simple and honest mind, had a dream in which he saw the Brahman, who said to him, "I am Maitreya Bodhisattva, and
916b fearing that artists could not imagine the holy features of the Buddha, I came in person to make the image. It is made with the right hand pointing downward, because when the Tathāgata was about to attain Buddhahood, Māra came to disturb him, and the earth gods informed him of Māra's arrival. One of the earth gods came out first to assist the Buddha in subjugating Māra, but the Tathāgata said to the god, 'Do not worry. I can surely subjugate him with my power of forbearance.' Māra said, 'Who will bear you witness?' The Tathāgata then pointed his hand to the earth while saying, 'This one here will bear me witness!' At that moment the second earth god emerged to bear witness. Therefore the image is made with the right hand pointing downward." The monks came to know that it

was a divine manifestation, and all of them were moved to tears. The unfinished spot above the breast was made good with various gems, and the image was adorned with a necklace of pearls, crowned with a coronet, and embellished with other valuable ornaments.

When King Śaśāṅka felled the Bodhi Tree, he also wished to destroy this image. But when he looked at the compassionate features of the image, he did not have the heart to do so. At the time of returning home, he told his attendant minister, "You had better remove this image of the Buddha and replace it with that of Maheśvara." Having received the king's edict, the attendant minister was afraid and said with a sigh, "If I destroy the Buddha's image, I shall suffer disaster for many kalpas, but if I disobey the king's order, I shall not only lose my own life but also incur the extermination of my entire family. What shall I do in this awkward plight?" Then he called some Buddhist believers to be his servants and had a brick wall built horizontally in front of the Buddha's image. As he was ashamed to see the image in utter darkness, he lit a lamp for it. On the front of the brick wall he drew a picture of Maheśvara, and when this was done he made a report to the king. Upon hearing the report, the king dreaded the consequences. He suffered from blisters all over his body, and his skin became cracked, and before long he died.

The attendant minister hurriedly went back to the image and demolished the screen wall. After many days the lamp was still burning without extinction. The image is now still in existence, and as it is in a profound chamber, lamps and torches are burning continually. One cannot see the compassionate features clearly unless one reflects sunlight with a big mirror into the chamber to see the divine statue early in the morning. Those who have the chance to see the image are struck with emotion.

The Tathāgata attained perfect enlightenment on the eighth day of the second half of the month of Vaiśākha of the Indian calendar, corresponding to the eighth day of the third month of our calendar, but according to the tradition of the Sthavira school, the event occurred on the fifteenth day of the second half of the month of

Vaiśākha, corresponding to the fifteenth day of the third month of our calendar. He was then at the age of thirty or thirty-five.

To the north of the Bodhi Tree is a place where the Buddha walked up and down. After achieving perfect enlightenment, the Tathāgata did not rise from his seat but sat in meditation for seven days. When he rose to his feet, he went to the north of the Bodhi Tree where he walked to and fro east and west for seven days. When he had walked over ten paces, signs of strange flowers followed his footprints at eighteen points. People of later times built a brick promenade about three feet high at this place. It is said in a previous record that this sacred site can foretell the length of
916c one's life. One should make a sincere vow before taking the measure. The length of the promenade varies with the possible duration of life of those who measure it.

To the north of the promenade, on a huge rock on the right side of the road, is a big shrine in which there is an image of the Buddha with its eyes gazing upward. Formerly the Tathāgata looked at the Bodhi Tree from this place for seven days without blinking his eyelids, looking at the tree attentively with a feeling of gratitude.

Not far to the west of the Bodhi Tree there is a great shrine with a brass image of the Buddha in the standing posture facing the east that is adorned with rare jewels. In front of the image is a blue stone with wonderful veins of various hues. This is the place where Brahmā built a hall with the seven precious substances and Indra made a seat, also of the seven precious substances, at the time when the Tathāgata first attained enlightenment. On this seat he sat in meditation for seven days and emitted an unusual light that shone upon the Bodhi Tree. The precious substances have become stone because the event occurred in the remote past.

Not far to the south of the Bodhi Tree is a stupa more than one hundred feet high built by King Aśoka. After having bathed himself in the Nairañjanā River, the Bodhisattva was going to the Bodhi Tree when he pondered what he should use for a seat. Then he got the idea of using some clean grass to make a seat. Meanwhile Indra transformed himself into a grass cutter, carrying a bundle of grass going on his way. The Bodhisattva said to him, "Can you favor me with some of your grass?" The transformed figure respectfully offered him some grass, and after receiving the grass the Bodhisattva proceeded on his way.

Not far to the northeast of the spot of receiving grass is a stupa built at the place where some blue birds (*Eophona personata*) and a drove of deer came as a good omen when the Bodhisattva was about to achieve Buddhahood. Among the signs of auspiciousness in India, their presence is the most lucky symbol. Thus in compliance with the custom of the human world, the celestial beings of the Pure Abode Heaven made the blue birds fly around the Bodhisattva to signal his spirituality and holiness.

To the east of the Bodhi Tree there are two stupas, one on the left and the other on the right side of the main road. This is the place where the King of Māras disturbed the Bodhisattva. When the Bodhisattva was about to attain Buddhahood, the King of Māras exhorted him to be a supreme ruler [instead of a Buddha]. As this device was ineffective, the King of Māras withdrew in deep sadness. His daughters volunteered to go to seduce the Bodhisattva, who with his divine power changed the beautiful girls into decrepit old dames. They retreated clinging to each other and holding sticks to support their skinny frames.

In a shrine to the northwest of the Bodhi Tree there is an image of Kāśyapa Buddha. Well known for its spirituality and sanctity, it often emits a bright light. It is said in a previous record that if a man walks around the image seven times with utmost sincerity, he may gain the wisdom of knowing where he was born in his past life.

To the northwest of the shrine of Kāśyapa Buddha, there are two brick chambers, each housing an image of an earth god. One informed the Buddha of the arrival of Māra, and the other one bore
witness for the Buddha. People of later times made these images of 917a
the gods in memory of their merits.

Not far to the west of the Bodhi Tree enclosure is a stupa more than forty feet high known as Saffron Stupa, built by a merchant lord of the country of Jāguḍa. Formerly in the country of Jāguḍa there was a great merchant lord who worshipped heavenly gods to pray for wealth and despised the Buddha-dharma, not believing in the law of causality. Once he led a group of fellow traders to do business and sailed to the South Seas, where they encountered a typhoon and lost their way. They drifted along with the roaring waves and sailed on the sea for three years until their rations became exhausted and they had nothing more to eat. All those who sailed in the same ship were in a precarious state, and they earnestly prayed to the gods they worshipped with one mind. When they were quite fatigued with their laborious prayer and failed to receive divine rescue, they suddenly saw a huge mountain with lofty cliffs and steep peaks under the light of two bright suns. The merchants said to comfort one another, "We are lucky to have come across this huge mountain. We should halt here to get peace and happiness." The merchant lord said, "It is not a mountain but a *makara* fish (a sea-monster). The lofty cliffs and steep peaks are its fins and whiskers, while the two bright suns are its eyes." When they had barely finished talking, their ship floated toward the monster. The merchant lord told his fellow traders, "I have heard that Avalokiteśvara Bodhisattva will bestow peace and happiness upon those who are in peril and adversity. Let us call his name with a mind of complete sincerity." Then they all repeated the name of the Bodhisattva in unison and sought refuge under his spiritual protection. The lofty mountain disappeared and the two suns submerged. In a moment they saw a Śramaṇa with a quiet and peaceful manner coming through the air with a religious staff in hand to rescue them from being drowned. Very soon they returned to their own country. Thence they cherished minds of resolute faith and tried to perform good deeds unweariedly. They built a stupa for making offerings and plastered the whole structure with saffron-clay.

Having cherished the mind of faith, the merchant lord led his fellow traders to worship the holy sites and visit the Bodhi Tree. They spent a whole month in pilgrimage before they thought of going home. The fellow traders while travelling together said among themselves, "Being separated by mountains and rivers, we are far away from our homeland. Since we are here, who will sweep and clean the stupa we have built?" Having said so, they came in a roundabout way to this place and suddenly saw a stupa. Being surprised at the sight, they went up to have a close look at the stupa and found that it was the one they had built at home. Thus it was named the Saffron Stupa in India.

At the southeast corner of the Bodhi Tree enclosure there is a banyan tree beside which are a stupa and a temple. In the temple is enshrined a sitting statue of the Buddha. Formerly when the Tathāgata had just attained Buddhahood, Mahābrahmā came here and entreated him to turn the wonderful Wheel of the Dharma. At each of the four corners inside the Bodhi Tree enclosure there is a great stupa. Formerly when the Tathāgata had received the auspicious grass, he went to the Bodhi Tree. He first came to the four 917b
corners and the earth quaked, and it became quiet and calm when he reached the Diamond Seat. Inside the enclosure there are many sacred sites located as closely as the scales of a fish, and it is difficult to describe them in full detail. At the southwest corner outside the Bodhi Tree enclosure is a stupa that marks the site of the old house of the two milkmaids who offered milk gruel [to the Buddha]. Beside it is another stupa, marking the place where the milkmaids cooked the gruel, and next to this stupa is the place where the Tathāgata received the gruel.

Outside the south gate of the Bodhi Tree enclosure is a big pond more than seven hundred paces in circuit, with clear and lucid water, in which dragons and fish dwell. It was dug by the younger brother of a Brahman under the order of Maheśvara. Next to the south is a pool that was magically produced by Indra when the Tathāgata wished to wash his clothes after having attained enlightenment. At the west of the pool is a big rock that was brought here by Indra from the Great Snow Mountains when the Buddha wished to dry his washed clothes in the sun. Beside the rock is a stupa where the Tathāgata mended his old clothes. Next to the south is a stupa in a wood, which was the place where the Tathāgata accepted the old clothes offered by a poor old woman as alms.

To the east of the pool produced by Indra, there is a wood in which is the pond of the dragon king Mucilinda; the water is clear and dark and tastes sweet. On the west bank is a small shrine in which is installed an image of the Buddha. Formerly when the Tathāgata had just attained enlightenment, he sat in meditation for seven days at this place. The dragon king protected the Tathāgata by surrounding him with his body in seven coils, while there appeared many heads looking down to serve as a canopy over him. On the east bank of the old pool is the chamber of the dragon king.

In a wood to the east of the dragon Mucilinda's pool is a shrine with an image of the Buddha in an emaciated condition. Beside the shrine is the place where he walked up and down. It is more than seventy paces long, and there are two pipal trees, one at the south and the other at the north side of the promenade. In the past and at present it is the custom of the local people to anoint the image with fragrant oil when they are afflicted with a disease, and in most cases they are cured of their illness. This was the place where the Buddha practiced austerities. In order to subdue the heretics and also at the request of Māra, he practiced asceticism for six years, eating only one grain of sesame and one grain of rice each day, reducing himself to a mere skeleton and becoming so feeble that he had to hold the branch of a tree to stand up to take a walk.

Beside the pipal tree where the Bodhisattva practiced austerities is a stupa at the place where Ājñāta-Kauṇḍinya and his four companions made their abode. When the Prince [Siddhārtha] renounced his home to wander in mountains and marshes and dwell in woods or by springs, King Śuddhodana sent these five persons to look after and serve him. Since the Prince practiced austerities, Ājñāta-Kauṇḍinya and the others also did the same diligently.

To the southeast of the abode of Ājñāta-Kauṇḍinya and the
917c others is a stupa where the Bodhisattva entered the Nairañjanā River to bathe. Not far from the river is the spot where the Bodhisattva accepted and ate the milk gruel. The stupa beside the spot is the place where two elders offered baked barley and honey [to the Buddha]. The Buddha was sitting cross-legged in silent meditation under a tree, enjoying the bliss of emancipation for seven days

before he emerged from the state of tranquillity, when two merchants passed by outside the wood. The god of the wood told the merchants, "The Prince of the Śākya clan is now in this wood. He has just attained Buddhahood and has been sitting in silent concentration with a fixed mind for forty-nine days without taking any food. If you offer him what food you may have with you, you will get great benefit." Then each merchant took out from his ration bag some baked barley and honey as offerings, which the World-honored One accepted.

Beside the place where the elders offered baked barley is a stupa where the four Deva-rājas offered alms bowls [to the Buddha]. When the merchants had offered baked barley and honey to him, the World-honored One considered what vessels he should use to contain the food. At that time, the four Deva-rājas came from the four quarters and each of them offered a golden bowl, but the World-honored One declined the offer by keeping silent, thinking that it was unsuitable for a mendicant to use such a bowl. The four Deva-rājas then took away the golden bowls and offered silver ones, and they even presented bowls made of crystal, lapis-lazuli, agate, coral, and pearls in succession, but the World-honored One declined them all. The four Deva-rājas then returned to their respective palaces and brought back stone bowls of a dark violet color with a brilliant luster. In order to avoid showing partiality, the World-honored One accepted all four bowls, which he piled one upon the other and pressed them into one bowl. That is why his alms bowl has four rims at the outside.

Not far from the place where the four Deva-rājas offered alms bowls is a stupa where the Tathāgata preached the Dharma for his mother. When the Tathāgata had attained perfect enlightenment with the title of Teacher of Celestial and Human Beings, his mother, Mahāmāyā, descended from her heavenly palace, and the World-honored One taught her according to her capacity for her benefit and happiness. Beside this place, on the bank of a dried-up pond, is a stupa where the Tathāgata once manifested supernatural powers to convert those who had the good causes to be present on the occasion. Beside the place of showing supernatural powers is a

stupa where the Tathāgata converted Uruvilvā-Kāśyapa and his two younger brothers together with their one thousand disciples. When the Tathāgata was spreading the good Way to conquer people as time arose, Uruvilvā-Kāśyapa's five hundred disciples wished to accept the Buddha's teachings. Kāśyapa said to them, "I shall also go with you to give up the erroneous way." So all of them came to the place where the Buddha was. The Tathāgata told them, "Throw away your deerskin garb and relinquish the utensils for fire worship." Acting according to the Buddha's holy instruction, the Brahmans cast their garments and utensils into the Nairañjanā River. On seeing the sacrificial utensils drifting away with the current, Nadī-Kāśyapa and his disciples waited to see what measures his elder brother would take next. When they saw that
918a his elder brother had changed his religion, they also followed his example and donned the dyed robes to become Buddhist monks. When Gayā-Kāśyapa and his two hundred disciples heard that his elder brothers had given up their practice, they also came to where the Buddha was and wished to lead the life of purity.

To the northwest of the place where the brothers Kāśyapa were converted is a stupa where the Tathāgata subdued the fire-dragon worshipped by the Kāśyapas. When the Tathāgata tried to convert a man, he first subdued the object of his worship. So he went to stay in the cave of the Brahmans' fire-dragon. Later in the night the dragon spouted smoke and flames, and the Buddha, who was sitting in meditation, also issued a glare, making the cave bright with the light of the furious flames and blazing fire. The Brahman teachers, fearing that the fire might hurt the Buddha, hurried to the spot, while wailing piteously. But Uruvilvā-Kāśyapa said to his disciples, "In view of the present situation, it may not be a fire. It may be the Śramaṇa subjugating the fire-dragon." The Tathāgata then put the fire-dragon into his alms bowl and showed it to the heretical disciples at dawn. The stupa beside this spot was the place where five hundred Pratyekabuddhas entered Nirvana simultaneously.

To the south of the pool of the dragon Mucilinda is a stupa where the Kāśyapas went to rescue the Tathāgata from drowning. The Kāśyapa brothers were highly esteemed for their supernatural powers and were respected for their virtue by people from far and near who had faith in them. In the course of exerting his great power in an appropriate way to guide and convert those who had gone astray, the World-honored One caused a dense cloud that poured down a torrential rain, but the Buddha's lodging alone remained dry. Upon seeing the cloud and rain, the Kāśyapas said to their disciples, "Might the lodging of the Śramaṇa not be flooded?" They sailed in a boat to rescue the World-honored One but saw that he was walking on the surface of the water just as if walking on earth, and that when he walked into the river, the water gave way to him and the sand on the bottom appeared. At this sight, the Kāśyapas went away convinced.

Two or three *li* outside the enclosure of the Bodhi Tree is the cave of a blind dragon. As this dragon had done evil deeds in its previous lives, it was born blind to suffer retribution. When the Tathāgata was proceeding from Prāgbodhi Mountain to the Bodhi Tree, he passed by the cave of the blind dragon. The dragon suddenly recovered its sight and saw that the Bodhisattva was on his way to the Bodhi Tree. It said to the Bodhisattva, "Kind Sir, you will soon gain perfect enlightenment. I have been blind for quite a long time. Whenever a Buddha emerges in the world, my eyes regain sight. When the past three Buddhas of the Bhadrakalpa appeared in the world, I recovered my sight on each occasion. Now you have come here and my eyes suddenly became perceptive. From this I know that you will become a Buddha."

Beside the east gate of the enclosure of the Bodhi Tree is a stupa where the King of Māras [tried to] frighten the Bodhisattva. Knowing that the Bodhisattva was going to achieve enlightenment and having failed in his temptation, the King of Māras did not know what to do and was worried. Then he called various gods to a meeting and arrayed his demonic troops, arranging them in proper order, to menace the Bodhisattva. A storm rose up; thun- 918b
der and lightening flashed in the dark night, fire blazed and smoke rose high, and sand and stones were raised and blown into the air. Spears and shields were fully prepared, and bows and arrows employed to the utmost. But the Bodhisattva sat in the meditation of

great compassion, and all the weapons turned into lotus flowers. Māra's troops became terrified and retreated in disorder. Not far from this place are two stupas, built by Indra and Brahmā.

Outside the north gate of [the enclosure of] the Bodhi Tree is Mahābodhi Monastery, built by a former king of the country of Siṃhala. The buildings consist of six courtyards and three storied pavilions, surrounded by walls thirty or forty feet high. The workmanship is most wonderful, and the decorative paintings are exquisitely done. The Buddha's image is made of gold and silver, and all the ornaments are embedded with gems and jewels. The stupas are lofty and spacious with wonderful adornments and contain relics of the Tathāgata. The bone relics are of the size of a finger joint, lustrous and pure white in color and semitransparent. The flesh relics, as big as pearls, are of a pinkish blue color. Every year on the full-moon day of the month of showing the Tathāgata's divine power of ubiquity (i.e., on the thirtieth day of the twelfth month in the Indian calendar, corresponding to the fifteenth day of the first month in China) these relics are shown to the public, and a light is issued or flowers fall down in showers. There are fewer than one thousand monks, who study the teachings of both the Mahayana and the Sthavira schools; they are strict in observing the Vinaya rules and pure in conduct and have moral integrity.

Formerly in the country of Siṃhala in the South Seas, the king was a devout Buddhist by birth. He had a cousin who had become a monk and desired to visit the holy traces of the Buddha. So he travelled far to India, where he sought lodging in various monasteries, but all the local monks despised him as a frontiersman. Then he returned to his homeland, and the king went out to a distance to welcome him. The Śramaṇa sobbed piteously and could not properly speak. The king said, "What is wrong with you that you are so sad?" The Śramaṇa said, "It was depending upon the prestige of our country that I travelled far to seek the Way. I sojourned in a foreign land and experienced the discomfort of cold and hot weather. I was often insulted for my behavior and was sneered at for my utterances. How could I be happy under such worrying and shameful conditions?" The king said, "If that is the case, what shall I do?" The Śramaṇa said, "I sincerely hope that Your Majesty will pay attention to the performance of good deeds and construct a monastery in India. That will not only glorify the holy site but also build a high reputation for yourself. The blessedness of the deed will do good to our forefathers and benefit our descendants as well." The king said, "That is a good idea. How is it that I hear of it so late?"

Then the king [of Siṃhala] offered all the treasures of his country to the king of India, who, after accepting the tribute and wishing to foster friendship with a distant ruler, said to the envoy, "What shall I give you to bring back as a return gift?" The envoy said, "The King of Siṃhala pays homage to the King of Great Auspiciousness of India. Your prestige and virtue extend far and your kindness and benevolence cover all living beings. A Śramaṇa of our humble land, out of respect and admiration for the morals and manners of your country, ventured to travel to your esteemed land to pay veneration to the holy sites. He looked for lodging in various monasteries, but none would house him. After going through 918c
uttermost difficulties, he returned home with shame. I humbly propose a far-reaching project that may serve as an example for coming generations, that is, to build a monastery in India so as to provide a resting place for travelling monks, in order to promote good relations between our two countries, and to let envoys be exchanged without intermission." The king said, "The tradition of the Tathāgata's subtle edification is still extant, and you may choose any one of the holy sites [for the construction]."

With this message the envoy returned home to make a report to the king [of Siṃhala]. The king's ministers prostrated themselves before him in congratulation. Then the Śramaṇas were convened to discuss the matter of constructing a monastery, and they said, "As the Bodhi Tree is the place where the past Buddhas attained and the future ones will attain Buddhahood, nowhere is there a better place among all suggestions." Then the treasures of the country were donated for the construction of this monastery with monks from the country [of Siṃhala] to look after it. A copper plate was inscribed with the following words: "Selfless alms-giving is the supreme teaching taught by all Buddhas, and rendering assistance to those who have the cause to receive it is the explicit instruction of former sages. I, this humble person, after having succeeded to the throne, have built this monastery to glorify the holy site and to render blessedness to my ancestors, as well as to benefit the common people. The monks of my country may have free access to it, and the people of the country where it stands may also enjoy the same privilege as the monks. This tradition is to be transmitted to posterity into the indefinite future." Thus most of the monks in this monastery come from the Land of Lions.

More than ten *li* to the south of the Bodhi Tree, the sacred sites are so closely neighboring on each other that it is difficult to tell of them in detail. Each year, when the *bhikṣus* end the rains retreat, monks and lay people, hundreds and thousands in number, come here from the four quarters, holding flowers, playing music, and wandering in the wood to perform acts of veneration and make offerings for seven days and nights.

According to the Buddha's holy teachings, the monks of India commence the rains retreat on the first day of the first half of the month of Śrāvaṇa, corresponding to the sixteenth day of the fifth month in China, and end the retreat on the fifteenth day of the second half of the month of Aśvayuja, corresponding to the fifteenth day of the eighth month in China. In India, as the months are named after the constellations, the course of time has not changed from ancient times to the present, and it is invariably accepted by all schools. It was probably due to misunderstanding or mistranslation from the foreign language that variance arose in the calculations for the division of time and the fixation of the months. Thus [in China] the rains retreat is started on the sixteenth day of the fourth month and terminated on the fifteenth day of the seventh month (one month earlier than in India).

End of Fascicle Eight

Fascicle IX

The Country of Magadha (2)

To the east of the Bodhi Tree and across the Nairañjanā River, 919a
there is a stupa in a great wood, and to the north of the stupa is a pond where the fragrant elephant attended on his mother. In the past, when the Tathāgata was practicing the deeds of a Bodhisattva, he was born as the son of a fragrant elephant, living on North Mountain, and once he came near the pond for pleasure. As his mother was blind, he drew pure water and fetched lotus roots to feed her with respect and filial piety; this he did over time. Once a man lost his way while travelling through the wood. He walked back and forth and wept piteously. Having heard the sound, the young elephant had pity upon the man, guided him out of the wood, and showed him the way home. When the man returned home, he reported to the king, "I know that a fragrant elephant is wandering about the pond in the wood. This is a rare animal, and you may go to catch it." The king accepted his words and sent soldiers to catch the elephant. The man proceeded before them as a guide, and at the very moment when he pointed out the young elephant for the king, his two arms fell down as if chopped off. Although the king was surprised by the sight, he still captured the young elephant and brought him home. After he was caught, for a long time the young elephant refused to eat grass or drink water. The stable keeper informed the king, who went personally to inquire into the matter. The young elephant said, "My mother is blind and is starving all day long. Now I am a captive; how can I enjoy delicious food?" Being moved by the elephant's filial sentiment, the king released him. In front of the stupa beside the pond is a stone pillar

where Kāśyapa Buddha had sat in meditation in the past. Beside it are places where the four past Buddhas sat and walked up and down.

After crossing the Mahā River to the east of the seats of the four past Buddhas, I reached a great wood in which there is a stone pillar marking the place where a heretic sat in meditation and made an evil vow. In the past the heretic Udraka Rāmaputra was a man aspiring to spiritual attainment and making his abode in the wilderness. In this wood of religious practice, he engaged his mind in meditation and lived in seclusion. As he gained the five supernormal powers and achieved the Samādhi of Neither Thinking nor Not-thinking, the king of Magadha highly respected him. At noon every day he always invited the hermit to the palace to have his meal. Udraka Rāmaputra travelled through the air to and fro without interruption, and the king of Magadha would look into the air and wait for him. Upon his arrival the king would receive him and give him a seat.

Once the king was about to go out for a pleasure trip, and he
919b intended to entrust somebody to serve the hermit. But nobody in the inner palace was competent to answer the purpose, except his own daughter, a young lady with a kind heart and prudence, who was courteous and well-behaved; nobody excelled her in amiability and virtue. The king of Magadha summoned his daughter and ordered her, "I am travelling to a distant place, and I have something to entrust to you. You should be careful to fulfill the duty to completion. The hermit Udraka Rāmaputra is a man whom I always venerate respectfully. When he comes at mealtimes, you should serve him as I do." Having given this instruction, the king started on his journey. Under the order of the king, the young maid waited for the hermit as usual, and upon his arrival she received him and took him to his seat. Having been in contact with a woman, Udraka Rāmaputra felt an impulse of desire and lost his supernormal powers.

After the meal was over, when he was to go back, he found that he was unable to fly anymore. Feeling shame in his mind, he said deceitfully to the maid, "I have been practicing the Way and sitting in meditation with a peaceful mind for many years, and I am used to flying to and fro through the air without any leisure moments. I heard long ago that the people of the country wished to see me. Previous teachers have taught us that we should work for the benefit of others as our duty. How can one stick to one's own good and forget about altruistic considerations? Now I wish to go out the door and walk on the earth, so that those who see me may gain bliss and benefit." Having heard these words, the princess made a public announcement. Thereupon, the people hurriedly sprinkled water and swept the thoroughfare clean, and hundreds and thousands of people stood still for a long time to wait for the arrival of the hermit.

Udraka Rāmaputra walked from the palace to the religious wood and sat down to practice meditation. But his mind was disturbed by the external environment. When he stayed in the wood, he heard the crowing and chirping of crows and other birds, and when he came near the pond, the splashing of fish and turtles annoyed him. His attention was distracted and his mind confused, and he lost his spirit and was unable to practice meditation. Thus he was enraged and made an evil vow, saying, "Let me be in the future a fierce and wicked animal with the body of a leopard and the wings of a bird, preying on living creatures. My body will be three thousand *li* in width and each of the wings fifteen hundred *li* in length. I shall haunt the forests to devour the feathered tribes and enter the waters to eat aquatic animals." After making this vow, his anger gradually abated. Through hard work he regained his original state of meditation shortly afterward. Before long he died and was reborn in the Heaven of Neither Thinking Nor Not-thinking, enjoying a life of eighty thousand kalpas. The Tathāgata predicted that after the conclusion of his heavenly life, the hermit would realize his original vow and be reborn as that ugly creature. Thenceforward he would turn in the evil states of transmigration without a period fixed for his release.

At the east of the Mahā River, I entered a great jungle, and going for more than one hundred *li*, I reached Kukkuṭapāda (known as Jizu, or Cock's foot, in Chinese) Mountain, also called Gurupāda (known as Zunzu, or Sage's foot, in Chinese) Mountain. The lofty peaks are extremely steep, and the deep valleys seem to be bottomless. At the foot of the mountain and among the brooks, there are tall trees in the valleys, and luxuriant green grass covers the rocks on the peaks and cliffs. There are three precipitous peaks, standing cloud-capped, nearly touching the sky. As the Venerable Mahākāśyapa entered Nirvana at this mountain, people of later times, not wishing to mention his name bluntly, called the mountain Guru's Foot Mountain.

919c Mahākāśyapa was a *śrāvaka* disciple [of the Buddha] who achieved the six supernatural powers and possessed the eight forms of liberation. When the Tathāgata had completed his career of edification and was about to enter Nirvana, he told Kāśyapa, "For innumerable kalpas I diligently practiced austerities seeking the supreme Dharma for the benefit of all living beings. Now as I have fulfilled my desire and expectation as I wished in the past, I am going to enter Mahanirvana, and I entrust the Dharma-piṭaka to you. You should preserve and spread it and never let it fall down. I shall leave behind the golden-thread *kaṣāya* that my aunt offered to me, to be transmitted to Maitreya when he becomes a Buddha in the future. All those who cultivate themselves in my bequeathed teaching, whether *bhikṣu*s, *bhikṣunī*s, *upāsaka*s (male lay devotees), or *upāsikā*s (female lay devotees), should be first delivered from the round of transmigration."

Having received the instructions of the Buddha, Kāśyapa upheld the right Dharma. In the twentieth year after the conclusion of the Great Council, he became tired of the impermanent world and wished to enter Nirvana. Thus he went to Kukkuṭa Mountain and climbed up the north side of the mountain; going by a roundabout way he reached the southwest ridge. The peaks are dangerous and difficult to climb, and the paths are tortuous and overgrown with weeds. He cleared the way with his pewter staff and cut down the weeds as if he were using a knife. When he had opened the mountain path, he proceeded along the roundabout way in a crisscross manner. After reaching the summit, he was facing the northeast. Standing in the midst of the three peaks, he held the Buddha's *kaśāya* with both hands. By the power of his vow, the three peaks closed together, leaving behind the three protuberant ridges we see now.

When Maitreya comes to the world as a World-honored One, he will preach the Dharma in three assemblies. After that there will still be numerous arrogant people who will ascend this mountain and come to the place of Kāśyapa. Maitreya will snap his fingers and the mountain peaks will open by themselves, and upon seeing Kāśyapa, the people will become all the more arrogant. At this moment Mahākāśyapa will hand over the *kaṣāya* [to Maitreya]. After making a speech and paying homage [to the new Buddha], Kāśyapa will rise into the air and manifest various divine transformations. A fire will burst forth to cremate his body, and in this manner he will enter Nirvana. Having seen this sight, the people will dispel their pride; thereupon they will become awakened and realize sainthood. Therefore a stupa has been built on the mountain, and on a quiet night one may see a burning torch from a distance, but when one goes up the mountain, nothing is to be seen.

Going more than one hundred *li* northeast from Kukkuṭapāda 920a
Mountain, I reached Buddhavana Mountain with its lofty peaks and steep cliffs. Among the rocks there is a cave in which the Buddha once stayed. Beside the cave is a huge rock, on which Indra and Brahmā pulverized oxhead sandalwood and rubbed the body of the Tathāgata with the powder. Even now there is a strong fragrance retained on the rock. The spirits of the five hundred Arhats remain here latently. Those who have the chance to meet them may see them appearing as *śrāmaṇera*s going to the villages to collect alms of food. Their miraculous deeds, whether secret or manifest, are difficult to relate in detail.

Going east for more than thirty *li* in the deep valleys of Buddhavana Mountain, I reached the Yaṣṭi Wood (known as Stick wood in Chinese), full of bamboos covering the mountain and the valleys. Formerly there was a Brahman who heard that the Śākya Buddha was sixteen feet tall, but he was in doubt and would not believe it. Thus he used a bamboo stick sixteen feet long to measure the height of the Buddha. Each time he did so, the Buddha's figure always exceeded the length of the stick by sixteen feet. In this manner the Brahman found the Buddha's height becoming higher and higher and could not ascertain his actual height. Then he cast off the stick and went away, and the stick took root [giving rise to a bamboo wood]. In the wood there is a great stupa built by King Aśoka. Formerly the Tathāgata showed great supernatural powers and preached the deep and subtle Dharma for various heavenly and human beings at this place for seven days.

In the Stick Wood there was recently an *upāsaka* named Jayasena (known as Shengjun, or Victorious army, in Chinese), who was a man of the Kshatriya caste of West India. He preferred to live a plain and simple life in the mountains and forests, and although he stayed in the world of illusion, his mind dwelt in the state of reality. He was learned in the subtle meanings of both Buddhist and heretical texts, being eloquent in discussion and perspicuous in thinking. Various Śramaṇas, Brahmans, heretical and heterodox scholars, kings, ministers, elders, and wealthy and powerful people approached him to seek his instructions with full conviction. His disciples were found in six families out of ten. When he was nearly seventy years old, he still devoted himself to arduous study without tiredness. He gave up all other subjects of learning and engaged himself solely in the study of Buddhist scriptures with mental and physical exertion both in the daytime and at night.

In India it is the custom to make miniature stupas five or six inches high with scented clay. Copies of scriptures are put inside these stupas, which are known as Dharma relics. When a large number of such stupas is accumulated, a great stupa is constructed to contain them all for perpetual veneration. Therefore when Jayasena was teaching his disciples, he orally inculcated them with the wonderful Dharma, while his hands were busy in making small stupas in order to accumulate supreme bliss. At night, he walked to and fro, or worshipped and recited scriptures, or sat in quiet meditation, having no time to sleep or take food, and never relaxed either in the daytime or at night. Even when he was one hundred years old, he did not slacken his effort, and in a period of thirty years he made seven *koṭis* of Dharma-relic stupas. Each time he completed one *koṭi* of stupas, he constructed a great stupa to contain all the small ones for people to make offerings to, and monks 920b were invited to celebrate religious functions. On each occasion a divine light shone brightly, an apparent spiritual manifestation, and after that a light issued from time to time.

More than ten *li* to the southwest of Stick Wood, there are two hot springs to the south of a great mountain. The water is very hot, and when the Buddha had caused these springs, he bathed in them. They are still in existence, and the flow of clear water has never diminished. People come here from far and near to bathe, and for those who suffer from chronic illness they may effect a cure. Beside the springs is a stupa built at a place where the Tathāgata walked up and down. Going southeast for six or seven *li* from Stick Wood, I reached a great mountain. In front of a ridge of the mountain, there is a stone stupa, and in the past the Tathāgata once preached the Dharma at this place for the three months of the rains. At that time King Bimbisāra wished to come to listen to the Dharma, so the mountain was cut to build a passageway with stone steps more than twenty paces wide and three or four *li* in length, leading forward.

Three or four *li* to the north of the great mountain is an isolate hill where the hermit Vyāsa once dwelt. The cave he excavated in the rock is still in existence. He imparted his teachings to his disciples, and the system of his learning is still prevalent. Four or five *li* to the northeast of this isolate hill is a smaller isolate hill. The size of the cave excavated in the rock of the hill is large enough to provide seats for over one thousand people. In the past the Tathāgata once preached the Dharma at this place for three months. Above the cave is a big rock, on which Indra and Brahmā ground oxhead sandalwood to rub the body of the Buddha with the powder. The fragrance lingering on the rock is still very strong.

At the southwest corner of the cave, there is a grotto known in India as the Asura's Palace. Once a mischievous man, who was skillful in the art of sorcery, invited [thirteen] bosom friends who had the same interests as he, and the fourteen of them went together into

the grotto. After going for thirty or forty *li*, they came out into an open, bright place and saw city walls, terraces, and pavilions all made of gold, silver, and lapis-lazuli. When they approached the city, some young maidens standing by the city gate welcomed them with pleasure and cordiality. Then they proceeded gradually and came to the inner city, where two maidservants, standing by the gate and each holding a golden tray full of flowers and incense, greeted them and said, "You must bathe yourselves in the pool, rub your bodies with incense, and wear garlands before you can be admitted in a proper manner; but the sorcerer may go in promptly." Then the thirteen others went to take baths. As soon as they entered the bathing pool they forgot everything and found that they
920c were sitting in a paddy field on a plain thirty or forty *li* to the north of the grotto.

Beside the grotto there is a viaduct more than ten paces wide and four or five *li* in length. In the past, when King Bimbisāra was about to go to the place of the Buddha, rocks were cleft to clear up the valley, precipices were cut down to dredge the stream, and stones were piled up and cliffs chiselled to make steps leading to the place of the Buddha.

From this great mountain going east for more than sixty *li*, I reached the city of Kuśāgrapura (known as Shangmaogongcheng, or Superior reed palace city, in Chinese). Kuśāgrapura, being at the center of the country of Magadha, was the capital of previous kings in ancient times. It is so called because it abounds in superior and lucky fragrant reeds. It is surrounded by hills as its outer walls, with a narrow path leading to the west and a passage opening to the north. It is long from east to west and narrow from south to north and more than one hundred fifty *li* in circuit. Karṇikāra (mayeng) trees grow everywhere on the mountain paths. The flowers have a special redolence and are golden in color. Late in spring the whole wood becomes golden colored.

Outside the north gate of the palace city there is a stupa built at the place where Devadatta, who was on intimate terms with Ajātaśatru, let out Dhanapāla, an intoxicated elephant, in an attempt to hurt the Tathāgata. But the Tathāgata produced five lions from the tips of five fingers to tame the drunken elephant before he proceeded on his way.

To the northeast of the place where the drunken elephant was subdued was the spot where Śāriputra attained sainthood upon hearing the Dharma preached by Bhikṣu Aśvajit (known as Masheng, or Victorious horse, in Chinese). When Śāriputra was a layman, he was well known for his high talents and broadmindedness, and he had disciples and pupils studying under his instruction. Once he was going to the great city of Rājagṛha when Bhikṣu Aśvajit was going round to beg for his food. Upon seeing Aśvajit at a distance, Śāriputra said to his disciples, "That man coming over there looks very graceful and refined in deportment. If he had not attained sainthood, he could not be so calm and quiet in demeanor. Let us wait a moment and see whither he is going." Bhikṣu Aśvajit, being an Arhat, was free from mental defilements and carried himself in a gentle and peaceful manner, holding a religious staff in hand. Śāriputra said to him, "Elder Sir, are you living in good health and happiness? Who is your teacher and what Dharma have you realized that you look so glad and contented?" Aśvajit said, "Do you not know that the prince of King Śuddhodana relinquished his position as a wheel-turning monarch and out of pity for all beings of the six paths of transmigration practiced austerities for six years and attained perfect enlightenment, so that he now possesses all-knowing wisdom? He is my teacher. As regards the Dharma, it is neither real nor void, and it is difficult to give a systematic exposition of it. It can be fully explained only by the Buddhas. How can I, a man of ignorance, discuss the matter in detail?" Then he uttered a stanza in praise of the Buddha-dharma. 921a
Upon hearing the stanza, Śāriputra attained sainthood.

Not far to the north of the place where Śāriputra attained sainthood, there is a big and deep pit beside which a stupa has been built. This was the place where Śrīgupta (known as Shengmi, or Auspicious secrecy, in Chinese) attempted to kill the Buddha in a fire pit, and with poisoned rice. Śrīgupta had faith in the heretics and held fast to erroneous views. Some Brahmans said to him, "As Gautama is respected by the people of the country, we have lost our supporters. Invite him to a meal at your home. Dig a big pit with fire burning in it at the gate of your house. Then cover the pit with some rotten timber and camouflage it with dry earth. Poison should be put into all food and drink. In case he escapes the fire pit, he will be poisoned to death." According to this suggestion, Śrīgupta prepared a meal of poisoned food. All the people in the city knew that Śrīgupta was intriguing against the World-honored One with an evil intention, and they all exhorted the Buddha not to go to take the meal. The World-honored One told them, "Do not worry! Nothing can harm the body of a Tathāgata." Then he accepted the invitation and went. As soon as his foot touched the doorsill, the fire pit turned into a pool full of lotus flowers growing out of clear and lucid water. At this sight, Śrīgupta was panic-stricken, but he said to his disciples, "Even if he has escaped the fire pit through magic power, there is still poisoned food for him." When the World-honored One had taken the meal, he preached the wonderful Dharma. Upon hearing the Dharma, Śrīgupta apologized for his misdeeds and took refuge in the Buddha.

At a bend of the mountain city to the northeast of Śrīgupta's fire pit is a stupa where the great physician Jīvaka (wrongly transliterated as Qipo in Chinese) built a preaching hall for the Buddha with flowers and fruit trees planted at the open spaces around the building. Remains of the structure and new sprouts of the old plants are still to be seen. When the Tathāgata was living in the world, he stayed mostly in this hall. Beside it is the site of Jīvaka's private residence, of which the remnant foundations and an old well still exist in ruins.

Going northeast for fourteen or fifteen *li* from the palace city, I reached Gṛdhrakūṭa Mountain (known in China as the Vulture peak or terrace, and formerly mistranscribed as Qishejue Mountain). It links with the south side of North Mountain, protruding all alone to a great height, where vultures perch, and also resembles a high terrace. The verdurous mountain presents a distinct color in contrast with the sky. During the fifty years of his missionary career, the Tathāgata stayed on this mountain on many occasions to preach the wonderful Dharma.

In order to hear the Buddha's preaching, King Bimbisāra sent men to build a road leading from the foot of the mountain to the summit, more than ten paces wide and five or six *li* in length, across valleys and over rocks, with stones piled up into steps. There are two small stupas on the way. One is known as the place of alighting, from where the king started to walk on foot to proceed on his way, and the other as the place of preventing ordinary persons from going further [with the king]. The summit is oblong from east to west and narrow from south to north. On the brink of the west side of the precipice is a brick shrine, high and spacious, built 921b
in a marvellous style, with its door opening to the east. The Tathāgata preached the Dharma in it many times. Now there is a life-size statue of the Tathāgata in the posture of delivering a sermon.

To the east of the shrine is an oblong stone on which the Tathāgata walked to and fro. Beside it is a great rock fourteen or fifteen feet high and more than thirty paces in circumference. This was the place where Devadatta hurled a stone from a distance to hit the Buddha. To its south and below the cliff was the place where the Tathāgata preached the *Saddharma-puṇḍarīka-sūtra* in olden times. To the south of the shrine and beside a steep rock is a cave where the Tathāgata sat in meditation in days of yore. To the northwest of the Buddha's cave there is another cave, in front of which is a huge rock where Ānanda was frightened by Māra. Once when the Venerable Ānanda was sitting in meditation at this place, Māra transformed himself into a vulture and occupied the huge rock one night in the black half of the month, flapping his wings violently and shrieking terrifically to scare Ānanda. The venerable monk was alarmed and terror-stricken. The Tathāgata, seeing him in trouble, stretched his comforting hand through the stone wall of the cave to stroke Ānanda's head and said to him with great compassion, "It is merely a phantom of Māra. Do not be frightened!" Having been consoled, Ānanda felt at ease and happy both physically and mentally. The traces left by the bird on the rock and the hole made in the stone wall in the cave still exist despite the long lapse of time. Beside the shrine there are several caves, in which Śāriputra and other great Arhats practiced meditation. In front of Śāriputra's cave is a big well; it is now dried up, but the mouth of the well still exists in the ruins.

A huge flat rock in the stony gully to the northeast of the shrine is the place where the Tathāgata sunned his *kaṣāya*. The stripes of the robe left on the rock are as distinct as if they were carved on it. Beside the rock are the footprints of the Buddha. Although the traces are obscure, the size is still discernible. On the top of North Mountain is a stupa at the place where the Tathāgata looked at the city of Magadha and preached the Dharma for seven days.

To the west of the north gate of the mountain city is Vipula Hill. I heard the local people say that on the north side of the cliff to the southwest of the hill, there used to be five hundred hot springs, but now there are only a few score, of which some are cold and some warm, so not all of them are hot springs. The source of these springs is Anavatapta Lake to the south of the Snow Mountains, and the water flows underground to this place. It is nice and clear and tastes the same as the water in the lake of origin. The water flows out in five hundred streams through the Small Hot Hells, and as the fire of the hells goes up it makes the water of the springs lukewarm. All the mouths of the springs have stone carvings in the shapes of heads of lions or white elephants; aqueducts lead the water below into tanks made of slabs of stone. People
921c come from various places in different regions to bathe in the tanks, and they can often wash away their old maladies. On both the right and the left sides of the hot springs, stupas and shrines were built with their foundations laid as closely together as the scales of a fish, and all of them are sites where the four past Buddhas sat and walked up and down in ancient times. As this is a place of mountains and streams, it is an ideal hermitage for wise and benevolent people to take up their abodes; so there must be many recluses living in seclusion in this locality.

To the west of the hot springs is the Pippala Cave, in which the World-honored One always made his abode. The cavern behind the back wall of the cave is the Asura's Palace. *Bhikṣus* who practiced meditation mostly resided in this cave. Strange phantoms in the shapes of dragons, snakes, and lions often appeared in this cave, and those who saw them would go insane. But as this is a well-known place where holy and spiritual persons stayed, people in admiration of their edification braved the danger and came here one after another. Recently a *bhikṣu* who was pure in observing the disciplinary rules and took delight in lodging at quiet and peaceful places desired to live in this cave to practice meditation. Someone advised him, "Do not go to that cave, which is full of disasters; many people have been killed. It will be difficult for you to gain mental concentration there, and you might even lose your life. You should take warning from former accidents and not cause yourself regret in the future." The *bhikṣu* said, "No, it is not so. I am aiming my efforts at attaining Buddhahood in order to subjugate the heavenly Māra. What is worth mentioning in such mischief?" He shook his pewter staff and went to the cave, where he prepared an altar and recited mantras. After ten days a young woman came out of the cavern and said to the *bhikṣu*, "Venerable Sir, you wear the dyed robe and keep the disciplinary rules so that living beings may take refuge under you, and you cultivate wisdom and practice meditation to be a good guide for living creatures. But now you stay here to frighten us. Is this what the Tathāgata has taught you to do?" The *bhikṣu* said, "I observe the pure rules in accordance with the Buddha's holy teachings, and I live in seclusion in the mountains in order to avoid the hubbub and excitement of social life. What is wrong with me that causes you to accuse me?" The woman said, "When you uttered mantras your voice made a fire burn from the outside into my dwelling and caused trouble to my kinsfolk. Will you have pity on us and not repeat mantras any more?" The *bhikṣu* said, "I recite mantras for self-protection and not for doing harm to others. In the past when monks stayed here to practice meditation in the hope of gaining sainthood, so as to save those who were suffering in the dark path of transmigration, they were scared to death by the sight of your terrific appearance. It was all your fault. What do you say to that?" The woman said in reply, "Heavy is my sin and shallow is my wisdom. From now onward I shall live in seclusion and keep myself within bounds. But I also hope that you, Venerable Sir, will not repeat mantras." So the *bhikṣu* practiced meditation in peace and was not harmed.

On Vipula Mountain is a stupa where the Tathāgata formerly preached the Dharma. Now many naked heretics stay at this place,
922a practicing austerities without negligence day and night, and from dawn to dusk they turn round to watch [the sun] in movement.

Going east for two or three *li* from the north side of the south cliff at the left side of the north gate of the mountain city, I came to a great cave in which Devadatta sat in meditation in olden times. On a flat rock not far to the east of this cave there are traces resembling stains of blood. Beside it is a stupa built at the spot where a *bhikṣu* who practiced meditation committed suicide and attained sainthood. Once a *bhikṣu* exerted his mental and physical effort in practicing meditation in seclusion. As he failed to attain sainthood through the passage of a long time, he blamed himself and said with regret, "I could not gain in time the perfect stage of sainthood with nothing more to learn. What is the use of keeping this body of mine, which is really a burden to me?" Then he came to this rock and cut his throat. At that very moment he realized Arhatship, ascended into the air, performed miraculous transformations, produced a fire to cremate his body, and entered Nirvana. This stupa was built in memory of his merits, to extol his sublime character.

On the cliff to the east of the place where the *bhikṣu* [cut his own throat and] attained sainthood is a stone stupa at the spot where another *bhikṣu* practiced meditation, threw himself down the cliff, and gained sainthood. Once at the time of the Buddha there was a *bhikṣu* who sat in the woods and the mountains to practice meditation in order to achieve sainthood. He worked hard for a long time but could not realize his wish. Both in the daytime and at night, he never forgot to fix his mind in tranquil meditation.

Knowing that the fundamental ability of the *bhikṣu* was about to be fully developed, the Tathāgata went to render assistance to him. He came from the Bamboo Grove to the foot of the cliff, snapped his fingers to call the *bhikṣu,* and stood there waiting for him. Looking at the holy monks from a distance, the *bhikṣu* was encouraged and jumped down the cliff with delight. As his mind was pure and he had faith in the Buddha's words, he gained sainthood before his body reached the ground. The World-honored One told him, "You should know it is the time now!" Then the *bhikṣu* ascended into the air and showed divine manifestations. In order to exalt his pure faith, this stupa was built as a memorial.

Going out of the north gate of the mountain city for about one *li,* I reached the Kalandaka Bamboo Garden, in which there is now a temple, a brick chamber built on stone bases with its door opening to the east. When the Tathāgata was living in the world, he spent much time in this temple, preaching the Dharma for the edification and guidance of the common people and converting the secular folk. There is a life-size image of the Tathāgata of recent origin. At the beginning there was an eminent elder named Kalandaka, well known for his nobility and enormous wealth. He presented this great Bamboo Garden to the heretics, but when he saw the Tathāgata and heard the Dharma with pure faith, he repented that he had given his garden as a lodging to the heterodox believers and now had nowhere to house the Teacher of Men and Heavenly Beings. At that time various gods and spirits, being moved by the elder's sincerity, expelled the heretics and told them, "The Elder Kalandaka wishes to build a temple for the Buddha in the Bamboo Garden. You should quickly go away so as to avoid mishap and disaster." The heretics quitted the garden in anger and resentment. So the elder built a temple in the garden, and 922b
when the construction was completed, he went in person to invite the Buddha, who then accepted the gift.

To the east of the Kalandaka Bamboo Garden is a stupa built by King Ajātaśatru (known in Chinese as Weishengyuan, or Enemy before birth, formerly abridged wrongly as Asheshi). After the Nirvana of the Tathāgata, various kings shared his relic bones, and King Ajātaśatru obtained his portion, for which he built this stupa with veneration to make offerings to the relics. Afterward when King Aśoka had faith in the Buddha-dharma, he opened this stupa and took out the relics for building more stupas. There are still some remnant relics in the stupa, which often emits a bright light.

In another stupa beside the one built by Ajātaśatru are entombed the relics of the Venerable Ānanda's half body. When the Venerable Ānanda was about to enter Nirvana, he left the country of Magadha and proceeded to the city of Vaiśālī. The two countries contended with each other [to keep Ānanda's body] and were on the brink of war. Out of pity for them, Ānanda divided his body. When the king of Magadha got his portion, he brought it back and built a stupa for it at this superior place. Beside it is the spot where the Tathāgata formerly walked up and down. Not far from here is a stupa built at the place where Śāriputra and Maudgalaputra stayed to observe the summer retreat during the rainy season.

Five or six *li* to the southwest from the Bamboo Garden and at the north of South Mountain, there is a large cave in a great bamboo grove. Mahākāśyapa and nine hundred ninety-nine great Arhats stayed here to collect the Tripiṭaka after the Nirvana of the Tathāgata. In front of the cave are the old foundations of a hall built by King Ajātaśatru for the great Arhats who took part in collecting the Dharma-piṭaka. At the beginning, when Mahākāśyapa was sitting at leisure in a mountain forest, he suddenly saw a brilliant light while the earth quaked. He said, "What does this strange phenomenon augur?" He observed with his divine eye and saw that the Buddha, the World-honored One, had entered Nirvana at the Twin Trees. Then he ordered his disciples to go with him to the city of Kuśinagara. On the road they met a Brahman holding some celestial flowers in his hand, and Kāśyapa asked him, "Where do you come from? Do you know where my great teacher is?" The Brahman said, "I have just come from the city of Kuśinagara, and I have seen that your great teacher has entered Nirvana. Men and heavenly beings in a great assembly are making offerings to him. These flowers in my hand are obtained from them."

Upon hearing these words, Kāśyapa said to his disciples, "The Sun of Wisdom has sunk and the world is rolled up in darkness. The Good Guide has relinquished us, and living beings will trip and fall." The indolent *bhikṣus*, however, felt happy and said to each other with joy, "Since the Tathāgata has entered Nirvana, we shall be able to live an easy life. If we commit any fault, nobody will reproach or restrain us any more." Having heard these words, Kāśyapa felt all the more sorrowful and thought of collecting the Dharma-piṭaka as a guiding principle to prevent the violation of moral regulations taught by the Buddha. Then he went to the Twin Trees to see and worship the Buddha.

After the demise of the King of the Dharma, men and heav- 922c
enly beings lost their Guide, and various great Arhats also entered Nirvana. At that time Mahākāśyapa considered that the Dharma-piṭaka should be collected in obedience to the Buddha's teachings. So he ascended Mount Sumeru, struck a big bell, and made an announcement, saying, "A Dharma affair is to be conducted in the city of Rājagṛha. All those who have attained sainthood should promptly assemble!" Kāśyapa's summons was carried by the sound of the bell to all the three thousand great chiliocosms, and on hearing the summons all those who had acquired supernatural powers came to the assembly. At that time Kāśyapa told the congregation, "As the Tathāgata has entered Nirvana, the world is empty now. We should collect the Dharma-piṭaka in order to repay the kindness of the Buddha. In collecting the Dharma, only a select number of persons may take part, so that they may work in quiet. How can we flock into a crowd to upset this sublime task? Only such superior persons as possess the three kinds of knowledge and the six supernatural powers, have heard and practiced what is not erroneous, and are eloquent without hindrance may be invited to take part in the collection, while those who have more to learn should return to their respective abodes." Then a total of nine hundred ninety-nine persons was selected. Ānanda was not included in the list, as he was still in the stage of learning. Mahākāśyapa called to him and said, "As you have not become spiritually perfect, it befits you to quit the holy assembly." [Ānanda] said,

"I attended on the Tathāgata for many consecutive years. Whenever there was a discussion on the Dharma, I never missed it. Now at the time of collecting the Dharma, I am not allowed to take part in the task. The King of the Dharma has entered Nirvana, and I have lost what I relied on." Kāśyapa told him, "Do not be vexed! It is true that you have been a personal attendant to the Buddha and have heard most of his utterances, but you are not free from the delusion of passion, and your bonds of habitual illusion have not been cut off." Ānanda was tongue-tied and went out. He went to a solitary place, desiring to gain the perfect stage of having nothing more to learn. Although he worked hard, he could not realize his ambition. When he felt tired, he went to take a nap, and at the moment he had not yet touched the pillow, he instantly attained Arhatship. Then he went to the assembly hall and knocked at the door to announce his arrival. Kāśyapa inquired, "Have you cleared off all your bonds? You should be able to utilize your supernatural powers and come in without opening the door." Accordingly, Ānanda entered through the keyhole. After paying homage to the monks, he withdrew and resumed his seat. This event occurred on the first full-moon day of the summer retreat.

Then Kāśyapa made a declaration, "Please listen to me attentively: Ānanda was praised by the Tathāgata for his all-round knowledge; let him collect the Sūtra-piṭaka. Upāli is well-known to all for his clear understanding of the monastic rules; let him collect the Vinaya-piṭaka. And I, Kāśyapa, shall collect the Abhidharma-piṭaka." When the three months of the rainy season came to an end, the collection of the Tripiṭaka was completed. As Mahākāśyapa was the elder among the monks and presided over the assembly, it was known as the Assembly of the Elder.

To the northwest of the place where Mahākāśyapa collected the Tripiṭaka is the spot where Ānanda came and sat in medita-
923a tion and attained Arhatship after he had been criticized by the monks and not allowed to take part in the gathering. He was permitted to join in the work after his realization of sainthood.

More than twenty *li* to the northwest of the spot where Ānanda attained sainthood is a stupa constructed by King Aśoka at the place where the Great Congregation of monks made their collection of the Buddha's teachings. Hundreds and thousands of Arhats and ordinary monks, who were not admitted to the assembly headed by Mahākāśyapa, came here and said among themselves, "When the Tathāgata was living in the world, we all studied under one teacher. Now that the King of the Dharma has entered Nirvana, we have been treated discriminatorily. In order to repay the kindness of the Buddha, we should collect the Dharma-piṭaka." Thus the ordinary and saintly monks gathered together, and sages and wise men joined in the meeting. They collected the Sūtra-piṭaka, the Vinaya-piṭaka, the Abhidharma-piṭaka, the Miscellaneous piṭaka, and the Dhāraṇī-piṭaka as a separate fivefold piṭaka. As this collection was made in an assembly participated in by both ordinary and saintly monks, it is called the Collection of the Great Congregation.

Going north for more than two hundred paces from the Bamboo Temple, I reached the Kalandaka Pool. Formerly the Tathāgata preached the Dharma at this place. The water was clear and clean and possessed the eight virtues. After the Buddha's Nirvana, the pool became dried up completely. Two or three *li* to the northwest of the Kalandaka Pool is a stupa built by King Aśoka. It is more than sixty feet high, and beside it is a stone pillar carved with an inscription narrating the events of constructing the stupa. It is more than fifty feet tall and has the figure of an elephant on its top.

Not far to the northeast of the stone pillar is the city of Rājagṛha (known in Chinese as Wangshe, or Royal house). Its outer walls are destroyed and there is no trace of them left; the inner walls, though ruined, still have foundations of some height. It is more than twenty *li* in circuit, with a gate on each side.

When King Bimbisāra made the city of Kuśāgrapura his capital, the registered inhabitants frequently suffered the calamity of fire. If one family was careless, the neighbors on the four sides would be involved in the disaster. As the people were busily engaged in preventing fires, they had no leisure to manage their properties. Thus they had a grudge against the situation and were living uneasily in their abodes. The king said, "It is because I am lacking in virtue that my subjects suffer adversities. What meritorious deeds should I do to avert their misfortune?" His ministers said, "O Great King! You rule over the country with mild virtue and magnanimity, and your governance and education are brilliant and discerning. As fires are caused by the imprudence of the humble people, a strict law should be proclaimed to prevent future accidents. When a fire occurs, the one who causes the accident should be thoroughly investigated and the chief offender be punished by being exiled to a *śītavana*, a place where corpses are disposed of, which is regarded by the people as an inauspicious locality, so that nobody would go to visit it. Once a man is banished to such a place, he will be no more than a discarded corpse. In order to avoid living at such a shameful spot, people will be more cautious to protect themselves." The king said, "Good! An announcement should be made to notify all the inhabitants."

Before long the palace itself caught fire, and the king said to his ministers, "I must remove my lodgement." Then he ordered the prince to act as regent to attend to state affairs, and for the
923b sake of upholding the impartiality of the national law, he made up his mind to move [to the cemetery]. At that time, upon hearing that King Bimbisāra was living in the cemetery in the wilderness, the King of Vaiśālī mustered his troops and made ready to launch a surprise attack. According to information sent back by his frontier guards, a city had been built [at the cemetery] called the City of the Royal House, and the king had moved there. Government officials and common people had also moved to live in the new city. It is also said that this city was built at the time of King Ajātaśatru. When prince Ajātaśatru ascended the throne, he made this city his capital, but when King Aśoka moved the capital to Pāṭaliputra, he gave Rājagṛha to the Brahmans. Hence there are no ordinary inhabitants in this city, only less than a thousand families of Brahmans.

At the southwest corner of the palace city, there are two small monasteries where guest monks from different countries may make a sojourn in the course of travelling. This was a place where the

Buddha once preached the Dharma. Further to the northwest is a stupa built at the native place of the Elder Jyotiṣka (known in Chinese as Xingli, or Heavenly body, formerly mistranscribed as Shutijia). On the left side of the road outside the south gate of the city is a stupa at the spot where the Tathāgata preached the Dharma and ordained Rāhula.

From here going north for more than thirty *li*, I reached Nālandā Monastery (known in Chinese as Shiwuyan, or Insatiable in alms-giving). I heard some old people say that in the mango grove to the south of the monastery there was a pond in which lived a dragon named Nālandā, hence the name of the monastery built beside the pond. But the fact was that when the Tathāgata was practicing Bodhisattva deeds in a former life, he was a great king with his capital founded at this place. As he had compassion on living beings and took delight in alms-giving, the people called him "The Insatiable in Alms-giving" in praise of his virtue. This monastery was then named after his appellation. The land for building the monastery was originally a mango grove; five hundred merchants purchased it with ten *koṭi*s of gold coins and presented it to the Buddha. The Buddha preached the Dharma at this place for three months, and thereupon the merchants attained sainthood. Not long after the Nirvana of the Buddha, Śakrāditya (known as Tiri, or Sun of Indra, in Chinese), a former king of this country, who esteemed the One Vehicle and honored the Triple Gem, selected this propitious spot by divination and constructed the monastery on it. When the construction work was started, the dragon's body was pierced through. A Nirgrantha (naked ascetic) who was a good diviner saw this and predicted, "This is a propitious site. The monastery built on it will certainly be prosperous and be a standard one for all the five parts of India. It will thrive all the more after a thousand years. Students of future generations in this monastery will easily gain achievements in their studies, but most of them will spit blood, because the dragon has been injured."

Śakrāditya's son, King Buddhagupta (known as Juehu, or Buddha-protected, in Chinese), succeeded to the throne to continue

the good works and built another monastery to the south of the original one. King Tathāgatagupta (known as Rulai, or Thus-come, in Chinese) earnestly followed the example of his predecessors and built one more monastery to the east. After ascending the throne,
923c King Bālāditya (known as Youri, or Morning sun) built a fourth one to the northeast. When the construction work was completed, a festive meeting was held to celebrate the occasion, at which both prominent and obscure persons were entertained with sincerity, and holy as well as ordinary monks were invited. Monks of the five parts of India travelled long distances to attend the meeting. When all the participants had been seated, two monks arrived late, and they were led to the third story. Someone asked them, "When the king prepared the feast, he first of all sent invitations to holy and ordinary monks. Why do you two virtuous ones arrive so late, and where do you come from?" They said, "We come from China. Because our teacher is ill, we served him his meal before we started the journey. As we have been invited by the king from a great distance, we have come to attend the meeting."

The inquirer was surprised to hear this and promptly made a report to the king, who, knowing that they were saints, went in person to greet them. But as he came too late to the storied pavilion, the two monks had gone somewhere unknown to the others. The king's faith was deepened, and he eventually relinquished his country to become a homeless monk. After becoming a monk, he was the lowest in rank in the community of monks. This made him unhappy and discontented. "When I was a king, I used to occupy the uppermost position. But now as a monk I am placed in a humble position at the end of all the monks." Then he went to tell his feelings to the monks, who called a meeting and made a rule that those who were not fully ordained might fix their priority by age, which became a tradition peculiar to this monastery.

This king's son, Vajra (known as Jingang, or Diamond, in Chinese), was a man of firm faith, and after his succession to the throne he built a monastery to the west. Later, a king of Central India built another great monastery to the north and constructed a lofty enclosure with one gate for all the monasteries. As the whole complex was constructed by the kings of successive dynasties, the buildings were erected by most exquisitely skilled carpenters, employing such tools as burins and curved chisels to make the architectural complex a really magnificent sight. In the great monastery built by King Śakrāditya, there is placed an image of the Buddha. Forty monks are assigned to take their meal every day in this monastery in requital for the kindness of the alms-givers. There are several thousand monks, all of whom are brilliant scholars of high learning; those whose virtue is esteemed by their contemporaries and whose reputation is known to foreign lands amount to several hundreds. They are pure in observing the monastic regulations and faultless in conduct according to the Vinaya rules. The monks have strict restrictions and all of them are chaste and spotless, so that the various countries in India look up to them as exemplars. They always ask for more instructions and deliberate on the abstruse theories incessantly all day long. They admonish each other day and night, and extend mutual help between the old and the young. Any who did not engage in discussion of the profound teachings of the Tripiṭaka would be ashamed of themselves. Thus foreign scholars who wish to win fame come here to clarify the dubious points they found in their learning before they can join the ranks of the well-reputed. Some go about under the name of this monastery and gain honor and consideration through fraudulence. But people of different regions and countries who desire to enter this monastery to hold discussions are mostly debarred from entering the establishment after a preliminary interrogation by the gatekeeper. Only those who are well-versed in both ancient and contemporary learning can gain admittance. Then the visiting students carry on debates with the resident monks, but seven or eight out of ten flee in defeat. The remaining two or three learned scholars may also be deflated of their arrogance, since their reputation can be damaged by the questions later raised by the resident monks. There are highly talented and versatile sages endowed with retentive memory and good virtue, who maintain the glory of the monastery 924a and follow in the wake of their predecessors. As regards Dharmapāla and Candragupta, who won their fame in the scope of the teachings bequeathed by the Buddha; Guṇamati and Sthiramati, whose good repute is well known even today; Prabhāmitra, skilled in theoretical discussion; Viśeṣamitra, fluent in elevated conversation; Jñānacandra of elegant demeanor and perspicacious discernment; and Śīlabhadra of sublime virtue and profound insight, they are all men of supreme quality and well known to all people, and their virtuous deeds excel those of their forerunners. They are well-versed in ancient learning, each having composed more than ten treatises that are widely popular and highly valued even today.

The sacred traces around the monastery are counted by the hundreds, of which I shall just cite two or three as brief examples.

Not far to the west of the monastery is a temple where the Tathāgata once stayed for three months and spoke extensively on the wonderful Dharma for various devas and men. More than one hundred paces to the south is a small stupa at the place where a *bhikṣu* coming from a distance saw the Buddha. Once a *bhikṣu* came from a distance and met the Tathāgata and the holy monks at this place. With a mind of veneration, the *bhikṣu* prostrated himself [before the Tathāgata] and wished to be a universal monarch. Upon seeing him, the Tathāgata told the assembly of monks, "This *bhikṣu* is very pitiful. As he is a man of great bliss and deep virtue with a mind of firm faith, he would have realized Buddhahood very soon if he had aimed at it. But now as he wishes to be a universal monarch, he will surely get the reward in his future lives and be a universal monarch for as many lifetimes as the atoms of dust from the place of his prostration down to the gold wheel beneath the earth. Because of his addiction to worldly pleasure, he is thus far removed from the realization of sainthood."

To the south is a standing statue of Avalokiteśvara Bodhisattva. Sometimes it has been seen proceeding to the Buddha's temple and going rightward around it with a censer in its hand. In the stupa to the south of the statue of Avalokiteśvara Bodhisattva are kept hair and fingernails of the Buddha shaven and clipped

over three months. Sick people often get cured of their illness by going round the stupa. The stupa beside the tank at the outside of the west wall of the enclosure was the place where a heretic, holding a small bird in his hand, asked the Buddha about the problem of life and death. More than fifty paces further to the southeast inside the enclosure is an extraordinary tree, eight or nine feet high with two branches. Once the Tathāgata chewed a piece of willow twig [to clean his teeth] and threw the used twig to the ground, where it then took root and grew into this tree. Although a long time has passed, the branches never increase or decrease in number. Next to the east is a great temple more than two hundred feet in height. Once the Tathāgata spoke on various wonderful Dharmas at this place for four months. More than one hundred paces further to the north is a temple in which is enshrined an image of Avalokiteśvara Bodhisattva. When pure devotees come to make offerings, they see it at variant places without a fixed position, either standing beside the gate or under the eaves outside the temple. Both monks and lay people come from different countries to make offerings to the image. To the north of the temple of Avalokiteśvara Bodhisattva is a great temple, more than three hundred feet high built by King Bālāditya. Its size and ornamen- 924b
tation and the Buddha's image inside it are similar to those of the great temple at the Bodhi Tree. The stupa to the northeast is the place where the Tathāgata once expounded the wonderful Dharma for seven days, while to the northwest is a sitting place of the four past Buddhas. To the south is the Brass Temple constructed by King Śīlāditya, but the work is unfinished. According to the drawing of the building, it is to be one hundred feet in height when completed. Further to the east, more than two hundred paces outside the enclosure, is a copper image of the Buddha in the standing posture, over eighty feet tall and sheltered by a pavilion as high as six stories. It was made by King Pūrṇavarman in olden times.

Two or three *li* north of the copper image of the Buddha made by King Pūrṇavarman is a brick temple in which is enshrined an image of Tārā Bodhisattva. It is tall in size and obvious in spiritual manifestation. On every New Year's Day profuse offerings are made to the image, and the kings, ministers, and wealthy people of neighboring regions, holding fragrant incense and flowers as well as precious canopies and parasols, come to join the ceremony performed amidst the harmonious music of bells, stone chimes, and string and wind instruments, lasting for seven days. Inside the south gate of the enclosure is a large well. Formerly when the Buddha was living in the world a group of merchants suffering from heat and thirst came to the place of the Buddha. The World-honored One pointed at the earth and said that water might be obtained from there. The lord of the merchants then dug the ground with the axle of a cart, and water gushed out from the depression in the earth. All those who drank the water and heard the Dharma became enlightened and attained sainthood.

Going southwest for eight or nine *li* from the monastery, I reached the town of Kolika, in which is a stupa built by King Aśoka. This was the birthplace of the Venerable Maudgalaputra. Beside it is another stupa built at the spot where the venerable monk entered final Nirvana; his relic bones were entombed in it. He was born of a great Brahman family and was an intimate friend of Śāriputra since their youth. Śāriputra was noted for his brilliant talent, while the Venerable Maudgalaputra was reputed for his fine discernment. They were equals in genius and wisdom and were always together whether travelling or staying at a place, forging lifelong friendship and vowing to take similar actions in their activities. Both of them became disgusted with the world, and they renounced their homes together and served Sañjaya as their teacher. When Śāriputra met with the Arhat Aśvajit, he heard the Dharma from the latter and attained sainthood. He immediately repeated what he had heard from the Arhat to the Venerable Maudgalaputra, who upon hearing the Dharma became enlightened and realized the first stage of sainthood. With his two hundred fifty disciples, Maudgalaputra came to the place of the Buddha. When the World-honored One saw him at a distance, he pointed at the newcomer and told the assembly of monks, "That person coming over there will become my disciple most noted for his miraculous powers." Having arrived at the Buddha's place, Maudgalaputra requested that he be admitted into the brotherhood of the Dharma. The World-honored One replied to him, "Welcome, *bhikṣu*! By living a pure life you will be free from the bondage of suffering." At the sound of these words, Maudgalaputra's beard and hair fell off 924c and his secular garments changed. He observed the disciplinary rules in a pure manner and behaved in the proper way. After seven days, he became free from the bondage of rebirth, attained Arhatship, and gained miraculous powers.

Three or four *li* to the east of the birthplace of Maudgalaputra is a stupa at the spot where King Bimbisāra welcomed the Buddha. At first when the Tathāgata realized Buddhahood, he sensed that the people of Magadha longed to meet him. Thus at the invitation of King Bimbisāra he dressed himself properly, took up his alms bowl one morning, and went to the city of Rājagṛha with one thousand *bhikṣus* around him. These *bhikṣus* had been old Brahmans who wore their hair in the shape of a conch on the top of their heads, and in admiration of the Dharma they donned the dyed robes to follow the Buddha. At that time Indra transformed himself into a *māṇava* (a young Brahman) wearing a topknot in the shape of a conch; he held a golden vase in his left hand and a precious staff in his right, and walked in the air four fingers above the ground, leading the way for the Buddha among the congregation. King Bimbisāra of the country of Magadha, together with the Brahmans, elders, and lay people in his country, hundreds and thousands in number, came out of the city of Rājagṛha to greet the group of holy monks.

Going southeast for more than twenty *li* from the place where King Bimbisāra welcomed the Buddha, I reached the town of Kālapināka, in which there is a stupa built by King Aśoka. This was the birthplace of the Venerable Śāriputra, and the well is still in existence. Beside the well is a stupa built at the spot where the venerable monk entered Nirvana, and his relic bones are preserved in the stupa.

The Venerable Śāriputra was born in a great Brahman's family. His father was a highly talented scholar of extensive knowledge, with deep insight into what was subtle and abstruse; he was well-read in various texts. Once his wife had a dream, and she told it to her husband, saying, "Last night I had a dream in which I saw a strange man clad in armor holding a diamond club in his hand. He demolished all the mountains, except one by which he stood in retirement." Her husband said, "It is a good dream. You will give birth to a son, who will be a learned scholar in the world and defeat all Śāstra-masters and refute their theories. He will be inferior to only one person and become his disciple." In the course of pregnancy, the woman suddenly became wise and intelligent and could carry on a discussion eloquently without stammering in her speech. When the Venerable Śāriputra was eight years old, his name spread far to the four quarters. He was honest and unsophisticated by nature and had a mind of compassion. He destroyed the bondage of rebirth and achieved wisdom. He was a friend of Maudgalaputra since their youth. They detested the world but did not know where to take refuge. So the two of them went to the place of the heretic Sañjaya for spiritual practice and cultivation. But they told each other, "What we are learning here is not the ultimate truth; it cannot free us from the scope of suffering. We should go each by a [different] way to seek for a brilliant teacher. Whichever of us tastes the sweet dew first must let the other one enjoy it also."

925a At that time the Arhat Aśvajit with alms bowl in hand was going to the city to beg for alms of food. On seeing that he was peaceful and elegant in demeanor, Śāriputra asked him, "Who is your teacher?" "The prince of the Śākya clan, who, being weary of the world, renounced his home and achieved full enlightenment, is my teacher." Śāriputra said, "What Dharma did he preach? Can I hear of it?" "As I have just started receiving instructions, I have not mastered the profound teachings." Śāriputra said, "I hope you will tell me just as much as you have heard." Aśvajit then expounded the Dharma as was suitable for the occasion. Upon hearing the Dharma, Śāriputra attained the first stage of sainthood, and together with his two hundred fifty disciples he came to the place of the Buddha. When the World-honored One saw him at a distance, he pointed at him and told the assembly of monks, "He will be the foremost in wisdom among all my disciples." Śāriputra saluted the Buddha and wished to follow the Buddha-dharma. The World-honored One said to him, "Welcome, *bhikṣu*!" Upon hearing these words, Śāriputra became a fully ordained monk, and half a month later when he heard the Buddha preaching the Dharma to the Long-nailed Brahman, he became enlightened and realized Arhatship.

Afterward, when Ānanda had heard about the time of the Buddha's [approaching] Nirvana, he spread the tidings to many people, who were grieved and sad. Śāriputra too was deeply saddened by the news, and as he could not bear the idea of the Buddha entering Nirvana, he asked permission of the World-honored One to allow him to die first. The World-honored One told him, "You should know that this is the right time for you to do so." Then [Śāriputra] departed from his disciples and returned to his native place. His attendant *śrāmaṇera* informed the inhabitants in the city and the towns of Śāriputra's intention. Thus King Ajātaśatru and the people of his country came in a great hurry and assembled together like the clouds. Śāriputra expounded the Dharma extensively for them, and after hearing the Dharma, the audience dispersed. Late in the night he concentrated his mind and entered the Samādhi of Complete Cessation of Sensation and Perception. When he came out of the *samādhi*, he passed into Nirvana.

Four or five *li* to the southeast of the town of Kālapināka is a stupa at the place where the disciples of the Venerable Śāriputra entered Nirvana. It is also said that at the time of Kāśyapa Buddha the great Arhat Trikoṭi (*koṭi* meaning "one hundred million" in Chinese) entered final Nirvana at this same place.

Going to the east for more than thirty *li* from the stupa of Śāriputra's disciples, I reached Indraśailaguhā Mountain (known as Dishiku, or Indra's cave, in Chinese). In that mountain the valleys are deep and quiet with exuberant flowers and trees. There are two prominent peaks on the top of the mountain, and on the south cliff of the west peak is a large cave, which is broad but not high. Formerly

the Tathāgata often stayed in it. In those days Indra carved marks on the rock concerning forty-two dubious points and inquired of the Buddha, and the Buddha gave him explanations. The marks are still there. The present image [in the cave] was made in imitation of the posture of the Buddha as he posed on that occasion. None of those who entered the cave to worship the image was not inspired with a feeling of awe and veneration. On the crag of the mountain
925b are sites where the four past Buddhas sat and walked to and fro. On the east peak is a monastery. It is said by the local people that in the night the monks of this monastery often see lamps and candles burning brightly before the image in the cave on the east peak.

In front of the monastery on the east peak of Indraśailaguhā Mountain is a stupa named Haṃsa (Wild goose). In this monastery the monks once practiced the Hinayana teachings. As these are gradual teachings, the monks were allowed to eat the three kinds of pure meat, and this habit was followed persistently. Later, the three kinds of pure meat became unobtainable, and a *bhikṣu*, while taking a walk, saw a flock of wild geese flying overhead. He said in jest, "Today the monks are running short of food for their midday meal. The Mahāsattva should know that this is the right time [to make a sacrifice]!" Before he had finished speaking, one of the wild geese flew back and dropped to the ground dead before the monk. Upon seeing this incident, the *bhikṣu* told it to all the monks, who were sad to hear about it and said among themselves, "The Tathāgata preached the Dharma according to the faculty of understanding of the audience in order to guide and induce them to enlightenment. We have been sticking to stupidity in following the gradual teachings. The Mahayana tenets are the right principles, and we should correct our former behavior and follow the holy teachings. This wild goose came to admonish us, and it is our clever guide. Its great virtue should be glorified and the event be transmitted to posterity." Thus a stupa was built in memory of its spirit of sacrifice, and the dead goose was buried under it.

Going northeast for one hundred fifty or sixty *li* from Indraśailaguhā Mountain, I reached Kapotaka (Pigeon) Monastery, where lived over two hundred monks, who study the teachings of the Sarvāstivāda school. To the east of the monastery is a stupa built by King Aśoka. Once the Buddha preached the Dharma to the monks at this place for a whole night, while a bird-catcher was catching the feathered tribe with a net in the wood. As he failed to get any birds for a whole day, he said, "I am a man lacking in good fortune, and whatever I do is always adverse to me." Then he came to the place of the Buddha and declared, "Today the Tathāgata is preaching the Dharma here, and I am unable to catch any birds with my net. What shall I do to feed my starving wife and children?" The Tathāgata told him, "Build a fire! I shall give you food." Then the Tathāgata took the shape of a pigeon and burned himself to death in the fire. The bird-catcher took the dead pigeon home and partook of it with his wife and children. Later, he came again to the place of the Buddha, who converted him in an appropriate way. Upon hearing the Dharma the bird-catcher repented of his misdeeds, made a fresh start in life by relinquishing his home for spiritual cultivation, and realized sainthood. Thus the monastery constructed at this place was named Pigeon Monastery.

Two or three *li* to the south of Kapotaka Monastery is an iso- 925c
lated hill that is tall and precipitous with luxuriant trees and is covered by splendid flowers and clear streams. On the hill there are many temples and shrines beautifully constructed with most exquisite carvings and engravings. In the central temple is enshrined an image of Avalokiteśvara Bodhisattva, which is small in size but august and mystical in spiritual manifestation. It holds a lotus flower in one hand and has a statuette on its forehead. Once some men fasted and prayed earnestly for seven days, a fortnight, or even one month, wishing to see the Bodhisattva in person. The one who had gained spiritual influence saw the Bodhisattva coming out of the image, a majestic and stately figure with a bright radiance to give him comfort and advice.

In former times, when the king of the country of Siṃhala in the South Seas looked in his mirror one morning, he did not see his own reflection but saw the image of this Bodhisattva in a wood of *tāla* trees on a small hill in the country of Magadha in Jambudvīpa. Deeply delighted, the king set out to seek the image. When he came to this hill, he found that the image here was similar to the one he had seen in his mirror, and so he built the temple and made various offerings to the image. The kings of later times followed his example and built more temples and shrines beside it; and offerings of incense, flowers, and music were made incessantly.

Going southeast for more than forty *li* from the image of Avalokiteśvara Bodhisattva on the isolated hill I reached a monastery with more than fifty monks, all of whom studied the Hinayana teachings. In front of the monastery is a great stupa that revealed miraculous signs many times. Formerly the Buddha preached the Dharma to Brahmā and others at this place for seven days. Beside it are ruins where the three past Buddhas sat and walked to and fro.

Going northeast for more than seventy *li* from the monastery, I reached a big village at the south of the Ganges, with a dense population of prosperous villagers. There are several deva-temples, all beautifully adorned with engravings. Not far to the southeast is a great stupa at the place where the Buddha once preached the Dharma for one night.

Going east from here through mountains and forests for over one hundred *li*, I reached Lāvaṇīla Village. The great stupa in front of the monastery here was built by King Aśoka. Once the Buddha preached the Dharma here for three months. Two or three *li* to the north of this place is a large lake more than thirty *li* in circuit with lotus flowers in four colors blooming all four seasons of the year.

Going east from here through great mountains and forests for more than two hundred *li*, I reached the country of Īraṇaparvata (in the domain of Central India).

End of Fascicle Nine

Fascicle X

Seventeen Countries, From Īraṇaparvata to Malakūṭa

1. The Country of Īraṇaparvata
2. The Country of Campā
3. The Country of Kajaṅgala
4. The Country of Puṇḍravardhana
5. The Country of Kāmarūpa
6. The Country of Samataṭa
7. The Country of Tāmraliptī
8. The Country of Karṇasuvarṇa
9. The Country of Uḍa
10. The Country of Koṅgoda
11. The Country of Kaliṅga
12. The Country of Kosala
13. The Country of Andhra
14. The Country of Dhānakaṭaka
15. The Country of Cola
16. The Country of Draviḍa
17. The Country of Malakūṭa

The country of Īraṇaparvata is more than three thousand *li* in 926a
circuit, and its capital city is more than twenty *li* in circuit. Agriculture is prosperous, and both flowers and fruits thrive. The climate is mild and pleasant, and the people are simple and honest by social custom. There are more than ten monasteries with over four thousand monks, most of whom study the Dharma of the Hinayana Saṃmitīya school. There are more than twenty deva-temples, and heretics live together. Recently the king of a neighboring country deposed the ruler of this country and presented the capital city as a gift to the monks. Two monasteries are built in this city, with less than one thousand monks living in each of them, and they study the Hinayana teachings of the Sarvāstivāda school.

Beside the capital city and near the Ganges is Īraṇa Mountain, which is enshrouded in mist and clouds, casting the sun and moon into shade. Both ancient and contemporary anchorites and holy persons come here one after another to practice meditation. Now there is a deva-temple that still follows the rules handed down from past generations. Once the Tathāgata also lived at this place and widely spoke on the wonderful Dharma for various devas and men. To the south of the capital city is a stupa where the Tathāgata preached the Dharma for three months. Beside the stupa are ruins where the three past Buddhas sat and walked up and down.

Not far to the west of the ruins where the three Buddhas walked up and down is a stupa built at the place where the *bhikṣu* Śruta-viṃśati-koṭi (Hearing two hundred [twenty?] *koṭi*, and formerly mistranslated as Koṭi ears) was born. In the old days there was an
926b elder who was enormously rich and powerful in this city. In his old age a son was born to him, and when a man brought the news to him, he gave the man two hundred *koṭi*s of gold coins as a reward, and so his son was named Two Hundred Koṭis on Hearing [the news]. When the child was growing up his feet never touched the earth, and thus hair grew out of his soles to about one foot long, soft and lustrous and golden in color. As the child was dearly beloved, all kinds of toys were provided for him. From his residence up to the Snow Mountains, posts were set up in a chain with pages and servants stationed all along the way. Whenever any good medicine was needed, a message was passed on by the servants to get the required material, which was then relayed back through the posts in good time. Such was the wealthy condition of his family.

When the Tathāgata knew that the good root of the young man was about to sprout, he ordered Maudgalaputra to convert him. After arriving at the gate of the elder's house, he had no pretext for making an announcement. As the members of the elder's family were sun-worshippers, they paid homage toward the east in the morning every day. At that moment, the venerable monk, employing his supernatural powers, descended from the disk of the sun and stood before them. Suspecting that he was the god of sun, the elder's son offered him some fragrant rice, which the monk took back home. The fragrance of the rice permeated the city of Rājagṛha, and King Bimbisāra, surprised by the strange scent, ordered a messenger to find out the cause. Then it was found that it was the rice brought back by Maudgalaputra of the Bamboo Grove Temple from the elder's house. Thus the king came to know that the elder's son had such a marvellous foodstuff, and he summoned him. Having received the king's order, the elder considered which was the safe way for his son to go. If he sailed in a boat, there might be the danger of a storm, and if he went in a cart or by riding an elephant, there might be the trouble of the cart turning over or the elephant stumbling down. Thus he had a canal cut to lead from his house up to the city of Rājagṛha, and he filled it with mustard-seeds, on which a boat was placed and towed by a long rope. [In this manner] the elder's son reached the city of Rājagṛha, where he first went to pay homage to the World-honored One. The World-honored One told him, "King Bimbisāra summoned you because he wished to see the hair growing under your soles. When you sit you should cross your legs to let the king see the hair. To stretch one's legs toward a king would incur the death penalty according to the law of the country." With this instruction, the elder's son went away, and he was ushered into the presence of the king when the latter wished to see the hair. The young man sat down with crossed legs. The king was pleased with his proper etiquette and became deeply fond of him. On his way back home, he came to the Buddha's place again, when the Tathāgata was preaching the Dharma for the edification of the listeners. Upon hearing the Dharma, the elder's son was awakened and became a monk on the spot. Thus he worked strenuously for spiritual cultivation in order to achieve sainthood. He walked up and down in meditation, so much so that his feet bled. The World-honored One told him, "Good man, when you were a layman at home, did you know how to play the zither?" "Yes," was the reply. "If that is so, I shall cite it as a parable. When the strings are too tight, the sound will not rhyme well, and if they are too loose, the tune will be inharmonious and ungraceful. Only when the strings are neither too tight nor too loose can one produce melodious music. It is the same in spiritual cultivation. When you are too strenuous, you

will get overtired and dispirited, but if you are too much relaxed, you will become sluggish in disposition and forget about your ambition." He accepted the Buddha's advice and worshipped him by
926c going round him. Before long he gained sainthood.

At the west side of the country is the Ganges, from which proceeding to the south I reached a small isolated hill with lofty peaks. Once the Buddha stayed here three months during the rainy season and subjugated the *yakṣa* Bakula. On a big rock below the cliff at the southeast of the hill is the trace where the Buddha once sat. It is about one inch deep into the rock, five feet two inches long and two feet one inch broad. A stupa was built there. On a rock further to the south is the trace where the Buddha placed his *kuṇḍikā* (a waterpot for bathing). The trace is about one inch deep, in the pattern of an eight-petalled flower. Not far to the southeast of the trace of the Buddha's seat is a footprint of the *yakṣa* Bakula, one foot five or six inches long, seven or eight inches broad, and less than two inches deep. Behind the footprint is a stone image of the Buddha seated, six or seven feet in height. Next, not far to the west is a place where the Buddha once walked up and down. At the top of the hill is the old chamber where the *yakṣa* once lived. Next to the south is a footprint of the Buddha, one foot eight inches long, more than six inches broad, and about half an inch deep. There is a stupa built over the footprint. Formerly the Tathāgata subjugated the *yakṣa* and bade him not to kill people to eat their flesh. He respectfully accepted the Buddha's admonition and was later reborn in heaven. West of here there are six or seven hot springs, the water of which is extremely hot. In the mountains and forests in the southern part of the country, there are many wild elephants with enormous bodies. From here going east for more than three hundred *li* along the southern bank of the Ganges, I reached the country of Campā (in the domain of Central India).

The country of Campā is over four thousand *li* in circuit, and its capital city, with the Ganges flowing at its back in the north, is more than forty *li* in circuit. The land is low and humid, producing rich crops. The climate is moderately warm, and the people are simple and honest by social custom. There are several score of monasteries, most of which are dilapidated, and the monks, amounting to over two hundred, study the Hinayana teachings. There are more than twenty deva-temples, and the heretics live together. The city wall of the capital was built with bricks to the height of several tens of feet. The foundation of the wall is raised above the ground, and the defenders can repulse an enemy from high and perilous positions.

At the beginning of the kalpa, when human beings first appeared in the world, they lived in the wilderness or in caves, not knowing how to build palaces or houses. Later an *apsaras* (female heavenly being) descended from the heavens and dwelt among mankind, and after bathing in the Ganges with self-admiration, she became pregnant by spiritual influence and gave birth to four sons. They divided Jambudvīpa, each occupying a district, and built capital cities and established towns, drawing demarcations over their territories. The city [of Campā] was the capital of one of the four sons and was the first city ever built in Jambudvīpa.

One hundred forty or fifty *li* to the east of the city there is a solitary islet with lofty peaks in the southern part of the Ganges. On the top of a peak is a deva-temple, and a deity often gives spiritual responses to prayers. Caves are excavated upon the cliffs, and water is led into ponds. There are flowery woods and exotic trees, 927a
and with its huge rocks and perilous peaks this islet is the abode of wise and benignant dwellers. It is so attractive that visitors might forget to go home. In the southern region of the country there are thousands of wild elephants and other fierce animals roaming about in groups in the mountains and jungles. From here going east for more than four hundred *li*, I reached the country of Kajaṅgala (the local name being Kayaṅgala, in the domain of Central India).

The country of Kajaṅgala is more than two thousand *li* in circuit. The land, irrigated by subterranean water, produces rich crops. The climate is humid and the social customs are agreeable. Much value is set upon brilliant talents, and learning is highly esteemed. There are six or seven monasteries with more than three hundred monks. Deva-temples are ten in number where the heretics live together. A few hundred years ago, the royal clan became extinct and the country fell under the control of a neighboring state. Thus the capital city has been lying in ruins, and most of the inhabitants live in villages and towns. This is why when King Śīlāditya travelled to East India, he built a palace with thatch on his arrival, for the management of state affairs, and when he left the place, he set fire to burn down the thatched house. In the southern region of the country there are many wild elephants. In the northern region, not far from the Ganges, is a great high terrace, built with bricks and stone. The foundation of the terrace is broad and tall and is adorned with exquisite engravings. All around the terrace are carved statues of various holy persons, and the Buddha's images are made different from the figures of heavenly beings. From here crossing the Ganges to the east and after travelling for six hundred *li*, I reached the country of Puṇḍravardhana (in the domain of Central India).

The country of Puṇḍravardhana is more than four thousand *li* in circuit, and its capital city is over thirty *li* in circuit. The numerous inhabitants are rich. Tanks, guesthouses, and flowery woods are often alternately located. The land is low and moist and the crops are abundant. Breadfruits are plentiful but nevertheless expensive. This fruit is as large as a white gourd, and when ripe it is yellowish red in color. When it is cut open, one can see several tens of smaller fruits inside, each as large as the egg of a crane. When these are cut open, yellowish red juice with a sweet and delicious taste oozes out. The fruits are borne on branches, just like other kinds of fruits, or they grow on the roots of the tree as *fuling* (*Poria cocos*) does. The climate is mild and pleasant, and the people are fond of learning by custom. There are over twenty monasteries with more than three thousand monks, who study both the Mahayana and the Hinayana teachings. Deva-temples are one hundred in number, and the heretics live together. Naked Nirgranthas are numerous indeed.

More than twenty *li* to the west of the capital city is Vāśibhā Monastery, consisting of spacious courtyards and halls and lofty terraces and pavilions, with over seven hundred monks, all of whom study the Mahayana teachings. Most of the great scholars and renowned monks of East India reside here. Not far from it is a stupa built by King Aśoka. In olden times the Tathāgata once preached the Dharma at this place to heavenly and human beings for three months, and the stupa often issues a brilliant light on 927b
fast days. Beside the stupa are traces where the four past Buddhas sat and walked up and down. Not far from here is a temple in which is enshrined an image of Avalokiteśvara Bodhisattva. Its divine influence extends to all without omission and its spiritual response is evident. People come here from far and near to fast and say prayers. From here going east for more than nine hundred *li*, I crossed a large river and reached the country of Kāmarūpa (in the domain of East India).

The country of Kāmarūpa is more than ten thousand *li* in circuit, and its capital city is over thirty *li* in circuit. The land is irrigated by subterranean water, and the seeds of crops are sown in the proper seasons. The breadfruit and coconut are plentiful, but they are nevertheless expensive. Rivers and lakes link up the towns and villages. The climate is mild and pleasant, and the people are simple and honest by social custom. They are short in stature and dark in complexion, and their language is slightly different from that of Central India. They have very hot tempers but are strenuous and diligent in study. They worship gods and do not believe in the Buddha-dharma. Therefore, since the rise of Buddhism up to the present day, no monastery has been built to invite Buddhist monks. Those who follow the pure faith just do so in private. There are several hundred deva-temples, and the heretics amount to several myriads.

The reigning king, being an offspring of Nārāyaṇa, is a Brahman by caste and is named Bhāskaravarman (Sun armor) with the title of Kumāra (Youth). Since the royal family occupied the territory and ruled over the country from generation to generation, he is the one thousandth monarch. His Majesty is fond of learning, and his subjects follow his example. Men of high talents, in admiration of the king's righteousness, come from distant places to visit him as guests. Although he does not earnestly believe in the Buddha-dharma, he treats learned monks with respect. The king heard that a Chinese monk had come from a great distance to Nālandā Monastery in Magadha to study the profound Dharma of the Buddha, and he repeatedly sent messengers cordially to invite the Chinese monk, but the monk did not accept the invitation. At that time, the Śāstra-master Śīlabhadra said to him, "If you wish to repay the kindness of the Buddha, you should disseminate the right Dharma. You had better go to the king; do not fear the long journey. King Kumāra professes the heretical religion by family tradition, and it is good of him to invite a Buddhist monk. Should he change his faith on account of your visit, it would be a great benefit with far-reaching influence. You cherished a great mind and made a solemn vow to come to a foreign land all by yourself to seek the Dharma at the risk of your life for the salvation of all living beings. Can you think only of your home country? You should forget about gain and loss and not care about honor or disgrace in spreading the holy teachings and enlightening those who have gone astray. Consider the advantage of others before you think of yourself, and forget about your own fame in the propagation of the right Dharma." I was then obliged to go with the messengers to meet the king.

King Kumāra said, "Although I am not a man of talent, I always pay respect to those who are learned. Upon hearing your fame as a man of learning and noble character, I ventured to extend an invitation to you." I said, "I am a man of little ability and
927c lacking in wisdom. It is a great honor to me that my humble name has reached your ears." King Kumāra said, "Excellent! You admired the Dharma and were fond of learning, and you regarded your body as a piece of floating cloud to travel over dangerous places to a distant foreign country. This was due to the edification of your king and the result of the general mood of advocating learning in

your country. Now in the various states of India, most of the people eulogize the Song of Triumph of the Prince of Qin in Mahācīna. I heard about this country long ago; is it your homeland?" I said, "Yes. That song is sung to praise the virtues of our monarch [when he was the Prince of Qin]." King Kumara said, "I did not know that you were from that country. I always admired the morals and manners of your country, and I have looked toward the East for a long time, but being blocked by mountains and rivers, I have had no means to pay my respects." I said, "The virtues of our great lord spread far and his benevolence extends widely. People of different regions with diverse customs and habits, coming to the imperial palace to acknowledge his suzerainty, are numerous." King Kumāra said, "Since such is the case with many countries in the world, I also wish to offer my tributary gifts. [But] now King Śīlāditya is going to conduct a great alms-giving convocation in the country of Kajuṅghira to achieve bliss and wisdom. All Buddhist monks, Brahmans and learned scholars from the five parts of India are invited to take part in the meeting. A messenger has come to invite me, and I hope we can go together." Thus I went with him.

In the eastern part of this country [Kāmarūpa] there is a chain of mountains and hills without a big city. It borders on the territory of the Yi tribe in the southwest [of China], and so the inhabitants are akin to the Man and Lao minorities. I made a detailed inquiry of the local people, who told me that a journey of about two months would take one into the southwest region of the state of Shu [in China], but that the mountains and rivers were difficult to pass, and that miasmal vapor permeating the air, poisonous snakes, and noxious plants would cause drastic harms. In the southeast part of the country, there are wild elephants trampling about in herds, and so the elephant troops are particularly strong in this country. Going south from here for one thousand two hundred or three hundred *li*, I reached the country of Samataṭa (in the domain of East India).

The country of Samataṭa is more than three thousand *li* in circuit, and as it borders on the sea, the land is low and humid.

The capital city is over twenty *li* in circuit. Crops grow profusely, and flowers and fruits are abundant. The climate is pleasant, and the social customs are agreeable. The people are upright and unyielding by nature. They are short in stature with dark complexions. They are fond of learning and are diligent of their own accord. They believe in both heterodox faiths and the right religion. There are more than thirty monasteries with over two thousand monks, all of whom study the teachings of the Sthavira school. Deva-temples are one hundred in number, and the heretics live together. Naked Nirgranthas are very numerous. Not far from the capital city is a stupa constructed by King Aśoka at the spot where the Tathāgata once preached the deep and wonderful Dharma to various men and heavenly beings for seven days. Beside it are traces of the sitting and walking up and down of the four past Buddhas. In a monastery not far from here is a green jade image of the Buddha eight feet high with all the perfect features and showing timely spiritual response.

928a Northeast of there in the valleys beside the great sea is the country of Śrīkṣetra; further to the southeast at a corner of the great sea is the country of Kāmalaṅka; further to the east is the country of Dvārapatī; further to the east is the country of Īśānapura; further to the east is the country of Mahācampā, which in our country is known as Linyi; and further to the southwest is the country of Yamanadvīpa. As these six countries are obstructed by mountains and rivers on the way, I did not go into their territories, but I got information about their customs and habits and the demarcations of their lands. From the country of Samataṭa going west for more than nine hundred *li*, I reached the country of Tāmraliptī (in the domain of East India).

The country of Tāmraliptī is one thousand four hundred or five hundred *li* in circuit, and its capital city is over ten *li* in circuit. As it is situated near the sea, the land is low and moist. Crops are planted in the proper seasons, and flowers and fruits are plentiful. The climate is mild and warm. The people are hot-tempered by custom and bold and courageous by nature. They believe in both heterodox religions and the correct one. There are more than ten monasteries with over one thousand monks. Deva-temples are over fifty in number, and heretics live together. The country borders on a bay and is a center of land and water communication. Rare and precious goods are collected here, and so the inhabitants are generally rich and prosperous. The stupa beside the city was built by King Aśoka, and by its side are traces where the four past Buddhas sat and walked to and fro. From here going northwest for more than seven hundred *li*, I reached the country of Karṇasuvarṇa (in the domain of East India).

The country of Karṇasuvarṇa is four thousand four hundred or five hundred *li* in circuit, and its capital city is over twenty *li* in circuit. The inhabitants are wealthy, and their families are rich and prosperous. The land is low and moist, and crops are planted in the proper seasons. Different kinds of flowers are abundant and precious fruits multitudinous. The climate is mild and pleasant, and the customs are honest and peaceful. The people are fond of learning and craftsmanship, and they believe in heterodox religions as well as the correct one. There are more than ten monasteries with over two thousand monks, who study the Hinayana teachings of the Saṃmitīya school. Deva-temples are over fifty in number, and the heretics are quite numerous. In three other monasteries milk curd is not taken as food, in accordance with the teaching of Devadatta.

Beside the capital city is Raktamṛttikā (Red clay) Monastery, of which the courtyards and houses are noticeable and spacious, and the terraces and pavilions lofty and sublime. All the talented and learned scholars and intelligent and well-informed men are assembled here in this monastery to help each other in the cultivation of morality. At first, when the Buddha-dharma was not professed in this country, a heretic of South India, wearing a copper belt around his waist, putting a lamp on his head, and holding a staff in his hand, walked proudly into the city, beating the drum of contention and demanding a debate. Someone asked him, "Why do your head and waist look so strange?" The heretic said, "Because my

928b belly is so full of knowledge that I fear it may burst at any moment! Out of pity for those who are in the darkness of ignorance, I wear a lamp for their illumination." After the lapse of ten days nobody accepted the challenge, and even among the most talented scholars no one suitable was found. The king said, "How is it possible that no brilliant scholar is to be found in the whole country? It will be a deep shame upon the nation if the guest's questions are not answered. We should seek a competent scholar among the hermits living in seclusion." Someone said, "In the great forest there is a strange man who claims to be a Śramaṇa and has earnestly engaged himself in study in seclusion for a long time. If he is not practicing the right Dharma in accordance with morality, how could he have been living in such a manner?" Upon hearing this, the king went in person to invite the Śramaṇa. The Śramaṇa said, "I am a native of South India, and in the course of travelling I have come and stayed at this place. Being a man of shallow learning, I fear that I am not as good as you have heard. Since I am honored by your invitation, perhaps I shall not insistently decline it. But if I am not defeated in the debate, I request that you build a monastery and summon monks to glorify the Buddha-dharma." The king said, "I have heard your words with respect, and I dare not forget your virtue."

At the invitation of the king, the Śramaṇa went to the place of discussion, where the heretic proclaimed his theories in thirty thousand words with deep meanings expounded in a concise manner, including all the names and substances of visible and audible objects in the world. Having heard the exposition only once, the Śramaṇa grasped the essence of the statements without misunderstanding and refuted them in a few hundred words. Then he proposed his own theories, and the heretic was dumbfounded and at his wits' end; he could not utter a word in reply. His fame being frustrated, the heretic retired in shame. With deep respect for the Śramaṇa, the king built this monastery, and after that the Buddha-dharma began to be spread in this country.

Not far from the monastery is a stupa built by King Aśoka. Once the Tathāgata preached the Dharma at this spot for seven days to enlighten the audience. Beside it is a temple, and there are traces where the four past Buddhas sat and walked up and down, as well as some more stupas, all built by King Aśoka to mark spots where the Tathāgata preached the Dharma. Going southwest from here for more than seven hundred *li*, I reached the country of Uḍa (in the domain of East India).

The country of Uḍa is more than seven thousand *li* in circuit, and its capital city is over twenty *li* in circuit. The land is fertile and the crops are abundant. All kinds of fruits are bigger in size than those of other countries. Marvelous plants and famous flowers are so rich in variety that I cannot give a full description. The climate is temperate, and the custom is tough and intrepid. The people are stalwart in stature with dark complexions. Their language and manners are different from those in Central India. They are tirelessly fond of learning, and most of them believe in the Buddha-dharma. There are more than one hundred monasteries with over ten thousand monks, all of whom study the Mahayana teachings. Deva-temples are fifty in number, and the heretics live together. There are over ten stupas built by King Aśoka at different places to mark the spots where the Tathāgata preached the Dharma.

Among the big mountains in the southwest part of the country 928c
is Puṣpagiri Monastery. The stone stupa of this monastery shows many spiritual signs, and on fast days it often issues a brilliant light. Thus pure believers come here from far and near to offer canopies of flowers in competition with each other. If the handle of a canopy is put under the dew basin or upon the body of the stupa in the shape of an inverted bowl, the canopy will stick to the stupa like a needle attracted by a magnet. The stupa in another monastery in the mountains to the northwest of this one shows the same strange phenomenon. It is because these two stupas were built by deities and spirits that they possess such wonderful manifestations.

In the southeast part of this country is the city of Caritra (Journey-starting) by the seaside. Being over twenty *li* in circuit, it is a passageway and halting place for seagoing merchants and distant travellers. The city wall is strong and high, and inside it there are many rare valuables. Outside the city there are five monasteries standing in a row. The terraces and pavilions of the monasteries are lofty, and the respected images are beautifully made. The country of Siṃhala is over twenty thousand *li* away to the south. On a calm night when I looked into the distance, I saw the precious pearl shining on the top of the Buddha-tooth stupa in that country, like a bright torch burning in the air. From this city travelling through a great forest to the southwest for more than one thousand two hundred *li* I reached the country of Koṅgoda (in the domain of East India).

The country of Koṅgoda is more than one thousand *li* in circuit, and its capital city is over twenty *li* in circuit. It borders on a bay of the sea, and its hills and mountains are rich and prosperous. The land is low and moist, and the crops are sown in the proper seasons. The climate is temperate and the custom is brave and intrepid. The people are big and tall with dark complexions. Roughly speaking, they are polite and righteous and are not very deceitful. As far as their written language is concerned, it is the same as that of Central India, but they speak in a quite different way. They respect the heretics and do not believe in the Buddhadharma. There are over one hundred deva-temples with more than ten thousand adherents. In the whole country there are several tens of small towns located close by the mountains or at the junctions leading to the sea. The city walls are strong and tall and the soldiers are valorous. As they are powerful and have influence over the neighboring countries, they do not have a strong enemy. As the country is situated at the seaside, it stores many rare and valuable goods, and cowries and pearls are used as money. It produces large darkish elephants that are capable of carrying heavy loads for long distances. From here going southwest for one thousand four hundred or five hundred *li* through a great wild jungle dense with tall trees that bedim the sun, I reached the country of Kaliṅga (in the domain of South India).

The country of Kaliṅga is more than five thousand *li* in circuit, and its capital city is over twenty *li* in circuit. The crops are sown

in the proper seasons, and both flowers and fruits are thriving. Woods and marshes extend to several hundred *li* at a stretch, and it produces darkish wild elephants valued by the neighboring countries. The climate is hot, and the people are irascible and violent by custom; most of them are rash and impetuous by nature, though 929a
they are trustworthy and faithful. They speak in a quick and fluent manner with correct pronunciation, but their phraseology is quite different from that of Central India. A few of them believe in the right Dharma, but the majority follow the heretics. There are more than ten monasteries with over five hundred monks who study the teachings of the Mahayana and the Sthavira schools. There are over one hundred deva-temples, and the heretics are numerous, most of them Nirgranthas.

In olden times Kaliṅga was a rich and prosperous country with such a dense population that pedestrians jostled in the paths and carts collided on the highways; when the people raised up their sleeves, a curtain would be formed. A *ṛṣi* possessing the five supernatural powers lived in the mountains in this country for mental cultivation. As someone insulted him, he became enraged, and his feeling of hatred caused him to lose his supernatural powers. He cursed the people of the country, whether old or young, wise or ignorant, and the country became depopulated for many years. Recently it has been gradually reinhabited, but it is still sparsely populated.

Not far to the south of the capital city is a stupa more than one hundred feet high built by King Aśoka. Beside it are traces where the four past Buddhas sat and walked up and down. On the great ridge of a mountain at the north frontier of the country is a stone stupa more than one hundred feet high. This is the place where a Pratyekabuddha entered Nirvana at the beginning of the present kalpa, when human life was countless years long. From here going northwest through mountains and forests for over one thousand eight hundred *li*, I reached the country of Kosala (in the domain of Central India).

The country of Kosala is more than six thousand *li* in circuit, and it is surrounded by mountains and ridges with woods and marshes linking with each other. The capital city is over forty *li* in circuit. The land is fertile and the soil productive. The towns and villages are situated within sight of each other, and the inhabitants are rich and substantial. They are physically stout and dark in complexion. The social custom is indomitable and fierce, and the people are bold and violent by nature. They believe in both erroneous religions and the correct one, and their learning and craftsmanship are outstanding. The king, who is a Kshatriya by caste, pays high respect to the Buddha-dharma, and his benevolence is deep and far-reaching. There are over one hundred monasteries with nearly ten thousand monks, all of whom study the Mahayana teachings. Deva-temples amount to over seventy, and the heretics live together.

Not far to the south of the city is an old monastery, beside which is a stupa built by King Aśoka. In olden times the Tathāgata, employing his great divine powers, subjugated the heretics at this place, and afterward Nāgārjuna Bodhisattva stayed in this monastery. The reigning king of this country, named Śātavāha (Leading right), respected Nāgārjuna and posted a guard at the door of his dwelling. At that time Deva Bodhisattva came from the country of Siṃhala in hopes of holding a discussion. He said to the guard, "Please announce my arrival." The guard did so accord-
929b ingly. Nāgārjuna, knowing well the name of Deva, filled a bowl with water and said to a disciple, "Take this water and show it to Deva." On seeing the bowl of water, Deva silently dropped a needle into it. The disciple took the bowl back in bewilderment. Nāgārjuna asked the disciple, "What did he say?" The disciple said, "He kept silence and simply dropped the needle into the water." Nāgārjuna said, "He is a man of wisdom indeed! He understands the deep meanings of things as cleverly as a divine being, and his perceptivity of subtle theories is second only to that of a saint. Such a virtuous man as he should be admitted immediately." The disciple said, "What does this mean? Is this the wonderful eloquence of reticence?" Nāgārjuna said, "Water is something that may be round or square according to the vessel containing it, and it can carry

away anything, whether it is clean or defiled. It flows to anywhere without interruption, and it is limpid but unfathomable. I showed him a bowlful of water to signify that my wisdom is all-round, and he dropped a needle into it to hint that he could get to the bottom of my knowledge. He is not an ordinary man. Quickly usher him in!"

Now Nāgārjuna was a man of austere deportment with a stern appearance, and whoever talked with him always drooped his head. Deva had heard about his ways and manners and had wished to study under his instruction for a long time. When he was about to receive Nāgārjuna's instruction, he flaunted his sublime wits at first, but when he saw the teacher he was awed by his austerity. After entering the hall, he took a seat in a corner and talked on abstruse topics in refined and elegant words for a whole day. Nāgārjuna said, "You are a prominent student, and your eloquence exceeds that of your predecessors. Being a feeble old man, I am happy to have met you, a brilliant scholar, to whom I may impart my knowledge as one pours water from one pitcher into another and transmit the Lamp [of the Dharma] without cease. The propagation of the Dharma depends upon such men as you. Please come closer, so that we may discuss the deep and abstruse teachings." Upon hearing these words, Deva felt self-conceit, and before starting the exposition of the profound theories, he first put forward an argumentation in a plausible and lengthy manner. When he raised his head to look at his opponent, he suddenly saw [Nāgārjuna's] awe-inspiring features, which rendered him dumbfounded, not knowing what to say. He stood up to apologize and begged to receive his instructions. Nāgārjuna said, "Be seated again! I shall teach you the supreme and wonderful truth, the real teachings of the King of the Dharma."

Deva then prostrated himself before Nāgārjuna and promised to devote his life and his whole mind to him, saying, "From now on I shall listen to your instructions."

Nāgārjuna Bodhisattva was skilled in pharmacology. By taking medicated nourishment he lived to be several hundred years of age with unfading mental and physical faculties. With the aid of such miraculous potions, King Śātavāha also reached the age of several centuries. His youngest son said to his mother, "When shall I be able to succeed to the throne?" The prince's mother said, "In view of the present situation, there is no fixed date. Your father, the king, is several hundred years old, and many of his offspring have predeceased him. This is all due to the power of bliss of Nāgārjuna plus his art of medication. When the Bodhisattva is no more, the king will certainly fall into extinction. Nāgārjuna Bodhisattva is a man of great wisdom and profound compassion. He renders service to all living beings and regards his own body as excrement. You may approach him and try to beg for his head. If you can succeed in the attempt, you will be able to fulfill your wishes."

Under his mother's instruction, the prince came to the monas-
929c tery, and as the guard had fled away in fear, the prince had free admittance to the premises. When Nāgārjuna Bodhisattva was walking up and down, reciting a eulogistic stanza, he suddenly saw the prince and stopped walking to ask him, "What is the cause of your arrival at the monastery this evening in such a hurry, as if some urgent and fearful thing had happened?" The prince said in reply, "I had a discussion with my compassionate mother, and I said that it was mentioned in the scriptures and proverbs that alms-givers gave alms to others for sustaining their precious lives, but that no one would give up his own body to someone who asked for it. My compassionate mother said, 'It is not so. The Sugatas (Well-departed ones) of the ten directions and the Tathāgatas of the three periods diligently seek the Buddha's way from their [first] mental initiation up to their attainment of Buddhahood. They acquire forbearance by observing the disciplinary rules; they lie down to feed beasts or cut their own flesh to ransom doves. King Candraprabha gave his head as alms to a Brahman, and King Maitrībala fed hungry *yakṣa*s with his own blood. Such instances are too numerous to cite, and examples can be found among the enlightened ones of all generations.' Now, Nāgārjuna Bodhisattva, you are a man cherishing high ambitions. I am in need of a human head, but for many years I could not find anyone who would voluntarily give

his head to me. If I kill a man by force, I would be deeply sinful, and to slaughter an innocent person is notoriously immoral. But you, a Bodhisattva, have practiced the sacred Way in expectation of attaining Buddhahood in the future, with your kindness benefitting all sentient beings without limit. You slight your body as a piece of shifting cloud and treat it with contempt as a rotten log. As it is not contrary to your original vow, I beseech you to grant me my request."

Nāgārjuna said, "What you have said is true. I seek the fruition of Buddhahood, and in imitation of the Buddha, I can forsake anything. This body of mine is [as impermanent] as an echo or a bubble. It rotates in the four forms of birth and transmigrates in the six ways of reincarnation. I have made a great vow that I should never go against others' wishes. But, my dear prince, there is one thing we should not do. What do you think about this? When I am dead, your father will also perish. Please consider the matter and see who can save him." But Nāgārjuna walked about to see what could be used to take his own life. Then he took a blade of dry cogon grass to cut his throat and severed his head as if by a sharp sword. Upon seeing this sight, the prince was terrified and fled. The palace gatekeeper reported to the king and informed him of everything. The king was so much grieved to hear the evil tidings that he died.

More than three hundred *li* to the southwest of the country is Bhrāmara-giri (Black bee) Mountain, which is lofty and has precipitous peaks and cliffs, and as it has no slopes to form a valley, it seems to be a whole rock. King Śātavāha chiselled the rocky mountain to build a monastery for Nāgārjuna. At a point more than ten *li* away from the mountain, a passageway was cut open, leading up to the foot of the mountain and then going upwards by excavating the rocks. In the monastery there are porches and verandas, lofty terraces and storied pavilions. The pavilions are arranged in five tiers, and in each tier there are four courtyards with shrines, and in each shrine is a golden life-size image of the Buddha carved with perfect workmanship. The other places are decorated with gold

and jewels. Water is channelled from the high peaks of the moun-
930a tain to flow down around the pavilions to link them with the corridors. Windows are cut in the rocky walls to illuminate the chambers.

In the course of constructing this monastery, King Śātavāha ran short of laborers, and his treasury became exhausted when the work was not yet half done; he was very much worried. Nāgārjuna said to him, "Why does Your Majesty seem to be heavy-hearted?" The king said, "I cherished a great mind and ventured to establish a deed of blessedness, hoping it would be everlasting up to the advent of Maitreya Buddha. But before the completion of the meritorious exploit, all my resources are expended. This is the cause of my worry that makes me sleepless and sit up waiting for daybreak." Nāgārjuna said, "Do not worry! A sublime deed of supreme bliss will produce endless advantages. With a great mind, no worrisome problem is insoluble. Be merry and happy when you return to your palace today. In the morning of the day after tomorrow, you may go out to sightsee in the countryside, and then come here to talk about the construction work." Having received this guidance, the king worshipped him by going round him.

Nāgārjuna dropped mystical potions onto the big rocks, and all of them turned into gold. While making an excursion, the king was delighted to have seen the gold. He drove his carriage to the place of Nāgārjuna, to whom he said, "Today while I was making a pleasure trip, I was beguiled by deities and spirits into seeing heaps of gold in the mountains and woods." Nāgārjuna said, "It is not a beguilement of spirits. It is due to your sincere devotion that the gold has come into existence. You should make use of it to accomplish your superior work." Thus the king used the gold for the construction of the monastery, and when the work was completed, there was still surplus gold, with which four big golden images were made on each of the five tiers. The remaining gold was used to replenish the bursary so that one thousand monks could be invited to live and carry out religious activities in the monastery. Nāgārjuna Bodhisattva collected and classified the teachings of the Buddha and the treatises composed by various Bodhisattvas, and he stored them in the monastery. In the top tier only the Buddha's images and various scriptures and treatises were placed. The lowest tier was used for dormitories for the monastic servants and storerooms for keeping property and miscellaneous things, while the three tiers in the middle were the lodgings of the monks. I heard some old people say that when King Śātavāha had completed the construction, it was estimated that the amount of salt consumed by the workers cost nine *koṭis* of gold coins.

Afterward the monks had a contention among themselves, and they went to the king for a settlement. Then the monastic servants said to one another, "The monks are quarrelling with each other in contradictory words, while some evil people are taking this opportunity to subvert the monastery." Thus they locked the doors from the interior to repulse the monks. Since then no monks have ever lived in this monastery. When one looks at the rocky mountain from afar, one cannot see the path leading to the gate. When physicians were invited to cure sick inmates, they were taken in and out blindfolded, so they did not know the way.

Going southwest from here for more than nine hundred *li* through a large forest, I reached the country of Andhra (in the domain of South India).

The country of Andhra is more than three thousand *li* in circuit, and its capital city, Veṅgīpura, is over twenty *li* in circuit. 930b
The land is good and fertile, yielding abundant crops. The climate is warm and hot, and the people are violent by custom. Their spoken language is different from that of Central India, but they follow the same rules of writing. There are more than twenty monasteries with over three thousand monks. Deva-temples are more than thirty in number with numerous heretics.

Not far from Veṅgīpura is a great monastery consisting of storied pavilions and multi-tiered terraces beautifully decorated with engravings; the images of the Buddha are most exquisitely made. In front of the monastery is a stone stupa several hundred feet high built by the Arhat Ācāra (Established rule of conduct). Not far to the southwest of the monastery of the Arhat Ācāra is a stupa built by King Aśoka. Once the Tathāgata preached the Dharma and showed great supernatural powers at this place and converted innumerable people.

Going southwest for more than twenty *li* from the monastery of the Arhat Ācāra, I reached a solitary hill. On the peak of the hill is a stone stupa built at the place where Dignāga (Given) Bodhisattva composed the *Hetu-vidyā-śāstra*.

Dignāga Bodhisattva became a monk clad in the dyed robe after the decease of the Buddha. He was endowed with great intelligence and resolution, and his power of wisdom was firm and strong. Having pity on the helpless world, he thought of propagating the holy teachings. Considering that the theories of *Hetu-vidyā* (logic) were profound in wording and extensive in reasoning, so that no student could complete the study of it without working hard, he retired to a secluded place in the mountains to fix his mind in meditation, pondering over the advantages and disadvantages of his writings, and thinking about the verbosity and conciseness of the textual meanings. At that time a sound echoed in the valley, and the mist and clouds changed color, while the mountain god raised the Bodhisattva to a height of several hundred feet and made an announcement, saying, "Formerly the Buddha, the World-honored One, who guided the people appropriately, spoke on the *Hetu-vidyā-śāstra* with a mind of compassion, comprehending all wonderful systems of reasoning and delving into the meanings of subtle sayings. After the decease of the Tathāgata, the great teachings became extinct. Now Dignāga Bodhisattva, having been endowed with bliss and intelligence for a long time, and deeply understanding the gists of the sacred teachings, is going today to propagate the *Hetu-vidyā-śāstra* again!" The Bodhisattva issued a brilliant light, shining upon those who were in darkness. At that moment, the king, upon seeing the light, suspected with a mind of deep respect [that the Bodhisattva] had entered the Diamond Samādhi and asked him to realize the Fruition of Birthlessness. Dignāga said, "I sit in meditation to think about how to shed light upon a profound text. What I expect to attain is perfect enlightenment [of Buddhahood], and I am not aiming at gaining the Fruition of Birthlessness [of Arhatship]." The king said, "The Fruition of Birthlessness is appreciated and admired by all holy persons, because it cuts off the desires of the three spheres of the world and makes one thoroughly master the three systems of learning; this is a great event. Please realize it without delay!"

At that time Dignāga was pleased with the king's request, and when he was about to realize the sacred fruition of having nothing more to learn, Mañjuśrī Bodhisattva knew his intention and had pity on him. Wishing to admonish him, Mañjuśrī said with a snap 930c
of his fingers, "What a pity! Why should you give up the broad mind to adopt a narrow and inferior ambition, and follow the line of selfishness instead of an altruistic intention? If you wish to perform benevolent deeds for others, you should widely propagate the *Yogācāra-bhūmi-śāstra* composed by Maitreya Bodhisattva, to guide younger scholars; this would be of great advantage." Dignāga Bodhisattva respectfully accepted the instruction and worshipped [Mañjuśrī] by going round him. Then he engaged himself in making a profound study to popularize the knowledge of *Hetu-vidyā*. As he feared that the meaning was too subtle and the wording too terse for the students, he wrote the *Hetu-vidyā-śāstra* to explain the principal gists and the subtle meanings in a comprehensive way for the guidance of younger students. After that he propagated the *Yogācāra-bhūmi-śāstra* extensively, and his disciples were well known to their contemporaries.

Going south from there through forests and wilds for more than one thousand *li*, I reached the country of Dhānakaṭaka (also known as Great Andhra, in the domain of South India).

The country of Dhānakaṭaka is more than six thousand *li* in circuit, and its capital city is over forty *li* in circuit. The soil is fertile and produces rich crops. There is much wasteland, and inhabited towns are few. The climate is humid and hot, and the people are dark in complexion, violent by nature, and fond of learning arts. There are numerous monasteries crowded together like scales of a fish, but most of them are deserted; only about ten are still in use, and they have more than one thousand monks, mostly studying the teachings of the Mahāsāṃghika school. There are over one hundred deva-temples with innumerable heretics.

On the hillside to the east of the capital city is Pūrvaśaila (East mountain) Monastery, and on the hillside to the west of the city is Avaraśaila (West mountain) Monastery. These were built for the Buddha by a former king of this country, who reclaimed the river to make a path and cut the rocks to build tall pavilions with corridors and passageways lying upon the steeps leading up to the peaks. Spirits and deities guarded these monasteries, which were frequented by saints and sages. During the millennium after the Buddha's Nirvana, one thousand ordinary monks came here to spend the rainy season every year, and on the day of dissolving the summer retreat they all attained Arhatship and flew away by supernatural power. After the termination of the millennium, ordinary and holy monks lived here together, but during the last one hundred years no monks have resided at these monasteries. The mountain gods changed themselves into the forms of jackals and wolves, or apes and monkeys, to scare off wayfarers, and that is why the monasteries became deserted of resident monks.

Not far to the south of the city is a great mountain cliff, which was the place where the Śāstra-master Bhāvaviveka (Clear discrimination) stayed at the Asura Palace to wait for the advent of Maitreya Bodhisattva as a Buddha. The Śāstra-master was a man of magnanimous disposition with deep and sublime virtues. Although he was outwardly clad in the garb of the Sāṃkhya sect, he inwardly glorified the theories of Nāgārjuna. When he heard that Dharmapāla Bodhisattva of the country of Magadha was spreading the teachings of the Dharma with a following of several thou-
931a sand disciples, he cherished the thought of having a discussion with him; and holding his pewter staff he went to see him. Upon arriving in the city of Pāṭaliputra, he came to know that Dharmapāla Bodhisattva was at the Bodhi Tree. The Śāstra-master said to his disciple, "Go to the Bodhi Tree, where Dharmapāla Bodhisattva is staying, and convey my message to him: 'The Bodhisattva

is preaching the bequeathed teachings of the Buddha to guide those who have gone astray. I have admired your virtue with an open mind for a long time. But owing to the nonfulfillment of my former resolve, I failed to come to pay respect to you—I vowed not to see the Bodhi Tree until I realized Buddhahood and became a teacher of men and heavenly beings.'" Dharmapāla Bodhisattva said to the messenger, "The human world is illusory and life is ephemeral. As I practice religion with diligence and sincerity all day long, I am short of time to have a discussion." The messenger went to and fro and brought back the message, but no interview was held.

The Śāstra-master returned to his own country and pondered quietly, "Until Maitreya Bodhisattva becomes a Buddha, who can solve my doubts?" Then he recited the *Mahā-kāruṇika-citta-dhāraṇī* before an image of Avalokiteśvara Bodhisattva. He refrained from taking food and only drank water for three years. Then Avalokiteśvara Bodhisattva appeared in a beautiful body and said to the Śāstra-master, "What is your aspiration?" "I wish to keep this body of mine so as to wait and see Maitreya Bodhisattva," was the reply. Avalokiteśvara Bodhisattva said, "As human life is fragile and the world is illusory, you should cultivate superior good deeds in order to be reborn in the Tuṣita Heaven, where you can speedily see and pay homage [to Maitreya]." The Śāstra-master said, "I shall not give up my idea, nor shall I change my mind." The Bodhisattva said, "If that is the case, you should go to the country of Dhānakaṭaka, where you can get your wish fulfilled by reciting the *Vajrapāṇi-dhāraṇī* at the place of the deity Vajrapāṇi on the mountain cliff to the south of the capital city." The Śāstra-master then went there accordingly and recited the incantation. After three years the deity said to him, "What is your wish, for which you have worked so hard and vigorously?" The Śāstra-master said, "I wish to preserve this body of mine to wait and see Maitreya. It was Avalokiteśvara Bodhisattva who directed me to come here. Are you the deity who will help me fulfill my desire?"

Then the deity told him the secret and said to him, "Inside the cliff is the Asura's Palace, and if you act in accordance with my

directive, the cliff will open. Once it is open, you should go in at once, and therein you may wait to see [Maitreya]." The Śāstra-master said, "If I am confined inside, how can I know when a Buddha has come into the world?" Vajrapāṇi said, "When Maitreya is born in the world, I shall inform you." The Śāstra-master then did as he was instructed and devoted himself to reciting the incantation for three more years. At first he did not have any other thought, and then he transmitted magic power to some mustard seeds and threw them so that they hit the cliff, which consequently opened wide. Hundreds and thousands of people witnessed the miracle and forgot to go back home. Standing at the entrance of the cave, the Śāstra-master said to the crowd, "I have prayed for a long time, wishing to wait and see Maitreya, and now my great desire is to be fulfilled by the spiritual assistance of holy deities. You may also come into the cave together with me to see the advent of a Buddha." The people were frightened and no one dared to step through the door, saying
931b that it was a cavern of venomous snakes and fearing that they might lose their lives. Upon repeated exhortation, only six men followed him in. The Śāstra-master turned back to wave farewell to the crowd and entered the cave in a composed manner, and the cliff closed behind him. The crowd felt sorry and repented of the faulty remarks they had made. From here going southwest for more than one thousand *li*, I reached the country of Cola (in the domain of South India).

The country of Cola is two thousand four or five hundred *li* in circuit, and its capital city is over ten *li* in circuit. The land and fields are empty and lying waste amid desolate marshes. There are few inhabitants, and bands of robbers run amok openly. The climate is mild and warm, while the people are fraudulent by custom and fierce by nature; they believe in heretical faiths. The monasteries are dilapidated and have very few monks. There are several tens of deva-temples with many naked heretics.

Not far to the southeast of the city is a stupa built by King Aśoka. Once the Tathāgata manifested great supernatural powers, preached the profound Dharma, subjugated the heretics, and converted many men and heavenly beings at this place.

Not far to the west of the city is an old monastery where Deva Bodhisattva held a discussion with an Arhat. Deva Bodhisattva had heard that in this monastery lived the Arhat Uttara (Supreme), who possessed the six supernatural powers and had attained the eight emancipations, and he came from afar to visit this Arhat. When he arrived at the monastery, he asked for lodging from the Arhat, but the Arhat was content with few desires and had only one bed. As he had no spare bed for Deva, he gathered a heap of withered leaves and invited Deva to sit on it. The Arhat then entered *samādhi*. When he emerged from the state of trance at night, Deva put his doubts to him for a solution, and the Arhat gave explanations to solve the queries point by point. But when Deva raised the seventh question in his repeated interrogations, the Arhat remained reticent and gave no reply; he went stealthily to the Tuṣita Heaven by supernatural power to seek the advice of Maitreya. Maitreya gave him the relevant explanations and told him, "Deva has cultivated himself in right practice for many kalpas in the past, and during the present Bhadrakalpa he will achieve Buddhahood. This was not known to you, but you should revere him with deep respect." In the time it takes to snap one's fingers, the Arhat returned to his seat and continued to talk about the wonderful theories and analyze the subtle sayings. Deva said to him, "What you have said is the exposition of the holy wisdom of Maitreya Bodhisattva. Is that why you can make a full elucidation?" The Arhat said, "What you have said is true." Then he stood up from his seat to worship Deva with respect and praise.

Going south from there through jungles and wilds for one thousand five hundred or six hundred *li*, I reached the country of Draviḍa (in the domain of South India).

The country of Draviḍa is more than six thousand *li* in circuit, and its capital city, Kāñcīpura, is over thirty *li* in circuit. The soil 931c
is fertile and the crops are plentiful. It abounds in flowers and fruits and yields precious substances. The climate is hot. The people are courageous and fierce by custom and are entirely worthy of trust. They are noble-minded and have wide learning. In writing

and speaking, their language is slightly different from that of Central India. There are more than one hundred monasteries with over ten thousand monks, all of whom study and practice the teachings of the Sthavira school. There are over eighty deva-temples, and most of the worshippers are naked heretics. When the Tathāgata was living in the world, he visited this country on several occasions to preach the Dharma for converting the people, and King Aśoka built stupas at all the holy sites.

The city of Kāñcīpura was the birthplace of Dharmapāla (Dharma-protection) Bodhisattva, who was the eldest son of a minister of this country. He had a magnanimous disposition since his childhood, and when he had grown up he was broad-minded. When he was twenty years old, a daughter of the king was betrothed to him, but on the evening when a banquet was held in celebration of the marriage, he felt distressed and prayed before an image of the Buddha. Being moved by his sincerity a deity carried him off to a mountain monastery several hundred *li* away from his home. He sat in the Buddha-hall, and a monk opened the door, discovered the young man, and suspected him to be a thief. Upon interrogation, the Bodhisattva told the monk everything and asked to become a monk. The community of the monks, being amazed by his career, gave him permission to satisfy his wish. Meanwhile, the king gave orders to seek for him far and near and came to know that the Bodhisattva had been carried away from the world by a deity. Having been informed of the fact, the king was most respectful and amazed. After he donned the dyed robe as a monk, he studied hard and well; his reputation and character have been narrated in a previous passage.

Not far to the south of the capital city is a great monastery in which the wise and intelligent people of the country assembled. There is a stupa more than one hundred feet high built by King Aśoka. Formerly the Tathāgata preached the Dharma, subjugated heretics, and widely converted men and heavenly beings at this place. Beside it are sites where the four past Buddhas sat and walked up and down. From here going south for more than three thousand *li* I reached the country of Malakūṭa (also called the country of Kumāri, in the domain of South India).

The country of Malakūṭa is more than five thousand *li* in circuit, and its capital city is over forty *li* in circuit. The land has saline soil, and agricultural yields are poor. Most of the precious products of the islands in the sea are collected in this country. The climate is very hot and the people are mostly dark in complexion. They are upright and indomitable in disposition and follow both the erroneous faiths and the right one. They do not uphold the learning of the arts but are good at making profit. There are many ruined foundations of old monasteries, but the existing ones are very few, and the monks are also few in number. There are several hundred deva-temples with many heretics, most of whom are naked ascetics.

Not far to the east of the city is an old monastery of which the buildings are desolate but the foundations are still in existence. It was constructed by Mahendra, a younger brother of King Aśoka. 932a
At the east side is a stupa of which the high foundation has sunk down, but the dome in the shape of an inverted bowl is still existent. It was built by King Aśoka. As the Tathāgata once preached the Dharma, showed great supernatural powers, and converted innumerable people at this place, it was built to mark the holy site. Although a long time has elapsed, it is all the more divine, and it can answer whatever prayer is said to it.

Near the sea in the south of the country is Malaya Mountain with its lofty cliffs and ridges and deep valleys and gullies. In the mountain there are white sandal trees and *candaneva* trees, the latter being similar to white sandal trees; indeed the two are indistinguishable. But at the height of summer, when one goes to a high place to look afar and sees a tree entwined by a large snake, one knows that it is a *candaneva* tree. As this species of tree is cool by nature, snakes like to twist on it. Having discovered the tree, one should shoot an arrow to mark it and come to cut it down after the winter solstice. While the trunk of the *karpūra* (camphor) tree is similar to that of the pine tree, the leaves as well as the flowers and fruits are different from those of the pine. When the wood is fresh after being cut down, it has no fragrant smell, but when it is dried and split along the grain, the aromatic substance is found in a form like mica and of the color of ice or snow. This is what is known as camphor.

To the east of Malaya Mountain is Potalaka Mountain, which has perilous paths and precipitous cliffs and valleys. On top of the mountain is a lake of clear water, issuing in a big river that flows twenty times round the mountain before passing into the South Sea. Beside the lake is a stone heavenly palace which is frequented by Avalokiteśvara Bodhisattva. Those who wish to see the Bodhisattva risk their lives to cross the river and climb up the mountain, regardless of hardship and danger, but only a few of them reach their destination. When the inhabitants living at the foot of the mountain pray to see the Bodhisattva, he appears either in the form of Maheśvara or as an ash-smearing heretic to console them and answer their prayers. At the seaside to the northeast of the mountain is a city located on the way to the country of Siṃhala in the South Sea. I heard the local people say that from here going southeast over the sea for more than three thousand *li* one can reach the country of Siṃhala (known in China as the Country of lions, not in the domain of India).

End of Fascicle Ten

Fascicle XI

Twenty-three Countries, From Siṃhala to Varṇu

The country of Siṃhala is more than seven thousand *li* in circuit, 932b
and its capital city is over forty *li* in circuit. The soil is fertile and the climate is warm and hot. The crops are sown and planted in the proper seasons, and flowers and fruits are plentiful. The country is densely populated with rich families. The people are short in stature and black in complexion with a rustic and fiery disposition, but they are fond of learning, advocate virtue, and promote the performance of good deeds in order to gain bliss.

This country is a precious island, producing many valuable gems, and it was originally occupied by spirits and deities. Once the

daughter of a king of South India was betrothed to a neighboring country. When the girl was sent to get married on an auspicious day, she met a lion on the way. The guards deserted her and fled, while the girl remained in her palanquin, waiting for sure death. But the lion king carried her to the remote mountains and provided her with venison and fruit daily. After some years she gave birth to a son and a daughter with human bodies but of animal extraction. When the boy grew up, he was so strong that he could wrestle with a fierce beast. At the age of twenty, his human intelligence was developed, and he said to his mother, "What am I, with a beast as my father and a human being as my mother? Since you are not of the same genus, how could you have lived with him?"
932c His mother then told him about the past, and he said, "Men and animals go on different ways. We should escape at once." His mother said, "I have tried to escape, but I have failed in the attempt." Her son then followed the tracks of his lion-father over mountains and ridges to find a way to flee from the calamity. When his father was away, he carried his mother and sister down to the region of human habitation. His mother said, "You two should be prudent and not say anything about our origin. If the people get wind of it, they will despise us." Then she and her children proceeded to her father's country, but it was no longer under the rule of her family, and her relatives had all gone. So she took lodging in the house of a townsman, who asked her, "Where do you come from?" She said, "I am a native of this country and have been wandering about in alien lands without a home. I have come back with my children to our homeland." The people felt sorry for them and provided them with sustenance.

When the lion king came back and found his dwelling empty, he was enraged by the loss of his family. Thus he went out of the valley to roam about the villages and towns, roaring with fury, making havoc for people and causing harm to living creatures. When the townsfolk came out, he would catch and kill them. They beat drums, blew conches, armed themselves with crossbows and spears, and they travelled in groups to avoid being injured. Fearing that this might jeopardize his sovereignty, the king sent hunters to capture the lion, while the king himself, commanding myriads of soldiers of the four divisions of his troops, lay in ambush in the dense forests and covered over the valleys. But the lion roared furiously, and both men and horses fled in terror. Having failed to seize the lion, the king posted a proclamation, saying that anyone who could capture the lion and rid the country of him would be handsomely rewarded in appreciation of his merit.

Upon hearing the order of the king, the lion's son said to his mother, "We are suffering very much from hunger and cold. I should respond to the king's call, and perhaps I can earn something to sustain you." His mother said, "No! You must not say so. Although he is an animal, he is still your father. How can we do him any harm simply because we are living a hard life?" The son said, "As man and animal belong to different genera, what principle of morality exists between the two? Since we have departed from him, what is to be anticipated in our minds?" He put a dagger into his sleeve and went to answer the call.

At that time hundreds and thousands of men and horses were assembled, and the lion was crouching in the forest, while nobody dared to approach him. But when his son came into his presence, he became tame and docile, and his parental affection appeased his anger. Then his son stabbed him in the abdomen with the dagger. Even then he was still affectionate to his son and had no feeling of resentment. His abdomen burst open and he died in pain.

The king said, "What sort of man is he, who has done such a strange thing?" Allured by promises of a reward, and threatened by severe punishment, the lion's son told the whole story in full detail. The king said, "How treacherous you are! You could kill even your father, so what about unrelated people? A man of animal blood is hard to tame, and his brutal sentiment is easily aroused. You have done a meritorious deed by ridding the people of the beast, but as you killed your father, your heart is treacherous indeed. I shall grant you a rich reward as payment for your 933a
merit, but I shall banish you to a far-off place as punishment for

your cruelty, so that the code of the country can be maintained while I do not break my promise." Then two big ships were prepared and furnished with a large amount of foodstuffs and rations. The mother was kept in this country and well looked after in reward of her merit, while her son and daughter each embarked on a ship to drift away with the waves. The son's ship sailed over the sea to this precious island, where he saw plenty of pearls and gems, and he settled down here. Later, when some merchants came to this island to collect gems, he killed the chief of the merchants and kept his daughter. Thus the people multiplied gradually and produced a large number of offspring. Then they established the system of king and subjects in superior and inferior positions. They constructed a capital city, built up villages and towns, and occupied the territory of the country, As their forefather was a seizer of a lion, they named their country by that title in commemoration of the merit of their origin. The daughter's ship floated to the west of Pārsa, where she was bewitched by a spirit and gave birth to a group of daughters, who then formed what is now called the Women's Country in the West. The inhabitants of the country of Siṃhala are short in stature and black in complexion with square cheeks and big foreheads. They are rustic and fiery by temperament and cruel and malignant in disposition, which are features inherited from the fierce animal. Therefore the people are mostly brave and stout. This is one of the traditions.

According to the Buddhist tradition, it is said that in the great iron city of this precious island, there lived five hundred *rākṣasīs* (demonesses). On the tower over the city gate two pennants were hoisted high to signify good or ill luck. When something good was going to happen, the auspicious pennant would flutter in the air, and when something evil was going to occur, the inauspicious one would quiver. The *rākṣasīs* always waited for merchants coming to the precious island, and they would change themselves into beautiful maidens to welcome and console the travellers with fragrant flowers and music and lure them into the iron city. After the merriment and feasting were over, the merchants would be confined in an iron prison to be eaten up gradually.

At that time, there was in Jambudvīpa a great merchant lord named Siṃha, whose son was named Siṃhala. As his father was getting old, Siṃhala assumed responsibility for family affairs. He led five hundred merchants to sail the seas to collect valuables, and they were driven to this precious island by wind and waves. As the *rākṣasīs* saw the auspicious pennant fluttering in the air, they held fragrant flowers and played music to receive the guests and entice them into the iron city. The young merchant lord joined with the queen of the *rākṣasīs* in happiness and merry enjoyment, while each of the other merchants found a spouse for himself, and after a year each of them had a son born to him. But the *rākṣasīs* became unfaithful to their paramours and intended to cast them into the iron prison and wait for the coming of other merchants. Siṃhala then had an evil dream, and he knew that it was an ill omen. He secretly sought a way of returning home. When he came by the iron prison, he heard the sound of pitiful wailing. So he climbed up a tree and asked, "Who imprisoned you, that you are crying so sorrowfully?" The prisoners said, "Do you not know that all the women in the city are *rākṣasīs*? Formerly they lured us into the city to make merry with us, but just before your arrival, they put us into this prison and began eating us as their food. Now most of us have been consumed by them. Before long you will suffer 933b
the same calamity." Siṃhala asked, "By what means shall I be able to escape from such a disaster?" The prisoners said, "We have heard that by the seaside there is a heavenly horse. If you say prayers with sincerity, it will surely rescue you."

Having heard this warning, Siṃhala secretly told it to his merchant companions, and so they faced the seaside and prayed earnestly for help. At that time the heavenly horse came and told them, "All of you should grasp my mane firmly and not look back. I shall carry you across the sea to save you from disaster, and send you home to Jambudvīpa." The merchants did as they were told and gripped the mane of the horse intently. The heavenly horse rose into the air and galloped along the road of clouds to the seaside. When the *rākṣasīs* found that their husbands were gone, they told the news to one another and asked where they had gone. They brought their infant sons with them and flew in the air to and fro. When they knew that the merchants were about to go across the sea, they called to each other to fly the long distance together. In a short time, they met the company of merchants with mixed feelings of grief and joy, shedding tears of emotion. Each of them covered her face and sobbed, saying to her husband, "I am lucky to have been acquainted with you, my goodman, and we lived together happily in conjugal affection for a long time. But now you are trying to go away, leaving your wife and child to live in solitude and to long for you in despair. How can you be so hardhearted? I hope you will stay and go back with us to the city." But the merchants would not listen to their entreaties. As the *rākṣasīs* failed in their tactful solicitation, they resorted to coquetry to seduce them with bewitchment. The merchants could not withstand their amorous fascination, and at the moment they hesitated whether they should go or stay, they dropped from the air. The *rākṣasīs* were overjoyed and returned home with the merchants.

As Siṃhala was a man of deep wisdom with no attachment in his mind, he succeeded in crossing the great sea and spared himself the disaster; so the queen of the *rākṣasīs* returned to the iron city empty-handed. The other *rākṣasīs* said to her, "Since you are devoid of wisdom and tact, you should not stay here." The queen then brought her son, flew to the presence of Siṃhala, and tried all means of feminine charm to persuade him to go back with her. Siṃhala recited an incantation while brandishing a sword, and shouted at her, "You are a *rākṣasī*, but I am a man. We go on different ways and are not compatible. If you importune me to go with you, I shall kill you at once." Knowing that she could not prevail upon him, the *rākṣasī* flew away to Siṃhala's home and lied to his father, Siṃha, saying, "I am a princess of a certain country; I married Siṃhala and had a son. When we were on our way returning to his home country with precious gifts, our ship was overturned in a hurricane, and the three of us barely escaped death. In the course of travelling over the obstacles of mountains and
933c rivers, we suffered the hardships of cold and hunger; but because

one word was uncongenial to Siṃhala, he forsook me, and using insolent language he slandered me as a *rākṣasī*. If I turn back to my own country, it is too far away, and if I stay here, I shall live in solitude. As I am in such a dilemma, I have come to state my case to you." Siṃha said, "If what you have said is true, then come in and live in my house."

Shortly after the *rākṣasī* took up her abode, Siṃhala came back, and his father said to him, "How is it that you value wealth, but slight your wife and son?" Siṃhala said, "She is but a *rākṣasī*!" And then he told everything to his father. His clansmen and relatives all came to expel her. The *rākṣasī* lodged an accusation against them before the king, and the king was ready to mete out punishment to Siṃhala, who said, "She is a *rākṣasī* full of feminine bewitchment." Considering his words untrue, the king was already attracted by the beauty of the *rākṣasī* and said to Siṃhala, "If you insist on deserting this woman, leave her in my harem." Siṃhala said, "I am afraid it will cause you disaster. The *rākṣasī*s are man-eaters!" But the king would not listen to Siṃhala's advice and took the *rākṣasī* to wife.

In the latter half of the night, she flew back to the precious island and summoned the five hundred *rākṣasī*s to come together to the palace. There they repeated evil incantations and committed cruelties, eating the flesh and drinking the blood of the people and animals in the palace. Then they brought the remnant corpses back to the precious island.

At dawn the following morning, when the ministers came to have an audience with the king, they found the palace gate tightly closed, and though they waited for a long time, they heard nobody speaking. So they broke the door open and entered the palace, and they found it empty, except for heaps of skeletons. They were startled at the sight and looked at each other helplessly, crying and wailing with grief, not knowing the cause of the calamity. When Siṃhala told them the story, the ministers realized that the king had suffered from his own actions.

Then the state assistants and old ministers, as well as senior officials and veteran generals, went in search of a virtuous and

talented person of sublime character to be king, and they all esteemed Siṃhala as a man of blessedness and wisdom. They discussed the matter, saying, "The nomination of a king should not be done at random. A king should be a man of congenital blessedness and wisdom, and he should be sensitive and sagacious. Without blessedness and wisdom, he cannot enjoy the throne, and without sensitivity and sagacity, how can he manage state affairs? Siṃhala is the person endowed with such qualities. He foresaw in a dream a presage of disaster and inspired the heavenly horse [to rescue him]. Out of loyalty, he pleaded with the king against the *rākṣasī*, and by his cleverness he preserved his own life. It is destined by heaven that he start a new dynasty." Siṃhala declined the honor, but his declination was not accepted, and he agreed to hold sway according to the principle of the golden mean, and after paying due respect to the ministers, he ascended the throne. Then he corrected former corrupt practices and commended sages and good people. He issued an order, saying, "My former merchant companions are still in the country of the *rākṣasī*s. I do not know whether they are alive or dead and their fate is unknown. In order to rescue them, we must reorganize our troops. It is a blessing of the country to
934a succor those who are in trouble and sympathize with those who are loyal. As to the collection of gems and valuables, this will also be to the advantage of the nation." Then he arrayed his troops and sent them across the sea.

At that time, the pennant of evil omen on the gate of the iron city shivered, and the *rākṣasī*s were frightened by the sight. So they came out to receive the troops, intending to cheat and tempt them with seductive bewitchment. Knowing their fraudulence well, the king, Siṃhala, ordered his soldiers to recite incantations and be brave in military action. The *rākṣasī*s tumbled in retreat, either escaping to hide in an islet or drowing in the great sea. Then the iron city was destroyed and the iron prison broken; all the merchants were released, and a large quantity of pearls and gems was obtained. Common people were invited to immigrate into the precious island, where they constructed a capital city and built up villages and towns.

Consequently a country was established, which was called by the name of Siṃhala after that of their king. This tale of Siṃhala is a story of the Śākya Tathāgata in one of his previous incarnations.

Formerly the inhabitants of the country of Siṃhala worshipped only inappropriate gods. During the first century after the demise of the Buddha, King Aśoka's younger brother Mahendra relinquished the secular life of passionate desire and aimed at the fruition of sainthood; he attained the six supernatural powers and possessed the eight emancipations. He walked on air and came to this country to propagate the right Dharma and spread the Buddha's bequeathed teachings. Since then the people have followed the faith of purity. There are several hundred monasteries with more than twenty thousand monks who follow the teachings of both the Mahayana and the Sthavira schools. More than two hundred years after the arrival of the Buddha-dharma, they were divided into two separate sects, each specializing in its own theories. One was the Mahāvihāra sect, which refuted the Mahayana teachings and advocated Hinayana tenets. The other one was the Abhayagiri sect, which studied the teachings of both *yānas* (vehicles) and propagated the Tripiṭaka. The monks, strict and pure in practicing the disciplinary rules, are experts in meditation and have brilliant wisdom. Many of them are model in conduct and serve as teachers of good behavior.

Beside the royal palace is the Temple of the Buddha's Tooth, which is several hundred feet high and decorated with pearls and rare gems. A signal post is installed on the temple, with a huge *padmarāga* (ruby) fixed on it that issues a refulgent light that shines brightly as a star when viewed at a distance day or night. The king bathes the tooth relic three times a day with scented water and burns powdered incense as an offering, in an extremely opulent manner.

Beside the Temple of the Buddha's Tooth is a small shrine, which is also decorated with various lustrous gems, and inside it is kept a golden image of the Buddha, which was cast after the size of a previous king of this country, with a precious gem embedded in the protuberance on the head. Afterward a thief intended

to steal the gem, and as the shrine was guarded by one door after another in enclosures of railings under close surveillance, he dug an underground passage and entered the temple through the tunnel. When he attempted to take the gem, the image rose higher and higher. As the thief could not reach the gem, he withdrew and
934b said with a sigh, "When the Tathāgata was practicing the Bodhisattva Way, he cherished a great mind and made a solemn vow that he would give, with a feeling of pity, everything including his life and country to the living beings of the four forms of birth. How is it that his image is so stingy as to be unwilling to part with the gem? I may well say that it does not know his past events." At these words, the image bent its head to give away the gem. Having obtained the gem, the thief went to find a purchaser. People who saw it said, "This is the gem on the protuberance of the golden image of the Buddha made by the previous king. Where did you get it? Are you trying to sell it here?" They seized him and reported to the king. The king asked him where he got it, and the thief said, "The Buddha gave it to me. I did not steal it." Thinking that the thief was dishonest, the king sent men to see the image and they found that its head was bending down. Upon seeing this spiritual manifestation, the king strengthened his faith. He did not punish the man but redeemed the gem for a large ransom. It was reset on the head of the image as an adornment for the protuberance. That is why the head of the image is still bending down up to now.

Beside the royal palace was built a great kitchen, which provided food for eighteen thousand monks every day. At mealtimes the monks came with their alms bowls to receive food, and after receiving their shares, they returned to their respective abodes. Since the time when Buddhism was introduced into this country, this tradition of making offerings to the monks was carried out from generation to generation up to the present age. But owing to the political turmoil and the lack of an established king in the last decade or so, this tradition has not been maintained.

Along the seacoast of this country, pearls and gems are produced. When the king came to pray to the gods, they would present him with extraordinary products. Townspeople come up and down to dig for gems, but the output varies according to one's luck. For whatever amount of gems they procure, they have to pay tax. At the southeast corner of the country is Laṅkā Mountain with its lofty cliffs and deep valleys that are haunted by spirits and ghosts. Once the Tathāgata came here and delivered the *Laṅkā-sūtra*.

Sailing south of this country for several thousand *li*, one reaches the island of Nārikela. The islanders are short in stature, about three feet tall. Although they have human bodies, their mouths are like the beaks of birds. They raise no crops and live on coconuts only.

Sailing westward from the island of Nārikela for several thousand *li*, one comes to a solitary islet, where on the eastern cliff there is a stone image of the Buddha over one hundred feet high, facing the east in a sedentary posture, with a moonstone as the protuberance on its head. When the moonlight shines upon it, water flows out from it over the rocky slope down to the valley. Once a company of merchants was driven by a hurricane to this solitary islet, and as the salty seawater was undrinkable they suffered thirst for a long time. It happened to be a full moon day, and water flowed down from the top of the image and saved all the merchants. They thought that they were saved by spirits moved by their sincerity. 934c
Thus they stayed there for a few days. When the moon was shaded by lofty cliffs, no water flowed down. Then the chief of the merchants said, "It may not be for the sake of saving us that the water flowed down. I have heard that when the moonstone is under the shining of moonlight, water flows out from it. Is it possible that a moonstone is on the top of the Buddha's image?" Then they climbed up the cliffs to have a look and saw that the protuberance on the head of the image was made of moonstone. A man who had witnessed the event told the whole story.

Sailing to the west from the country [Siṃhala] for several thousand *li*, one reaches a great precious island, which is not inhabited by men but is merely an abode of deities. On a quiet night one may see at a distance the mountains and rivers brightly illuminated. Many merchants visited this island, but none of them obtained anything.

From the north of the country of Draviḍa, entering a wild jungle and passing by isolated cities and small towns where evil people caused trouble to wayfarers, I travelled more than two thousand *li* and arrived in the country of Koṅkaṇapura (in the domain of South India).

The country of Koṅkaṇapura is more than five thousand *li* in circuit, and its capital city is over thirty *li* in circuit. The land is fertile, yielding rich crops, and the climate is warm and hot. The people, who are impetuous by custom, are dark in complexion and fierce and tough in disposition, but they are fond of learning and uphold virtue and arts. There are more than one hundred monasteries with over ten thousand monks, who study and practice the teachings of both the Mahayana and Hinayana schools. Deva-temples number several hundred, and heretics of different faiths live together.

Beside the city of the royal palace is a great monastery with over three hundred monks, all of whom are men of outstanding virtue and talent. In the monastery is a great temple more than one hundred feet high in which is preserved a precious crown of Prince Sarvārthasiddha, less than two feet high, adorned with precious jewels and kept in a precious chest. On each fast day, it is taken out and placed on a high dais, and incense and flowers are offered to it. It sometimes emits a bright light.

In the great monastery beside the city, there is a temple more than fifty feet high in which is enshrined a statue of Maitreya Bodhisattva carved out of sandalwood, which is over ten feet tall. On fast days, it sometimes issues a divine light. It was made by the Arhat Śrutiviṃśatikoṭi.

Not far to the north of the city is a wood of *tāla* (fan-palm) trees more than thirty *li* in circuit. The leaves of this kind of tree are long, broad and glossy, and in various countries they are used as writing paper. In the wood there is a stupa that marks a site where the four past Buddhas sat and walked up and down. Beside it is another stupa in which the relics of the Arhat Śrutiviṃśatikoṭi are preserved.

Not far to the east of the city is a stupa of which the base has sunk; the remaining part is about thirty feet above the ground. I heard some old people say that it contains relics of the Tathāgata that occasionally emit a divine light on fast days. Once the Tathāgata preached the Dharma at this place and manifested supernatural powers to convert a mass of people. 935a

Not far to the southwest of the city is a stupa more than one hundred feet high built by King Aśoka at the spot where the Arhat Śrutiviṃśatikoṭi showed great supernatural powers to convert living beings. Beside it is the ruined base of a monastery constructed by that Arhat. From here going northwest and entering a great wild jungle infested with ferocious animals and harassed by cruel bandits in gangs, I journeyed for two thousand four hundred or five hundred *li* and reached the country of Mahārāṣṭra (in the domain of South India).

The country of Mahārāṣṭra is more than six thousand *li* in circuit, and its capital city, bordering on a large river in the west, is over thirty *li* in circuit. The land is fertile, yielding plenty of crops. The climate is warm and hot, and the people, simple and honest by custom, are tall and sturdy in stature and are proud and carefree by nature. They are grateful for kindness and revengeful for injustice. If anyone insults them, they will risk their lives to avenge themselves. To those who come to seek refuge in distress they extend help selflessly. When about to take vengeance, they notify their opponent beforehand, so that both parties can put on armor to fight a duel. On the battlefield they chase after defeated enemies, but they do not kill those who have surrendered. For defeated soldiers and generals no punishment is meted out, but they are given women's costumes to shame them into committing suicide. The state keeps several hundred warriors. Before each decisive battle, they become intoxicated with wine, and one of them leading the van of the fighters can frustrate the bellicose spirit of a host of enemies. If they injure the inhabitants, the state will not punish them. Each time they come out for an excursion, drums are beaten by the vanguard. Moreover, they rear several hundred violent elephants, which are also fed with wine before taking part in an engagement. They rush and stampede wildly and break down all resistance before them. Relying on the strength of these warriors and elephants, the king looks down upon the neighboring countries.

The king, named Pulakeśin, is a Kshatriya by caste. He is a man of farsighted resource and astuteness who extends kindness to all, and his subjects serve him with perfect loyalty. The great King Śīlāditya has invaded east and west, and a number of countries far and near have either pledged allegiance to him or become his vassals, but this country [Mahārāṣṭra] alone has refused to acknowledge his suzerainty. On several occasions, Śīlāditya led the armed forces of the five parts of India and summoned heroic fighters of various countries under his personal command to invade this country, but he failed to win a victory. Such is the militancy of this country. But its social custom is quite different. The people are fond of learning and profess both heterodox and orthodox doctrines. There are more than one hundred monasteries with over five thousand monks who study comprehensively both the Mahayana and Hinayana teachings. Deva-temples are counted by the hundreds and the heretics are quite numerous.

935b Within and without the great city, there are five stupas built by King Aśoka to mark sites where the four past Buddhas sat and walked up and down. The other stone and brick stupas are too numerous to be named in detail. Not far to the south of the city is an old monastery in which is enshrined a stone image of Avalokiteśvara Bodhisattva that possesses latent spiritual power and often answers prayers.

In the eastern part of the country, there is a great mountain with peaks joining together to form a screen, and steep cliffs rising in a range. There is a monastery built in the deep valley, with lofty halls and spacious houses upon the peaks at the back, and storied pavilions and terraces of many tiers, standing before the cliffs and facing the gully. This monastery was built by the Arhat Ācāra (known as Suoxing or Behavior in Chinese), who was a native of West India. After his mother was dead, he observed where she had been reborn and saw that she was reborn as a girl in this country. So the Arhat came here with the intention of guiding and taking her [into the path of Buddhism] as the occasion arose. He entered the village to collect alms and came to the house where his mother had been reborn. When the girl came out to offer him food, her breasts yielded milk. As her kinsfolk thought it inauspicious, the Arhat told them the cause of the phenomenon, and thereupon the girl realized the fruition of sainthood. In order to repay the kindness of his mother for giving birth to him in her previous life as a result of karmic forces, the Arhat built this monastery out of gratitude for her deep virtue.

The great temple of the monastery is more than one hundred feet high; in it is enshrined a stone image of the Buddha over seventy feet tall. Above the image are overhung seven tiers of stone canopies that are neither attached nor supported, each being separated from the one above it by the space of about three feet. I heard some old people say that the canopies were supported by the willpower of the Arhat, or by his supernatural powers, or by the efficacy of drugs and magic. I made an actual investigation but could not find out the real cause. All around the temple there are engraved on stone walls figures depicting the events of the Tathāgata when he was praticing the Bodhisattva Way in his previous lives, such as the good omens of his realization of sainthood and the spiritual signs of his entering Nirvana, including all major and minor items carved in full detail. Outside the gate of the monastery, at the south and north and on the right and left, there are stone elephants each standing at a point. I heard some native people say that these elephants have occasionally trumpeted and caused earthquakes. Formerly Dignāga Bodhisattva spent most of his time in this monastery. From here going west for more than one thousand *li,* and after crossing the Narmadā River, I reached the country of Bharukacchapa (in the domain of South India).

The country of Bharukacchapa is two thousand four hundred or five hundred *li* in circuit, and its capital city is over twenty *li* in circuit. The soil is saline and plants are sparse. Salt is produced

by boiling seawater, and the sea provides profitable occupations. The climate is hot, with abrupt cyclones blowing violently. The
935c people are stingy by custom and deceitful in disposition. They are ignorant of learning and arts and believe in both heterodox and orthodox doctrines. There are over ten monasteries with more than three hundred monks, who study the Mahayana and the Sthavira teachings. Deva-temples are more than ten in number, and the heretics live together. From here going northwest for more than two thousand *li*, I reached the country of Mālava (i.e., the country of South Lāṭa in the domain of South India).

The country of Mālava is more than six thousand *li* in circuit, and its capital city, over thirty *li* in circuit, is situated on the southeast bank of the Mahī River. The land is fertile, producing rich crops, and vegetation is luxuriant with plenty of flowers and fruits. The soil is specially good for growing winter wheat, and so the inhabitants mostly eat pancakes and baked wheat flour. The people are benign by nature and are generally intelligent. They speak a refined language and are well educated. In all the five parts of India, two countries lay emphasis on learning, one being the country of Mālava in the southwest, and the other one the country of Magadha in the northeast, in which the people prize virtue and advocate loving-kindness, and being diligent and clever, they work hard at learning. In this country [Mālava] both heterodox and orthodox doctrines are followed, and there are several hundred monasteries with more than twenty thousand monks who study the teachings of the Hinayana Saṃmitīya school. Deva-temples are several hundred in number, and the heretics are really numerous, mostly being ash-smearing ascetics.

It is recorded in the local history that sixty years ago the king named Śīlāditya was a man of brilliant wisdom and resourcefulness with broad and profound knowledge. He protected and fostered all living beings and venerated the Triple Gem. From his birth up to his old age he was never angry with anybody and never killed living things. He was so kind that even drinking water for elephants and horses was filtered before it was given to them to drink, lest insects in the water should be injured. During his reign of more than fifty years, wild animals were friendly with men, and in the whole country the people never killed or harmed them. Beside the royal palace was a temple built by the most adroit workmen and decorated with all kinds of adornments. Inside the temple were kept the images of the seven Buddhas. An unlimited assembly was held regularly every year, to which monks were invited from the four quarters to receive offerings of the four monastic requisites, or the three types of robes and the seven kinds of precious gems. This good deed has been done from generation to generation without interruption.

More than twenty *li* to the northwest of the great city, one comes to a Brahmanic village. Beside it is a pit, which never overflows even under the excessive rains lasting ten days at a stretch during the autumn and summer seasons, when water flows into it from different sources. Beside the pit was built a small stupa. I heard some old people say that this was the place where an arrogant Brahman of yore fell into hell alive.

Formerly in this village there was a Brahman who was a man of erudition, the most prominent among his contemporaries, and he was learned in both Buddhist and heretical texts; moreover he was an expert in the art of calendrical calculation and astronomy. As a man of lofty character, his fame spread far. The king respected him appreciatively and the people venerated him as a teacher. His disciples, who were counted by the thousands, followed his theories and admired his way of teaching. He often said, "I was born 936a
into the world to transmit the teachings of the sages in order to guide ordinary people. None of the former sages or future philosophers can be my equal. The people are enthusiastic in propagating the theories of Maheśvaradeva, Vāsudeva, Nārāyaṇadeva, and the World-honored Buddha, and they draw pictures of them for pious worship. But now I surpass them all in virtue, and my reputation is dominant at the present time. I should be different from them all, otherwise how can I distinguish myself?" Then he carved images of Maheśvaradeva, Vāsudeva, Nārāyaṇadeva, and the

World-honored Buddha in red sandalwood and made a seat with four legs, which was carried wherever he went. Such was his attitude of overweening pride.

At that time there was in West India a *bhikṣu* called Bhadraruci (known as Xianai, or Friendly affection in Chinese), who was a highly learned logician, having fully mastered the theories of heretical treatises. He was pure in conduct and observed the disciplinary rules in such a perfect manner that his moral influence affected others as the strong fragrance of flowers does. He had little desire and was quite contented, never seeking material welfare. Having heard about the arrogant Brahman, the *bhikṣu* said with a sigh, "What a pity! At present the world is devoid of a great teacher, so that an ignorant man dares to commit treacherous deeds."

So he carried his pewter staff and travelled far to this country. He told his intention to the king, who saw him dressed in a shabby robe and did not have any feeling of veneration for him; but for his lofty ambition, the king was obliged to pay him due respect. He prepared debating seats and invited the Brahman, who said with a smile, "Who is that man daring to cherish such an ambition?" He ordered his disciples to come to the debating ground, where hundreds and thousands of people assembled to listen to the argumentation. Bhadraruci, wearing his shabby robe, sat on a heap of grass spread on the ground, while the Brahman sat on the seat which he carried with him, refuting the right Dharma and propagating erroneous theories. The *bhikṣu* debated fluently for several rounds, and at last the Brahman was defeated. The king said, "With your false repute, you have cheated the king and beguiled the people for a long time. It is laid down in the ancient code that the defeated party in an argumentation should be killed." A piece of hot iron from a stove was made ready for the Brahman to sit on, and the Brahman, being pressed in such an awkward predicament, took refuge in Bhadraruci and pleaded for his help. The *bhikṣu* said to the king, "The influence of Your Majesty's kindness spreads far, and your good reputation is known to all. Please be compassionate and do not resort to cruel punishment. Pardon him for his mistakes and let him go wherever he wishes." The king ordered the Brahman to ride on a donkey to announce his defeat all around the city. Being put to such shame, the Brahman felt so much insult that he spat blood. Upon hearing this, the *bhikṣu* went to comfort him and said, "You are learned in both Buddhist and heretical lore and your fame reaches far and near. Concerning the matter of glory or insult, you should know how to deal with it. What is substantial in the matter of fame?" The Brahman was so indignant that he rebuked the *bhikṣu*, slandered the Mahayana teachings, and scorned the ancient saints. Before he had finished his blasphemy, the earth cracked and he fell alive into the crevice. The site still remains there. From there rounding a cape and going northwest for two thousand four hundred or five hundred *li*, I reached the country of Aṭali (in the domain of South India). 935b

The country of Aṭali is more than six thousand *li* in circuit, and its capital city is over twenty *li* in circuit. The inhabitants are rich and prosperous, having plenty of pearls and gems. Although they pursue farming, trading is the preferred calling. The soil is sandy and saline, yielding few flowers and fruits. The country produces pepper trees, the leaves of which are like those of the pepper tree growing in the region of Shu [in China], and it also produces the *xunlu* (frankincense) tree with leaves resembling those of the birch-leaf pear. The climate is hot and windy and there are dust storms. The people are mean by nature, and they value wealth and despise virtue. Their writing and spoken language, as well as manners and laws, are generally the same as in the country of Mālava. Most of them do not believe in gaining happiness [by performing meritorious deeds]. Even those who believe in it also worship heavenly deities. There are over ten houses of worship, and the heretics live together. Going northwest from the country of Mālava for a journey of three days, I reached the country of Kiṭa (?) (in the domain of South India).

The country of Kiṭa is more than three thousand *li* in circuit, and its capital city is over twenty *li* in circuit. It has a large population of wealthy households. It has no sovereign lord and is under the jurisdiction of the country of Mālava, and its natural conditions and products are similar to those of that country. There are over ten monasteries with more than one thousand monks, who study and practice the teachings of both the Mahayana and the Hinayana schools. There are scores of deva-temples, and the heretics are numerous. From here going northward for more than one thousand *li*, I reached the country of Valabhi (i.e., the country of North Lāṭa, in the domain of South India).

The country of Valabhi is more than six thousand *li* in circuit, and its capital city is over thirty *li* in circuit. The native products, climatic conditions, social customs, and temperament of the people are similar to those of the country of Mālava. The inhabitants are rich and prosperous, possessing enormous wealth. More than one hundred families have each accumulated property worth one hundred *koṭi*s of coins. Many rare goods from distant places are gathered in this country. There are more than one hundred monasteries with over six thousand monks, most of whom study the Dharma of the Hinayana Saṃmitīya school. Deva-temples number several hundreds, and the heretics are quite numerous.

When the Tathāgata was living in the world, he repeatedly visited this country, and King Aśoka erected monuments and built stupas to mark the places where the Buddha had sojourned. Sites where the three past Buddhas sat, walked up and down, and preached the Dharma are located at intervals. The reigning king, called Dhruvapaṭu (known as Changrui or Permanent acuteness, in Chinese), is a Kshatriya by caste and is a nephew of the former King Śīlāditya of the country of Mālava and the son-in-law of the present King Śīlāditya of the country of Kanyākubja.

He is a man of hot temper and shallow intellect, but he sincerely believes in the Triple Gem. Every year he convokes a great assembly for seven days to offer the best of delicious food to the monks and present them with the three types of clerical robes and medicine as well as the seven kinds of valuable gems and jewels. After the presentation of the gifts, he redeems them with a payment of a double amount of money. He esteems virtue, honors good people, respects the Way, and lays emphasis on learning. He pays special reverence to eminent monks coming from afar. Not far from 936c the city is a great monastery built by the Arhat Ācāra, in which the Bodhisattvas Guṇamati and Sthiramati lodged and composed treatises that are widely circulated. From here going northwest for more than seven hundred *li*, I reached the country of Ānandapura (in the domain of West India).

Ānandapura is more than two thousand *li* in circuit, and its capital city is over twenty *li* in circuit. It has a large population of wealthy households. It has no sovereign lord and is under the jurisdiction of the country of Mālava; its natural products, climatic conditions, language, and laws are similar to those of that country. There are more than ten monasteries with less than a thousand monks, who study the teachings of the Hinayana Saṃmitīya school. Deva-temples are counted by scores, and the heretics live together. From the country of Valabhi going westward for more than five hundred *li*, I reached the country of Suraṭṭha (in the domain of West India).

The country of Suraṭṭha is more than four thousand *li* in circuit, and its capital city is over thirty *li* in circuit, with the Mahī River at its west. It has a large population of rich households under the jurisdiction of the country of Valabhi. The soil, being saline, yields few flowers and fruits. Although the cold and hot seasons alternate normally, the weather is often windy. The people are stingy by custom and frivolous and impetuous by nature. They are not fond of learning and believe in both heterodox and orthodox doctrines. There are more than fifty monasteries with over three thousand monks, most of whom study Mahayana teachings and the theories of the Sthavira school. Deva-temples are over a hundred in number, and heretics live together. As the country is situated on the way to the West Sea, the inhabitants procure profit from the sea by doing trade and commerce.

Not far from the city is Ujjanta Mountain, and on its top is a monastery, the cells and corridors of which are mostly excavated on cliffs amidst luxuriant trees and meandering streams. This was a place that saints and sages frequented and divine *ṛṣi*s dwelt. Going northward from the country of Valabhi for more than one thousand eight hundred *li*, I reached the country of Gūrjara (in the domain of West India).

The country of Gūrjara is more than five thousand *li* in circuit, and its capital city, called Bhillamāla, is over thirty *li* in circuit. The native products and social customs are the same as those in the country of Suraṭṭha. It is thickly inhabited, and the people are rich and prosperous. Most of them serve the heretics as their teachers, but a few believe in the Buddha-dharma. There is one monastery with more than a hundred monks who study the teachings of the Sarvāstivāda sect of Hinayana Buddhism. There are several tens of deva-temples, and the heretics live together. The king, a Kshatriya by caste, is a young man of sublime wisdom and courage. He deeply believes in the Buddha-dharma and is lofty in character and endowed with extraordinary talents. From here going southeast for more than two thousand eight hundred *li*, I reached the country of Ujjayanī (in the domain of South India).

937a The country of Ujjayanī is more than six thousand *li* in circuit, and its capital city is over thirty *li* in circuit. The natural products and social customs are the same as those in the country of Suraṭṭha. It is thickly inhabited, and the people are rich and prosperous. There are several tens of monasteries, most of which are dilapidated, only three to five remaining intact. There are over three hundred monks who study and practice the teachings of both the Mahayana and the Hinayana schools. There are several tens of deva-temples, and the heretics all live together. The king, a Brahman by caste, is well read in heterodox books and does not believe in the right Dharma. Not far from the city is a stupa built to mark the place where King Aśoka made a hellish prison. From here going northeast for more than one thousand *li*, I reached the country of Zhizhituo (in the domain of South India).

The country of Zhizhituo is more than four thousand *li* in circuit, and its capital city is fifteen or sixteen *li* in circuit. The soil is fertile and crops are abundant. It is good for growing pulse and wheat, and there are plenty of flowers and fruits. The climate is pleasant and the people are of a benign and affable disposition. Most of them believe in heterodoxy and a few respect the Buddhadharma. There are several tens of monasteries, but few monks. Devatemples are over ten in number, and there are more than one thousand heretics (priests). The king is a Brahman by caste, earnestly believes in the Triple Gem, and esteems men of virtue. Many learned scholars of various places assemble in this country. From here going northward for more than nine hundred *li*, I reached the country of Maheśvarapura (in the domain of Central India).

The country of Maheśvarapura is more than three thousand *li* in circuit, and its capital city is over thirty *li* in circuit. The natural products and social customs are similar to those of the country of Ujjayanī. The people venerate heretics and do not believe in the Buddha-dharma. There are several tens of deva-temples, mostly belonging to the ash-smearing ascetics. The king is a Brahman by caste and does not respect the Buddha-dharma very much. From there I returned to the country of Gūrjara, and again going northward through wilderness and dangerous desert for more than one thousand nine hundred *li* and crossing the great Sindhu River, I reached the country of Sindhu (in the domain of West India).

The country of Sindhu is more than seven thousand *li* in circuit, and its capital city, named Vichavapura, is over thirty *li* in circuit. The land is good for growing cereals, and millet and wheat are abundant. It produces gold, silver, and brass, and it is suitable for rearing cattle, sheep, camels, mules, and other domestic animals. The camels are small in size and have only one hump. It produces plenty of red salt, the color of red rock, while its white and black salt and white rock salt are used as medicine by people of distant foreign countries. The people are violent but upright by nature and are pugnacious and abusive. In learning, they do not aim at becoming erudite, but they deeply believe in the Buddhadharma. There are several hundred monasteries with more than ten thousand monks, all of whom study the teachings of the Saṃmitīya school of Hinayana Buddhism. They are mostly indolent

937b people with a corrupt character. The good and assiduous monks live apart in quiet and secluded mountains and forests, and many of them, working hard day and night, realize sainthood. There are more than thirty deva-temples, and the heretics live together. The king, a Sudra by caste, is a man of simplicity and honesty, and he respects the Buddha-dharma. Formerly the Buddha visited this country several times, and therefore King Aśoka built several tens of stupas at the holy sites. The great Arhat Upagupta visited this country many times to preach the Dharma to guide the people. At all the places where he sojourned, monasteries, stupas, or both were erected as monuments to mark the sites, of which I had brief information.

In a district of slopes and marshes extending to more than a thousand *li* beside the Sindhu River there live several hundred, nearly a thousand, families of ferocious people who made slaughtering their occupation and sustain themselves by rearing cattle, without any other means of living. All the people, whether male or female, and regardless of nobility or lowliness, shave off their hair and beards and dress in religious robes, thus giving the appearance of being *bhikṣu*s (and *bhikṣunī*s), yet engaging in secular affairs. They persistently hold Hinayana views and slander Mahayana teachings. I heard some old people say that in the old days the people of this place were cruel and evil by nature. There was then an Arhat who had pity on their degeneration and came flying through the air in order to edify them. He manifested great supernatural powers and performed wonders to induce their faith. Through his gradual teaching, the people respected him with delight and were willing to accept his instructions. Knowing that the people had become obedient, the Arhat told them to take refuge in the Triple Gem, quenched their ferociousness, and stopped them from killing living beings. They shaved off their hair, put on the religious robes, and respectfully practiced the instructions of the Dharma. But after the lapse of a long time and the changes of the world, they became imperfect in doing good deeds and returned to their evil habits. Although they were dressed in religious robes, they did not observe the disciplinary rules, nor did they practice good deeds. The custom has been handed down from generation to generation and has become a prevailing tradition. From there going east for more than nine hundred *li*, I crossed the Sindhu River, reached the east bank, and arrived in the country of Mūlasthānapura (in the domain of West India).

The country of Mūlasthānapura is more than four thousand *li* in circuit, and its capital city is over thirty *li* in circuit. The country is densely populated with rich families, and it is subject to the country of Ṭakka. The soil is fertile and the climate is mild and good for agriculture. The people are honest and upright; they like learning and esteem virtue. Most of them worship heavenly deities, but a few believe in the Buddha-dharma. There are more than ten monasteries, mostly dilapidated, with few monks, who do not specialize in the theories of any particular school. There are eight deva-temples, and the heretics live together.

There is a beautifully decorated Temple of the Sun God. The image of the god is made of gold and adorned with precious ornaments. It has spiritual perception and the power of penetration, and its divine merits protect all secretly. Female musicians play music incessantly, and candles are kept burning day and night. Incense and flowers are always offered without interruption. The kings and grand men of all the five parts of India come here to give alms of jewels and valuables, and they establish rest houses to
distribute food, drink, and medicine for the relief of the poor and 937c
the sick. There are always a thousand people coming from different countries to say prayers. Around the temple there are ponds and flowery woods that provide a very delightful resort. From there going northeast for more than seven hundred *li*, I reached the country of Parvata (in the domain of North India).

The country of Parvata is more than five thousand *li* in circuit, and its capital city is over twenty *li* in circuit. The country is thickly inhabited and is subject to the country of Ṭakka. It yields plenty of dry rice, and the soil is good for growing pulse and wheat. The climate is mild and pleasant, and the people are honest and upright by custom, though hot-tempered by nature; they use vulgar words in their speech. Their learning is deep and broad, and they believe in both heterodoxy and orthodoxy. There are more than ten monasteries with over one thousand monks who study and practice the teachings of both the Mahayana and the Hinayana schools. There are four stupas, built by King Aśoka. Deva-temples number twenty, and the heretics live together. Near the city there used to be a great monastery with over one hundred monks, all of whom studied Mahayana teachings. This was the place where the Śāstra-master Jinaputra (meaning Son of victory) composed *The Commentary on the Yogācāra-bhūmi-śāstra*, and it was also the place where the Śāstra-masters Bhadraruci and Guṇaprabha became monks. This great monastery was reduced to ruins by fire from heaven. Going southwest from the country of Sindhu for one thousand five hundred or six hundred *li*, I reached the country of Audumbatira (in the domain of West India).

Audumbatira is more than five thousand *li* in circuit, and its capital city, named Kacchešvara, is over thirty *li* in circuit. It is situated in the remote western region, near the Sindhu River and close to the great sea. The houses are beautifully decorated, and there are many jewels and gems. In recent years the country has had no sovereign king and is subordinate to the country of Sindhu. The land is low and moist and the soil is saline; wild weeds grow profusely, and few fields are cultivated. Although the country produces all kinds of cereals, pulse and wheat are particularly abundant. The climate is somewhat cold, and hurricanes blow violently. Cattle, sheep, camels, mules and the like are reared. The people are hot-tempered by nature and do not like learning. Their language is slightly different from that of Central India, and they are by custom simple and honest and respect the Triple Gem. There are more than eighty monasteries with over five thousand monks, most of whom study the teachings of the Saṃmitīya school of Hinayana Buddhism. There are ten deva-temples, mostly inhabited by ash-smearing ascetics. In the city is a temple of Maheśvara, which is adorned with engravings, and the image of the god has spiritual influence. It is frequented by ash-smearing ascetics. In the old days, the Tathāgata visited this country on several occasions to preach the Dharma to convert the people, guiding ordinary men and benefitting the secular inhabitants. Thus King Aśoka built six stupas at the holy sites. From here going west for less than two thousand *li*, I reached the country of Laṅgala (in the domain of West India).

The country of Laṅgala is several thousand *li* on each of the four sides, and its capital city, called Sthūlīśvara (?), is thirty *li* in circuit. The land is fertile and crops are abundant. The climate 938a
and social customs are the same as in the country of Audumbatira. It is a populous country and rich in precious jewels and gems. Situated at the seaside, it is on the way to the West Women's Country. It has no supreme ruler, and in each valley the people have their own leaders who are independent of one another, but all being subject to the country of Pārsa. Their written language is generally the same as that of India, but their spoken language is slightly different. The people believe in both heterodoxy and orthodoxy. There are over one hundred monasteries with more than six thousand monks who study and practice both Mahayana and Hinayana teachings. There are several hundred deva-temples, and ash-smearing heretics are extremely numerous. Inside the city is a temple of Maheśvara, which is magnificent and beautifully decorated; it is held in great esteem by the ash-smearing heretics. Going northwest from there, one would reach the country of Pārsa. (Though it is not in the domain of India, I passed by it and put it here as an appendix. It was formerly known as Bosi in abbreviation.)

The country of Pārsa is several myriad *li* in circuit, and its capital city, named Surasthāna, is over forty *li* in circuit. Since the territory is vast, the climate is different at different localities; generally speaking it is warm. Water is channelled into the fields, and the people are rich and prosperous. The country produces gold, silver, brass, quartz, crystal, and other precious and unusual substances. Large pieces of brocade, fine ramie cloth, woolen carpets, and the like are exquisitely woven. There are many good horses and camels. Large silver coins are used for currency. The people are hot-tempered by nature and have no etiquette by custom. Their spoken and written languages are different from those of other countries. There are no scholars or artists, but there are many skillful technicians whose products are much valued by the people of neighboring countries. They practice mixed marriage, and corpses are mostly discarded. They are tall and stout in stature and crop their hair short to expose the top of the head. They wear clothes made of fur, ramie, and colored cotton. A household tax is levied at the rate of four silver coins per head. There are numerous deva-temples, highly honored by the heretics of Dinapati (the Lord of the Day, i.e., the sun). There are two or three monasteries with a few hundred monks, all of whom study the teachings of the Sarvāstivāda school of Hinayana Buddhism. The alms bowl of the Śākya Buddha is kept in the palace of the country. In the eastern part of the country is the city of Ormus, the inner city of which is not wide; the outer city is more than sixty *li* in circuit. The inhabitants are numerous and wealthy. The northeast region borders on the country of Hrum, the topography and social customs of which are the same as those of Pārsa, but the features of the people and their language are different. Having plenty of jewels and gems, it is also a rich country.

To the southwest of the country of Hrum is the West Women's Country, which is an island. In it there are only female inhabitants without a single male. It produces various valuable goods, and is a dependency of Hrum. Thus the king of Hrum sends men to mate with the female inhabitants every year, as it is their custom not to bring up any male baby born to them.

Going northward from the country Audumbatira for more than seven hundred *li*, I reached the country of Pātāsila (in the domain of West India).

The country of Pātāsila is more than three thousand *li* in circuit, and its capital city is over twenty *li* in circuit. It is well populated but without a sovereign lord, and it is subject to the country
938b of Sindhu. The land is sandy and salty, and chilly winds blow hard. There are plenty of pulse and wheat but few flowers and fruits. The people are rustic and hot-tempered by nature, and their language is different from that of Central India. They are not fond of learning the arts, but they have pure faith. There are more than

fifty monasteries with over three thousand monks, all of whom study the teachings of the Saṃmitīya school of Hinayana Buddhism. Deva-temples are over twenty in number, all belonging to the ash-smearing heretics. In a large wood, fifteen or sixteen *li* to the north of the city, there is a stupa several hundred feet high built by King Aśoka. It contains a relic bone that occasionally emits a bright light. This is the spot where the Tathāgata, as a *ṛṣi* in a previous life, was killed by a king. Not far to the east from here is an old monastery built by the great Arhat Mahākātyāyana. Beside it stupas were built to mark sites where the four past Buddhas sat and walked up and down. From here going northeast for more than three hundred *li*, I reached the country of Avaṇḍa (in the domain of West India).

The country of Avaṇḍa is two thousand four hundred or five hundred *li* in circuit, and its capital city is over twenty *li* in circuit. It has no sovereign lord and is subject to the country of Sindhu. The soil is good for growing crops, and pulse and wheat are particularly abundant. There are not many flowers or fruits, and vegetation is sparse. The climate is windy and cold, and its people are rustic and violent by nature. Speaking a simple and plain language, they do not uphold learning, but they fix their mind to and have pure faith in the Triple Gem. There are over twenty monasteries with more than two thousand monks, most of whom study the teachings of the Saṃmitīya school of Hinayana Buddhism. There are five deva-temples belonging to the ash-smearing heretics.

In a great bamboo grove not far away from the city are the ruins of an old monastery. This is the place where in the days of old the Tathāgata gave permission to the *bhikṣus* to wear jifuxi (boots). Beside the ruins is a stupa built by King Aśoka. Although the foundation has sunk down, the remaining structure is still over one hundred feet high. In a temple beside the stupa is enshrined a standing image of the Buddha made of blue stone. On fast days it often emits a divine light. Further away to the south for over eight hundred paces, in a wood, is a stupa built by King Aśoka. Once the Tathāgata stayed at this place, and as it was cold in the night, he covered himself with all three of his robes, one over the other. The following morning he permitted the *bhikṣus* to wear double robes. In this wood there is a site where the Buddha walked up and down. There are also other stupas built close to each other to mark spots where the four past Buddhas sat and walked to and fro. In one of the stupas are preserved the hair and nail relics of the Tathāgata, which often emit a bright light on fast days. From here going northeast for more than nine hundred *li*, I reached the country of Varṇu (in the domain of West India).

938c The country of Varṇu is more than four thousand *li* in circuit, and its capital city is over twenty *li* in circuit. It is thickly populated and is subject to the country of Kāpiśī. The land is mountainous with many woods, and crops are sown in season. The climate is somewhat cold, and the people are rustic and violent by nature and vulgar and mean in disposition. Their language is rather similar to that of Central India. They believe in both heterodoxy and orthodoxy and are not fond of learning. There are several tens of monasteries, mostly dilapidated, with more than three hundred monks, all of whom study Mahayana teachings. There are five deva-temples with many ash-smearing heretics. Not far away to the south of the city there is an old monastery. In the past the Tathāgata preached the Dharma at this place to teach the people for their welfare and enlightenment. Beside it are sites where the four past Buddhas sat and walked up and down. I have heard some local people saying that the west side of the country borders on the country of Kaikānān, which is located among big mountains, where there are chieftains at different valleys and no sovereign ruler. It has many sheep and horses, and the good horses are particularly large; they are of a rare breed highly valued by neighboring regions. From here again going northwest, crossing great mountains and wide rivers and passing small towns on a journey of more than two thousand *li*, I came out of the domain of India and reached the country of Jāguḍa (also known as the country of Caoli).

End of Fascicle Eleven

Note on Siṃhala

by Zeng He

The country of Siṃhala, known as the Land of Lions in olden times, and also called the Country of No Sorrow, is south of India. As it produces plenty of rare gems, it is also named the Precious Island. Formerly, Śākyamuni Buddha transformed himself into a man named Siṃhala, and as he was a man possessing all virtues, he was made king by the people of the country. Therefore it was also called the country of Siṃhala. With his great supernatural powers, he destroyed the great iron city, annihilated the *rākṣasīs*, and rescued the victims who were in peril. Then he constructed a capital city and built towns to convert and guide the local people. After having propagated the right teaching, he passed away, leaving a tooth behind in this country. It is adamantine and will last for many kalpas without being damaged. It issues a precious light like a brilliant star, like the moon shining in the night, or the sun brightening the daytime. Whenever a prayer is said to it, it responds as swiftly as an echo. In times of natural disaster, an earnest prayer will bring instant divine auspiciousness. What is now called the Mountain of Ceylon was the country of Siṃhala in ancient times. Beside the royal palace is a temple for the Buddha's tooth relic, decorated with various gems and shining with great brilliance. It has been worshipped from generation to generation without negligence. The reigning king A-lie-ku-nai-er (Bhuvanaikabāhu V, r. 1372–1408 C.E.) is a native of Soḷī. He worships heretics, does not venerate the Triple Gem, is a brutal and tyrannical ruler, has no feeling of pity for his people, and blasphemes the Buddha's tooth relic. 939a

In the third year of the Yongle period (1405 C.E.) of the great Ming dynasty, the Emperor dispatched the eunuch Zheng He as an imperial envoy to send incense and flowers to that country and make offerings [to the tooth relic]. Zheng

He exhorted King Bhuvanaikabāhu V to respect Buddhism and keep away from heretics. The king was enraged and intended to kill the envoy. Having got wind of the intrigue, Zheng He went away. Afterward he was sent again to bestow gifts on various foreign countries, and he visited the king of the Mountain of Ceylon, who was all the more arrogant and disrespectful, and attempted to kill the envoy. The king mobilized fifty thousand troops to fell trees to obstruct the road and sent a contingent to ransack the seagoing vessels. At that juncture a subordinate official leaked the secret, and Zheng He and his men, having realized the situation, at once tried to return to their ships. As the road had been cut off, they could only secretly send some men out, but the captors of the ships would not allow them to go on board. Zheng He, commanding three thousand soldiers, made an assault by a shortcut at night and took possession of the royal city.

The native troops who had captured the ships joined forces with the native soldiers on land and launched a counterattack from all four sides. They besieged the royal city with a tight encirclement and fought for six days. Zheng He and his men captured the king and opened the city gate, and after cutting down trees to make a way, they moved away while fighting. Going for more than twenty *li*, they reached their ships in the evening. They brought the Buddha's tooth relic on board with due ceremony. It emitted a brilliant light in a most unusual manner as mentioned above, while a peal of thunder rumbled with such a loud crash so that people at a great distance saw the lightning and hid themselves. The ships sailed on the great sea without encountering a windstorm, [and they were as safe] as if they were walking on dry land. Ferocious dragons and mischievous fishes emerged before the ships but caused no harm. All the people on board the ships were safe and happy.

On the ninth day of the seventh month in the ninth year of Yongle (1411 C.E.) they returned to the capital, and the Emperor ordered that a precious diamond seat be prepared in the imperial city for the tooth relic, in order to make offerings to it for the benefit of living beings and the welfare of the people, so that they might perform countless meritorious deeds.

Fascicle XII

Twenty-two Countries, From Jāguḍa to Gostana

The country of Jāguḍa is more than seven thousand *li* in circuit, 939b and its capital city, named Hexina (Ghazni), is over thirty *li* in circuit; but the capital is sometimes located in the city of Hesaluo (Guzar), which is also over thirty *li* in circuit, both cities being strongly fortified in invulnerable positions. The mountains and valleys are rich in natural resources, and the cultivated farmlands, divided by ridges, are high and dry. Crops are sown in proper seasons. Winter wheat is abundant, and vegetation is luxuriant with profuse flowers and fruits. The soil is good for growing aromatic turmeric, and it produces the *hiṅgu* herb (*Ferula asafoetida*), which grows in the Rama-Indu Valley. In the city of Hesaluo there are gushing springs, the water of which flows to all sides, and the people

make use of it for irrigation. The climate is severely cold with much frost and snow. The people are frivolous and impetuous by nature and deceitful in disposition. They are fond of learning and are skillful in many kinds of crafts. They are clever, if lacking in discernment, and can recite a work of several myriads of words in a day. Their writing and spoken language are different from those of other countries. They produce more empty talk than real action. Although they worship various gods, they respect the Triple Gem. There are several hundred monasteries with more than ten thousand monks, all of whom study Mahayana teachings. The reigning king is a man of pure faith who inherited a throne handed down through many generations. He has engaged himself in performing meritorious deeds and is intelligent and studious. There are more than ten stupas built by King Aśoka. Deva-temples number several tens,
939c and the heretics, who are in the majority, live together. Their disciples are extremely numerous, and they worship the god Śuna.

Formerly the god moved from Aruṇa Mountain in the country of Kāpiśī to the Śunāśīra Mountain in the south of this country, and acting like a tyrant and doing evil deeds he rode roughshod over the inhabitants. Those who have faith in him and seek his protection have their wishes fulfilled, and those who despise him incur calamity. Thus the people, far and near and high and low, revere him with awe. The kings, ministers, officials, and common people, who observe different customs in neighboring countries, come here without making appointments on an auspicious day every year. They either offer gold, silver, and rare gems or present sheep, horses, and other domestic animals to the god in competition with each other to show their piety and sincerity. Therefore gold and silver are scattered all over the ground, and sheep and horses fill up the valley. Nobody dares to covet them, for everyone is eager to make offerings to the god. To those who respect and serve the heretics and practice asceticism whole-heartedly, the god imparts magical incantations, of which the heretics make effective use in most cases; for the treatment of disease, they are quite efficacious. From here going northward for more than five hundred *li*, I reached the country of Vṛjiṣṭhāna.

The country of Vṛjiṣṭhāna is more than two thousand *li* from east to west and over one thousand *li* from south to north. Its capital city, named Hubina, is over twenty *li* in circuit. The native products and customs are the same as in the country of Jāguḍa, but the language is different. The climate is very cold, and the people are rustic and violent by nature. The king is of Turkish stock and has deep faith in the Triple Gem, and he advocates learning and respects men of virtue.

Proceeding northeast from this country over mountains and across rivers, I passed several tens of small frontier towns in the country of Kāpiśī and reached the Bālasena Range of the Great Snow Mountains. The range is extremely lofty and precipitous, with dangerous and sloping stone steps on a tortuous path winding among the cliffs and peaks, and sometimes going down to a deep ravine and coming up to a high precipice. Even in the height of summer, it is frozen and one has to break ice while proceeding on the way. After a journey of three days, I reached the top of the range, where the cold wind is strong and piercing, and the accumulated snow fills the valley. When travellers pass this place, no one can make a halt. Even a falcon cannot fly over the range and has to alight and walk across it and then continue its flight. When one looks down the mountains, they appear to be small mounds, so this is a very high range in Jambudvīpa. On the range there are no trees but many rocky peaks that stand closely together resembling a forest. After a journey of three more days, I came down the range and reached the country of Andarāb.

The country of Andarāb, which is an old territory of the country of Tukhāra, is more than three thousand *li* in circuit, and its capital city is fourteen or fifteen *li* in circuit. It has no sovereign ruler and is a dependency of the Turks. Mountains and hills connect with one another, and the plains are narrow and limited. The climate is very cold with strong wind and heavy snow. Crops are abundant, and the land is good for growing flowers and fruits. The people are rustic and violent by nature, without moral discipline. They have no idea of sin 940a
or merit and are not fond of learning. They just erect deva-temples, but a few of them believe in the Buddha-dharma. There are three

monasteries with a few tens of monks, all of whom study the teachings of the Mahāsāṃghika school. There is one stupa built by King Aśoka. Going northwest from there, entering valleys, crossing rivers, and passing a number of small towns on a journey of more than four hundred *li*, I reached the country of Khost.

The country of Khost, which is an old territory of the country of Tukhāra, is less than one thousand *li* in circuit, and its capital city is over ten *li* in circuit. It has no sovereign ruler and is a dependency of the Turks. There are many mountains, and the plains are narrow and limited. The climate is windy and cold, and there are abundant crops and plenty of flowers and fruits. The people are rustic and violent by nature, without legal institutions. There are three monasteries with few monks. From here going northwest, crossing mountains and valleys, and passing a number of towns and villages in a journey of more than three hundred *li*, I reached the country of Huoh.

The country of Huoh, which is an old territory of the country of Tukhāra, is more than two thousand *li* in circuit, and its capital city is over twenty *li* in circuit. It has no separate ruler and is under the control of the Turks. The land is flat, and crops are sown in the proper seasons. Vegetation is luxuriant with profuse flowers and fruits. The climate is mild and pleasant, and the social customs are simple and honest. The people are of a rash and fiery disposition, and they wear garments made of felt and hempen cloth. Most of them believe in the Triple Gem, and a few worship various gods. There are over ten monasteries with several hundred monks, who study and practice the teachings of both the Mahayana and Hinayana schools. The king is a Turk who rules over the various small countries south of the Iron Gate and is always migrating from one country to another without a permanent city of government.

From here going eastward I entered the Cong Ling (Onion Range), which is the center of Jambudvīpa. On the south it connects with the Great Snow Mountains, on the north it reaches the Hot Sea and the Thousand Springs, on the west it borders upon the country of Huoh, and on the east it adjoins the country of Wusha. On each side there are hundreds of cliffs and ridges lining up in a row several thousand *li* in length. The deep valleys are perilous and precipitous with accumulated ice and snow that never melt, and the cold wind is strong and piercing. As many fistular onions are grown on the mountains, it is called the Onion Range, or it is so called because of the onion-green color of the cliffs. Going east for more than one hundred *li*, I reached the country of Mungān.

The country of Mungān, which is an old territory of the country of Tukhāra, is more than four hundred *li* in circuit, and its capital city is over fifteen or sixteen *li* in circuit. The native products and social customs are generally the same as in the country of Huoh. It has no sovereign ruler and is a dependency of the Turks. To the east is the country of Alini.

The country of Alini, which is an old territory of the country of Tukhāra, is located on both banks of the Oxus, with a circumference of more than three hundred *li*, and its capital city is over
fourteen or fifteen *li* in circuit. The native products and social cus- 940b
toms are generally the same as in the country of Huoh. To the east is the country of Rāhu.

The country of Rāhu, which is an old territory of the country of Tukhāra, borders on the Oxus in the north and is more than two hundred *li* in circuit; its capital city is over fourteen or fifteen *li* in circuit. The native products and social customs are generally the same as in the country of Huoh. From the country of Mungān going east over high ranges, across deep valleys, and passing several cities in the plains on a journey of more than three hundred *li*, I reached the country of Krisma.

The country of Krisma, an old territory of the country of Tukhāra, is more than one thousand *li* from east to west and over three hundred *li* from south to north. Its capital city is fifteen or sixteen *li* in circuit. The native products and social customs are generally the same as in the country of Mungān, the only difference being that the people are violent and malicious in disposition. To the north is Pārghar.

The country of Pārghar, which is an old territory of the country of Tukhāra, is more than one hundred *li* from east to west and over three hundred *li* from south to north. Its capital city is over twenty *li* in circuit. The native products and social customs are generally the same as in the country of Krisma. Going east from the country of Krisma over mountains and across rivers on a journey of over three hundred *li*, I reached the country of Himatala.

The country of Himatala, which is an old territory of the country of Tukhāra, is more than three thousand *li* in circuit. The land has a chain of mountains and valleys, and the soil is fertile, good for growing crops and producing abundant winter wheat. Vegetation of diverse kinds thrives, and fruits of every variety are profuse. The climate is bitterly cold, and the people are violent and impetuous in disposition, not knowing what is iniquitous and what meritorious. They are short and ugly in their features, and their ways and manners, as well as their garments made of felt, fur, and hempen cloth, are quite the same as those of the Turks. Their married women wear a wooden horn about three feet high as a headdress, with two branches in front to represent their husbands' parents, the upper branch indicating the father and the lower one standing for the mother. When one of the parents is dead, the branch indicating the deceased person is removed, and when both are dead, the horn headdress is discarded altogether.

Formerly this was a powerful country and the royal lineage was of Śākya stock. Most of the states west of the Cong Ling were subject to this country. As the land is linked with the territory of the Turks, the people of this country are influenced by Turkish customs. As they have to guard their own land against invasion and pillage, they wander about leading a vagrant life in different regions. There are several tens of strong cities, each having its own ruler. The people live in domed felt tents and move from place to place, up to the border of the country of Krisma in the west. Going east in a valley for more than two hundred *li*, I reached the country of Badakshān.

The country of Badakshān, which is an old territory of the country of Tukhāra, is more than two thousand *li* in circuit, and its capital city, built on the cliff of a mountain, is six or seven *li* in circuit. In this land there are mountains and valleys connected in a chain, and the earth is covered with sand and stone. The soil is

good for growing pulse and wheat, and there are plenty of such fruits as grape, walnut, pear, and crab apple. The climate is fiercely cold, and the people are staunch and violent by nature. They observe no etiquette and do not learn arts or crafts. Their features 940c
are ugly and vulgar, and they mostly wear felt and hempen garments. There are three or four monasteries with very few monks. The king is a plain and honest man who deeply believes in the Triple Gem. Going southeast from here in a valley for more than two hundred *li*, I reached the country of Invakan.

The country of Invakan, which is an old territory of the country of Tukhāra, is more than one thousand *li* in circuit, and its capital city is over ten *li* in circuit. It has a chain of mountains and valleys with narrow plains and cultivated land. The native products, the climate, and the characteristics of the people are the same as in the country of Badakshān, but the language is slightly different. The king is a tyrannical person who does not distinguish between good and evil. From here going southeast over mountains and across valleys for more than three hundred *li* by perilous paths in the canyons, I reached the country of Kuraṇa.

The country of Kuraṇa, which is an old territory of the country of Tukhāra, is more than two thousand *li* in circuit. The land and the topographical and climatic conditions are the same as in the country of Invakan. There are no legal institutions, and the people are vulgar and violent by nature. Most of them do not perform meritorious deeds, but a few believe in the Buddha-dharma. They are ugly and unsightly in features, and they mostly wear felt or hempen clothes. There is a rocky mountain from which much crystal is produced. The people break the rocks to obtain the mineral. There are a small number of monasteries with few monks. The king is a plain and honest man who respects the Triple Gem. From here going northeast, climbing over mountains and traversing valleys for more than five hundred *li* in a hard and dangerous journey, I reached the country of Dharmasthiti (also called Zhenkan or Humi).

The country of Dharmasthiti, lying between two mountains, is an old territory of the country of Tukhāra; it is one thousand five hundred or six hundred *li* from east to west and four or five *li* broad, the narrowest point being less than one *li*. It winds along the Oxus. The land is uneven with mounds and hummocks, and the earth is covered with shifting sand and stone; the cold wind is rude and strong. Only wheat and pulse are planted, with few trees, and there are no flowers or fruits. The country produces many good horses; though small in size, they are capable of undertaking hard journeys. The people have no sense of etiquette and righteousness, and they are rustic and violent by nature, with ugly and unsightly features. Their garments are made of felt and hempen cloth, and their eyes are of a dark green color different from those of the people of other countries. There are more than ten monasteries with few monks.

The city of Khamdādh is the capital of this country, in which is a monastery built by a former king of this country. Cliffs were hewn down to fill up the gully in order to prepare a site for building the halls and houses of the monastery. Formerly this country was not Buddhist, and the people only worshipped heretical gods. It was a few hundred years ago that the Dharma began to spread in this country. Once the beloved son of the king of this country was ill, and as the physicians were unable to cure him, his illness became worse and worse. The king then went in person to a deva-temple to seek the help of the god, and the priest in charge of the temple, speaking on behalf of the god, said that the prince would surely be cured and that there was no need to worry. The king was
941a pleased to hear this, and on his way back home he met with a Śramaṇa with a noticeable demeanor. Surprised to see the mendicant's appearance and garments, the king inquired where he had come from. This Śramaṇa, who had realized sainthood, wished to spread the Buddha-dharma, which was why he was dressed as he was. He answered the king, saying, "I am a disciple of the Tathāgata, a *bhikṣu* as people say." Having worries in his mind, the king eagerly said to him, "My son is sick, and he is in critical condition." The Śramaṇa said, "Even the spirits of your ancestors may be brought back to life, but it will be difficult to save your beloved son." The king said, "The god has said that my son will not die, yet

this Śramaṇa says that he is near his end. How can I believe the words of such a humbug?" When he returned to his palace, he found that his son was dead. The king kept it a secret and did not send out an obituary, but he went to see the priest, who still said that his son would not die and that his disease would be cured. The king was enraged and had the priest bound, and he rebuked him, saying, "You fellows live in a group doing a lot of evil and cheat people with your influence to gain advantages. My son is already dead, and yet you are still saying that he will be cured of his illness. Your fraudulence and swindling are intolerable. The priest should be killed and the temple demolished." Thus the priest was put to death and the image of the god was removed and thrown into the Oxus. After that the king started to return home, and on his way back, he again met with the Śramaṇa. He was glad to meet the mendicant, showed him respect, and paid homage to him, saying, "Formerly, as I had no sagacious person to guide me, I set foot on the wrong path. Although it has been a long tradition, it is time now for a reformation. I hope you will condescend to come to my residence."

At the invitation of the king, the Śramaṇa came with him to the royal palace. After the burial of the prince the king said to him, "The human world is an entanglement of the cycle of rebirths. When my son was ill, I inquired of the god about his fate, and the god said falsely that my son would certainly be cured of his illness. Then I heard your information, which proved to be true. From this I know that your Dharma is believable. Please have pity on me and guide this deluded disciple." Then he invited the Śramaṇa to make a plan for the construction of a monastery according to established rules. Since then the Buddha-dharma began to prosper. The temple of the old monastery was built for the Arhat.

In the great temple of the monastery is a stone image of the Buddha, over which is suspended a gilded copper canopy adorned with various precious things. When a man pays homage to the Buddha's image by going round it, the canopy also turns round with the worshipper, and when the man stands still, the canopy stops turning too. Nobody knows about the mystery. I heard some old people say that the canopy is suspended by the willpower of a saint, or that it is operated by some mechanical device. I noticed that the stone walls of the hall were high and strong, and I could not tell which of the stories was true. Going north over a great mountain in this country, I reached the country of Śikni.

The country of Śikni is more than two thousand *li* in circuit, and its capital city is over five or six *li* in circuit. Mountains and valleys connect together, with sand and stones spreading all over the wilderness. The country produces much winter wheat, but there are few other cereals. Trees are rare, and flowers and fruits are scarce. The climate is very cold, and the people are rustic and bold
941b by custom, being cruel in slaughtering and making theft their profession. They do not know about ritual and righteousness and make no distinction between good and evil. They hold wrong ideas about future calamity and happiness, and they fear disasters in their present life. They are vulgar and unsightly in their features and wear fur or hempen clothes. Their written language is the same as that of the country of Tukhāra, but they speak in a different way. Going south over a great mountain in the country of Dharmasthiti, I reached the country of Shangmi.

The country of Shangmi is two thousand five hundred or six hundred *li* in circuit, with alternating mountains and valleys, as well as high and low hills. All sorts of cereals are grown, and pulse and wheat are particularly abundant. It yields a large amount of grapes and produces orpiment, which is obtained by breaking the rocks cut down from the cliffs. The mountain gods are fierce and malicious and have repeatedly caused calamities. Travellers may be safe and have a happy journey if they worship the gods with offerings before entering the mountains; otherwise they may encounter abrupt windstorms and hail. The climate is cold, and the people are impetuous by custom, but they are simple and honest in disposition. They have no idea of etiquette and righteousness. Their wisdom and resourcefulness are limited, and their crafts are shallow and superficial. Their written language is the same as that of the country of Tukhāra, but they speak in a different way. They mostly wear felt and hempen clothes. The king is of the Śākya stock and respects the Buddha-dharma; the people following his edification are all pure Buddhists. There are two monasteries with very few monks.

Going over mountains and across valleys through dangerous regions in the northeast part of the country for more than seven hundred *li*, I reached the Pamir Valley, which is more than one thousand *li* from east to west and over one hundred *li* from south to north, the narrowest point being less than ten *li*. It is situated between two snow mountains, and the cold wind is fierce and strong, blowing day and night; snow falls in the spring and summer. The soil is saline and has much gravel; it is uncultivable and so there are scarcely any plants. It is an empty and dreary locality without human habitation.

In the Pamir Valley there is a great Dragon Lake more than three hundred *li* from east to west and over fifty *li* from south to north. Lying among the ranges of the Cong Ling Mountains in the center of Jambudvīpa, this lake is in the highest position. The water is pure and clear, of an unfathomable depth, and bluish black in color with a very sweet and refreshing taste. In the water dwell sharks, hornless dragons, fish, normal dragons, soft-shelled turtles, alligators, and tortoises; and floating on the water are mandarin ducks, swans, wild geese, and bustards. The huge eggs laid by various birds are left in the wilds among the marshes, or on sandy islets.

The lake has a large outlet on the west side with water flowing westward to the eastern boundary of the country of Dharmasthiti, where it joins the Oxus and flows west. All streams on the right side of this point flow to the west. On the east of the lake, another large stream flows northeast to the western boundary of the country of Kasha, where it joins the Sītā and flows east. All streams on the left side of this point flow to the east. Across a mountain in the south of the Pamir Valley is the country of Balūra, where much gold and silver are produced, and the gold is of a fiery color. From this
valley going southeast for more than five hundred *li*, climbing over 941c

mountains by dangerous paths, which are without human habitation all along the way but full of ice and snow, I reached the country of Kabhanda.

The country of Kabhanda is more than two thousand *li* in circuit, and its capital city, founded on a large rocky ridge with the Sītā at its back, is over twenty *li* in circuit. The mountains and ridges of the country connect together, and the valleys and plains are small and narrow. There are few varieties of cereals, but pulse and wheat are abundant. Trees are rare, and flowers and fruits are scarce. The plains and swamps lie waste, and the cities and towns are desolate. The people have no idea of etiquette and righteousness by custom, and they seldom learn crafts. They are rustic and violent by nature and are valiant and brave as well. Their features are ugly and unsightly, and they wear felt and hempen clothes. Their writing and spoken language are generally the same as in the country of Kasha. But they have pure faith and respect the Buddha-dharma. There are over ten monasteries with more than five hundred monks, who study the Hinayana teachings of the Sarvāstivāda school. The present king is a simple and honest man, who venerates the Buddha-dharma, has a composed and refined demeanor, and is devoted to learning. Many years have elapsed since the establishment of the country. The king professed himself a descendant of *Cīna-deva-gotra* (Chinese–sun-god stock) [see below].

Formerly the country was a wild valley in the ranges of the Cong Ling Mountains. Once in the past a Persian king obtained a Chinese lady for his queen. While the bride was being taken to Persia, she passed this place at a time when a rebellion was taking place. As the road leading from the east to the west was blocked, the king's bride was lodged on an isolated peak, which was so steep and lofty that ladders had to be used for going up and down. Guards were posted around the peak, keeping watch day and night. After three months the uprising was quelled, but when the bride was about to resume the journey, she was found to be pregnant. The envoy who escorted her was terror-stricken and said to his followers, "The king ordered us to fetch the bride back, but we met with the revolt and remained in a precarious state in the wilds, not knowing what would befall us. Thanks to the virtuous influence of our king, the insurgency has been put down. But at this juncture, resuming our return journey, the king's bride is found to be in gestation. I am worried about the situation, not knowing where I will die. We should find the chief culprit so that he can be put to death later." They made a clamorous interrogation but could not find out the true criminal. At this moment the bride's maidservant told the envoy, "Do not condemn anybody. It is due to her union with a god. Every day at noon a man came out of the disc of the sun to this place on horseback." The envoy said, "If that is so, how can we rid ourselves of the blame? If we go back we shall be put to death, and if we stay here, troops will be sent to attack us. What shall we do in such awkward circumstances?" They all said, "This is not a trivial matter. Who would go to suffer the punishment of death? We had better stay abroad to linger away our days."

Hence they built a palace and other houses on the top of a rocky peak more than three hundred paces in circuit. They constructed a city wall around the palace and made the Chinese lady their queen. Officials were appointed and a legal system was proclaimed. When the time was ripe, she gave birth to a son, who grew up into a handsome lad and received the title of king; his mother acted as regent. He could fly about in the air and had control over winds and clouds. His prestige and virtue spread far, and his fame and edification extended to a great distance; all the neighboring regions and countries became his vassal states. When at 942a
length this king died at a ripe age, his corpse was entombed in a cave in the mountains over one hundred *li* to the southeast of the capital. The corpse has become a mummy and is still intact, resembling an emaciated figure fast asleep. Its garments are changed from time to time, and sweet flowers are always placed before it by his descendants from generation to generation up to the present time. As their ancestor on the maternal side was a Chinese lady, while on the paternal side he was the sun god, they professed themselves the descendants of Chinese–sun-god stock. The features of

the members of the royal clan are similar to the countenances of the Chinese people, and they wear square caps, but they dress in the attire of the Hu people. Their offspring degenerated and suffered oppression from powerful countries.

When King Aśoka prospered in the world, he built a stupa in the palace, and the king [of this country] removed to live in the northeast corner of the palace. He converted his old palace into a monastery for the venerable Śāstra-master Kumaralāta. The terraces and pavilions were lofty and spacious with solemn images of the Buddha installed in them. The venerable monk, being a native of the country of Takṣaśilā, was intelligent since his childhood, and he left the world at an early age to engage in study of the scriptures and to fix his mind on the abstruse doctrines. Every day he recited thirty-two thousand words and wrote them down as well. Thus he was prominent in learning among contemporary scholars and enjoyed a high reputation in his time. He upheld the right Dharma and crushed erroneous views; in his brilliant discussions there was no question he could not answer. In all the five parts of India he was highly esteemed. His writings amounted to several tens of books, all of which were popular works studied by all scholars. He was the founder of the Sautrāntika school. In his time, Aśvaghoṣa in the east, Deva in the south, Nāgārjuna in the west, and Kumaralāta in the north were called the Four Brilliant Suns. So upon hearing of this venerable monk's great fame, the king of this country mobilized his troops, attacked the country of Takṣaśilā, and captured him. It was to show respect to him that this monastery was constructed.

More than three hundred *li* away to the southeast of the capital is a great rocky cliff with two caves in it. In each of the caves one Arhat entered the Samādhi of Complete Extinction, sitting erect and immovable in the shape of an emaciated man with skin and skeleton undecayed. They have been there for more than seven hundred years and their hair is constantly growing, so the monks shave their hair and change their garments once a year.

From the great cliff going northeast over ranges by a dangerous path for more than two hundred *li*, I reached the Puṇyaśālā

(Charity house), located at the center of a depression about one hundred *qing* in area (1 *qing* = 6.67 hectares), surrounded by four mountains of the eastern ridges of the Cong Ling Mountains. Snow accumulates in the winter as well as in the summer season, and the cold wind blows hard and strong. The fields are of saline soil and do not grow crops. There are no trees but only small grasses. Even in the hot seasons, snowstorms are likely to occur. When travellers have just entered this region, they may be enshrouded by clouds and mist at once. This is a dangerous place dreaded by travelling merchants. I heard some old people say that once in the 942b
past a group of more than a myriad of merchants, with several thousand camels laden with goods to gain profit, encountered a snowstorm at this place, and both men and animals lost their lives. At that time a great Arhat in the country of Kabhanda saw the catastrophe from a distance, and having pity on the merchants caught in danger, he intended to rescue them by supernatural power. But when he arrived at the spot, the merchants were already dead. So he collected the jewels and valuables and all their property to build a house in which he stored various commodities. He also purchased a piece of land in the neighboring country to make a settlement in the frontier city and hired people to live there to look after travellers. Hence at present all wayfarers and merchants are provided with daily necessaries. From here going eastward down the eastern ridges of the Cong Ling Mountains, climbing over perilous ranges and across deep valleys, through dangerous paths in the gorges, and braving continuous wind and snow, I proceeded for more than eight hundred *li* and emerged from the Cong Ling, arriving in the country of Wusha.

The country of Wusha is more than one thousand *li* in circuit, and its capital city is over ten *li* in circuit. It borders on the Sītā in the south, and the land is fertile, producing abundant crops. The trees are luxuriant with plenty of flowers and fruits. It yields much jade of different hues, such as white, jet, and sapphire. The climate is mild with good weather favorable to the growth of crops. The people are lacking in etiquette and righteousness and are strong-willed and rustic in disposition, being deceitful and having little sense of shame. Their written and spoken language are somewhat similar to those of the country of Kasha. Their features are ugly and unsightly, and their clothes are made of fur and hemp. But they believe in and respect the Buddha-dharma. There are some ten monasteries with less than one thousand monks, who study the Hinayana teachings of the Sarvāstivāda school. For several hundred years, the royal lineage has been extinct; thus this country, having no sovereign ruler of its own, is subject to the country of Kabhanda.

Going westward from the capital for more than two hundred *li*, I reached a great mountain, where the vapor of the mountain rises high and turns into clouds upon touching the rocks. The precipices are lofty and steep, as if they were broken, and seemed likely to collapse at any moment. The stupa built at the summit affords a splendid sight. I heard some local people say that several hundred years ago a cliff of the mountain collapsed and exposed a *bhikṣu* sitting with closed eyes behind the rocks. He was tall in stature but emaciated in appearance. His beard and hair covered his face and shoulders. A hunter saw him and reported the case to the king. The king came in person to see and worship the *bhikṣu*, and the inhabitants and officials in the capital also came of their own accord to vie with one another in offering incense and flowers. The king asked, "Who is this man, so tall in stature?" A *bhikṣu* said in reply, "This man with long beard and hair, clad in religious robes, is an Arhat absorbed in the Samādhi of Mental Extinction. One who is absorbed in such a *samādhi* has prelimited the length of remaining in the trance; or he may be aroused by the sound of a musical instrument, or by the shining of sunlight; with such signals he may be wakened from the abstract meditation. If there is no disturbance, he will remain motionless. The power of *samādhi*
942c sustains his body from decaying, but when he is out of *samādhi*, his physical body, which is composed of food, may become feeble and fragile. We should infuse him with ghee to nurture his body before we wake him up from mental concentration." The king said, "Let it be so!"

Then a musical instrument was struck. As soon as the instrument was sounded, the Arhat was awakened, and after looking around for a while he said, "Who are you, of such base appearance and wearing religious robes?" The monk said, "I am a *bhikṣu*." The Arhat said, "But where is my teacher, Kāśyapa Tathāgata?" The monk said, "He entered Mahanirvana a long time ago." Upon hearing this, the Arhat closed his eyes, disappointed. Then he asked again, "Has Śākyamuni Tathāgata come into the world yet?" The monk said in reply, "He has passed away after having been born into the world to guide living beings." When the Arhat had heard this information, he drooped his head. After a long while he ascended into the air and cremated himself with a fire produced by his supernatural power. His ashes dropped to the ground; the king collected them and built a stupa for them. Going northward from here for more than five hundred *li* over mountains, deserts and wilderness, I reached the country of Kasha (formerly called Shule, which is the name of the capital city. To be correct, it should be called Śrīkrītati, which indicates that the name of Shule is apparently wrong).

The country of Kasha is more than five thousand *li* in circuit, consisting mostly of deserts and having little cultivable land. Crops are abundant and there are plenty of flowers and fruits. It produces fine felt and hemp, as well as exquisitely woven cotton cloth and woolen carpets. The climate is mild and the weather changes according to the seasons. The people are rustic and violent by nature and deceitful by custom. They have little sense of etiquette and righteousness, and their learning is superficial. It is their custom to compress the heads of their newborn babies into a flat shape. They are vulgar and coarse in appearance, tattoo their bodies, and have green eyes. Their written language evolved after the fashion of the language of India. Although there are deletions and aberrations, the linguistic structure and function are mainly preserved. The diction and accent of their dialect are different from those of other countries. They piously believe in the Buddha-dharma and diligently perform meritorious deeds. There are several hundred monasteries with over ten thousand monks who study the Sarvāstivāda school of the Hinayana teachings. The monks do not delve into the doctrines, but they can recite by heart most of the texts. Therefore many of them are reciters of the Tripiṭaka and the *Mahā-vibhāṣā-śāstra*. From here going southeast for more than five hundred *li*, crossing the Sītā and a great sandy range, I reached the country of Cukuka (formerly called Juqu).

The country of Cukuka is more than one thousand *li* in circuit, and its capital city, which is over ten *li* in circuit, is in an impregnable position with a large number of registered inhabitants. There is a chain of mountains and hillocks covered with stone and gravel. As there are two rivers winding in the country, the land is good for cultivation. Such fruits as grapes, pears, and crab apples are in abundance. The seasonal wind is cold. The people are rude and deceitful by custom, and robbery is committed openly. Their writing is similar to that of Gostana [see below], but the spoken language is different. They have little sense of etiquette and righteousness, and their learning is superficial, but they piously believe in the Triple Gem and are fond of performing meritorious deeds. There are several tens of
943a
monasteries, but most of them are in ruins. The monks, about one hundred in number, study Mahayana teachings.

In the southern part of this country, there is a great mountain with lofty peaks and ranges standing one behind the other. The grass and trees are cold resistant, and they are always the same whether in spring or in autumn. The streams in the gullies flow rapidly in all directions. Upon the cliffs there are caves and rock cells, scattered all over the precipices. Many Indians who achieved sainthood came here by their supernatural power of levitation from a great distance and settled at this place. As many of the Arhats died here, a large number of stupas were built in the mountain. There are still three Arhats living in the caves, absorbed in the Samādhi of Mental Extinction. They look emaciated, but their beards and hair keep on growing all the time. So the monks go to shave them regularly. In this country a large number of Mahayana scriptures in particular are stored, and of all the places where Buddhism has prevailed, none can surpass this country in its collection of scriptures. Books consisting of one hundred thousand stanzas each amount to more than ten titles, and those of fewer stanzas are widely circulated indeed. Going eastward from there for more than eight hundred *li* over ranges and across valleys, I reached the country of Gostana (which is the elegant form of the local dialect, meaning "earth-nipple." In the vulgar language it is called Huanna, while the Huns call it Yudun. In the other Hu languages, it is designated as Qidan, and in India it is named Qudan. Its old form, Yutian, is incorrect).

The country of Gostana is more than four thousand *li* in circuit, and more than half of the country is desert. There is only a limited area of cultivable land, which yields cereals and diverse kinds of fruits. The country produces woolen carpets and fine felt, and the people are skillful in spinning and weaving silk. It also yields white and black jade. The climate is pleasant, but there are dust whirls. The people have a sense of etiquette and righteousness and are genial and polite in disposition. They are fond of learning the classics and the arts, and they are conversant with various crafts. The common people are wealthy and happy, and the registered families live in peace and security. The state promotes music, and the people love singing and dancing. A few of them wear woolen, hempen, felt, or fur clothes, but the majority use silk and white cotton for their dress. They are graceful in deportment and well-disciplined in behavior. Their system of writing follows that of India, with slight alterations and some reforms, and their spoken language is different from that of other countries. They esteem the Buddha-dharma, and there are over a hundred monasteries with more than five thousand monks who mostly study Mahayana teachings. The king is a very brave man, and he holds the Buddhadharma in high estimation. He claims to be a descendant of the deity Vaiśravaṇa.

In the past, when this country was uninhabited, the deity Vaiśravaṇa stayed here. When King Aśoka's prince had his eyes gouged out in the country of Takṣaśilā, the king angrily reproached his ministers and exiled some of the powerful and influential families to live in the desert valleys to the north of the Snow Mountains. In the course of moving from place to place in search of

pasture, the people in exile came to the western region of this country and elected their leader to be king. Meanwhile, a son of the emperor of a land in the east was condemned to banishment, and
943b he removed to live in the eastern region of this country. At the instigation of his followers, he made himself king. For a long time, the two kings were not in touch with each other. But once, in the course of hunting, the two of them met in the wilderness, and each inquired of the other about his ancestral lineage. Then they had a dispute over the question of who was superior to the other in rank. Their voices became hotter and hotter, and they came to the brink of resorting to force. Someone advised them, "Why should we fight a decisive battle in the course of hunting, when we have not fully mobilized our troops? We should go back to arrange our fighters in battle array, and then make an appointment to meet again." Thus the two kings returned to their respective countries, had their soldiers drill and practice the arts of war, and boosted their morale. On the appointed day the two armies met with colors flying and drums beating on the battleground, and they engaged on the following day. The lord from the west was defeated, and in the course of retreating he was decapitated. The lord from the east, in his victorious march, comforted and recollected the inhabitants of the defeated country. He moved his capital to the central part of the country and planned to build city walls. But he was worried by not knowing where the ground was clay and feared that he could not succeed in his plan. He made an announcement to invite learned soil scientists from far and near, and an ash-smearing ascetic carrying a big calabash of water came up to recommend himself to the king, saying, "I know the structure of soil." He dripped the water to mark the ground in a roundabout way twice, and then he fled and disappeared. Along the water marks, the foundations of the city walls were laid down, and this became the seat of the government. It is in this city that the present king has made his capital. Although it is not in a lofty and invulnerable position, it is strong and difficult for attackers to capture. Since ancient times, nobody has ever occupied it in a war.

When the king had moved his capital to the newly built city for the establishment of his government and the settlement of his people, he was already getting old after many achievements and exploits. As he was childless, he feared that the ancestral line would become extinct. So he went to the place of the deity Vaiśravaṇa to pray for a son, and a baby burst out from the forehead of the image of the deity. The king carried the baby home to the delight of the whole country. But as the baby refused to drink milk, the king feared that it might not live long, and he went again to the temple to seek nourishment for the baby. The earth in front of the deity's image suddenly bulged into the shape of a nipple, from which the baby sucked milk until he grew up. He became an unprecedentedly brave and brilliant man whose influence spread far, and he renovated the temple in honor of his forefather. Since then the royal lineage has continued from generation to generation without cessation. That is why the temple is full of jewels and gems, and worshipping ceremonies and sacrifices are regularly offered to the deity without neglect. As their ancestor was nursed with milk from an earth-nipple, the people named their country after it.

About ten *li* to the south of the royal city is a great monastery constructed by a previous king of this country for the Arhat Vairocana (meaning Universal shining in Chinese). Formerly, when the Buddha-dharma had not spread to this country, the Arhat came here and stayed in the wood, sitting in meditation. Someone saw him and was amazed by his appearance and garment. He reported the matter to the king, who came in person to see the Arhat and said, "Who are you staying alone in the solitary wood?" The Arhat 943c
said, "I am a disciple of the Tathāgata, and I am living alone practicing meditation. O King, you should perform meritorious deeds to propagate the Buddha's teachings and build a monastery for the assembly of monks." The king said, "What are the virtues of the Tathāgata, and what divine powers does he possess that made you dwell like a bird in the wood and practice his teachings assiduously?" The Arhat said in reply, "The Tathāgata has compassion on all creatures of the four kinds of birth and guides all living

beings of the three realms, either overtly or covertly, in the states of existence or extinction. Those who follow his Dharma will get rid of birth and death, while those who do not believe in it will be entangled in the net of passion." The king said, "Truly, as you have said, this matter is beyond verbal discussion. Since he is a great saint, he may as well appear in physical form for me to see him. Once I have seen him, I shall build a monastery, believe in him as my refuge, and propagate his teachings." The Arhat said, "When you have completed the construction of a monastery, you will get his spiritual response." The king in hope of this agreed to build a monastery. When the construction was completed, people from far and near assembled to celebrate the occasion as a religious function, but the instrument to be sounded for summoning the monks was lacking. The king said to the Arhat, "Now the monastery is completed, but where is the Buddha?" The Arhat said, "Work with utmost sincerity; the holy evidence is not far off." The king then prayed and worshipped, and suddenly an image of the Buddha descended from the air and handed an instrument to him. Thenceforth the king piously believed in the Buddha and propagated his teachings.

More than twenty *li* to the southwest of the royal city is Gośṛṅga (meaning Cow's-horn) Mountain, with two peaks rising high and surrounded by precipitous cliffs. In the valley a monastery was constructed, in which the Buddha's image often emitted a bright light. In the past the Tathāgata once came here and briefly preached the essence of the Dharma to men and heavenly beings. He prophesied that a country would be founded here and that the people would revere his teachings and follow Mahayana tenets. Upon the rocks of Cow's-horn Mountain, there is a large cave in which an Arhat is absorbed in the Meditation of Mental Extinction, waiting for the advent of Maitreya Buddha. For several hundred years offerings have been made to him without cease. Recently the rocks collapsed and blocked the entrance to the cave. The king sent his soldiers to clear away the fallen stones, but a swarm of black wasps flew out to sting them. Thus up to now the entrance has not been opened.

About ten *li* to the southwest of the royal city is Dīrghabhāvana Monastery, in which the standing image of the Buddha, made of ramie and lacquer, came by itself to this place from the country of Kuci. Once a cabinet minister of this country was banished to live in Kuci, and while he was in exile he always worshipped this image. Afterward he was recalled back to his own country, and he continued to remember and venerate the image from a distance. One night the image suddenly came to him. The man offered his residence for the construction of this monastery.

Going westward from the royal city for more than three hundred *li*, I reached the city of Bhagya. In this city is an image of the 944a
Buddha seated, about seven feet in height, with consummate features, quiet and dignified, and with a precious crown on its head that occasionally emits a bright light. I heard the local people say that this image was originally in the country of Kaśmīra and was transported to its present place. Once in the past a *śrāmaṇera*, who was a disciple of an Arhat, desired to eat some fermented rice cake when he was on his deathbed. The Arhat saw with his supernatural power of clairvoyance that this kind of cake was obtainable in the country of Gostana, and he went there by his faculty of divine feet and got some for his disciple. Having eaten the cake, the *śrāmaṇera* wished to be reborn in that country after death. His wish was actually fulfilled, and he was reborn as a prince of that country. After his succession to the throne, his prestige spread far and near, and then he crossed the Snow Mountains to invade the country of Kaśmīra. The king of Kaśmīra concentrated his troops to resist the invaders at the frontier, when the Arhat exhorted him, "There is no need to resort to force. I can repulse them." Then the Arhat went to speak on the essence of various Dharmas to the king of Gostana, but at first the king would not listen to him and still wished to send his army to the battleground. The Arhat then produced the robe that the king had worn when he was the *śrāmaṇera* in his previous life. At the sight of the robe, the king gained the supernatural faculty of remembering past events, and so he apologized to the king of Kaśmīra and withdrew his troops after conciliation. He also brought back with his army the Buddha's

image that he had worshipped when he was a *śrāmaṇera* in his former life. When the image was brought to this place, it refused to be moved any further, and so a monastery was built to enshrine the image where it was. Monks were invited to live in the monastery, and the king's precious crown was put on the head of the image. The present crown on its head is the one offered by the previous king.

Along the main path, in a great desert one hundred fifty or sixty *li* to the west of the royal city, there are mounds that are actually heaps of earth dug out by rats from their holes. I heard the local people say that the rats in the desert were as large as hedgehogs, and that the ones with golden or silvery hair were the chiefs, and that each time they came out of their holes, the other rats always followed them as attendants. Once the Hun people led hundreds of thousands of troops to attack the frontier city [of Gostana], and they were stationed beside the rat mounds. At that time the king of Gostana had only a few tens of thousands of soldiers under his command and feared that his force was not strong enough to resist the enemy. He always knew that the rats in the desert were marvellous animals, but he did not regard them as divine beings. When the invaders arrived, both the monarch and his subjects were greatly surprised and did not know how to deal with the situation. They tried as a temporary expedient a sacrificial ceremony to pray to the rats in the hope that they might help strengthen their army. That night the king of Gostana dreamed
944b that a giant rat said to him, "I wish to assist you, and I hope you will get your men ready for battle at an early hour. If you engage the enemy tomorrow, you will certainly win the day." Knowing that he had spiritual assistance, the king of Gostana mobilized his troops and ordered them to launch a surprise attack before dawn. Upon hearing this news, the Hun invaders were frightened. When they rushed to put on armor and mount horses and chariots, they found that their saddles and equipment, the strings of their bows and the ties for the armor, and all such belts and links, had been gnawed through by the rats. Then the defenders arrived abruptly, and the Hun people were taken aback and suffered capture and

massacre; the commanders were killed and the soldiers taken prisoner. The Hun people were struck with awe, thinking that their opponents had the help of divine beings. Out of gratitude toward the rats, the king of Gostana built a temple to offer sacrifices to them, and this tradition was carried down from generation to generation with a deep and special feeling of wonderment. From the monarch above down to the common citizen, everybody performed sacrificial ceremonies to gain blessedness. Whenever they came by the rat holes, they alighted from their horses and carriages to worship the rats and offer clothes, bows and arrows, or fragrant flowers and delicious food to them, so as to pray for happiness. As they did so with sincerity, they gained benefit in most cases. If no sacrifice was offered, one might meet with calamities.

Five or six *li* to the west of the royal city is Samājñā Monastery, in which is a stupa more than one hundred feet high that shows frequent spiritual signs and occasionally emits a divine light. Once in the past an Arhat came from a distance and stayed in the wood, issuing a bright light by his supernatural power. From a storied pavilion the king saw the light shining brightly in the wood at night and inquired of his attendants about it, and they all said, "A Śramaṇa has come from a distance and is now sitting in the wood, manifesting his supernatural powers." Then the king ordered his driver to prepare his carriage and went in person to see the monk. When he saw the sage, he cherished a feeling of respect for him, and in admiration of the monk's demeanor, the king invited him to go to the palace. The Śramaṇa said, "Everything has its own appropriate position, and each person has his particular inclination. A secluded wood with marshes and streams is the place I appreciate, while lofty halls and grand mansions are not what I should accept." The king respected him all the more and treated him with greater honor. A monastery was built with a stupa in it, and the Śramaṇa was invited to stay there.

Before long the king obtained, to his great delight, several hundred grains of relic bones through his profound devotion. He regretted that the relics as a spiritual response came a bit too late,

otherwise they would have been enshrined in the stupa, which would consequently have become a superior holy site. He went to the monastery and told his idea to the monks. The Arhat said, "O king, do not worry! I can place the relics under the stupa for you. You should put the relics in golden, silver, copper, iron, and stone cases one by one." The king ordered craftsmen to make the required cases, and they completed the task in a few days' time. The cases were sent to the monastery in precious carriages, and hundreds of heralds, attendants, and officials from the palace escorted the relics, and
944c tens of thousands of people watched the procession. The Arhat lifted up the stupa with his right hand and placed it in his palm, saying to the king, "You may store the relics now." Then the ground was dug up for the cases, and when this had been done, the stupa was put back without any damage or slanting. Those who witnessed the event said with admiration that they had never seen such a sight before. Their faith in the Buddha became more sincere, and their mind of respecting the Dharma more steadfast.

The king said to his group of officials, "I have heard that the Buddha's power is inconceivable and that his divine faculties are unfathomable. He can appear in hundreds of myriads of bodies simultaneously and be born either in the human world or in heaven. He can lift up the world in his palm, without making living beings feel agitation. He expounded the nature of the Dharma in normal language to enable all creatures to reach enlightenment in different ways according to their varying classifications. His divine power is incomparable, and his wisdom is beyond description. Although his corporeality has vanished, his teachings have been handed down, so that we can enjoy the peace of his doctrine, live under the influence of his virtue, taste the flavor of the Way, and admire his characteristic style of life. It is also owing to his blessing that we have now obtained these holy relics. Do your utmost, all of you, to pay deep respect to the Buddha. You will then understand that the Buddha-dharma is abstruse and profound."

Five or six *li* to the southeast of the royal city is Maza Monastery, which was established by a concubine of a former king of this country. In the past neither the mulberry tree nor the silkworm was known in this country. Upon hearing that a certain country in the east had mulberry trees and silkworms, [the king] dispatched a messenger to seek for them. But the monarch of the eastern country kept them hidden and would not grant the request. He gave orders to the frontier guards to prevent the smuggling of mulberry seeds and silkworms out of the country. The king of Gostana then humbly proposed to enter into a matrimonial alliance with the eastern country. As the king of the eastern country had the ambition to exert his influence over distant lands through mollification, he readily agreed to the proposal. The king of Gostana appointed an envoy to fetch the bride and said to him, "Tell the daughter of the monarch of the eastern country that in our country we have no silk floss, nor have we mulberry trees or silkworms. Let her bring some seeds with her to make silk garments for herself." Upon hearing these words, the daughter of the monarch secretly obtained some mulberry seeds and silkworms, which she kept inside the cotton of her hat. When she arrived at the frontier, the guards searched all her belongings but dared not inspect her hat. In this manner she entered the country of Gostana and lodged at the place where Maza Monastery is standing now. She was then taken to the royal palace with proper rites and ceremony, and the mulberry seeds and the silkworms were kept at the palace. At the beginning of the spring, the mulberry seeds were planted, and in the month of breeding silkworms the leaves of the mulberry trees were plucked to feed them. At the beginning of their arrival, they were also fed with leaves of miscellaneous trees. From then onward, the mulberry trees thrived, their luxuriant foliage casting shadows in patches. The king's concubine made an inscription on a stone tablet to lay down a rule forbidding the people to hurt the silkworms. It was only when the silk moths had all flown away that the cocoons might be reeled, and the gods would not protect those who dared to infringe this rule. This monastery was built in memory of the first group of silkworms. There are several withered mulberry trees, said to be the first mulberries planted there.

Thus silkworms are not killed in this country, and if anyone stealthily reeled silk [from cocoons with larvae inside], he would reap a poor harvest in sericulture in the following year.

945a More than one hundred *li* to the southeast of the [royal] city is a large river flowing northwest, and the people made use of it for irrigation. At one time it dried up, to the great surprise of the king, who rode in his carriage to inquire of an Arhat monk, saying, "The water of the large river is usually drawn and used by the people; what is the fault that has made it dry up? Am I unjust in managing state affairs, or are my virtuous deeds not extending to all? Otherwise why is the punishment from above so severe?" The Arhat said, "Your Majesty is ruling the country in peace and good order. The drying up of the river is caused by the dragon [in the river]. It befits Your Majesty quickly to offer sacrifice and say prayers to him, and then the lost advantages may be recovered." The king returned to his palace and performed a sacrificial ceremony for the dragon in the river. Suddenly a woman came over the waves and said to the king, "As my husband has been dead for a long time, I am unable to carry out your order. That is why the river has become dried up and the farmers have lost the advantage of irrigation. If you can select one of your noble ministers to be my husband, the river will flow with water as usual." The king said, "Please do as you wish." The dragon [woman] looked at the ministers and was delighted with one of them. After returning to the palace, the king said to his ministers, "My ministers are the pillars of the state, and agriculture is the source of food for sustaining our lives. If I lose my ministers, the state will be endangered, but without food all of us will die. What shall I choose, the endangerment of the state or death?" The minister [chosen by the dragon woman] came out of his seat and knelt down, saying in reply, "I am an incompetent person unworthy of my important position, and I have always been thinking of dedicating myself to the service of my country, but I have not had such a chance. Now, having been selected [to take up the appointment], how dare I refuse to bear the important responsibility? If it is for the benefit of the masses of people, what is there to be reluctant about in sending away a minister? A minister is merely an assistant of the state, while the people are the foundation of the country. I hope Your Majesty will not hesitate any more. And I shall be fortunate if a monastery can be constructed as a good deed done on my behalf." The king consented to his request, and the work was done in no time.

The minister then asked permission to go to the dragon's palace at an early date. All the officials and common people in the whole country held farewell banquets accompanied by the performance of music in honor of him. The minister, dressed in white and riding on a white horse, bade adieu to the king and expressed thanks to his countrymen before he rode into the river. The horse walked on the surface of the water without sinking down. When it came to midstream, the minister waved his whip to cut the water and made an opening, through which he dropped into the river. After a short while, the white horse floated out of the river, carrying a sandalwood drum on its back together with a letter in which it was said in brief, "Your Majesty did not despise me as a humble person and gave me the chance to be selected by the goddess. I hope you will perform more meritorious deeds for the benefit of your country and people. The big drum is to be hung at the southeast of the city. Before the approach of invaders, it will sound of itself to give a warning." Since then water has flowed again in the river, and the people have made use of it up to now. Because of the long lapse of time, the original dragon drum is no longer in existence. At the place where it was hung, another drum has been put as a substitute. The monastery beside the pond is deserted and in ruins, and there are no monks living there.

More than three hundred *li* to the east of the royal city is a large expanse of marsh several tens of *qing* in area, the earth of which is reddish black in color; it bears no vegetation whatsoever. I heard some old people say that this was the place where the army [of this country] was defeated. Once in the past a country in 945b
the east raised a million troops to make an invasion to the west. At that time the king of Gostana prepared an army of several lakhs

strong to resist the enemy from the east. The two armies met at this place and engaged in battle in which the soldiers of the west were defeated by the troops from the east, while the latter, advancing in the flush of victory, slaughtered people cruelly, captured the king [of Gostana], killed his generals, and massacred the soldiers, sparing not a single one. The ground was stained with blood, and the traces are still visible.

Going eastward for more than thirty *li* from the battleground, I reached the city of Bhīmā, in which there is a standing image of the Buddha carved in sandalwood, over twenty feet high, which has shown spiritual responses many times and often emits a bright light. If someone who is suffering from a painful ailment pastes a piece of gold foil on the image at the part corresponding to his ailing point, he may be instantly relieved of the pain; and if one says prayers to the image with earnest devotion, one's wishes are fulfilled in most instances. I heard the local people say that this image was made by King Udayana of the country of Kauśāmbī when the Buddha was living in the world. After the decease of the Buddha, this image came through the air from that country to the city of Araurak in the north of this country [Gostana].

When the image first came to this city, as the inhabitants were living in happy and wealthy conditions and were deeply attached to erroneous views, they did not treasure or respect it. Though they heard that it came by itself, they merely regarded it as a miracle and did not venerate it as an unusual object of worship. Later, an Arhat came to worship this image, and the people, amazed to see his strange garb, hurriedly went to make a report to the king, who ordered that they should scatter sand and earth over the strange figure. The Arhat was then smeared with sand and earth, and no food was supplied to him. At that time a man who always worshipped the image with veneration could not bear to see the Arhat being starved and secretly offered food to him. When the Arhat was about to leave, he told the man, "Seven days from now there will be a sandstorm that will fill up the whole city, and no one will remain alive. You should know this and prepare an exit for yourself. This disaster will be caused by their casting sand and earth on me." After saying these words, the Arhat went away and disappeared all of a sudden.

That man entered the city and told the tidings to his relatives and friends, but those who heard his information sneered at him. On the following day a big gale rose rapidly and blew away the filthy dust, while various kinds of gems and precious substances rained down all over the roads and thoroughfares, and so the people berated their informant all the more. But the man knew that disaster was a certainty, and he secretly opened a tunnel leading out of the city and made it a cellar. After midnight on the seventh day sand and earth rained from the air and filled up the city. The man came out through the tunnel and went east to this country [Gostana], where he stayed in the city of Bhīmā. No sooner had he arrived than the image also came. At this place it was worshipped with offerings and nobody dared to remove it. I heard some prophet say that by the end of Śākyamuni's Dharma, the image will enter the dragon's palace.

Now the city of Araurak has become a big mound. Kings and powerful persons of many countries have attempted to dig out the precious treasure, but each time they have come to the side of the
mound, a strong gale has broken out violently, raising up a shroud 945c
of mist and cloud, in which they lose their way.

From the east of the valley of Bhīmā, I entered a desert. After going for more than two hundred *li*, I reached the city of Nina, which is three or four *li* in circuit, situated in a vast marsh. The marsh is hot and humid, and it is difficult to go through it. This region is overgrown with reeds and wild grass and has no track or path. As this is the only passageway leading to the city, travellers have to go to and fro by this way. Gostana made this city a frontier station in its eastern region. Going east from there I entered the Great Desert, in which the shifting sand gathers together and scatters apart with the wind. As no trace of wayfarers can remain visible on the sand, travellers often lose their way in the vast wilderness and do not know what to do. Therefore they have collected the skeletons of the dead to serve as landmarks. Water and pasture are scarce in the desert, and the wind is hot, and whenever the hot wind blows, men and animals fall into a swoon and become sick. The sound of singing and shouting, or wailing and crying, is sometimes heard, but when one looks around to locate the source of the sound, nobody can tell where it comes from. This phenomenon often causes death, as it is mischief wrought by ghosts and devils.

Going further for more than four hundred *li*, I reached the old country of Tukhāra, which has been deserted for a long time; all the cities are in ruins. From here proceeding to the east for more than six hundred *li*, I reached the old country of Calmadana, that is, the Land of Jumo. The lofty city walls are still there, but there is no trace of human habitation. Continuing my journey toward the northeast for more than one thousand *li*, I reached the old country of Navāp, namely, the Land of Lulan.

The purpose of composing this book has been to describe the mountains and valleys [of the Western Regions], to investigate and collect data on the conditions in different lands, to narrate in detail the upright and flexible customs of various countries, and to record the climatic and topographic situations in diverse localities. As circumstances were always changing, I laid emphasis on different points at different times. Although it was difficult for me to trace the origin of everything I described, I by no means resorted to conjecture or fabrication. But I could write only in a brief manner about what I saw or heard on my journey and keep a record of the spread of the edification of Buddhism. Up to the place where the sun sets, all people are living under the beneficence of the Emperor, whose ultimate virtue is admired by all within the reach of his moral influence. As the whole empire is a great unity and the world the manifestation of oneness, am I a mere solitary envoy going in a single carriage, passing through travellers' rest stations for a distance of ten thousand *li*?

Eulogy of the Buddha

The Eulogy says: Great is the King of the Dharma, who appeared in the world with his spiritual edification working secretly and his divine Way leading to voidness. His form and mentality disappeared in as many worlds as the grains of sand in the Ganges, and he ceased to rise and fall for kalpas as innumerable as atoms in the world. As his form and mentality have disappeared, his birth has no reality of birth, and as he has ceased to rise and fall, his extinction has nothing of extinction. Could his birth at Kapilavastu have been a real fact? His passing away between the *śāla* trees was merely a means of his secret edification. We should know that he manifested his traces in the world at opportune moments in accordance with circumstances to show the effect of his spirituality.

He was born in a Śākya family of the Kshatriya caste. He should have succeeded to the throne of his native country, but he devoted his life to religious activities. He gave up the prospect of being a universal monarch of the golden wheel and preferred to rule over the world of the Dharma; and from the white curl between his eyebrows he shed a light to comfort all living beings. His Way pre- 946a
vails in the ten directions, and his wisdom comprehends everything. Although he is from the unknowable universe, he provides shelter to those who are in the discernible world. He turned the Wheel of the Dharma of the three classifications in the great chiliocosm, and he expounded his doctrine in one and the same diction to teach all the masses. His teachings are classified into eighty-four thousand gates, the essence of which is summed up in the twelve divisions of the scriptures. Therefore wherever they are under the protection of his teachings, the people can move about freely in the wood of blessedness, and wherever they are inspired by his morals and discipline, all men live in the region of longevity. Glorious are his saintly and sagacious deeds, and perfect is his goodness toward men and heavenly beings! But he gave up both mobility and immobility in the wood of *śāla* trees and nullified the conception of coming and going in illusory existence, and nobody could succeed him to glorify his doctrine of nothingness.

In order to repay the kindness of the Buddha, the Venerable Mahākāśyapa selected a group of Arhats to collect the precious Dharma, consisting of the four *Āgamas* explaining its origin and ramifications and the Tripiṭaka giving its essential theories. Although various schools and sects have arisen, the essence of the great Dharma remains unchanged. From his birth up to his decease, he showed a thousand transformations of his holy traces and manifested propitious omens in ten thousand ways. His limitless spirituality became more and more apparent, and his teachings of nonaction were always pure and new. All these are preserved in the scriptures and are written down in records and commentaries. But different opinions became confused and tangled, and dissident discussants spread their own diverse views. The original and fundamental theories are scarcely interpreted in the correct way. Even in such writings as are based on concrete facts, there are many variant views, let alone in the texts that deal with the abstruse and profound right Dharma and delve into the deep meanings of the abstract and recondite principles, where there are many incomplete points in exposition. This is because previous sages of virtue remained only in the track of translation, and brilliant scholars of later times followed the course shown by incomplete texts. Thus the great doctrine was hidden in obscurity, and the subtle sayings were missing and unknown to the world.

The teachings of the Dharma have been spreading for quite a number of years. Beginning with the Han dynasty and up to the present reign of the Tang, the glorious task of translation has been carried on in a fluent and graceful manner as splendidly as the conjoined shining of the sun and moon. But the abstruse Way was not revealed in its entirety, and the true essence was still obscure. This was not because the holy teachings were sometimes active and at other times inactive, but because of untimely royal patronage.

But since the great Tang has held sway over the empire, it has won the confidence of the foreign countries. The old rules formulated by the saints have been scrutinized, and the outdated codes laid down by former monarchs amended. The teachings of the Image

Period of Buddhism are exuberantly expounded as great instructions. The Way does not exist in vain, but its propagation depends on the illustration of virtue. This is why the abstruse doctrines of the Three Vehicles were buried in oblivion for the last thousand years, and the spiritual efficacy of the Buddha's ten powers of wisdom were shut out ten thousand *li* away. It is true that the divine Way has no directional limitations in its spread, but the holy teachings have to depend on circumstances for their appearance.

Eulogy of Xuanzang

The genealogical origin of the Dharma-master Xuanzang may be traced back to Emperor Shun, who once fished at Leize and later married the two daughters of Emperor Yao at the Gui River, and whose descendants adopted the surname of Chen. He is the embodiment of the good omen of superior virtue and contains the perfection of medium harmony. He follows the right Way in accordance with virtue and abides by chastity to rectify his behavior. As he had planted the cause of blessedness in his previous birth, he was born into this life during a time of prosperity. His conduct surpassed that of the world, and he stayed quietly at learning centers to receive the correct instructions taught by former teachers
and to admire the virtues of previous philosophers. In the course 946b
of wandering to pursue his studies, he travelled to the regions of Yan and Zhao and visited the states of Lu and Wei. After leaving the district of the Three Rivers at his back, he entered the interior of the region of Qin. He proceeded from the three prefectures of Shu and arrived at the state of Wukuai. He approached all learned scholars to ask for instructions, and in the presence of distinguished personages he repeatedly avowed his intention of going abroad to acquire the Dharma. He heard the discussions of various schools and made a study of their propositions, finding that they were vying with each other to emphasize their own specific theories and were jealous of the teachings of their rivals. This aroused his desire

to go to the root of the doctrine of Buddhism, and he determined to make a thorough study of the matter.

At a time when the empire within the four seas was in good order and the distant lands in the eight directions were free from troubles, he tidied himself and started the journey, with his travelling staff in hand, on the morning of the first day of the eighth month in the third year of the Zhenguan reign (629 C.E.). With the prestige of the Emperor, he made his way, and under the protection of deities, he travelled in solitude. He went out of the strategic passes at the Iron Gate and the Rocky Gate and climbed over the perilous Icy Mountains and Snow Mountains. In the course of time, he reached India, where he publicized Chinese civilization in a foreign land and propagated the great teachings in an alien country. He studied Sanskrit texts under the instruction of learned scholars, and the dubious points he had in his mind were solved by reading the books. As regards the profound doctrines, he sought the elucidation of highly talented teachers. He opened his mind to understand the ultimate truth and clarified his spirit to realize the Way. He heard what he had never heard before and acquired what was unacquired previously. He became a beneficial friend in Buddhist circles and was indeed a master in the gate of the Dharma. From this we may know that his religious fame was prominent and his deeds of virtue were lofty and noble. His store of knowledge was accumulated in three years, and his reputation spread ten thousand *li*. The scholars of India respected him for his great virtue, calling him Basket Full of Scriptures or General of the Dharma. The Hinayanist disciples named him Mokṣadeva (Deity of emancipation), while the Mahayanist followers called him Mahāyānadeva (Deity of the Great Vehicle). These were titles bestowed on him in honor of his virtue, eulogistic epithets used to show respect to his personality. As regards the abstruse theories of the three classifications of the turning of the Wheel of the Dharma and the subtle sayings spoken by the Buddha after three inquiries, he did profound research into their roots and acquired a full understanding of the leaves and branches. He promptly became

intellectually enlightened and happily clarified his theoretical entanglements. The dubious points he had raised were recorded in certain works. After having made a deep study of the theoretical principles and having mastered the lore of metaphysics, with his repute widely spreading as an erudite scholar, and having achieved great virtue, he started to tour the country, visiting the towns and their vicinities. He left the city of Kuśāgrapura and entered the Deer Park, and after visiting Yaṣṭivana Forest, he took rest at Kukkuṭārāma Monastery. He looked around the country of Kapilavastu and had a glimpse of the city of Kuśinagara. The old site of the Buddha's birthplace had turned into a plain of fertile land, and the other sites of secret spirituality lay in ruins in vast wildernesses. When he looked at the divine traces, his remembrance of the past glories increased, and he sighed with regret while recalling the Buddha's teachings with admiration. He was not merely like Jizi who sang the *Ode to Flowering Wheat* in sorrow over the fallen dynasty of Yin, nor was he similar to the senior official at the court of Zhou who composed the *Lyric of the Millet Shoots* in lament for the collapse of the house of Zhou. But he narrated in detail the stories of Śākyamuni Buddha and gave an account of many historical facts of India. He also recounted the manners and 946c
customs of various places and wrote down the strange legends. Time elapsed swiftly, and he sojourned in India several years. Although he was much attached to the Land of Happiness, he did not forget to return to his homeland.

He procured one hundred fifty grains of the Tathāgata's relic bones; one golden image of the Buddha one foot six inches high including the seat and the halo, an imitation of the shadow image in the dragon's cave at Prāgbodhi Mountain in the country of Magadha; one golden image of the Buddha three feet three inches high including the seat and the halo, an imitation of the image of the Buddha in the posture of turning the Wheel of the Dharma for the first time at the Deer Park in the country of Bārāṇasī; one sandalwood image of the Buddha one foot five inches high including the seat and the halo, an imitation of the sandalwood portrait made by King Udayana of the country of Kauśāmbī when he longed to see the Tathāgata; one sandalwood image of the Buddha two feet nine inches high including the seat and the halo, an imitation of the image of the Tathāgata descending by a precious stairway from the heavenly palace to earth in the country of Kapitha; one silver image of the Buddha four feet high including the seat and the halo, an imitation of the image of the Buddha as he was preaching the *Saddharmapuṇḍarīka* and other scriptures on Vulture Peak in the country of Magadha; one golden image of the Buddha three feet five inches high including the seat and the halo, an imitation of the shadow portrait left by the Buddha when he had subdued a venomous dragon in the country of Nagarahāra; one sandalwood image of the Buddha one foot three inches high including the seat and the halo, an imitation of the Buddha's image in the posture of making a tour in the [capital] city of the country of Vaiśālī to edify the inhabitants; two hundred twenty-four Mahayana scriptures; one hundred ninety-two Mahayana treatises; fourteen scriptures, disciplinary texts, and treatises of the Sthavira school; fifteen scriptures, disciplinary texts, and treatises of the Mahāsāṃghika school; fifteen scriptures, disciplinary texts, and treatises of the Saṃmitīya school; twenty-two scriptures, disciplinary texts, and treatises of the Mahīśāsaka school; seventeen scriptures, disciplinary texts, and treatises of the Kāśyapīya school; forty-two scriptures, disciplinary texts, and treatises of the Dharmagupta school; sixty-seven scriptures, disciplinary texts, and treatises of the Sarvāstivāda school; thirty-six texts on Hetuvidyā (logic); and thirteen texts on Śabdavidyā (grammar): altogether six hundred fifty-seven books bound in five hundred twenty bundles.

In order to propagate the supreme teachings, he prepared his carriage for his return journey along the perilous way. He came out of the old country of Śrāvastī and left the former suburbs of Gayā. After climbing the dangerous path over the Cong Ling Mountains and traversing the hazardous way in the desert, he arrived in the capital in the first month of the spring of the nineteenth year (of the Zhenguan reign, 645 C.E.) and had an interview with the Emperor at Luoyang, who ordered him to translate the Sanskrit texts into Chinese. He summoned scholars to work with him to achieve a superior deed by joint effort. The Cloud of the Dharma again cast a [protective] shade, and the Sun of Wisdom issued a brilliant light anew. The edification that the Buddha taught at Vulture Peak prevailed in the Chinese capital, and the teachings brought out from the dragon's palace were expounded in the metropolitan district. This was a time of prosperity in the spread of Buddhism during its Image Period.

The Master is dexterously conversant with the Sanskrit language, with which he praised the profound Buddhist texts. He reads Sanskrit books as if they were his own compositions, and his intonation is still echoing in the air. Strictly sticking to the Buddha's 947a
meanings, he does not add any embellishments to his translations. Unknown dialects and Sanskrit terms without previous translations are carefully studied and weighed through research and mutual collation with the passages of classical Buddhist texts lest deviations should occur.

A gentleman garbed in the dress of an official came up to the Master and said earnestly to him, "India is a country where divine beings and saints assembled and men of virtue were born. Their writing is that of the gods, and their language that of the deities, with graceful and well-constructed diction rhythmically pronounced, with one word having many meanings, and one meaning being expressed in different words. There are falling and rising intonations, and voiced as well as voiceless consonants. The translation of the profound Buddhist texts has to depend on brilliant scholars, and the abstruse essences of the scriptures are to be explained by men of great virtue. If deletions are made in a translation or if the words are tuned according to musical notation, it is really inappropriate, and it cannot truly be regarded as good work. The exposition of the profound essences of the scriptures must be made easily understandable. So long as it is not contradictory to the original meaning, it may be considered well done. Excessive embellishments would render a translation too flowery in style, but if it is too simple it would be inelegant. Only when it is done in a plain style without ornamentation and written elegantly without being dull can a work be free of grave blunders and be counted as a good translation. Laozi said, 'Florid sayings are not trustworthy, and trustworthy words are not florid.' And Hanzi said, 'When one's reason is justifiable, one's speech is straightforward; if one talks in ornate language, one is hiding the truth.' From these maxims we may know that the principle is applicable to all things alike. It is hoped that obscure and unintelligible points may be expurgated for the advantage and delight of the readers. It is highly harmful to deviate from the original meanings so as to give place to ornamental verbiage, and adherence to obsolete rules is what the Buddha strongly objected to." Both the monks and the laity said unanimously, "Yes! What has been said is really true!" Formerly, when Confucius was in a position to hear litigation, he used to write verdicts jointly with others and never did so alone by himself. But in writing his *Spring and Autumn Annals*, he wrote what should be written and deleted what should be cut out, and even such learned literati among his disciples as Ziyou and Zixia could not aid him to write a word. The Master did his translation in the same way. He is not like Kumārajīva, who translated Buddhist texts at the Garden of Leisure and Repose, allowing his disciples Daosheng, Sengzhao, Daorong, and Sengrui to make deletions as they pleased. How can we add or cut out anything of the Buddha's teachings in an age when the angles of a square are cut off to make it round, and when ostentation is discarded and simplicity upheld?

Note by Bianji

I, Bianji, a descendant of a remote progenitor who believed in high culture, cherished the ambition while I was a child to lead the life of seclusion. When I had just reached school age I cut my hair, changed into religious robes, and became a disciple of the Venerable Daoyue of the Sarvāstivāda school in the great Zongchi Monastery.

Although I met a learned teacher, my stupidity rendered me as useless as rotten wood that could not be carved into shape. I was lucky to have entered the stream of the Dharma, but I failed to saturate myself in the moisture of learning and simply ate my fill all day long and did nothing but face the wall to pass the years. Fortunately the time came for me to take part in this fine gathering of intellectuals, where with my ability as meager as that of a sparrow, I worked at the end of a file of brilliant scholars resembling lofty swans in writing this *Record* with my smattering of literary knowledge. I am not a student well versed in ancient writings, and my compositions are devoid of ornamental phrases. I worked just like one carving a piece of rotten wood with a blunt 947b
burin, toiling through as laboriously as a lame man. I respectfully listened to the words, committed them to writing, and put them in proper order. Under the orders of the Secretary of State, I compiled the *Record* as it is presented here. Due to the shallowness of my wisdom and the narrowness of my ability, I must have made many unintentional omissions, and there must be surplus words that ought to have been deleted. Formerly, when the highly talented historian Sima Zichang wrote his *Historical Records*, he was succeeding to his father's task as grand historian, and even he sometimes only mentioned the given name of a person and neglected his second name. As regards places, he often only denoted the name of the county without indicating that of the prefecture. So it is said that even a discreet scholar when working alone on a heavy and complicated task is apt to be neglectful, let alone a man of slow wits and poor capability such as I. How can I expect to be perfect and consummate in my work? The different topographical conditions and social customs, the territorial limits and native products, the temperament and intelligence of different peoples, as well as the cold and warm climates of the four seasons in a region have been ascertained and are described in detail, good or bad, according to the actual facts. As regards the personal names of the people of different tribes, they are given together with the names of their countries of origin, and Indian customs and teachings are divided

into two categories, namely, the religious and the secular. All these are briefly narrated, but a full description can be found in the preceding preface. Such matters as social etiquette, ceremonies, household registration, brave warriors, and religious recluses are not related in detail.

As the Buddha contacted people through the employment of supernatural powers and taught them with spiritual admonition, it is said that his divine Way is deep and mysterious, with its principles alien to the human world, and that whatever profundities he exposed in his spiritual admonitions are concerned with things beyond the sky. For all places where the Buddha had left his auspicious traces, and for the ruins connected with the good names of former sages, brief accounts have been given with succinct notes. The roads wound and zigzagged, and the boundaries of different countries interlocked with one another jaggedly. Descriptions have been made about the places of the Master's journey in sequence, without editorial arrangement. The different parts of India, irrespective of the national boundaries, have been indicated at the end of the description of each country, just to give a rough idea of its whereabouts. Where the word "going" is used in the narration, it means that the Master visited the place in person, and the word "reaching" signifies that he merely gathered information for his record. It is either written straightforwardly according to facts, or in a mild and roundabout way to put it in a graceful style with well-balanced words, so as to submit a trustworthy record to His Supreme Majesty the Emperor.

In the seventh month in the autumn of the twentieth year (of the Zhenguan reign, 646 C.E.) I completed the compilation, wrote it down on pure white silk, and presented it to the Emperor for his perusal, despite my uncertainty whether it would meet His Majesty's expectations. However, the risky journey to a distant land was actually undertaken under the prestige of the imperial court, and the composition of a topographical record of foreign countries was done with curiosity under His Majesty's inspiration. It was not only Kuafu who had the strength to chase the sun to the remotest realms; and the opening up of the Western Regions can by no means be solely the merit of the Marquis of Bowang. Vulture Peak is made known in China through this *Record*, and the Deer Park is rendered as familiar as the outer garden of the imperial palace. It enables one to visualize what happened a thousand years ago and see the sights along the ten thousand *li* journey as if one visited the places in person. All these were not heard of since the remote past, nor were they recorded in previous books. The Emperor's supreme virtue covers all, and different countries with diverse customs have come to offer allegiance. The tradition of honesty and magnanimity has spread to far regions, not excepting wild and out-of-the-way localities. This *Record* may serve as a supplement to the *Book of Mountains and Seas*; let it be published as a chronicle and distributed for their general reference to the authorities concerned.

End of Fascicle Twelve

Glossary

Abhidharma piṭaka: the section of the Buddhist canon containing systematic accounts of the teachings of the Sutras.

absolute truth: the ultimate, beyond words and conceptualization. It is generally contrasted with relative truth, the conventional truth that can be put into words. Mahayana teachings insist that both relative truth and absolute truth are equally valid.

Ānanda: the Buddha's cousin, close disciple, and personal attendant. He was renowned for his ability to recite all of the Buddha's sermons from memory.

Anāthapiṇḍika: a wealthy lay follower and donor to the Buddha. Also called Sudatta.

Arhat: a saint who has freed himself from the bonds of samsara by eliminating all passions. The ideal of the Hinayana (q.v.).

Avalokiteśvara: the celestial Bodhisattva who embodies compassion.

āyatana: seat. There are twelve: six senses and six objects of the senses.

bhikṣu: a Buddhist monk.

bhikṣuṇī: a Buddhist nun.

Bodhisattva: the seeker after Buddhahood who gradually perfects the virtues of wisdom and compassion for the sake of liberating all sentient beings from suffering. The ideal of the Mahayana (q.v.)

Bodhi Tree: the tree under which the Buddha attained enlightenment.

Buddha-dharma. *See* Dharma.

deva: a god.

Dharma: the doctrine taught by the Buddha; Buddhist teachings.

dhātu: a sphere or realm. There are eighteen: twelve *āyatana*s (q.v.) and six corresponding consciousnesses.

doctrine of voidness (*śūnyatā*): the doctrine, one of the central tenets of Mahayana Buddhism, that all things exist only in dependence on a complex web of causes and conditions. All things are empty of any essence.

eight emancipations: emancipation from attachment to forms and desires through eight types of meditation.

Ekayāna (One Vehicle): also called the Buddhayāna (Buddha Vehicle); the Mahayana (q.v.), which contains the final and complete Dharma of the Buddha and is not merely a part, or a preliminary stage, as is the Hinayana (q.v.). Basically, it teaches that all beings will eventually become Buddhas. It is emphatically maintained in the teaching of the *Lotus Sutra*.

emptiness: *See* doctrine of voidness.

five desires: desires for the objects of the five senses.

five branches of mundane knowledge: grammar, mathematics, medicine, logic, and philosophy.

Five Precepts: (1) not to kill, (2) not to steal, (3) not to commit adultery, (4) not to speak falsely, and (5) not to drink intoxicants.

four forms of birth: the four possible ways that a being can be born—(1) birth from a womb, (2) birth from an egg, (3) birth from moisture, and (4) birth from metamorphosis.

four monastic requisites: the four things needed by a monk—clothing, food, bedding (or a dwelling), and medicine.

Four Noble Truths: (1) life is suffering; (2) defilements are the cause of suffering; (3) all suffering can be ended; (4) the way to end suffering is by following the Buddha's Eightfold Noble Path (i.e., right view, right thought, right speech, right action, right livelihood, right effort, right mindfulness, and right concentration).

Hinayana (Small Vehicle): a derogatory term applied by Mahayanists to various schools of Buddhism that exalt as their ideal the Arhat (q.v.). *See also* Mahayana.

Image (Counterfeit) Period: the second period in Buddhist historical theory (usually said to begin one thousand years after the Buddha's death and to last for a thousand years), during which conditions are not so favorable for practice as in the earlier period but are still better than in the third and final period.

Jambudvīpa: this world.

Jātaka stories: tales of the Buddha's previous lives as a Bodhisattva.

kalpa: an immense period of time, an aeon.

kaṣāya: a Buddhist monastic robe.

koṭi: an extremely large number, usually ten million, sometimes one hundred million.

li: approximately one-third of a mile.

Mahāsattva: a Bodhisattva with great wisdom and compassion (q.v.).

Mahayana (Great Vehicle): teachings on the attainment of enlightenment or Buddhahood in which the ideal is the Bodhisattva (q.v.). *See also* Hinayana.

Maitreya: the future Buddha, presently in the Tuṣita heaven.

Māra: the Devil; the tempter. The personification of human temptation to adhere to this world.

Nāgārjuna (ca. 150–250): a Mahayana teacher who is acknowledged as founder by the Mahayana schools in the Buddhist tradition. His teachings emphasized the doctrine of voidness (q.v.).

Nirvana: the final goal of Buddhists, a state in which passions are extinguished and the highest wisdom attained.

prajñā: transcendent wisdom. Knowledge of absolute truth (q.v.).

Pratyekabuddha: a self-enlightened Buddha, who does not teach others. A solitary Buddha.

rākṣasa: an ogre.

rākṣasī: an ogress.

ṛṣi (seer): a sage.

śāla trees: the kind of trees under which the Buddha passed away into final Nirvana.

samādhi: a deep trance.

Śāriputra: one of the original disciples of the Buddha, called "the foremost of the wise."

śarīra: relic(s).

Sarvāstivāda: an early school of Buddhism.

śāstra: a Buddhist treatise, a scholastic work, sometimes a commentary on a Sutra.

six supernatural powers: (1) supernatural vision, (2) supernatural hearing, (3) the power to know others' thoughts, (4) the power to know the past lives of oneself and others, (5) the power to perform miracles, such as appearing anywhere at will, and (6) the power to eradicate defilements.

skandhas: aggregates. There are five: matter, feeling, perception, volition, and consciousness.

Śramaṇa: a Buddhist monk.

śrāmaṇera: a male novice.

stupa: a tope, a reliquary; a large hemispherical structure enshrining relics.

Sudatta: Anāthapiṇḍika (q.v.)

Sutra: a discourse of the Buddha.

Tathāgata (Thus-come or Thus-gone): an epithet of a Buddha.

Ten Good Deeds: (1) not to kill, (2) not to steal, (3) not to engage in illicit sexual practices, (4) not to lie, (5) not to utter harsh words, (6) not to utter words that cause enmity among people, (7) not to engage in idle talk, (8) not to be greedy, (9) not to be angry, and (10) not to have wrong views.

ten powers: the ten powers of a Buddha, giving him complete knowledge of (1) what is right or wrong; (2) the past, present, and future karmas of all sentient beings; (3) all forms of meditation; (4) the powers and faculties of all sentient beings; (5) the desires, or moral direction, of every being; (6) the different levels of existence; (7) the results of various methods of practice; (8) the transmigratory states of all sentient beings and the courses of karma they follow; (9) the past lives of all sentient beings and Nirvana; and (10) the destruction of all evil passions.

three evil paths: the three evil realms in which sentient beings transmigrate as retribution for evil deeds, namely, (1) hell, (2) the realm of hungry spirits, and (3) the realm of beasts.

three [clear] insights: (1) insight into the conditions of self and others in previous lives; (2) heavenly insight into future conditions; and (3) nirvanic insight into present suffering to overcome all passions.

three realms: the three worlds in which sentient beings transmigrate—(1) the world of desire, (2) the world of pure form, and (3) the world of non-form.

Three Vehicles: the three paths to enlightenment, which are (1) the Śrāvaka vehicle (for followers of the Hinayana), (2) the Pratyekabuddha (q.v.) vehicle, and (3) the Bodhisattva vehicle, otherwise known as the Mahayana.

Tripiṭaka (Three baskets): the Buddhist canon: Sutra, Vinaya, and Abhidharma.

Triple Gem: the Buddha, the Dharma (q.v.), and the Sangha (the Buddhist community).

Twelvefold Causation: the twelvefold cycle of causes and conditions that make up the human condition, namely (1) ignorance, (2) volitional activity, (3) consciousness, (4) name and form, (5) the six senses, (6) contact, (7) perception, (8) love, (9) attachment, (10) existence, (11) rebirth, and (12) decay and death.

upāsaka: a male lay devotee.

upāsikā: a female lay devotee.

Vasubandhu (fl. ca. 300–400): a Buddhist teacher who was an important expounder of the Abhidharma (q.v.) and the Vijñānavāda.

Vihāra: a hall, a monastery.

Vinaya: disciplinary rules for Buddhist monks.

yakṣa: a kind of spirit or demon.

Bibliography

Xuanzang is responsible for the contents of three books that deal with his journey to India. The earliest English translations of the three seem to be the following:

Hsüan-tsang. *She-kia-fang-che*. Translated by Prabodh Chandra Bagchi. Visva-Bharati Research Publication. Santiniketan: Santiniketan Press, 1959. This is Taishō No. 2088. The author Daoxuan had access to Xuanzang's travelling accounts while he was working as an assistant at the latter's translation center. This text is sometimes listed with Hsüan-tsang as the author.

Hsüan-tsang. *Si-Yu-Ki: Buddhist Records of the Western World*. Translated from the Chinese of Hiuen-tsiang (A.D. 629) by Samuel Beal. 2 vols. London: Trübner, 1884. Many subsequent editions.

Huili. *Life of Hsüan-tsang*. Translated by Samuel Beal. New ed. London, 1911. Huili may have written to Xuanzang's dictation.

Based on all three of these is T. Watters. *On Yuan Chwang's Travels*. London, 1904. Many subsequent editions.

Based on the *Si-Yu-Ki* and the Huili book is *In the Footsteps of the Buddha* by R. Grousset. This is an abridged version of a French original; see the review by E. Conze in his *Thirty Years of Buddhist Studies*.

French translations from the Chinese of two of the above are:

Hui-li. *Histoire de la vie de Hiouen-Thsang et de ses voyages dans l'Inde, depuis l'an 629 jusqu'en 645, par Hoei-li et Yen-thsong: Suivie de documents et d'eclaircissements geographiques tirés de la relation originale de Hiouen-Thsang.* Translated by Stanislas Julien. Paris: Imprimerie Impériale, 1853.

Hsüan-tsang. *Mémoires sur les contrées occidentales, traduits du sanscrit en chinois, en l'an 648, par Hiouen-thsang.* Translated by Stanislas Julien. Paris: Imprimerie Impériale, 1857–58. (Actually the book may have been originally written in Chinese by Hsüan-tsang.)

Li Rongxi has twice translated the Huili book, once with the additions of Shi Yancong:

Hui-li. *The Life of Hsüan-tsang, the Tripitaka-Master of the Great Tzu En Monastery.* Translated by Li Yung-hsi. Peking: Chinese Buddhist Association, 1959.

Huili and Shi Yancong. *A Biography of the Tripiṭaka Master of the Great Ci'en Monastery of the Great Tang Dynasty.* Berkeley: Numata Center for Buddhist Translation and Research, 1995.

See also Waley, Arthur. *The Real Tripitaka.* London: Allen and Unwin, 1952; accounts of the travels of Faxian (Fa-hsien) and Songyun (Sung-yun), translated in Beal's *Si-Yu-Ki* above; accounts of the journey of Yijing (I-tsing).

Index

334–36, 339, 342, 344, 346, 348, 349, 351, 352, 358, 370, 372–74, 381, 382
built by King Aśoka, 151, 156, 163, 168, 178, 180, 183–85, 191, 196, 206, 208, 210, 266, 279, 286, 287, 291, 299, 304, 308, 313, 318, 351, 360
stone, 42, 71, 78, 88, 98, 99, 109, 110, 118, 196, 242, 267, 274, 305, 307, 313, 314
Subhadra (Śākyamuni's disciple), 187, 188
Śubhavastu River, 83, 84
Subhūti (Śākyamuni's disciple), 138
Sudāna (prince), 78, 79
Sudatta (Śākyamuni's disciple), 165–67, 171
Śuddhodana (Śākyamuni's father), 174–76, 178, 179, 200, 254, 269
Sudra(s) (caste), 59, 128, 346
Sūma Stupa, 87
Sumeru, Mount, 17, 277
Śuna (god), 358
Śunāśīra Mountain, 42, 43, 358
Surasthāna (city), 349
Suraṭṭha (country), 323, 343, 344
Sūrya (monk), 151
Sushe (river), 26–28
Sutrūshana (country), 15, 29
Suvarṇagotra (country), 134
Śvetapura Monastery, 215, 216
Śyāmaka (Bodhisattva), 78

Ṭakka (country), 113, 130
Takṣaśilā (country), 83, 93, 95, 99, 370, 375
Talaqān (country), 15, 36, 37
Tamasāvana-saṃghārāma (monastery), 119
Tāmraliptī (country), 6, 293, 302
Tārā (Bodhisattva), 235, 285
Taras (city), 28
Tathāgata(s) (epithet of Buddha), 36, 45–47, 51, 57, 66–74, 78, 81, 84–88, 91, 92, 94, 95, 99–103, 106, 108, 118, 119, 121–24, 126, 127, 131, 135–38, 148–53, 155, 156, 160, 161, 163–69, 171, 173, 176, 178, 181, 184–91, 193, 196–99, 201, 202, 205, 206, 208–11, 213, 214, 216, 218, 219, 223, 225, 226, 229, 235, 236, 243–45, 247–50, 253–59, 261, 263–67, 269–79, 281, 284, 285, 287, 290, 291, 294–96, 299, 302, 304, 305, 308, 310, 314, 318, 320, 321, 331–33, 335, 337, 342, 348, 351, 352, 364, 373, 377, 378, 393, 394
Tathāgatagupta (king), 282
Tattvasaṃcaya-śāstra, 110
taxes, 63
tigress, starving, 99
Tilaḍhāka Monastery, 235
time, units of, 50-1
Tirmidh (country), 15, 32
Tokhāra (country), 106
tooth, Buddha's. *See* Buddha's Tooth, Temple of
tooth relic. *See under* relic(s)
transformation(s), 265, 274, 390
transmission(s), 141
Trapusa (city), 35, 36
Trāyastriṃśa. *See under* heaven(s)
Treatise on the Essential Truth of the Holy Teaching, 163
Tripiṭaka, 1, 3, 9, 12, 74, 75, 103–5, 132, 215, 234, 236, 276, 278, 283, 331, 374, 390
truth(s), 6, 7, 10, 20, 56, 57, 76, 81, 131, 148, 149, 155, 157, 163, 201–3, 219, 236, 237, 241, 288, 309, 392, 396
of Bhūtatathatā, 6
conventional, 118
Four Noble, 236
supreme, 131
ultimate, 12, 97, 133, 148, 155, 201, 202, 241, 288, 392

A List of the Volumes of the BDK English Tripiṭaka (First Series)

Abbreviations

Ch.:	Chinese
Skt.:	Sanskrit
Jp.:	Japanese
T.:	Taishō Tripiṭaka

Vol. No.	Title	*T.* No.
1, 2	*Ch.* Ch‘ang-a-han-ching (長阿含經) *Skt.* Dīrghāgama	1
3–8	*Ch.* Chung-a-han-ching (中阿含經) *Skt.* Madhyamāgama	26
9-I	*Ch.* Ta-ch‘eng-pên-shêng-hsin-ti-kuan-ching (大乘本生心地觀經)	159
9-II	*Ch.* Fo-so-hsing-tsan (佛所行讃) *Skt.* Buddhacarita	192
10-I	*Ch.* Tsa-pao-ts‘ang-ching (雜寶藏經)	203
10-II	*Ch.* Fa-chü-p‘i-yü-ching (法句譬喩經)	211
11-I	*Ch.* Hsiao-p‘in-pan-jo-po-lo-mi-ching (小品般若波羅蜜經) *Skt.* Aṣṭasāhasrikā-prajñāpāramitā-sūtra	227
11-II	*Ch.* Chin-kang-pan-jo-po-lo-mi-ching (金剛般若波羅蜜經) *Skt.* Vajracchedikā-prajñāpāramitā-sūtra	235

Vol. No.		Title	*T.* No.
29-I	*Ch.*	Ta-fang-kuang-yüan-chio-hsiu-to-lo-liao-i-ching (大方廣圓覺修多羅了義經)	842
29-II	*Ch.*	Su-hsi-ti-chieh-lo-ching (蘇悉地羯羅經)	893
	Skt.	Susiddhikaramahātantrasādhanopāyika-paṭala	
29-III	*Ch.*	Mo-têng-ch'ieh-ching (摩登伽經)	1300
	Skt.	Mātaṅgī-sūtra (?)	
30-I	*Ch.*	Ta-p'i-lu-chê-na-ch'êng-fo-shên-pien-chia-ch'ih-ching (大毘盧遮那成佛神變加持經)	848
	Skt.	Mahāvairocanābhisambodhivikurvitādhiṣṭhāna-vaipulyasūtrendrarāja-nāma-dharmaparyāya	
30-II	*Ch.*	Chin-kang-ting-i-ch'ieh-ju-lai-chên-shih-shê-ta-ch'eng-hsien-chêng-ta-chiao-wang-ching (金剛頂一切如來眞實攝大乘現證大教王經)	865
	Skt.	Sarvatathāgatatattvasaṃgrahamahāyānābhi-samayamahākalparāja	
31–35	*Ch.*	Mo-ho-sêng-ch'i-lü (摩訶僧祇律)	1425
	Skt.	Mahāsāṃghika-vinaya (?)	
36–42	*Ch.*	Ssŭ-fên-lü (四分律)	1428
	Skt.	Dharmaguptaka-vinaya (?)	
43, 44	*Ch.*	Shan-chien-lü-p'i-p'o-sha (善見律毘婆沙)	1462
	Pāli	Samantapāsādikā	
45-I	*Ch.*	Fan-wang-ching (梵網經)	1484
	Skt.	Brahmajāla-sūtra (?)	
45-II	*Ch.*	Yu-p'o-sai-chieh-ching (優婆塞戒經)	1488
	Skt.	Upāsakaśīla-sūtra (?)	
46-I	*Ch.*	Miao-fa-lien-hua-ching-yu-po-t'i-shê (妙法蓮華經憂波提舍)	1519
	Skt.	Saddharmapuṇḍarīkopadeśa	
46-II	*Ch.*	Fo-ti-ching-lun (佛地經論)	1530
	Skt.	Buddhabhūmisūtra-śāstra (?)	
46-III	*Ch.*	Shê-ta-ch'eng-lun (攝大乘論)	1593
	Skt.	Mahāyānasaṃgraha	
47	*Ch.*	Shih-chu-p'i-p'o-sha-lun (十住毘婆沙論)	1521
	Skt.	Daśabhūmika-vibhāṣā (?)	

Vol. No.		Title	*T.* No.
48, 49	*Ch.*	A-p'i-ta-mo-chü-shê-lun (阿毘達磨俱舍論)	1558
	Skt.	Abhidharmakośa-bhāṣya	
50–59	*Ch.*	Yü-ch'ieh-shih-ti-lun (瑜伽師地論)	1579
	Skt.	Yogācārabhūmi	
60-I	*Ch.*	Ch'êng-wei-shih-lun (成唯識論)	1585
	Skt.	Vijñaptimātratāsiddhi-śāstra (?)	
60-II	*Ch.*	Wei-shih-san-shih-lun-sung (唯識三十論頌)	1586
	Skt.	Triṃśikā	
60-III	*Ch.*	Wei-shih-êrh-shih-lun (唯識二十論)	1590
	Skt.	Viṃśatikā	
61-I	*Ch.*	Chung-lun (中論)	1564
	Skt.	Madhyamaka-śāstra	
61-II	*Ch.*	Pien-chung-pien-lun (辯中邊論)	1600
	Skt.	Madhyāntavibhāga	
61-III	*Ch.*	Ta-ch'eng-ch'êng-yeh-lun (大乘成業論)	1609
	Skt.	Karmasiddhiprakaraṇa	
61-IV	*Ch.*	Yin-ming-ju-chêng-li-lun (因明入正理論)	1630
	Skt.	Nyāyapraveśa	
61-V	*Ch.*	Chin-kang-chên-lun (金剛針論)	1642
	Skt.	Vajrasūcī	
61-VI	*Ch.*	Chang-so-chih-lun (彰所知論)	1645
62	*Ch.*	Ta-ch'eng-chuang-yen-ching-lun (大乘莊嚴經論)	1604
	Skt.	Mahāyānasūtrālaṃkāra	
63-I	*Ch.*	Chiu-ching-i-ch'eng-pao-hsing-lun (究竟一乘寶性論)	1611
	Skt.	Ratnagotravibhāgamahāyānottaratantra-śāstra	
63-II	*Ch.*	P'u-t'i-hsing-ching (菩提行經)	1662
	Skt.	Bodhicaryāvatāra	
63-III	*Ch.*	Chin-kang-ting-yü-ch'ieh-chung-fa-a-nou-to-lo-san-miao-san-p'u-t'i-hsin-lun (金剛頂瑜伽中發阿耨多羅三藐三菩提心論)	1665
63-IV	*Ch.*	Ta-ch'eng-ch'i-hsin-lun (大乘起信論)	1666
	Skt.	Mahāyānaśraddhotpāda-śāstra (?)	

Vol. No.		Title	T. No.
63-V	*Ch.* *Pāli*	Na-hsien-pi-ch'iu-ching (那先比丘經) Milindapañhā	1670
64	*Ch.* *Skt.*	Ta-ch'eng-chi-p'u-sa-hsüeh-lun (大乘集菩薩學論) Śikṣāsamuccaya	1636
65	*Ch.*	Shih-mo-ho-yen-lun (釋摩訶衍論)	1668
66-I	*Ch.*	Pan-jo-po-lo-mi-to-hsin-ching-yu-tsan (般若波羅蜜多心經幽賛)	1710
66-II	*Ch.*	Kuan-wu-liang-shou-fo-ching-shu (觀無量壽佛經疏)	1753
66-III	*Ch.*	San-lun-hsüan-i (三論玄義)	1852
66-IV	*Ch.*	Chao-lun (肇論)	1858
67, 68	*Ch.*	Miao-fa-lien-hua-ching-hsüan-i (妙法蓮華經玄義)	1716
69	*Ch.*	Ta-ch'eng-hsüan-lun (大乘玄論)	1853
70-I	*Ch.*	Hua-yen-i-ch'eng-chiao-i-fên-ch'i-chang (華嚴一乘教義分齊章)	1866
70-II	*Ch.*	Yüan-jên-lun (原人論)	1886
70-III	*Ch.*	Hsiu-hsi-chih-kuan-tso-ch'an-fa-yao (修習止觀坐禪法要)	1915
70-IV	*Ch.*	T'ien-t'ai-ssŭ-chiao-i (天台四教儀)	1931
71, 72	*Ch.*	Mo-ho-chih-kuan (摩訶止觀)	1911
73-I	*Ch.*	Kuo-ch'ing-pai-lu (國清百録)	1934
73-II	*Ch.*	Liu-tsu-ta-shih-fa-pao-t'an-ching (六祖大師法寶壇經)	2008
73-III	*Ch.*	Huang-po-shan-tuan-chi-ch'an-shih-ch'uan-hsin-fa-yao (黄檗山斷際禪師傳心法要)	2012 A
73-IV	*Ch.*	Yung-chia-chêng-tao-ko (永嘉證道歌)	2014
74-I	*Ch.*	Chên-chou-lin-chi-hui-chao-ch'an-shih-wu-lu (鎭州臨濟慧照禪師語録)	1985
74-II	*Ch.*	Wu-mên-kuan (無門關)	2005

Vol. No.		Title	*T.* No.
74-III	*Ch.*	Hsin-hsin-ming (信心銘)	2010
74-IV	*Ch.*	Ch'ih-hsiu-pai-chang-ch'ing-kuei (勅修百丈清規)	2025
75	*Ch.*	Fo-kuo-yüan-wu-ch'an-shih-pi-yen-lu (佛果圜悟禪師碧巖録)	2003
76-I	*Ch.* *Skt.*	I-pu-tsung-lun-lun (異部宗輪論) Samayabhedoparacanacakra	2031
76-II	*Ch.* *Skt.*	A-yü-wang-ching (阿育王經) Aśokarāja-sūtra (?)	2043
76-III	*Ch.*	Ma-ming-p'u-sa-ch'uan (馬鳴菩薩傳)	2046
76-IV	*Ch.*	Lung-shu-p'u-sa-ch'uan (龍樹菩薩傳)	2047
76-V	*Ch.*	P'o-sou-p'an-tou-fa-shih-ch'uan (婆藪槃豆法師傳)	2049
76-VI	*Ch.*	Pi-ch'iu-ni-ch'uan (比丘尼傳)	2063
76-VII	*Ch.*	Kao-sêng-fa-hsien-ch'uan (高僧法顯傳)	2085
76-VIII	*Ch.*	T'ang-ta-ho-shang-tung-chêng-ch'uan (遊方記抄:唐大和上東征傳)	2089-(7)
77	*Ch.*	Ta-t'ang-ta-tz'ŭ-ên-ssŭ-san-ts'ang-fa-shih-ch'uan (大唐大慈恩寺三藏法師傳)	2053
78	*Ch.*	Kao-sêng-ch'uan (高僧傳)	2059
79	*Ch.*	Ta-t'ang-hsi-yü-chi (大唐西域記)	2087
80	*Ch.*	Hung-ming-chi (弘明集)	2102
81–92	*Ch.*	Fa-yüan-chu-lin (法苑珠林)	2122
93-I	*Ch.*	Nan-hai-chi-kuei-nei-fa-ch'uan (南海寄歸内法傳)	2125
93-II	*Ch.*	Fan-yü-tsa-ming (梵語雜名)	2135
94-I	*Jp.*	Shō-man-gyō-gi-sho (勝鬘經義疏)	2185
94-II	*Jp.*	Yui-ma-kyō-gi-sho (維摩經義疏)	2186
95	*Jp.*	Hok-ke-gi-sho (法華義疏)	2187

Vol. No.		Title	T. No.
96-I	*Jp.*	Han-nya-shin-gyō-hi-ken (般若心經秘鍵)	2203
96-II	*Jp.*	Dai-jō-hos-sō-ken-jin-shō (大乘法相研神章)	2309
96-III	*Jp.*	Kan-jin-kaku-mu-shō (觀心覺夢鈔)	2312
97-I	*Jp.*	Ris-shū-kō-yō (律宗綱要)	2348
97-II	*Jp.*	Ten-dai-hok-ke-shū-gi-shū (天台法華宗義集)	2366
97-III	*Jp.*	Ken-kai-ron (顯戒論)	2376
97-IV	*Jp.*	San-ge-gaku-shō-shiki (山家學生式)	2377
98-I	*Jp.*	Hi-zō-hō-yaku (秘藏寶鑰)	2426
98-II	*Jp.*	Ben-ken-mitsu-ni-kyō-ron (辨顯密二教論)	2427
98-III	*Jp.*	Soku-shin-jō-butsu-gi (即身成佛義)	2428
98-IV	*Jp.*	Shō-ji-jis-sō-gi (聲字實相義)	2429
98-V	*Jp.*	Un-ji-gi (吽字義)	2430
98-VI	*Jp.*	Go-rin-ku-ji-myō-hi-mitsu-shaku (五輪九字明秘密釋)	2514
98-VII	*Jp.*	Mitsu-gon-in-hotsu-ro-san-ge-mon (密嚴院發露懺悔文)	2527
98-VIII	*Jp.*	Kō-zen-go-koku-ron (興禪護國論)	2543
98-IX	*Jp.*	Fu-kan-za-zen-gi (普勧坐禪儀)	2580
99–103	*Jp.*	Shō-bō-gen-zō (正法眼藏)	2582
104-I	*Jp.*	Za-zen-yō-jin-ki (坐禪用心記)	2586
104-II	*Jp.*	Sen-chaku-hon-gan-nen-butsu-shū (選擇本願念佛集)	2608
104-III	*Jp.*	Ris-shō-an-koku-ron (立正安國論)	2688
104-IV	*Jp.*	Kai-moku-shō (開目抄)	2689
104-V	*Jp.*	Kan-jin-hon-zon-shō (觀心本尊抄)	2692
104-VI	*Ch.*	Fu-mu-ên-chung-ching (父母恩重經)	2887